Dances with Devils

Dances with Devils

A JOURNALIST'S SEARCH FOR TRUTH

Jacques Pauw

Published by Zebra Press
an imprint of Random House Struik (Pty) Ltd
Company Reg. No. 1966/003153/07
80 McKenzie Street, Cape Town, 8001
PO Box 1144, Cape Town, 8000, South Africa

www.zebrapress.co.za

First published 2006
Reprinted in 2006, 2007 and 2008

5 7 9 10 8 6 4

Publication © Zebra Press 2006
Text © Jacques Pauw 2006

PUBLISHER: Marlene Fryer
MANAGING EDITOR: Robert Plummer
EDITOR: Marléne Burger
PROOFREADER: Ronel Richter-Herbert
COVER DESIGN: Michiel Botha, Flame Design
TEXT DESIGN: Natascha Adendorff-Olivier
TYPESETTER: Monique van den Berg
INDEXER: Robert Plummer
PRODUCTION MANAGER: Valerie Kömmer

Set in 10 pt on 13.5 pt Minion

Reproduction by Hirt & Carter (Cape) (Pty) Ltd
Printed and bound by Paarl Print, Oosterland Street, Paarl, South Africa

ISBN: 9 781770 073302

To my mother and Sam

Contents

Preface

THOSE WHO FARED ON CONGO RIVER BOATS BEFORE ME DESCRIBED them as stinking, noisy, overheated, overcrowded African markets. In the space of twenty-four hours, the MS *Tshopo* went from being exactly that to a mute and crippled disaster in the making. None of the passengers had slept the night before. The boat-whores had been singularly luckless, makeshift hair salons had no clients and kiosk proprietors didn't even light their paraffin stoves.

The captain, drunk and witless, had steered the ungainly, overcrowded craft into an island and we had narrowly escaped death by drowning or being devoured by the monstrously big crocodiles that patrol the murky waters in search of prey.

I was supposedly fulfilling a lifelong dream, inspired by Joseph Conrad's epic voyage more than a century earlier, when he wrote: 'Going up that river was like travelling back to the earliest beginnings of the world, when vegetation rioted on the earth and the big trees were kings.'

My bubble of illusion had been rudely burst. I wasn't even looking at the Congo River any longer. I drew the Stetson-style hat that I had bought in Kinshasa low over my eyes and fantasised about large platters of scrumptious food and bottles of chilled chardonnay. I hadn't eaten for three days, because I didn't dare utilise one of the two toxic *pissoirs* on board.

Sitting next to me was Jan de Klerk, my virtuous travel companion and cameraman *extraordinaire*. He put his hand on my shoulder, gave me a reassuring squeeze and said: 'Lighten up, *broer*. We'll make it.'

Together we had prevailed in African danger zones such as Rwanda, Burundi, Ethiopia, Eritrea, Algeria and Sudan, but this trip had me petrified. I didn't answer Jan. I knew he was really just trying to console himself. Then he said: 'You know what you should do?'

'What?'

'If we survive this, why don't you write a book?'

I didn't respond and I gave his suggestion not a moment's thought. Of course, we did survive, eventually limping into a lawless and isolated backwater called Bumba, where we were promptly arrested. We extricated ourselves from that predicament by stuffing greenbacks into a sleazy official's grimy paw until it hurt. Ten days later, we flew back to Johannesburg.

Five years earlier, in the West African country of Sierra Leone, I had interviewed rebel leader Foday Sankoh, one of the worst human beings that Africa ever spat out. I spent more than an hour trying to evoke some sense of responsibility or token of remorse from him for the brutal maiming and murder of thousands of women, men and children. Afterwards, exhausted and frustrated, I slumped into a chair at a Lebanese restaurant on Freetown's beachfront. My local researcher and interpreter, Allieu Kamara, looked at me pensively, then said:

'You know what you did today?'

'What?' I asked dispiritedly.

'You danced with the devil.'

'What do you mean?'

'You danced with the devil,' he said. 'You took Foday for a leap and a hop around the dance floor. I watched you. You waltzed with him. You went backwards and forwards and left and right, but you kept dancing. That's how you managed to get so much out of him.'

When I asked Allieu where on earth he got this metaphor, he said his journalism lecturer had used it often. He told his students that as journalists they should be prepared to dance with anyone, including the devil. And if necessary, they must dance close and all night long.

'My teacher always said that doctors doctor, lawyers do law, teachers teach and auditors audit. But journalists? They dance.'

Allieu's teacher was either an avid ballroom dancer or an astute philosopher, but either way, the image stayed with me, because it's true. As journalists, we dance. In the endless quest for The Story, I've cavorted and gambolled and jived and quickstepped with riff-raff and rabble that I would not normally give the time of day.

With Dirk Coetzee, I shared a slow and intimate shuffle. I led and he followed as we made our way through many a night and into the next day. With Ferdi Barnard, I did a hot and steamy tango, edging him ever closer to a gaping void. With many I whirled around in a crafty two-step, guiding them towards the confessional while making them believe we were actually dancing to the same tune.

Fifteen months after my *pas de deux* with death on the Congo, my girlfriend Sam left me (fortunately, only temporarily) and I plunged into a therapeutic bout of writing. Television, unrivalled in its power and influence, is an exceptionally shallow and trivial medium. I've sometimes spent a month in a faraway location or hunted down a villain or ruffian for weeks in order to claim thirty or sixty minutes of a viewer's time and attention. That is the nature of television documentaries and current affairs programmes, but no matter how visually evocative they are, they don't reveal what happens behind the scenes or what I've smelt or felt or endured on the journey into people's living rooms.

Most of the stories in this book are the untold anecdotes, epics and narratives that lie behind my years as a television journalist. This is not an autobiography in the style or grandeur of Max du Preez's *Pale Native* or Aidan Hartley's *The Zanzibar Chest*, but rather a collection of events and encounters with extraordinary people in places where 'ordinary' people generally don't go. The journey stretches from the last, dark days of apartheid and its aberrations to the apocalyptic events in several African states around and since the dawn of the new millennium. Juxtaposed between these cataclysmic developments are what I call the *whores, hoods and hooligans* – gangsters and their molls, con men and their rackets, opiates and their slaves. There are also tales of *inyangas* (black witches) concocting muti from human flesh and innocent girls being trafficked into prostitution.

In addition to Jan, who first came up with the idea, and Allieu, who unwittingly provided the title, far too many people have in some way contributed to this book to name here. Among them are outstanding editors, distinguished colleagues and supportive friends, to say nothing of a host of remarkable people, from near and far and both good and bad, that I've been privileged to meet and spend time with and who, sometimes, became the subject of my stories.

Some have been friends and colleagues for a very long time and I can only laud their support and understanding. Some have had a remarkable influence on my career, while others have stood by me through turbulent times. Only some are identified on the pages that follow, but all their names are engraved on my heart.

A special mention is due to Sam for so much love and understanding, especially during my long periods of absence while writing this book.

A brilliant team at Zebra Press stands behind *Dances with Devils*. A special word of appreciation to Marlene Fryer, Robert Plummer and, above all, Marléne Burger. I came to know Marléne B a long time ago as a resolute journalist; now she's proven herself an outstanding editor as well.

This is not necessarily a collection of my best stories, merely those that have remained glued to my mind. In each and every one there is something or someone I will remember for the rest of my life. In twenty years of finding and exposing the very worst that humanity has to offer, I have seen and touched and encountered things that no education can prepare one for. Quite recently, a colleague wrote of me: 'If it is indeed the case that a journalist's hands are dirty, those of Jacques Pauw must be filthy. In fact, I suspect his whole body is covered in a layer of grime, having spent so much time in the sewers of society.'

Thankfully, though not nearly often enough, I have also found purity and goodness and hope and caring along the way. Many times, fox-trotting and doing the hustle with despicable human beings knotted my guts and forced puke to my throat.

But in the end, I took their hands and we danced.

JACQUES PAUW
Johannesburg
August 2006

Abbreviations

ALIR: Army for the Liberation of Rwanda
ANC: African National Congress
AWB: Afrikaner Weerstandsbeweging (Afrikaner Resistance Movement)
BBC: British Broadcasting Corporation
CCB: Civil Cooperation Bureau
CIA: Central Intelligence Agency
CNN: Cable News Network
DCC: Directorate of Covert Collection
DEA: Drug Enforcement Administration
DOP: director of photography
DRC: Democratic Republic of Congo
FAR: Armed Forces of Rwanda
FRELIMO: Mozambican Liberation Front
ICTR: International Criminal Tribunal for Rwanda
Idasa: Institute for a Democratic Alternative for South Africa
Medunsa: Medical University of South Africa
MRND: National Revolutionary Movement for Development
NATO: North Atlantic Treaty Organisation
NG Kerk: Dutch Reformed Church
NI: National Intelligence
PAC: Pan Africanist Congress
Pebco: Port Elizabeth Black Civic Organisation
PFP: Progressive Federal Party
RENAMO: Mozambican National Resistance
RPF: Rwandan Patriotic Front
RPG: rocket-propelled grenade
RUF: Revolutionary United Front
SAA: South African Airways
SABC: South African Broadcasting Corporation
SADF: South African Defence Force
SAP: South African Police

SPLA: Sudan People's Liberation Army
TRC: Truth and Reconciliation Commission
UN: United Nations
UNAMIR: United Nations Mission to Rwanda
UNHCR: UN High Commission for Refugees
Wits: University of the Witwatersrand

CHAPTER 1

Rites of passage

If a person is not talented enough to be a novelist, not smart enough to be a lawyer, and his hands are too shaky to perform operations, he becomes a journalist. — **Norman Mailer**

'COME WITH ME,' SAID THE SCHOOL PRINCIPAL. 'I'LL SHOW YOU the lock-up room. It's nothing special. Just a small room. There's nobody in it at the moment and you can see it for yourself.'

We walked out of his office and crossed a parade ground. It was late in May, and a weak and dreary winter sun cast elongated and jesting shadows across the concrete surface. A short distance away a pair of white hockey nets protruded from a lustreless and brown grass field.

Jan van Aswegen was a tall and dapper man, dressed in a grey three-piece suit with a striped blue tie. His bespectacled face was clean-shaven, his Brylcreamed hair clipped short and his fingernails immaculately groomed. My father was also a school principal and I could see something of the one in the other. That's how headmasters were made in those days.

Van Aswegen was one of the education department's favourite sons. He was seen as young, dynamic and devoted, and had been selected for a year of further study in the United States. His National Party member of parliament and the local *dominee* (Van Aswegen was a deacon in the Dutch Reformed Church) had endorsed his bursary application. They saluted him in references as God-fearing, patriotic and astute.

We turned into a dimly lit passage. Van Aswegen looked at me over his shoulder. 'The lock-up has great disciplinary value,' he babbled. 'It's like a mental purgative. Once a girl has been in there for some time, she's much more amenable to fresh ideas. It calms them down and cleans them out. Don't believe what some of them tell you. They lie.'

He stopped in front of a reinforced door. A key turned in the lock and the door swung open. We stepped into the bare room. 'See, it's nothing much,' he said. 'A mattress, blankets and a bucket. They're safe here and we feed them like all the other girls.'

'How long do you lock them up for?' I asked.

He seemed vague. 'Hmm, maybe a day, two days. Sometimes longer. It depends.'

'On what?'

'On their psychological profile,' he answered curtly.

'Sir, would you mind if I took a photograph?' I asked respectfully.

'No, no, no,' he said firmly. 'That would be inappropriate. I don't have permission for that.'

Back in his office, I pushed a wee bit further the reason I had made the two-hour drive from Johannesburg to the dreary Highveld town of Standerton.

'The girl also claims, sir,' I said, 'that you hit her.'

He raised his eyebrows. 'What does she mean by hit?'

'That you beat her.'

'Yes, but in accordance with the prescriptions set down by the department.'

'She said you beat her with a strap.'

'And what else did she have to say?'

'That she first had to put on a pair of pants decorated with blue and white flowers. She had to bend over.'

'Remember, they lie!' he protested indignantly.

'She said you lifted her school dress and then beat her with a strap called Sannie. Is it true, sir?'

This was to be my first exposé in print. It was a simple story of abuse. Abuse of power and abuse of industrial schoolgirls, or 'govvie-chicks' as they referred to themselves. They were problem children, often from broken homes in which the abuse had its genesis.

These girls were birds with broken wings who needed to be nourished and nurtured back to health. Instead, they were entrusted to a headmaster who treated them like putrid objects wrapped in human skin and who resorted to disgusting violence when confronted with their delinquency and errant behaviour.

Worse, the system condoned his methods. Brute that Jan van Aswegen was, he was nonetheless rewarded with a bursary to study in America and lauded as a dedicated and unyielding disciplinarian. Nobody frowned upon his style of punishment, because violence had become so routine and accepted.

When I stumbled upon this story in the winter of 1985, I was incredibly naive. I had not yet made the acquaintance of the inherent evil and brutality lurking within my white and privileged world. I had no concept of living in an authoritarian society where problems were solved through the barrel of a gun, disputes settled with a clenched fist and disorderliness crushed under a heavy boot.

I tell this story not only because it was my first foray into investigative journalism, but because it was my crude awakening to the real world. To a certain extent, this story blew the dust of gullibility from my eyes and impregnated me with a sense of incredulity that I have harboured ever since.

I tackled the story with a tireless fervour and determination. On the one hand, I was an overzealous twenty-five-year-old reporter with a burning ambition to show my mettle in the rigorous and cutthroat realm of newspapers. On the other hand, the plight of the girls hit a chord and stirred an aversion I'd had since childhood to adults assaulting children under the pretext of *'n goeie pak slae* (a good hiding).

I grew up in Pretoria, the heartland of Afrikanerdom, where I attended the foremost government schools. I was an average and relatively diligent pupil, yet was beaten and thrashed by my teachers on a weekly and sometimes daily basis.

I couldn't do maths, and the more I grappled with an inability to measure angles or add values, the more savage the floggings became. The maths teacher's name was Koos du Plessis, and he baptised his cane Leonardo (after Da Vinci, I suppose, though I doubt he knew much about him). Pock-skinned and tight-lipped, Du Plessis was stocky and built like a stunted cattle farmer. I closely analysed his technique. As he reached the top of his stroke, he would pause for a moment and give a peculiar hop and a skip – probably to gain some height – before launching a mighty and meaningful downswing. I remember to this day the sadistic smirk plastered across his face as Leonardo thudded down on my bony buttocks. I clenched my fists and vowed not to cry. I never gave him that satisfaction.

As a schoolboy I fantasised about horrifying misfortune and anguish befalling my maths teacher. My preference would have been an accident resulting in the amputation of his right arm.

Du Plessis promised me and several other paltry maths students: '*Vir julle bliksem ek deur matriek!*' (I will thrash you through matric!) Of course the beatings didn't help. I scored an F for maths in my final exam.

But he wasn't the only teacher who merrily swung a cane. The headmaster beat us when we lost a cricket match. The biology teacher clobbered us with a stick thicker than my thumb. I thought it was normal. I never dreamt of complaining to my parents, as I didn't want to be a crybaby. School was an environment hostile to frailty and vulnerability; there wasn't space for the weak or the sissy.

Corporal punishment was the norm. What I didn't realise at the time was that it was merely a manifestation of something much more malevolent, and that violence had become endemic throughout my beautiful land.

It looked as if mice had nibbled at her badly cropped and spiky blonde hair, I thought, when I first saw her. 'I've cut my hair myself to change my look,' she said defensively. She was skinny and petite, no more than a centimetre or two over a metre and a half. She was shabbily dressed, her lips cracked and her fingernails gnawed to stumps. As a chronic nail-biter myself, someone's hands are almost always the first thing I notice.

She said her name was Jenny and she was sixteen years old. I took her to the Wimpy for breakfast. I don't think she ordered anything and repeatedly glanced over her shoulder. She had called *Rapport* the previous day and the switchboard operator put the call through to me. It was sheer coincidence that our paths crossed.

The girl on the line said she was a runaway and wanted to speak to a journalist. Runaway from where, I asked. From an industrial school for girls, she said. What's an industrial school? A reformatory, she said, adding that it was a school where juvenile courts sent problem children. Why do you want to see me? Horrible things are happening at the school, she said, and I want you to write about it.

Early the next morning, I drove the 120 kilometres or so to the Western Transvaal town of Potchefstroom. I waited for about twenty minutes at a pre-arranged spot in the centre of town before my eyes fixed on the forlorn and dejected-looking teenager slowly walking towards me. I'm Jenny, she said. Are you the journalist?

It turned out she had escaped from an industrial school by the name of Die Vlakte (the plains) in the south-eastern Transvaal town of Standerton. As I tucked into my breakfast, she gushed out her story. The headmaster locks us up in a cell, beats us with a strap and belittles us, she said. He forces us to wear an odd pair of pants and we have to bend over in front of him. He snuffed out a cigarette butt on my friend's head.

I later discovered that Jenny was the product of a callous and perverted father and a drunken stepmother. Her early childhood was a haze of alcoholic stupors, domestic brawls and perpetual beatings. Child Welfare intervened and took her away. She was put in a place of safety but repeatedly ran away, and was finally committed to Die Vlakte.

Jenny befriended a girl who smoked, but before long the housemother nabbed them in the act. She lost all privileges and was thrown out of the *Volkspele* (traditional Afrikaner dancing). Devastated, she ran away. Before she could reach Johannesburg, the police arrested and sent her back to Standerton.

Jan van Aswegen sentenced Jenny to nine days of solitary confinement. 'It's a small room, with bars in front of the window,' she said. 'Just like a cell. There's only a mattress and a bucket. And a Bible.'

When she emerged, she wasn't allowed to wear the standard orange school uniform, but had to don a blue dress that branded her a runaway and trouble-maker. A week later, she absconded again. Arrested and sent back once more,

Jenny was locked up for fourteen days this time and Van Aswegen ordered her to wear the blue dress for a month.

In order to reinforce his iron grip on the hapless inmates, the headmaster decided to beat Jenny into submission. 'Mr van Aswegen told me to put on the *blommetjiesbroek* (flowered pants),' she said. 'The girls called those pants the *strafbroek* (punishment pants). I bent over and he lifted my dress. He beat me with a strap called Sannie. I refused to cry. I closed my eyes and bit my lip.'

Jenny said over a period of less than two years she ran away eight times and spent a total of fifty-nine days in solitary confinement. She was on the receiving end of Sannie at least five times. Whenever Van Aswegen ordered her to bend over, she said, it was 'six of the best'. He once gave her twelve strokes. The strap split her skin and she bled, she claimed.

During the Easter holidays in 1985, Jenny and seven other girls managed to force open the burglar bars in front of a hostel window and jumped out. After a few days on the run, one girl, aged sixteen, was raped and murdered. When her corpse was brought back to the school, Van Aswegen forced the other runaways, who had meanwhile been apprehended and sent back, to look at their dead schoolmate. 'You see?' he said. 'This will happen to all of you if you don't listen.'

My childhood was perfectly ordinary – unremarkable and entirely normal for the time, place and people concerned, including the beatings at school. My parents were decent, middle-class, productive and God-fearing citizens. They instilled in me a sense of responsibility and respect for others.

I don't know if my father was aware of the level of brutality stalking his own society. I never discussed it with him. By the time I realised something was horribly wrong, he was on his deathbed, his emaciated body devoured by cancer.

My father beat me only once, and that was when I threw my shoes at Martha, our domestic worker. I had no idea where Martha came from, what her surname was or whether she had a husband and children, but I had to treat her with respect. I remember standing at the kitchen window one night and watching as the police dragged someone out of her tiny room in the backyard. My father told me to go to bed and the incident was never spoken about.

As a child, and even as a teenager, I was no more than vaguely aware of things like the pass laws or the Group Areas Act. My family, friends and I used the dreaded *kaffir* word, although my parents preferred to call blacks *naturelle* (natives). My mother called petrol attendants and other black men 'John'. There seemed to be an awful lot of *naturelle* named John.

My parents installed a shower for Martha so that she could keep herself clean. I think they even helped her to build a house somewhere in a homeland. She was as close to me as my mother, but ate from a tin plate and drank from a tin cup and cooked her own 'boys' meat' – cheap offcuts sold by butchers for consumption by servants. I sometimes sat with her in her room, where she fed me *pap* and *morogo* (maize porridge and indigenous wild spinach).

Max du Preez wrote in *Pale Native*: 'From the time I was very young I had a gut instinct that the leaders of my ethnic group were lying to me.' At a tender age, he said, he felt outrage when his father made a racist remark. He keenly followed the Rivonia Trial and romanticised the *Boere-kommunis* (Boer communist) Bram Fischer.

I had no such experiences. My father wasn't a racist, but the only black people besides the maid and the gardener with whom he ever interacted were the caddies on the golf course. His school was white, our neighbourhood was white, the city was white and the church was white. It was a beautiful but delusional snow-white world.

When *jeugdige opstokers* (youthful agitators) took to the streets of Soweto on 16 June 1976, I was still at school and obsessed with the All Black rugby team touring South Africa. It was a Wednesday afternoon, and I think the New Zealanders were playing a university side at Loftus Versfeld, temple of rugby in Pretoria. As we drove home after the match, my father switched on the car radio. There was *klipgooiery* (stone throwing) in the townships.

'What's going on?' I asked him.

'Don't worry,' he said. 'The police have everything under control.'

'Why are they burning their own schools down?' I asked.

'Bad people are inciting them,' he responded. I don't think he grasped the tide of anger in the townships any more than I did.

I duly attended catechism classes every Sunday. I'm not sure I really believed in God, but on confirmation night (when young people became fully fledged congregants and took holy communion for the first time) there was a thunderstorm and the power went out. The ritual was conducted by candlelight, but when it was my turn to place the small cube of bread – the body of Christ – on my tongue, the lights miraculously flickered back to life for a few seconds. To her dying day, my grandmother believed I was a blessed child.

When I was sixteen and in Standard 9, I registered as a conscript for the two years of national service I would be required to do after school in the South African Defence Force. Throughout high school I was a member of the cadet corps, where we learnt basic military parade ground drills in our khaki uniforms with short pants and listened to real soldiers who came to tell us about real war. They spoke about the Border war in South West Africa (later Namibia) and a communist-backed terrorist organisation called SWAPO that abducted schoolchildren and slaughtered innocent civilians. Communists, I thought, must be extremely grim people.

Most of my friends couldn't wait to get to the 'operational area', or even Angola, where they anticipated an exhilarating adventure. Conscription was regarded as a form of initiation: you had to go through it in order to become a man. National servicemen barely old enough to vote or get a driving licence who made the ultimate sacrifice were hailed as heroes. Their photographs were shown on television while the national anthem softly hummed in the background.

I was my mother's *witbroodjie* (favourite child), and in order to escape the harsh reality of the border conflict, she suggested I go to university after school. The University of Pretoria was lily-white and a beacon of Christian National Education, notwithstanding the fact that the students drank like fish and that when the jacarandas bloomed each October, *Boerepoppies* (Afrikaner dolly birds) popped out scores of unwanted babies conceived during the unbridled annual fun of Rag. But at least, unlike its traditionally English counterparts, the campus was untainted by communists or agitators or rowdy lefties.

My lecturers were drab, dull and conservative. My anthropology professor was one of the architects of the right-wing Conservative Party's policy, while another lecturer, Koos Botha, was in later years involved in a series of right-wing bomb explosions.

I was bored and skipped at least half my classes. I befriended a group of art students, smoked pot and enrolled for sculpting classes in order to gawk at naked models. I felt quirky and eccentric and dated a slutty bank teller who had her own flat and did yoga and listened to Dire Straits. I was sure I was living on the edge.

In my political science class there was a blind student who had a black youth to carry his books and help him around. The boy was not allowed to use the student toilets. Then some students complained about his presence in the lecture rooms and he had to wait outside. I was outraged, but did nothing. The first vote I ever cast was for the Progressive Federal Party (PFP). When I grow up one day, I thought, I want to be like PFP leader Frederik van Zyl Slabbert.

I stretched a silly and inconsequential three-year BA degree over five years to avoid going to the army. When I eventually had to report to 4 Infantry Battalion in Middelburg, I was armed with a false medical certificate. It stated that I had had tuberculosis as a child and had suffered permanent lung damage. I couldn't venture onto the shooting range or the parade ground. I never drilled or fired a single shot. My parents were friends with a prominent army brigadier, and before long I was a journalist at the SADF's official magazine, *Paratus*. It was the cushiest job in the army.

I screwed and bullshitted the army wherever I could. Now and then I travelled to the Border to snap pictures of dead SWAPO guerrillas and captured 'communist' weaponry. I wrote flowery propaganda about the army's 'iron fist bloodying SWAPO's terrorist nose' and crushing the Red Bear in Angola. It didn't bother me in the least, as long as I could escape combat and hardship. I was even given a rank and elected the best national serviceman at *Paratus*.

I'm not sure why I became a journalist. I suppose there wasn't much else to do with a degree in political science. The Sunday newspaper *Rapport* advertised for trainee reporters. I applied.

'Do you believe her?'

'Yes, I do. I have no doubt she's telling the truth.'

'I'm not convinced. You can't just believe her. We have to make sure.'

'What do we do?'

'Go to Standerton and have a nice and friendly chat with Mr van Aswegen. Let's see what he says.'

Seated opposite me was Martin Welz, my colleague at *Rapport*. No one had a more significant influence on my early journalistic career than this wiry, somewhat eccentric man with his Napoleonic nose. At the tip of that nub perched a pair of reading glasses. In a bony hand he perpetually clutched a lighted cigarette. His shirt tail was mostly draped over his pants, which, in turn, hung like a loose sack around his hips.

His office resembled a whorehouse in the aftermath of a vigorous police raid. Files, documents, notes, empty cigarette boxes, half-eaten apples and old newspapers were strewn across the floor. Martin never met any deadline, and there were times when he wasn't just hours late with copy, but days!

My office was next to his. I was in awe of being in such close proximity to a man whose journalistic accomplishments included the so-called Info Scandal. Martin was one of a small group of journalists in the late seventies to expose high-level corruption in the Department of Information, which forced the resignation of information minister Connie Mulder and contributed to the downfall of Prime Minister John Vorster. He subsequently exposed massive medical malpractice, unmasked an Italian multimillionaire as a Mafioso and laid bare apartheid South Africa's sanctions-busting arms deals.

I've never encountered anyone who could poke as doggedly and incisively as Martin. The phone was forever plastered to his ear, and he was relentless, merciless and, in a journalistic sense, ruthless. He taught me a golden rule: never believe anyone, he warned, and especially not politicians, lawyers, senior civil servants or businessmen. Martin was convinced that almost every fortune hid a crime.

The news editor, exasperated by Martin's inability to deliver on time, appointed me as his assistant. It brought me even closer to the master. I spent most of my time on my knees sifting through documents, scouting for a lost telephone number, trying to organise his unruly mind or typing while he dictated.

We started breaking stories together and shared bylines. When an Afrikaner businessman devised the biggest pyramid scheme in the history of South Africa and swindled his gullible countrymen out of hundreds of millions, Martin despatched me to face disillusioned investors. Convinced that *Rapport* was responsible for their financial collapse, they viciously turned on me. Police had to protect me and whisked me away from the marauding masses.

Martin set a trap for a corrupt cabinet minister (he later went to prison) who was engaged in dubious real estate deals. I had to pretend to be an estate agent. The minister swallowed my bullshit hook, line and sinker, and before long I was sitting in his official black Merc haggling about property prices.

And so, when Jenny phoned me, I turned to Martin for advice and we were soon on our way to Standerton. He had an uncanny ability to persuade someone he was on his or her side. Van Aswegen, convinced we were batting for the same team, ate out of our hands. Short of showing us Sannie and the *strafbroek*, he confirmed virtually everything Jenny had said.

The following Sunday, *Rapport* blasted the story across the front page and dedicated two inside pages to Van Aswegen's ornate pants, the feared and loathed strap, and the lock-up with the bucket. It became one of the single biggest investigations in the newspaper's history. For more than six months, week after week and Sunday after Sunday, I highlighted the plight of what the paper dubbed: 'South Africa's forgotten children'.

A journalist? Why a journalist? Is it a worthy profession?

My father, having suffered a stroke prior to being diagnosed with lung cancer, had lost his speech and the use of the right side of his body. Through hand movements and an almost inaudible slur he calmed down my mother when I told them that I wanted to be a journalist.

Although I think he wasn't completely averse to the idea, journalism shouldn't have been his only son's chosen profession. Theology and tuition bubbled in my family's blood. My great-grandfather was a missionary professor from Holland who arrived on Africa's southern shores, spawned something like twelve children and founded the NG Sendingkerk (Dutch Reformed Mission Church) for coloured people. My grandfather was also a clergyman, but my father chose teaching and rose to become headmaster of a leading Pretoria school. One of my uncles was also a headmaster, while the other was a respected Afrikaner businessman. My mother was a pedagogue who wrote books on remedial teaching. My only sister also became a teacher.

Journalism didn't seem like a *real* job. It paid badly. It was widely seen as a degrading trade whose practitioners had a reputation for excessive boozing, dodgy moral values and loose living. That was probably what attracted me to the profession. I thought I was going to get paid for having fun while at the same time bringing the government to its knees.

I slowly awakened to the world around me. A few days after reporting for duty, I was despatched to a Hillbrow flat where a father had gassed his family. For the first time in my life I was confronted with dead people, among them a baby girl with a waxen skin and tightly shut eyes.

I launched an investigation into the plight of the elderly. I scrounged decrepit and gloomy flats in Hillbrow and downtown Johannesburg. I walked into dumps where old people were eating dog food and pissing in their pants and dying of neglect. Of course they were all white, but nonetheless I was seeing things I'd never even imagined existed.

As my frame of reference expanded, I was assigned to cover extreme right-wing politics. The first meeting I attended was addressed by Afrikaner Weerstandsbeweging (AWB) leader Eugene Terre'Blanche. When *die volk* (the people) rose to sing 'Die Lied van Jong Suid-Afrika' (The Song of Young South Africa, unofficial anthem of the AWB), I stayed in my seat. As the meeting drew to a close, two pubescent *stormtroepe* (storm troopers), generations of inbreeding glaringly evident in their pimpled and moronic faces, rushed to the press table and threatened to beat me up. Terre'Blanche, still on the stage, ordered them to leave me alone.

A week or so later, the AWB had a gathering at Vryheid in Natal. I was again threatened – *Rapport* was truly hated by the right wing – and Terre'Blanche once more saved my skinny arse. The *uitverkorene* (chosen one) walked over and shook my hand. The following week we had lunch at a Pretoria restaurant, where he ordered a rib-eye steak and red wine.

The Boer leader warmed to me. He was reminiscing about the invincibility of the Boer people when he suddenly told me I must not lose the twinkle in my blue eyes. As he murmured the words, he leant across the table, put his hand on my shoulder and rubbed my neck. I was too startled to move, and for a moment thought he might try to kiss me. He reeked of stale sweat.

Of course I was repelled and dismayed, but we gulped down another glass of wine and he told me about AWB training camps. It was the lead story in the next edition of *Rapport* – although he denied it in the daily newspapers the day after.

I met Terre'Blanche again a few weeks later. I dragged a colleague with me, both as a deterrent and a witness. Unperturbed, the perverse old fart recited a poem and shuffled even closer. After this he was the one who phoned and proposed lunch. I met him once or twice more, and then wrote a story about two AWB *penkoppe* (cubs) who claimed they had been sexually assaulted by members of the movement's top brass.

I never spoke to Terre'Blanche again, and I couldn't attend meetings or gatherings any longer as I had received too many death threats. That was when I teamed up with Martin Welz.

Sixteen-year-old Mareloo walked into my office with her arm covered in burns and cuts. She had run away from an industrial school after spending fourteen days in the lock-up with only a Bible. The headmaster had instructed her to learn Psalm 119 by heart.

Mareloo emerged from the cell unable to recite the text. The headmaster threatened to lock her up again, and for longer. She took a cigarette and burnt her forearms and slit her wrists with a blade. She was taken to a hospital, where she escaped. She saw the articles in *Rapport* and came to the newspaper.

Mareloo was one of a drove of runaways roaming the streets of Hillbrow who were all too willing to recount their stories of horror and neglect. She took me to a tiny flat that belonged to a Hillbrow nurse named Magda Nunes. The flat was crammed with runaways, mostly from industrial schools, whom Nunes fed, clothed and tried to keep off the streets. Magda was one of those benevolent and nurturing people with a heart as big as an oil tanker.

The 'govvie-chicks' all had similar stories: corporal punishment, solitary confinement, emotional and physical abuse. Girls told me of headmasters who would stop beating them only once they either begged for mercy or cried. Others told of housemothers who demanded lesbian favours in return for additional privileges.

Girls were locked up for days without being able to wash or speak to anyone. Another runaway from Van Aswegen's school claimed she was raped, and when she reported the incident to him, he told her to stop lying, despite the fact that she had contracted a venereal disease. The manhandling of industrial-school pupils was widespread, common and institutionalised.

At the time, there were eighteen industrial schools around the country for whites and two reformatories, one for boys and one for girls. Juvenile courts referred 'problem children' to industrial schools, supposedly not as harsh as reformatories, although they turned out to be no less cruel or depraved.

The girls were no angels. A seventeen-year-old swallowed an overdose of pills in Magda's flat and I had to rush her to hospital. When she was discharged two days later, she refused to go back to the flat.

My flatmate was overseas and I allowed the girl to stay at my place until I could work out what to do with her. After a day or two, I found used condoms in the refuse bin. When I arrived home early the next day, I walked in on a brothel, with the runaway and a client cavorting on my bed!

What went on behind the barbed-wire fences surrounding industrial schools was protected under the Children's Act, and the Department of Education and Culture denied any wrongdoing at their institutions. The furthest officialdom would go was to announce the 'modernisation' of lock-ups in order to minimise the impression of a prison cell. In future, the department said, the rooms would be fitted out with toilets, washbasins and an intercom to enable headmasters to play soothing music to their troubled inmates. Corporal punishment for girls had been abolished a year earlier, though principals and teachers blatantly ignored the ban.

The department claimed that 80 per cent of all industrial-school pupils were successfully rehabilitated, despite research from the University of Cape Town's criminology department showing that 36 per cent of white prison inmates had spent time at such schools.

The state also stood by their man. Jan van Aswegen was described as a model educator who cared deeply about his pupils. He and his entire teaching staff laid charges of malicious and untrue reporting against me with the Press Council.

A few weeks into the exposé, I was summoned to the office of the Minister of Education and Culture. I had earlier requested an interview with Piet Clase, but it was bluntly refused. The issue was by then becoming a hot potato, with other newspapers getting in on the action and questions being asked in parliament.

Tall and hawk-like with a thin mouth and gold-rimmed glasses, Piet Clase was an arch-conservative National Party stalwart. He hardly looked up as I strutted into his office with Martin Welz and a photographer in my wake. As we sat down at a polished desk, he leant towards me menacingly, poked his finger in my face, and lashed out: '*Vir jou, jong man, dônner ek!*' (I will beat you up, young man!)

I was startled and didn't respond. He continued his diatribe, his finger pointing at me like the barrel of a gun: '*Ek laat nie met my manne mors nie!*' (I won't let you mess with my people!) As Clase uttered these words, the photographer snapped a picture.

That Sunday, the indignant politician was on the newspaper's front page and his belligerent statement the headline. War had been declared between *Rapport* and the education department. Clase issued a statement lambasting the newspaper's handling of his interview. He reiterated that corporal punishment was forbidden and lock-ups used for 'therapeutic purposes' only.

The state was fighting back. Police arrested Jenny, who had by then found refuge in Magda's flat. Soon afterwards the nurse was also picked up. It was against the law to harbour 'govvie-chicks'.

Jenny was kept in police cells for four days before being transferred to a place of safety. Van Aswegen announced that she was a troublemaker and he didn't want her back at his school. Nunes was detained for two days before being charged with contravening the Children's Act.

The department released a statement saying Jenny was being transferred to the girls' reformatory in Cape Town. She would have a fresh opportunity to be rehabilitated, the department said, adding that this would hopefully bring an end to all the negative publicity.

How wrong they were. When Magda Nunes appeared in the Johannesburg Magistrate's Court, it wasn't she who was put on trial, but a sadistic headmaster with a pair of floral pants and a strap called Sannie in his briefcase. Ultimately, it was the department and its employees who had to answer for their perverse and archaic policies that had traumatised generations of deprived and destitute children.

Rapport had mustered considerable resources to fight the charges against Magda Nunes. Her defence was that circumstances at Die Vlakte were so desperate that she had had no option but to harbour Jenny.

When Jan Daniël van Aswegen took the witness stand to tell magistrate LS du Toit what a difficult and uncontrollable child Jenny was and of his laudable attempts to rehabilitate her, a panel of three psychologists, a psychiatrist and two criminologists, as well as a pack of highly skilled and aggressive lawyers, confronted and challenged him.

In preparing for the case, one of *Rapport*'s psychologists and the psychiatrist visited Jenny at the reformatory and put her through a battery of tests. They found she was depressed and on the verge of suicide. Her experience at Die Vlakte had left her distrustful, suspicious and dejected. What Van Aswegen had done to her, the experts concluded, was inhuman and criminal.

When he stepped down three days later, his initial arrogance and self-conviction had dissipated into disgrace and indignity. His reputation was in tatters, and his bursary to study in the United States was gone. Instead, his own department turned on him and ordered a disciplinary inquiry. The police instituted criminal charges. Van Aswegen returned to Standerton with an empty briefcase. The magistrate ordered Sannie and the florid pants destroyed.

Rapport subpoenaed Van Aswegen's punishment pants, his strap, and the registers for his lock-up and corporal punishment. Like most diligent bureaucrats, he had kept an impeccable record of his disciplinary diet. As he produced the lock-up register, *Rapport*'s senior advocate Piet Henning asked: 'Are you still using the lock-up room?'

Van Aswegen: 'Yes, but in the meantime we have put beds in.'

Henning: 'Did they previously sleep on the floor?'

Van Aswegen: 'Yes, on mattresses.'

Henning: 'And what else? Reading material?'

Van Aswegen: 'Yes, they can request that.'

Henning: 'Anything else? We have a mattress, blankets and a pillow. What else?'

Van Aswegen: 'That's basically all. Except that they also get a bucket for their toilet needs.'

Henning: 'A bucket?'

Van Aswegen: 'Yes, a bucket.'

Henning: 'Is there water in the room?'

Van Aswegen: 'They regularly get water.'

Henning: 'Is there a tap in the room?'

Van Aswegen: 'No.'

Henning: 'Do your dogs at home have water?'

The magistrate ordered Van Aswegen to show the court his strap and the pants girls had to don before a thrashing.

Henning: 'Why is it necessary for girls to wear these flowery pants?'

Van Aswegen: 'It is improper for a girl to bend over in her school dress.'

Henning: 'Oh really?'

Van Aswegen: 'Yes, I deemed it necessary that they wear something more decent.'

Henning: 'Did you also hit them in winter?'

Van Aswegen: 'If it was necessary, yes.'

Henning: 'What do the girls wear in winter?'

Van Aswegen: 'Long pants.'

The punishment register revealed that the headmaster had administered up to ten lashings to a single girl. Henning asked him: 'Do you regard corporal punishment as therapy?'

Van Aswegen: 'Yes. If the child feels punishment on her body, it's more effective. Many come from homes where corporal punishment is nothing strange.'

Henning: 'And this girl [Jenny], you gave her seven lashes?'

Van Aswegen: 'Yes, she signed for seven. Not twelve as she suggested.'

Henning: 'Did you feel pain [when you did it]?'

Van Aswegen: 'Yes. In my soul.'

Henning: 'Did you hit with love?'

Van Aswegen: 'Yes, I did.'

Henning: 'Have you ever heard of assault committed with love?'

Van Aswegen: 'No.'

Henning: 'The only difference between corporal punishment and assault is that the one is legally permitted and the other not. It's therefore nonsense to talk of applying corporal punishment with love.'

Van Aswegen: 'I do not agree with you.'

Henning: 'With that strap, sir, you have thrashed a girl until she bled!'

Van Aswegen: 'I'm not aware of that. I don't know how that would be possible.'

Henning: 'Do you want to act as a guinea pig so that we can test it?'

Van Aswegen: 'If it's done with the same attitude, yes.'

Magistrate du Toit rejected the state's case and said in his judgment that Van Aswegen's behaviour had created a crisis at his school. Jenny had had no option but to flee and Magda Nunes had merely shielded her from further abuse. He condemned the headmaster for hitting children, locking them up, slapping a child, and ignoring two suicide attempts and an alleged rape.

Under immense pressure to act, a stolid Piet Clase caved in and appointed two commissions of inquiry to investigate industrial schools and reformatories.

Four months later, the commissions reported 'shocking conditions' and inadequate and often non-existent rehabilitation. They made more than a hundred recommendations to upgrade reform and care, including a total ban on corporal punishment and solitary confinement as methods of punishment.

As the department announced a new deal for South Africa's 'forgotten children', the court also ordered Jenny's release from the reformatory. One of *Rapport*'s lawyers adopted her.

My first 'black' story was as much of an eye-opener as the industrial school exposé. I met a clergyman by the name of Willie Cilliers. He was an astute curmudgeon and a preacher in the African branch of the Dutch Reformed Church family.

Cilliers was one of a small group of prominent and enlightened Afrikaner theologians – others were Beyers Naudé and Nico Smith – who had many years earlier broken away from the white mother church and found a home on the 'black' pulpits from where they advocated religious non-racialism and spoke out against National Party doctrine.

He gave me a book, written by a black theologian about apartheid's migrant labour system. Black men from the Bantustans were permitted to work in the cities, but had to leave their families behind in the rural areas. They were forced into single-sex accommodation scattered around the townships.

Cilliers took me to the Nancefield Hostel in Soweto – my first visit to the sprawling township. Thousands of blank-faced men existed in conditions not fit for animals. Nancefield was nothing but an overcrowded, decrepit, demeaning, grimy and diseased human garbage heap.

I spent several days with Cilliers at Nancefield and started speaking to the residents. They were cleaners and gardeners and garbage collectors and truck drivers and street sweepers and office workers. Just ordinary people, eking out a living in what I called 'apartheid's rubbish dump' in my articles.

After publication, the Department of Cooperation and Development – the government division responsible for the daily affairs of black people – announced it was going to upgrade the ablution facilities at Nancefield.

Was that it, I thought.

Next, I did a story about Mozambicans flocking to South Africa in an attempt to escape the civil war raging in their country. In the border town of Komatipoort, a senior police officer drove me in his Land Rover to the banks of the Komati River to show me what he called *krok-worsies* (crocodile sausages). They turned out to be the half-eaten corpses of refugees who had attempted to cross the river by night and fallen prey to crocodiles.

In a tasteless reference to a chicken fast-food advertisement, he smacked his lips and chortled with delight: '*Vinger-lek lekker!*' (Finger-licking good!)

Gone was my gullibility. I was discovering the real world. And it was cruel, arrogant, intolerant and bigoted. I might have been a *boereklong* (Afrikaner boy) from white and middle-class Pretoria, but my eyes were slowly being prised open.

I left the Dutch Reformed Church, joined the PFP (that's as far left as I thought it was possible to go) and had political arguments with my family. They didn't seem too concerned. Just wait, my mother said, you'll grow up one day.

I scoffed at the *totale aanslag* (total onslaught) ideology and did stories on PW Botha's declaration of a state of emergency. I covered the so-called Delmas Treason Trial, and searchingly looked at Popo Molefe and Terror Lekota (Mosiuoa Patrick Lekota, currently Thabo Mbeki's defence minister) in the dock. Was that how communists and agitators looked, I wondered.

But it had still not dawned on me that while I was writing these stories, phantom-like demons were traversing the length and breadth of our country to arrange for the disappearance of the Pebco Three and the 'permanent removal from society' of the Cradock Four. South Africa was littered with the remains of those who had dared to oppose an ideology that fostered and nurtured hate, division and oppression.

Their deaths cloaked apartheid's ultimate weapon. When all else had failed – detention without trial, torture, state of emergency regulations and security legislation – a group of men were sent in stealth from a farm west of Pretoria to 'solve the problem'.

I was about to learn this most closely guarded secret. It happened one night towards the end of 1985, when an open-faced and clean-shaven Afrikaner by the name of Dirk Coetzee told me: 'I was in the heart of the whore.'

Minutes after I had met Coetzee, he picked up the telephone and spat out a tirade that went something like this: 'Jaap, you stupid fucking stinking cunt, you must go to Jesus Christ! And you, Johan Coetzee, you and that pig's head of a minister, I am going to fuck you up!'

Jaap was a police general and head of the Criminal Investigation Division. Johan Coetzee was the commissioner of police. Dirk wasn't finished, though. He accused another general of having a sleazy affair with the wife of a Supreme Court judge. He claimed another two top policemen were engaged in wife-swapping, and that a third blew his salary on prostitutes.

When he eventually slammed down the phone, he turned to Martin Welz and me and said: 'That will teach them a lesson!' He was in an ebullient mood and from time to time exploded in a kind of manic snicker.

The police were tapping Coetzee's phone. He explained that as soon as he lifted the handset – before even dialling a number – the tape recorder at Security Branch headquarters started running and policemen monitoring his calls had to listen to his vulgar tirades.

He dragged us off to a storeroom in his backyard where he kept documents and old police records. He slowly opened the door and warned me not to step inside. Somewhere in the room lurked a deadly puff adder, waiting for uninvited guests to try to snitch his documents.

When Martin and I drove home that night, he asked me: 'And so, what do you think?'

'I think he's mad,' I told him.

'No, he's not,' said Martin. 'He's just very angry.'

In years to come, platoons of lawyers would fall over one another to brand Dirk Coetzee a seriously disturbed liar. Politicians and policemen tagged him deranged and embittered.

He was none of those things. How would his detractors have behaved after years of burning bodies on wooden stakes and ordering point-blank executions with a Makarov pistol? Considering what he had done, Coetzee was surprisingly normal.

When I shook his hand that first night, I had no inkling that he would eventually play a major role in my life. Initially, he was nothing but a scorned cop venting his anger in an unorthodox manner. His pleasant face belied the dark and ominous secrets he sheltered.

He had hit the headlines long before we met. When he discovered that his phone being was tapped, he compiled a report about telephone tapping and sent it to the leader of the official opposition, Van Zyl Slabbert. The report caused an outcry and was published on the front page of most newspapers. The police denied they were illegally listening in on his telephone conversations and said he was merely a security policeman who had fallen out with the system and was under investigation for misconduct.

It was difficult to believe that Coetzee had once been one of the brightest stars in the South African Police galaxy. He was the best student of his intake and quickly rose to the rank of captain. In August 1980 he was hand-picked to set up a security police counter-insurgency base on a farm called Vlakplaas outside Pretoria. He started the unit with seventeen 'rehabilitated and turned' ANC and PAC activists – the police called them askaris – and a handful of white policemen.

Coetzee commanded Vlakplaas for two years before falling into disfavour. It later emerged that he had bungled a kidnapping from Swaziland that caused a diplomatic row. By 1984, he was a rogue cop harbouring deep embitterment against the generals. He soon faced a host of internal charges, ranging from insubordination to distributing a pornographic video among his colleagues.

Martin Welz met Coetzee during this time and dragged me with him, probably as company on the drive between Johannesburg and Pretoria. After meeting Coetzee a second and third time, I decided I liked the security policeman. He seemed to be a bit of a gossipmonger and merrily chattered on about the police. But he never once uttered the words *death squad* or *hit squad* or *murder* or *eliminate*. That came only many months later.

The night Coetzee told me he was a police death squad commander is vividly etched in my memory. He was in Johannesburg for some reason and we went drinking. By then he had told us that he had commanded Vlakplaas and that it was a base for captured terrorists or askaris who had been coerced, blackmailed or tortured into becoming security police operatives. Martin was with me, and as we got into the car, we pestered him. 'Oh, come on Dirk, tell us what you really did at Vlakplaas.'

I already knew Coetzee as a blabbermouth. Such individuals are the fantasies of which journalism is made. They can't help themselves. Secrets ooze out of every pore and, without being able to hold back, they bleed themselves dry. God bless their souls.

Dirk Coetzee was no exception. Once he started talking, information poured from him in a torrent. As we drove around in circles, I attempted to make mental notes.

Vlakplaas, he said, was nothing but a death farm. It was a base from where hit squads operated to kill opponents of the apartheid state. One white policeman was in charge of a team of three or four askaris, who were often used to perform the assassinations.

He mentioned a name. Mxenge. A lawyer. Stabbed how many times and finished off on a soccer field near Durban. That was one of the names that I remembered the next day. The other was that of a student activist, Siphiwo. He'd been poisoned and kidnapped while he was in a wheelchair.

'I was in the heart of the whore,' Coetzee said. His words later became the title of my first book. When I asked him what he meant, he said it was his own phrase to describe how deeply entrenched he had been in the inner workings of the security police.

Was I surprised? No. Was I appalled? No. Did I realise that I was being handed the biggest news scoop in many a year? No. Was Coetzee telling the truth? Martin had no doubt he was, and I trusted my colleague implicitly.

The next morning, I delved into the *Rapport* library and pulled out clippings on assassinations and disappearances. I soon recognised the Durban attorney as being Griffiths Mxenge and the poisoned student leader as Siphiwo Mtimkulu. Coetzee had described their deaths in detail. How could he have known if he wasn't involved?

I later discovered that Coetzee had told not only me about Vlakplaas. In fact, at one juncture he was blabbing his secrets to anyone who was prepared to listen. He told a senior and *verligte* (enlightened) National Party member of parliament, Wynand Malan (who later served on the Truth and Reconciliation Commission). Malan said he would discuss the matter with a cabinet minister. Coetzee never heard from him again.

He also briefed the PFP spokesman on police. He spent two days with the politician, but again nothing came of the meeting. He also confided in a prominent Afrikaans newspaper editor, who listened but did nothing.

There was no possibility that *Rapport* would publish the allegations. The editor at the time was Willem de Klerk, older brother of FW. Although he was a man of great integrity and on the left of the ruling party, the newspaper was still a government-supporting publication. I'm not sure if Welz ever told De Klerk about Coetzee, but he suggested to me that we should keep his revelations to ourselves until an opportunity arose to break the story.

At his internal inquiry, Coetzee had been found guilty on various charges of misconduct. On compassionate grounds, he was allowed to retire as medically unfit (he had diabetes), albeit on a reduced pension.

Coetzee left the force bent on vengeance. He had to depend on the charity and goodwill of friends and family and scraped together a living by doing odd jobs. Former police friends shunned him and he became a pariah.

Investigative journalists feast on outcasts with a score to settle. Although they tend to exaggerate when venting their disdain, they are invaluable sources of information and form the core of many an exposé.

Dirk Coetzee, however, was nothing less than a time bomb waiting to explode.

CHAPTER 2

Scratching the lion's testicle

Between a rock and a hard-on. The weird and wonderful world of the
Boere-left.   **– Max du Preez describing**
                                    Vrye Weekblad in *Oranje Blanje Blues*

'WHAT? WORK FOR MAX?' SAID A MUTUAL FRIEND WHEN I TOLD
him I wanted to join *Vrye Weekblad*. 'He's not normal. He's erratic
and short-tempered. There are rumours he's got brain damage.'

It was a given that Max du Preez wasn't sane. Only lunatics start a newspaper without money. The next time I spotted him at my local watering hole,
the Yard of Ale, I studied Mad Max – as he was widely known – closely. He'd
apparently never been the same after sustaining a nasty bump on the head in a
near-fatal aircraft crash in what was then South West Africa. He was scruffy. His
beard and hair needed scissors and a brush. I was convinced there was a manic
glaze in his eyes. He portrayed a pronounced go-fuck-yourself attitude.

I was nonetheless eager to join *Vrye Weekblad*, but Max wasn't too keen on
me initially. He was looking for a top-notch team of hard-arsed journalists to
tackle Afrikanerdom and its political and social excesses head-on. I didn't fit
the profile. I was a feature writer with the Afrikaans human-interest magazine,
Huisgenoot, where I churned out cheap and nasty drivel.

I had left *Rapport* at the beginning of 1987 after Willem de Klerk was forced to
resign as editor because of his enlightened political leanings. He was replaced by
a *verkrampte* (conservative) for whom I refused to work. When I quit, *Huisgenoot*
offered me a job.

My daily bread came from stories like Fransie Geringer's birthday bash in his
Western Transvaal hometown of Stilfontein. For those who don't remember,
Fransie was a young boy trapped in the body of a geriatric. He suffered from
progeria, a rare disease that causes rapid ageing and gives children the appearance
of wizened old men and women. By his early teens, the wrinkled and shrivelled
little boy was already about 120 years old!

I made several trips to Stilfontein to update *Huisgenoot*'s readers on Fransie's
flight into senility. On the way, I usually stopped in Potchefstroom to chronicle
the valiant progress of Elize, a young girl whose hands had been amputated
in an accident and who had to learn to dress and feed herself using artificial
limbs.

Max was rather brusque at first and didn't pay much attention to my attempts to woo him. But he wasn't exactly flooded with applications for *Vrye Weekblad*'s two or three journalistic slots. Everybody, it seemed, supported the concept of an independent and anti-apartheid Afrikaans newspaper, but few were prepared to put their money where their mouths were. He eventually had no option but to give me a job.

Max could offer little more than a dream. There was no prospect of long-term employment or benefits such as medical aid or pension funds. I felt I had nothing to lose and was utterly bored at *Huisgenoot*. The newspaper at least promised to be an adventure.

In the end, Max was forced to settle for a handful of odd and offbeat journalists. I was rather taken aback when I saw my colleagues for the first time. I arrived dressed in a jacket and tie at 153 Bree Street, the bank building that Max had transformed into newspaper offices. The editor himself had the semblance of a ducktail. The rest appeared equally threadbare and clearly hadn't had an income or steady work for some time. I wasn't sure I would fit into this decidedly strange-looking bunch of journalistic outcasts.

I had never imagined working in such a peculiar place. In his book *Pale Native*, Max rightly called his staff 'a bunch of foul-mouthed, ill-mannered individualists and anarchists'. They had respect for nothing and no one. There was always an argument brewing in one corner and a debate raging in another. Like the people who worked there, the office was a mess.

'It was the most wonderful, creative, exciting space I had ever been in or heard of,' writes Max. 'It was close to my dream of the ideal newsroom: no rules, no formalities – just a free flow of ideas.'

I have to pause for a moment to acknowledge Koos Coetzee. He was the crankiest of the lot. Max and Koos had worked together before, but since then the latter had been bogged down by severe depression. Max found Koos somewhere in a semi-paralytic state, dusted him off and dragged him to *Vrye Weekblad* as the chief subeditor. It was his first job in a long time.

Koos was a sinewy, unshaven and somewhat musty character sporting a pair of glasses with thick black frames. He was cynical and glum and seemed to resent life. Koos was homeless and kept a sleeping bag at the office, where he lived for some time. There was no bathroom, and the place reeked of Koos and Koos reeked of the office. He was a brilliant, albeit frightening, subeditor.

I was initially petrified of Koos, especially when he ordered me to stop writing in florid *Huisgenoot* style. He stuttered, most noticeably when he was pissed – which was all the time. He would look at my copy, get a disdainful expression on his unshaven face and roar in a thunderous voice: *Jakkie, w-w-w-wat se p-p-p-p-poes is dit al weer hierdie?* I'm not sure how to translate *poes*. It's loosely the Afrikaans for cunt, so an approximate English equivalent of his dismissive comment would be: Jackie, w-w-w-what c-c-c-c-cunt is this again?

But underneath his base demeanour I later discovered a warm and genial fellow with a heart of gold, and we became close friends. A few years on, Koos finally lost his battle against depression and committed suicide.

As for Max, he was the anarchist incarnate. Brusque, *bedônnerd* and short-tempered – extremely, some would say – he demanded results. Crooks, killers, racists, assassins, anything that would sell the newspaper, damage the Afrikaner establishment, expose apartheid and make others take notice of us. He drove us like slaves but dangled an irresistible carrot: the space to practise honest, frank and uncompromising journalism.

I didn't join *Vrye Weekblad* because of any political conviction. I was no longer the naive reporter who had joined *Rapport* nearly five years earlier, but I still didn't grasp what non-racialism meant. The ANC, the Communist Party and even the United Democratic Front were as outlandish to me as they were to most of the newspaper's readers.

On the eve of 4 November 1988, we managed to scrape together the first edition of *Vrye Weekblad*. Earlier in the day I had sneaked into a proper newspaper's library under false pretences to filch photographs of people such as PW and Pik Botha, Magnus Malan, FW de Klerk, Adriaan Vlok and others who promised to frequently grace our front pages.

It was close to deadline and we didn't have a lead story yet. Max dictated and I typed. 'Nelson Mandela,' we wrote, 'will definitely be a free man soon. The date of 14 November is widely tipped as the day of his release.'

I don't think we had a source. I have no idea where the date of 14 November came from. Quite honestly, it was a bit of a thumbsuck! But as Max would afterwards say: '*Vrye Weekblad* was always ahead of its time!'

The important thing was that the newspaper was going to press, and we later got horribly drunk at the Yard. As happened often, Koos fell asleep in the bar's only toilet and it took us hours to wake him up and drag him out.

I again teamed up with my former colleague and friend Martin Welz, who had meanwhile also left *Rapport*. For the first edition of the newspaper he produced an exposé of a prominent Afrikaans businessman from Bloemfontein who was implicated in a housing scam. The man, a close friend of PW Botha, was extorting money from poor whites.

I had helped Martin with the story. When it hit the streets that Friday morning, the businessman left his office with *Vrye Weekblad* tucked under his arm, got into his luxury car and gassed himself and his gay lover outside the city.

Shaken, I phoned Martin when I heard the news. Unperturbed, he said:

'That's how you fuck someone up!' He's always denied those were his exact words, but I remember them as though he spoke them yesterday.

For one of the first editions of the newspaper, Martin and I wrote a story about a secret meeting between PW Botha and a notorious Italian Mafia boss who lived in South Africa. The Mafioso and the state president apparently discussed the possibility of a healthy contribution to the National Party's election coffers in return for his unhindered residence in the country. Botha denied the story and threatened to sue *Vrye Weekblad* for defamation. Suddenly, the rest of the media took notice and the president's indignation was the lead story on the state broadcaster's TV news that night. When the dreaded article was flashed on the screen, my byline was clearly visible.

The telephone rang. I somehow knew it was my mother. 'I wonder what your late father would have said about this,' she said through her tears. She suggested I write under a pseudonym in future to avoid further disgracing the good name of the family. We had a somewhat strained relationship for some time, although in later years she became my staunchest supporter.

Vrye Weekblad became one of the most prosecuted and persecuted newspapers in South Africa's history, turning Max into a virtual habitual criminal. Most Afrikaners branded us traitors, while the government regarded the newspaper as a threat to national security.

Max and I became extremely close. We developed the same camaraderie that soldiers share once they've spilt blood in battle together or ducked bullets side by side in foxholes. His public image was that of a hard-arsed, uncompromising, angry and maverick journalist who was always on the warpath. It was in many ways just a facade. I discovered a vulnerable and sensitive man who, like the rest of us, was full of insecurities and foibles.

One night, someone hammered on the newspaper's front door. Only Max and I were in the office, and I peeked through a window. Two rather ferocious-looking men the size of tree trunks stood outside.

The previous Friday I had written an exposé on an extremist and fascist white church after covertly attending one of their services in the Western Transvaal. The church regarded blacks as 'mud people' and advocated a so-called 'white man's Bible'.

I knew the two men at the door were from the church, as we had received calls earlier that day warning us they were on their way to *Vrye Weekblad* to beat us up. Whenever I received threatening calls, I burst into a diatribe of abuse – in the mould of Dirk Coetzee during his phone-tapping days – and slammed the receiver down. 'Fuck off, you cunt!' was my standard rebuttal. Koos said not even he could do better.

However, when it came to confronting my adversaries face to face, I wasn't nearly as brave. Neither, I discovered, was Max. We switched off the lights and tried to hide behind a cupboard. By now the men were peeking through the window and saw movement in the office. They threatened to break the door down and ordered us to come out.

We negotiated with them through the closed door. They were indeed from the church and demanded to speak to us. They promised not to get physical. We hesitantly opened the door. It was a mistake. Once inside, the burly beasts each took a pistol from the briefcases they carried and placed the weapons neatly on the table in front of them.

'Now,' they said, 'you're going to listen.'

We nodded our heads vigorously, and for the next hour or so listened to a most tormenting dissertation on why the Negroid lacked intellectual capacity and could never inherit the Kingdom of Christ. The Caucasian, by contrast, had a much larger brain and was therefore intellectually superior. Before they ran out of steam at long last and disappeared into the night, they warned us that if we belittled their church again, they would not be so amicable.

In time, the *Vrye Weekblad* office was bombed, and when we finally began exposing the death squads, there were numerous occasions when minibuses were ominously parked throughout the night in front of our homes. Our cars were broken into and we received countless death threats and constant hate mail.

But working for Max wasn't all *Sturm und Drang*. Shortly after the first edition, an elderly Afrikaner woman called me from a retirement home and said I had to come and see her. I thought she had mistaken *Vrye Weekblad* for *Landbou Weekblad* (an agricultural magazine), and hesitantly made my way to the dreary industrial town of Vereeniging, which was also FW de Klerk's 'safe' National Party constituency.

A grey-haired woman was waiting for me in the garden. She'd never seen or read *Vrye Weekblad*, but had overheard someone saying we didn't like the government and they didn't like us. She glanced around to make sure there weren't nosy eyes or ears focused on our exchange and shoved a mini-cassette into my hand. 'Go and listen to that!' she said.

'What is it?' I asked her.

'A speech Marike made to us.'

It was a story that brought me immense merriment: Marike de Klerk's infamous 'non-people' speech to a group of Vaal Triangle pensioners. Marike, remembered for her sour expression and the perpetual frown on her forehead, was not just FW's spouse, but also a member of the National Party's Federal Council.

For some reason the elderly woman, or someone she knew, had recorded

Marike's address. Max and I later listened to it with our mouths hanging open.

'The Coloureds,' said the future First Lady in a patronising tone, 'are a negative group. They are not black, they are not white and they are not Indian. In other words, they are non-people. They are those who remained behind when the others had been sorted out. They are the leftovers.'

Marike told her audience that just the week before, she had attended a performance by the Kaapse Klopse (a traditional Coloured song-and-dance troupe). 'I sat watching them and my heart bled. No two of them had the same features. We know we look European. But them? Some look Indian, some Chinese, some white, some black. And that is their dilemma.'

She was slightly more charitable towards Indians. 'They do need a bit of supervision,' she warned. She told her aged audience not to be concerned about the future. 'White supervision and domination are enshrined in the new dispensation.'

Needless to say, FW was never a great supporter of *Vrye Weekblad*, and later branded Max his enemy.

There was even a time at *Vrye Weekblad* when, believe it or not, I was in uniform again! I had completed my two years of national service in 1983. In March 1989, more than five years later, I was suddenly called up for a month-long military camp. Citizen Force members could be called up at any time if their services were required, but for the most part it was operational troops whose lives were regularly punctuated by the call to arms. Administrative types like me generally didn't warrant the paperwork involved, but I was nevertheless ordered to report to an army unit in Windhoek that produced propaganda for the SADF.

Vrye Weekblad deemed it harassment and a blatant attempt by the state to put an end to my mischief-making at the newspaper. Our lawyer took up the case, but the army stood firm: report for duty or face imprisonment. I was (sort of) prepared to go to jail, but Max came up with a better idea. Why don't you go, see what's going on, sniff around and write us a story? Be our correspondent in Windhoek for a month, he said.

It was an interesting period in Namibia's history. South Africa had finally committed itself to implementation of United Nations Resolution 435, which paved the way for democratic elections and independence. The UN was deploying peacekeepers and observers all across the country, while the SADF had to start withdrawing its forces and SWAPO had to demobilise.

I wriggled and jiggled myself into my corporal's uniform and reported for duty, as ordered, to the Army Information Unit. The commander was an SABC journalist and obviously a seasoned propagandist. Even then – and this was before the death squad exposé – I was a bit of an outcast among my fellow journalists staffing the unit as 'campers'. Nobody spoke to me or gave me anything to do.

I stayed with one of Max's friends and soon fell into the rhythm of jubilant Namibians celebrating the dawn of nationhood. There were parties around town, booze was free and plentiful, and my association with Max, who had lived and worked in South West Africa for a long time, gave me a ticket to join the fun.

I stopped reporting for duty or wearing a uniform, but during the time I had spent in the unit, I'd noticed my co-campers working frenetically on some project. They would often have meetings to which I wasn't invited.

I sneaked into the office early one morning – I had an access card – and scratched through their drawers, ransacked their tables and accessed their computer files. I discovered details of a massive campaign to discredit SWAPO. At a time when the SADF was supposed to be neutral and preparing to withdraw, they were producing pamphlets, a video and other election material on behalf of the so-called 'democratic' opposition parties that would contest the Namibian election.

I continued partying for another week or so while slipping into the office for early-morning raids. I flew back to Johannesburg and wrote the story. The SADF threatened to have me prosecuted under the Official Secrets Act. 'Welcome to the club,' Max observed wryly.

He and I signed a national register of conscientious objectors. A bit like slamming the stable door after the horse had bolted, admittedly, but Max insisted it would have symbolic value. The SADF didn't charge me. Instead, they wrote me a letter informing me that my attendance would not be required at any future camps.

If there was one story we were determined to publish, it was the existence of the security police's Vlakplaas hit squad. Max and I had agreed on this even before the ink was dry on *Vrye Weekblad*'s inaugural edition. I had no doubt he had the balls to do it, but the first year was a constant struggle for survival and there was little time to plot a way of dealing with Dirk Coetzee's revelations.

Everybody knew by then – or at least strongly suspected – that an official death squad existed, and fingers pointed at the security police, but there was no tangible evidence. Bombs went off and activists disappeared or turned up dead in mysterious circumstances. None of these crimes were ever solved and the police's standard rebuttal was that casualties were due to ANC 'infighting' or strife between the ANC and PAC.

In September 1989, SWAPO executive committee member Anton Lubowski was gunned down in front of his Windhoek house. We had no doubt that apartheid hit men had 'permanently removed him from society'. It later emerged he was murdered by a military-controlled death squad that we didn't even know existed at the time. Max told me to renew my acquaintance with Dirk Coetzee.

A day or so after the Lubowski murder, I wined and dined the former policeman at a Portuguese restaurant in Pretoria. I plied him with *vinho verde* and, when his blood sugar was sky-high, urged him to tell me more about Vlakplaas.

I already knew that Vlakplaas was a death farm and that the two murders Coetzee had previously mentioned were almost certainly the handiwork of his men. Now I wanted to know more – much more. He looked at me for a while, put his knife down, and asked: 'How much time do you have?'

'All night,' I replied.

When we stumbled out of the restaurant a few hours later, Coetzee had laid out the whole two years he had been the Vlakplaas commander. It was a bloodcurdling tale that spanned three countries and included six murders, attempted murder and conspiracy to murder, arson, sabotage, kidnapping, assault, housebreaking and car theft.

When he first arrived at Vlakplaas, Coetzee was one of the blue-eyed boys in the security police. His official car's registration was D J C 036 T – his initials and age when he set up the death squad. He drove around routinely with enough firepower in the boot of his car to start a small war. There were forty kilograms of explosives, a case of Russian hand grenades, five hand-held machine guns, a shotgun, and Makarov and Tokarev pistols with silencers. He also had body bags and strychnine in his car – just in case.

Coetzee had used strychnine to poison Griffiths Mxenge's dogs. He never needed the body bags. His favourite method of getting rid of activists was to take them to the banks of the Komati River and burn them to ashes. He did so three times. He was also involved in a bomb explosion in Swaziland and several more raids into the neighbouring state.

Coetzee also raised the spectre of Nazi Germany's 'Doctor Death', Joseph Mengele, when he told me that he had made a number of trips to the police forensic laboratory in Pretoria to fetch poison from the country's third most senior policeman, General Lothar Neethling. Ironically, the poison – designed to simulate a heart attack – didn't work, and he had to resort to a Makarov after all.

As he munched away on a steak, Dirk told me how he and his team had 'eliminated' two captured ANC cadres named Vusi and Peter. Like all assassins, Coetzee never used words like murder or kill. The covert conspiracy generated its own lexicon, one that contained no nasty references to blood, pain, death or suffering. Heaven forfend that any conversation should suggest a heinous crime was being committed!

So the killers and their bloodthirsty commanders spoke softly and in euphemisms: make a plan with; take him out; get rid of; permanently remove from society.

It was late afternoon when Peter and Vusi were taken to the banks of the Komati River. Coetzee added sedative drops to their cold drinks, and when the two men dozed off, a policeman stepped forward, placed his foot on the neck of one of the captives, pressed the muzzle of a Makarov against his head and pulled the trigger. Seconds later, the other man was executed in the same manner. 'Just a little jerk,' Coetzee told me, 'and then blood seeped out of their heads.'

In a dry ditch on the slightly elevated riverbank, a pyre was assembled from wood and old tyres. As the sun set over the Eastern Transvaal bushveld, two fires were lit, one to burn the bodies to ashes, the other for the security policemen to sit around and braai meat while drinking themselves into a stupor.

'It was just another job to be done,' Coetzee said as he mopped up the last bit of gravy from his plate with a chunk of bread. 'In the beginning it smells like a normal braai, but by the end all you can smell are the burning bones. It took about seven to nine hours to reduce the bodies to ashes.'

I asked him under what circumstances he would be prepared to have us publish his story in *Vrye Weekblad*. 'Get me out of the country and find me a safe place where my family and I can live in peace. Then I will tell the whole world what I did and what I know.'

It was Max who came up with the idea of sending Coetzee to the ANC in exile. I gaped at him as if he were mad. I told him so. 'Come up with a better idea,' he said. 'But come hell or high water, this is one story we are going to do.'

I didn't answer him. I had exhausted my brain trying to find a solution. I had no doubt Coetzee was ready to spill the beans, purely because he still wanted revenge and blamed the police high command for the fact that he'd been sidelined and was out of work. Our dilemma, however, was what to do with a self-confessed apartheid assassin. We didn't have the money to send him abroad. Max could barely meet the monthly payroll. One weekend he had simply disappeared to 'comfort' a lonely and frustrated woman in Cape Town whose stinking-rich husband had recently passed away. He came back with only half the amount of money needed, though he has always disputed this! Max somehow always found a way to pay salaries, albeit on occasion late.

Even if we could raise the money to get Coetzee out of the country, where would he go? No other country would be willing to accept him, and how the hell would we protect him, anyway?

The ANC was banned and outlawed and handing Coetzee over to the 'enemy' constituted a grave criminal offence. A whole lot of people had landed behind bars for lengthy periods for furthering the ANC's aims. When I pointed this out to Max, his answer was blunt. 'Do you want to do the story or not? And think about it, you'll be famous!'

I undertook to try to sell the idea to Coetzee. As we left the Yard, Max laughed and said: '*Nou krap ons die leeu se bal!*' (Now we are scratching the lion's testicle!)

He loved the idea. I was shit-scared. I thought about my recently bought house, my two dogs, my girlfriend and her young son, and the long and promising life and career I had envisaged for myself. I wasn't ready to sacrifice everything for the sake of a story, no matter how big or significant.

'I sensed that I was experiencing an important moment that could change the history of my country,' wrote Max in *Pale Native*. 'Perhaps this was why the universe had wanted me to launch an impossible newspaper project.'

Coetzee was surprisingly composed when I raised the possibility of him placing himself in the ANC's hands. He thought for a moment, then said: 'They'll kill me. I'll be a dead man.'

'They won't. They're not killers. Everything will be arranged,' I said. 'If anything happens, we'll write about it.'

'That might be a bit late, don't you think?' he replied.

Nevertheless, he agreed at least to talk to someone acting on behalf of the organisation, but before he could do so, events took a dramatic, even bizarre turn. On the eve of his execution, a death row prisoner swore an affidavit.

'I'm a 32-year-old male presently under sentence of death. My execution is scheduled for tomorrow morning, 20 October 1989, at 07h00. I wish to hereby reveal facts about my past which, I respectfully contend, might very well have had a bearing on my conviction.'

I was staring at the *Weekly Mail*. Its headline read: 'Death-row policeman tells of Special Branch hit squad.'

According to the story, Constable Butana Almond Nofemela had made a last-minute appeal for clemency the day before in order to escape the hangman's noose. In his affidavit, Nofemela said he had been a member of a police death squad. 'I served under Captain Dirk Coetzee, who was my commanding officer in the field.'

In September 1987, Nofemela was sentenced to death for murdering a white farmer. It wasn't an official 'hit' – simply a cold-blooded murder for personal gain. Nevertheless, he had hoped that his security police colleagues would save his skin, but when they abandoned him and his date with the hangman was fixed, he summoned a human rights lawyer and launched an urgent court application for a stay of execution. It was granted. He had told the court and the *Weekly Mail*: 'Sometime during late 1981 I was briefed by Brigadier Schoon and Captain Coetzee to eliminate a certain Durban attorney, Griffiths Mxenge. I was told by these superiors that Mxenge was to be eliminated for his activities within the ANC. I was involved in approximately eight other assassinations during my stint in the assassination squad, and also numerous kidnappings.'

It was an extraordinary coincidence. Nofemela's confession provided vital corroboration, as Coetzee had often mentioned his name as one of the killers from Vlakplaas. The details Nofemela provided about the Mxenge murder tallied in every salient respect with Coetzee's version: the dogs that had first been poisoned, the Okapi knife the squad had bought earlier in the day, how the lawyer had been abducted and taken at gunpoint to a soccer field, how he fought back before his throat was slit and his head bashed in with a wheel spanner.

Nofemela was on death row, and there was no way that he and Coetzee could have concocted a false account together. There was no longer any doubt that Coetzee was telling the truth.

The fact that Nofemela was a convicted murderer practically guaranteed an attack on the credibility of his claims. The security police would have discredited him without breaking a sweat, simply by filing a few false affidavits and dismissing him as a condemned man, desperate to save his own arse. But seen in conjunction with Coetzee's revelations, Nofemela's confession had the undeniable ring of truth. And the security police knew that.

When I saw an ashen-faced Coetzee on the day Nofemela's confession was made public, he was resigned. 'This is it,' he said. 'I think I've had enough. I told them a long time ago to look after Nofemela because he could bring all of us down with him.'

He agreed to meet André Zaaiman, a stern-faced director at the Institute for a Democratic Alternative for South Africa (Idasa), a long-standing friend and leftie Afrikaner. Max and I thought he was the obvious person to negotiate with the ANC on Coetzee's behalf. His work frequently took him to Lusaka in Zambia, where he dealt with the banned organisation's top leadership. Coetzee also undertook to contact his former gardener, David 'Spyker' Tshikalanga, whom he had elevated to the status of assassin and placed on the Vlakplaas payroll so that he could earn more money.

A few nights later, Max, Zaaiman and I met Coetzee and Tshikalanga on a smallholding outside Johannesburg. It was one of the most ominous nights of my life. The charcoal-skinned Tshikalanga – his nickname, the Afrikaans word for nail, was a tribute to his sexual prowess – had travelled from Venda to recount how he had slit lawyer Griffiths Mxenge's throat. His slow, monotone voice added to the eeriness of the dark-moon night. He explained how he had cut deep, right to the bone, then twisted the knife. Every now and then Coetzee giggled shrilly. 'You see,' he babbled, 'I told you!'

Dirk reiterated what he had previously told me about Vlakplaas, his voice droning on for hours. In *Pale Native*, Max later wrote that he was paralysed and rendered speechless by what he heard. 'I had a sudden panic attack. A part of me wished I had never heard this conversation. There was no way in the world, having heard this story, that we could ignore or keep it quiet. But I also knew that the story would be one of the most dangerous to be published since the National Party came to power in 1948. It could mean the end of our newspaper, and possibly have serious personal security implications for my colleagues and myself.'

The next morning, Zaaiman (he later told me he had slept in the bath that night) smuggled a cryptic message to ANC intelligence chief Jacob Zuma, and a few days afterwards flew to Zambia to brief the exiled Political Military Council on Coetzee's revelations and persuade them to offer the former policeman asylum.

Time was of the essence. While waiting to hear from Zaaiman, Coetzee was visited by a senior security police officer and told exactly what to say in order to neutralise Nofemela's dramatic admissions. Intuitively, he realised that unless he did as he was told, he would be singled out as the scapegoat, the fall guy for the very generals that he despised. The ANC agreed to shelter him, and Coetzee told me: 'Let's do it. I want to leave.'

Two weeks after the Nofemela bomb had burst, a forlorn Dirk Coetzee stood outside his house at six o'clock on a Sunday morning with two suitcases. He picked up his two poodles and hugged them close to his chest. 'I'm going to miss the dogs,' he said as he got into the car. 'I'm so fond of them.'

It had been an eventful forty-eight hours. The situation was tense, and it was getting to me. It was a massive responsibility to smuggle Coetzee out of South Africa and to safety with the ANC. Not only was it illegal, but anything could go wrong. He could get killed or simply vanish. The police might be waiting for us at the airport. His family could be targeted. Above all, in a country desperate for justice, we were helping an apartheid assassin to evade the law.

I could no longer think straight. On the afternoon of Friday 3 November, a purple Highveld sky disgorged a mighty deluge as I was driving from Johannesburg to Pretoria. The highway was slick and my thoughts a million miles away. I rear-ended the car in front of me, causing a major chain reaction as one vehicle thudded into another. As I slowly got out of my car and saw several pairs of angry eyes staring at me, I decided I couldn't handle this drama in addition to Coetzee's imminent departure. I gathered my things from my car, scampered across the freeway and jumped over the fence of the Kyalami golf course bordering the highway. I scurried across the fairways, navigated a small water hazard and ran to the clubhouse, from where I phoned Max to come and fetch me. I left my car on the highway, and to this day I don't know what happened to it.

The enormity of what he was doing caught up with Coetzee that day as well. His father was almost blind and seriously ill, and he thought the old man might not survive the shock of his son defecting to the ANC. He was also, quite understandably, concerned about the safety of his family. That night he confided in his elder brother Ben, the one person he had always trusted to help him make difficult decisions.

After my accident, Max, Koos and I waited at the Yard of Ale for Coetzee to call. It was quite late when he did, telling me: 'I'm ready to go.' Koos immediately poured a celebratory round. The story was on. Concerned that we might have a police spy in our office – which later turned out to be true – Max and I had been pretending for more than a fortnight at the office that it was business as usual. We had confided only in Koos, who would have to do the final editing of the Vlakplaas saga. Already mentally planning the layout and headlines, he reminded me more than once that night: 'Straight r-r-reporting, J-j-jakkie. No *Huisgenoot* drivel!'

Coetzee was not just an apartheid serial killer. He held the key to some of the country's most puzzling assassinations and disappearances. Names rolled off his tongue: Ruth First, Maputo, 1982. Parcel bomb. Sent to her by Major Craig 'Superspy' Williamson of the security police's foreign desk. Jeanette and Katryn Schoon, Angola, 1984. Another parcel bomb sent by Williamson. Siphiwo Mtimkulu, poisoned with thallium, his body burnt to ashes. Eastern Cape security police. The bombing of the ANC offices in London, 1982. Williamson again. After that operation, said Coetzee, police minister Louis le Grange had personally handed medals to those involved.

Even after leaving the police force, Coetzee had stayed in contact with one or two of the askaris. 'If you think I was bad,' he said, emitting a long, slow whistle, 'you ain't seen nothing yet!' His successor at Vlakplaas, he said, was a major by the name of Eugene de Kock. 'He's got thick black glasses and I hear the askaris call him *Brille* (spectacles). He's apparently very cruel and a great killer.'

For some reason Coetzee deeply resented De Kock – possibly because he knew that the latter led a far more effective killing machine than he had done. Coetzee had issued orders and rarely pulled the trigger himself. De Kock, he'd been told, personally carried out many executions.

Though the two men did not meet until the mid-1990s, when Coetzee testified against De Kock in court, their animosity was mutual. In De Kock's biography, written by journalist Jeremy Gordin, he disparaged Coetzee's description of having been 'in the heart of the whore'. 'If you want to use this metaphor,' he said, 'Coetzee was the kind of man who visits a brothel but stays in the parlour: he always had others do his dirty work for him. Furthermore, compared with me, he hadn't visited all that often. I doubt whether the whore would have recognised Coetzee in the street.'

On the morning of 5 November, Koos Coetzee drove Dirk and me to the airport. We had horrible hangovers after a debauched celebration of *Vrye Weekblad's* first birthday the night before. The cream of Johannesburg's anarchists and revolutionaries (or at least those not in exile or prison), Afrikaner lefties, avant-garde punks, academics and diplomats had toasted the newspaper's unexpected survival for a full year. In *Oranje Blanje Blues*, Max reminded me: 'Jacques Pauw, very unsteady on his feet and with a wild gaze in his eyes, ran around with a keg of red wine that he threw out on politicians and diplomats.'

While we drank as if there was no tomorrow, Dirk was taking his sons, Dirkie and Calla, to stay with friends because he couldn't face bidding them farewell. He was too distraught to call his parents and tell them that he might be away for a long time. Nor did he tell his wife where he was going or that he was placing himself in the ANC's hands. She would not have understood, he told me later.

Dirk and I were booked on a South African Airways flight to Mauritius. The plan was to stay on the island for a few days while I wrote his story, drew up an affidavit and took photographs of him. Then Coetzee would fly to London, where André Zaaiman would meet and deliver him to the ANC, which had undertaken to ensure his safety, give him sanctuary and look after his family.

On the way to the airport, Koos mumbled repeatedly: '*J-j-jakkie, f-f-f-fok hulle op*! (Fuck them up!) This is the big one!'

CHAPTER 3

Warm paper, wet ink

It is dangerous to be right when the government is wrong.
— Voltaire

E VERY YEAR SINCE 1989, I HAVE PAUSED FOR A MOMENT ON
17 November and cast my mind back to probably the greatest day of my
career. As the sun came up that morning Max, Koos and I were waiting at the
printers for the first copies of *Vrye Weekblad* to roll off the press. A printer in
blue overalls rushed over and placed them in our eager hands.

The paper was still warm and the ink still wet, but it smelt like freshly baked
bread. It was as if I was holding a newborn baby about to give its first cries
of life. As the distribution truck carrying our precious cargo made its way to
points of sale around Johannesburg, we followed and helped put posters up
on lamp posts.

That edition was one of the most beautiful things I'd ever cast my eyes
upon. The front page showed a photograph of Dirk Coetzee and the startling
headline: *'Bloedspoor van die SAP'* (Bloody trail of the SAP). The sub-headline
enticed readers to 'Meet Captain Dirk Johannes Coetzee, commander of an SA
Police death squad. He tells exclusively the full and gruesome story of political
assassinations, poisoned cocktails, foreign bomb blasts and letter bombs.'

Koos had excelled himself. Inside, over six pages, was my handiwork: a
chronicle of Coetzee's murder-and-mayhem career as the founder and man in
charge of Vlakplaas. The main story started with his infamous words: 'I was
the commander of the police death squad. I was in the heart of the whore.'

We also exposed Eugene de Kock as the current head of Vlakplaas. We said
he'd been there for six years, was implicated in many more 'eliminations' than
Coetzee, and might be killing so-called enemies of the apartheid state at that
very moment. We gave details of eleven people he had already 'taken out', though
it later emerged that he had actually killed more than ten times as many. We
revealed the existence of Daisy, another secret police farm, from where another
notorious apartheid agent, Craig Williamson, had plotted the murders – among
others – of Ruth First, Jeanette Schoon and her daughter Katryn.

As the good people of Johannesburg headed for their desks that morning,
we went to Fontana in Hillbrow for coffee. We were exhausted and quiet. Koos
reeked of rum and his eyes were bloodshot, but we were all elated. This was

the defining moment in *Vrye Weekblad*'s short history, the exposé that would catapult the newspaper into a publication of international repute.

When we got to our offices later that morning, telephones were ringing non-stop and foreign correspondents were camping on the doorstep. The night before, we had given translations of the stories to the correspondents of the *Independent* and *Guardian* in London, and the *Christian Science Monitor* and *New York Times* in the United States. All of them ran the Coetzee revelations on their front pages or as headline news that day.

As expected, the police immediately launched a massive damage-control exercise. They vehemently denied the existence of a hit squad and slammed *Vrye Weekblad* for its attempt to besmirch the South African Police. They admitted that Vlakplaas existed, but said it was nothing more than a safe house for 'rehabilitated terrorists'. A select group of journalists were taken on a guided tour of the property.

Watching the SABC television news that night, I felt like puking. The bulletin began with a benign shot of ducks swimming on a pond, then showed a smiling, mild-mannered askari testifying to how happy he was to have seen the error of his ways and now be opposing communism.

It would be years before the truth came out regarding the panic and chaos that had reigned at Vlakplaas that morning. The askaris were sent to Swaziland to hide. Thirty steel cases of weapons and ammunition were hastily trucked to the other nearby police farm, Daisy, and hidden. Incriminating documents and false identity books and passports were burnt in a 210-litre drum. By the time the press arrived, the farm was a haven of peace and tranquillity.

But Eugene de Kock later testified: 'This was the end of my career in the South African Police. It destroyed my self-image and integrity. I knew I would never wear a uniform again.'

Each and every grain of muck that could impugn Dirk Coetzee's credibility was unearthed, raked over and dished up to the malleable media. Transcripts of his telephone tirades were splashed across front pages. Rants like: 'You cunts think you are Christians, but God, Jesus is going to fuck all of you up!' didn't go down well.

Confidential details of his internal disciplinary inquiry were supplied to show that he had left the police under a dark cloud, distributed pornographic material among his colleagues and levelled false allegations of extramarital affairs against senior officers. 'Informed sources' said diabetes had diminished his mental capacity.

The National Party mouthpiece *Beeld* said one had to be mad to believe Coetzee. *Rapport*, for which I had worked only a few years earlier, disclosed 'exclusively' that Coetzee had never left South Africa but was hiding on a farm outside Pretoria. He was sick, without medication and semi-comatose, the newspaper authoritatively informed its readers. Even the *Sunday Times* batted briefly for the police. Coetzee phoned them a week after we broke the story and offered them an interview. They declined and instead provided the security police with information he had given them.

Within hours of *Vrye Weekblad* going on sale that Friday, Max and I were summoned telephonically by a police general. He said he'd been ordered to investigate the death squad allegations. Max and I were curious, and on Sunday morning we made our way to police headquarters in Pretoria.

Wiry and thin-lipped, General Krappies (his nickname means scratchy) Engelbrecht greeted us like long-lost brothers and vowed to get to the bottom of the scurrilous allegations. He wanted the tapes of our interviews and said he would like to speak to Coetzee himself. Would we tell him where he was? Max and I feigned total ignorance about Coetzee's whereabouts and refused to hand over any of our raw material. The whiff of a major cover-up hung heavy in the air of the slimy policeman's office.

As we left, Max said loudly enough for Engelbrecht to hear: '*Fokken valsgat!*' (Fucking false arse!). In due course, the general was indeed exposed as not only masterminding the official cover-up, but of having personally ordered assassinations by the Vlakplaas mob and sharing liberally in the spoils of the police slush fund that De Kock and his men had looted for years. Of course Krappies wanted to know where Coetzee was – forty-eight hours after our newspaper hit the streets, De Kock and his most trusted lieutenants had already decided to hunt down and kill the cop who had turned on his own.

They tapped Coetzee's home phone in an effort to try to find out where he was. Vlakplaas agents monitored conversations between Dirk's wife Karin, his lawyer in Johannesburg and me. In a particularly devious move, the cops planted a young Pretoria law student on Karin. Gullible and vulnerable as she was, she had an affair with him. I warned her that he was a police agent, but infatuated by the attention of a man half her age, she wouldn't listen. The *Sunday Times* got hold of the information and blasted it all over their front page. Coetzee was in exile and the story drove him up the wall.

Still unable to pinpoint his arch-enemy's location, De Kock despatched an old family friend and security policeman by the name of Peter Casselton to play the role of loyal and sympathetic supporter, win Karin's confidence and find out where the hell Coetzee had gone to ground.

Casselton, implicated by Coetzee in the 1982 bombing of the ANC's London office, called Karin and arranged to meet her at a Pretoria restaurant. She in turn called me and told me about the rendezvous, but Vlakplaas was listening and knew that Max and I would be there.

A paranoid De Kock thought we might try to abduct Casselton. The restaurant was swarming with Vlakplaas policemen. Ray-Bans and short-sleeved polyester shirts are hardly the most convincing disguise. What we didn't realise, though, was that we effectively came face to face with De Kock himself that night, seated with his wife at a strategically positioned table. Three vehicles, one a minibus full of black men – obviously askaris – were conspicuously parked outside.

Casselton, a bloated and ruddy-faced Englishman who hero-worshipped De Kock, arrived wired with the most modern listening device – which apparently didn't work. We had armed Karin with a micro-cassette tape recorder, but that didn't work either!

While we were in the restaurant, a security guard called us and said two men in a pickup truck had been trying to break into our car. Max marched straight to the pickup, in which were two bearded men. In retrospect, I was fairly sure that one was Vlakplaas killer Snor Vermeulen – his nickname means moustache – and the other Duiwel Brits, whose nickname means devil. One of them had a two-way radio on his lap, while the other was holding a dossier. We approached them from behind, and they didn't know we were there until Max roared: 'Were you trying to break into our car?'

The man with the file flung it on the floor while his companion tried desperately to stash the radio under the seat. 'Negative,' the one with the radio answered.

Max: 'Were you ever near our car?'

Policeman: 'Negative.'

Max: 'Are you a policeman?'

Policeman: 'Negative.'

Max: 'You talk like one.'

Policeman: 'Negative.'

Max: 'You look like one.'

Policeman: 'Negative.'

Max carried on for a while before ending with: '*Meneer, dink jy ek's 'n poephol?*' (Sir, do you think I'm an arsehole?)

Policeman: 'Negative.'

When we returned, Casselton was leaving the restaurant. Moments later, he sped away with the Vlakplaas cars on his tail. We tried to follow them, but they skipped a few red traffic lights and were gone.

We were in high spirits as we drove home, but later that night Max called me. The minibus of askaris was parked in front of his house. After a while, I noticed that it was now parked outside mine. This went on all night. I was terrified, and I think Max was, too. My only 'protection' was Joe, a Jack Russell, and Nelson, a springer spaniel. Max lived alone and didn't even have that.

For a while after exposing the police hit squad, we lived – as per the enigmatic Chinese curse – in interesting times, which included unexpected encounters and bemusing job offers. Out of the blue, two top National Intelligence (NI) officials invited Max and me for lunch. One of them was Maritz Spaarwater, who had initiated talks with the ANC in Switzerland in the mid-1980s. We met them on home territory at the Yard. They were fulsome in their praise of the sterling work *Vrye Weekblad* was doing to prepare Afrikaners for a new South Africa. Max and I shifted uncomfortably in our chairs and glanced at one another.

We're actually on the same side, said the spooks, so why don't the two of you work for us? We could use progressive and bright Afrikaners like you to bring about positive change.

I couldn't believe what I was hearing, and choked on my chardonnay (they were paying), while Max nearly tumbled off his chair. Rumours abounded at the time that Max or I or both of us were NI spies and that the agency had fed us the death squad exposé in order to accelerate reform within the security forces. The first thing that went through my mind when NI tried to recruit us was that we were being set up.

I could think of only one thing to do: make their offer public, and do so as soon as possible. There and then I turned towards the other restaurant patrons and shouted: 'Hey, all of you, listen up! These guys are from National Intelligence and they've just tried to recruit us as spies!' Needless to say, lunch ended abruptly and we never heard from NI again.

I was often asked if Max or I or anybody else was in danger at that time. I honestly don't know and never liked to entertain the thought. I find it tedious when journalists whine or boast about the perils of the profession. They usually exaggerate, but the point is, some measure of personal risk comes with the job. You can't build a career on publicly exposing crooks or covering conflict and expect to remain unscathed, but if you dwell on your own safety, you'll never write a single story.

There were numerous threats against us and I was told afterwards of plots to bump us off. Most of them, I suspect, were hatched around a roaring braai fire and washed down with copious amounts of *polisiekoffie* (police coffee – a glass of rum or brandy topped up with the tiniest splash of Coke). By the time the big-talking would-be assassins woke up the next day, they probably couldn't recall a single sinister strand of their late-night fantasies.

Max and I talked sometimes about the need for security precautions, but pragmatically, we knew that if the Vlakplaas squad or anyone else wanted us dead, they'd get us. We couldn't stop them. Besides, I always suspected that our enemies were much more resentful of Max – a seasoned agitator – than of me, a gullible young man whom they believed he had beguiled into becoming his partner in crime. The wheel nuts of Max's prehistoric Lancia were loosened three times and there was a mock raid on his house early one morning, with people hammering loudly on the doors and windows. He phoned the police, but they never came. He phoned friends, and when they arrived, a police van sped away.

Not long after the Coetzee story broke, someone left me a note at the Yard of Ale. It said I should go to a Roodepoort shopping centre the next day and wait in front of a certain store. The author said he had information for me.

There I met a short, stocky man. He was a security policeman, and for more than an hour he talked non-stop about the operations he had been involved in. Clearly, police atrocities had not been confined to the men from Vlakplaas.

The next time I met my informant was in an alley next to *Vrye Weekblad*'s office. He unceremoniously dumped a small arsenal of weapons on me: an R1 assault rifle with a bag of ammunition and extra magazines, an assassination pistol with a telescope and a throwing knife.

He said they were 'unofficial' weapons and that he no longer wanted to keep them at his house. I stashed them in the boot of my car. Max was livid and convinced it was a trap to get me arrested. Admittedly, it was idiotic of me to accept the stuff and I could think of only one way to dispose of it – dump the whole lot on André Zaaiman! But he was out of town and I had to drive around with the arms and ammunition in my car boot for ten days! André eventually hid them at the home of Van Zyl Slabbert, who was on a study trip abroad, before turning them over to someone else.

The cop who had given me the weapons turned out to be the first in a deluge of confessions. Week after week I was contacted by outcasts who wanted to come clean. In many cases I couldn't write their stories, either because they wouldn't allow me to identify them in print or because I had no way of corroborating their accounts.

Why did they speak to me at all when I was generally perceived to be anything from a communist to a government spy? Certainly not out of remorse or to ease the burden of a heavy heart. When FW de Klerk unbanned the ANC in February 1990 and released Nelson Mandela, he opened the floodgates of confession. The foot soldiers felt abandoned, betrayed and left to fend for themselves.

Members of apartheid South Africa's death squads were once closer than brothers, bound by the blood they had spilt rather than inherited. Like the Sicilian Mafia, treason was punishable by death. But when this closest of fraternities was pierced by the advent of democracy and the truth began to surface, brother turned on brother, loyalty made way for contempt, and respect turned to revulsion.

Although they hated what *Vrye Weekblad* stood for, those with dark secrets knew that we were not afraid to publish. It almost certainly helped that I was born an Afrikaner and we could converse in our mother tongue.

'I only followed orders. The generals knew everything. I was just a soldier,' most would say as they pointed the finger of culpability at their superiors. Some spoke out of fear of prosecution or tried to justify their deeds. 'It was a war ... they were killing us and we were killing them ... I did it for *volk en vaderland*' (my people and fatherland).

Vrye Weekblad's offices became renowned for a diversity of visitors. At any given time there might be an assassin in my corner, a dissident Afrikaans musician or revolutionary author sitting on the couch at the cultural desk, and United Democratic Front leader Terror Lekota chatting to Max.

Lekota was a great fan, but gravely lamented our lack of security. A week or two after the first Coetzee stories, I was talking to a young constable who had been on duty in the charge office at the Piet Retief police station in 1988 when Eugene de Kock and his men assassinated eight activists who were returning to South Africa after a period of asylum in Swaziland. As the policeman told me how the Vlakplaas men had celebrated their killing orgy with Old Brown sherry in the morgue, Lekota walked into the office. The two shook hands, had a conversation, and there and then, at 153 Bree Street, we had a mini Truth and Reconciliation Commission! The policeman left South Africa shortly afterwards and joined the ANC in Zambia.

I was asked many times, by many people, about the men of the death squads. What was it like dealing with them? Most seemed no different to anyone I had grown up with or rubbed shoulders with on a daily basis in Pretoria. I quickly learnt that assassins and evil-doers do not wear some or other mark of Cain on their foreheads.

What caused these souls to become so dark? What made perfectly ordinary men become so evil? Were they intrinsically bad and mentally ill? I'm no psychologist and haven't spent enough time with most killers to form a judgment. Evil, complicity and remorse are complex issues. But I spent more time with Dirk Coetzee than anyone else I ever did a story about, and I came to know him reasonably well. Besides all the time we spent together in South Africa, we shared a hotel room in Mauritius for about ten days, a flat in London for two weeks and another hotel room for several days at the Victoria Falls near Livingstone in Zambia.

The son of a postmaster, he had had a simple, stable upbringing in the

Northern Cape. His brother was a highly educated scientist. I never once heard Dirk Coetzee utter a racist remark. Whatever had turned him into a killer, it wasn't hatred of black people.

I know of no childhood trauma that he'd suffered. Some psychologists hold the view that certain people are more inclined to be violent as a result of experiencing shock, cruelty or abuse in their formative years. For them, say the experts, acting violently is almost a way of seeking revenge and getting their own back on early injustice.

Coetzee did not fit into that group. He was, if anything, utterly normal. He lived in a modest house in a middle-class suburb. His two young sons romped around and laughed a lot. Two perfectly coiffed poodles jumped onto their master's lap at every opportunity. His wife was a well-groomed suburban woman, always immaculately dressed with not a hair out of place. The Coetzees were a perfectly ordinary Afrikaner family.

In Hannah Arendt's report on Nazi killer Adolf Eichmann's trial, she observed that evil becomes widespread not so much because its proponents are profoundly diabolical, but because their work has become so routine, so banal, that they can do it without thinking of morality.

'The trouble with Eichmann was precisely that so many were like him, and the many were neither perverted nor sadistic, but they were, and still are, terribly and terrifyingly normal,' she wrote in *Eichmann in Jerusalem: A Report on the Banality of Evil.* 'This normality was much more terrifying than all the atrocities put together.'

Like most assassins, Coetzee's body housed a dual persona. One was that of the God-fearing, family-loving patriot who braaied on Saturday night and prayed on Sunday morning. The other was that of a cold-blooded killer, hidden from his family, friends and most of his colleagues.

I believe Coetzee killed because of his drive and zeal to reach the highest echelons of the police. He saw himself as commissioner material, and in reaching for the top, he was prepared to obey any order diligently and without flinching. The more notches on his security police belt, he believed, the more reward the generals owed him. He was prepared to kill his way to the top.

But, again like all assassins, Coetzee believed deeply in what he did, on the one hand because the political leaders convinced and assured him they were fighting communism, and on the other because even the traditional Afrikaans churches stood shoulder to shoulder with the warriors in what was propounded as nothing less than a holy war. How hard it must have been for an underling to listen to his conscience, provided he had one, of course, when he regularly saw cold-blooded killers, regarded as heroes in at least some police circles, being decorated and promoted by the generals for their good work.

Coetzee was probably right to believe that what he did would elicit the support of his people. I think most white South Africans, both Afrikaans and English, would have silently endorsed a policy of extermination, because the end – the greater good, getting rid of communists – justified the means. It was a grim but necessary solution, honest men and women would likely have said if asked. I couldn't help wondering how my own father would have reacted had he known death squads were roaming the land with impunity. 'It's not right,' I think he would have said, 'but it's none of our business.'

In order to survive, apartheid needed unquestioning foot soldiers like Dirk Coetzee to 'permanently remove' from white-dominated society those elements that posed the direst threat to the system. It was an unpleasant, distasteful and bloody business for almost every death squad member I ever met, but their reward was medals, promotions, respect within the tightly closed ranks of those who chose and commanded them, and financial compensation – literally blood money – from the secret fund into which they regularly dipped their tainted hands.

Their demeanour was uncompromising and macho, but when I met them individually and face to face, they never lived up to their bloodcurdling reputations. They usually hunted in packs and killed as a group. Underneath their veneer of normality skulked deeply damaged men.

Many executions were performed with a Makarov or Tokarev pistol in one hand and a glass of *polisiekoffie* in the other. In order to muster the guts to kill at close range or – as happened – within your own ranks, heavy boozing preceded many operations. Accomplished missions were almost always followed by another alcoholic orgy. This not only enabled the killers to numb their senses and comfort one another, but if one happened to physically throw up in revulsion at what he had just done, it could always be blamed on too much booze.

As an Afrikaner raised in the milieu of 'total onslaught', 'Reds under the beds' and 'black peril', could I have become a Dirk Coetzee? Of course I think not, if only because it is an inherent part of my nature to question, to seek answers and not to follow others blindly. In a society that rejected 'otherness' so profoundly that it had laws to keep people apart, I grew up to be a non-conformist; in a dispensation where the majority of whites abdicated their free will and trusted the government and the church to make the best and right decisions for them, I rebelled against authoritarianism. So no, I don't believe I could have become a Dirk Coetzee.

In her book, *The Haunted Land: Facing Europe's Ghosts After Communism*, Tina Rosenberg says, 'We who write and interview and judge, we are clear-eyed about the system's evil ... We know how we would have behaved. It is extreme good fortune that we will never face this test.'

I believe Coetzee made a conscious decision at some point to become a criminal, to lay himself open to guilt. Regardless of the circumstances, whatever the motivations, the ultimate choice was his, and he elected to be evil.

But Coetzee was by far not the most heinous killer of my acquaintance. Several others twisted my guts into knots and caused bile to rise up in my gullet, none more so than a podgy man who boasted about making gravy from a future judge's arm.

Pieter Botes was not a policeman, but a member of an SADF death squad exposed shortly after Coetzee spoke out. Under immense pressure to act on the Vlakplaas revelations, the police suddenly arrested a suspect for the May 1989 gunning-down of anti-apartheid activist and anthropologist David Webster, and blamed his death on the innocuously named Civil Cooperation Bureau (CCB). The ploy worked, and attention was momentarily diverted from Vlakplaas.

By the first half of 1990, I was reporting on the CCB, a debauched organisation that was out of control, employed criminals and thugs, and operated with complete impunity. Botes, the most senior member of the CCB to ever talk, headed up the Mozambican region until he fell out over money with Joe Verster, the Special Forces colonel who commanded the covert unit. When a bomb was planted at his business premises in Centurion outside Pretoria, Botes wanted revenge, and called me. We met in a pub, I plied him with liquor and convinced him that if he wanted to spill the beans, I was his man.

Seated opposite me, he sliced a chunk off his steak and crammed it into his jaws. For a few seconds the only audible sound was that of the meat being torn apart in his mouth. He washed it down with a Castle and dabbed his clammy lips with a napkin. It was as if he deliberately waited until the prime beef had settled somewhere near his well-fed middle before he nonchalantly remarked:

'*Ek het 'n sousie van Albie se armpie gemaak*' (I made a little sauce out of Albie's arm).

I was dumbstruck. Afterwards I thought he had chosen that exact moment over lunch, the sharing of an almost solemn ritual, to augment the shock, optimise the nausea. It was as if he basked and wallowed in arousing revulsion.

'You what?'

By the time I found my voice and asked the question, the next slab of steak was heading for his oral cavity and I had to wait while he chewed and swallowed. His knife was slicing another mouthful before he answered.

'I made a little sauce out of Albie's arm.'

Glee. Delight. Smugness. A tour de force. The triumph drooled off his lubricated tongue. I just stared at him. I was neither shocked nor surprised. Just appalled.

I realised he was talking about Albie Sachs, the one-armed activist who later became a judge in the new South Africa's Constitutional Court. On 7 April 1988, Sachs was an ANC activist and law professor at the Eduardo Mondlane University in Maputo, Mozambique. He was on his way to the Costa do Sol beach for a jog, but as he opened his car door, the Avenido Julio Vinti Quatro became an inferno. For many seconds after the blast, the only sound was that of red-hot metal falling into the flames.

A Mozambican journalist who was nearby filmed the scene. His footage showed one of the most harrowing moments of the anti-apartheid struggle: Sachs, surrounded by crumpled metal, his right arm dangling helplessly from his shoulder, trying to push himself up from the scorched tarmac.

A team of Soviet and Cuban doctors fought for seven hours to save his life. Apart from his mutilated right arm, he had four broken ribs, a fractured right heel, a severed nerve in his left leg, a lacerated liver, scores of shrapnel wounds and ruptured eardrums.

'Why did you blow Sachs up?'

'I'd never met Albie and had nothing personal against him, but we knew he was working for Umkhonto [we Sizwe, the ANC's military wing]. It was a war, and soldiers shouldn't cry.'

'He wasn't a soldier, he was an academic!'

'Albie was a soldier, no matter what he said.'

'How did you do it?'

'One of my black operatives set the bomb under the car.'

'Was it a success?'

'You know, in a war it's sometimes better to maim than to kill the enemy. We knew that everywhere Sachs went in Maputo, people would see the *stompie* (stump) where his arm once was and say: "Look, the Boers blew it off," knowing we could do the same to anyone we choose.'

'How many assassinations were you involved in?' I asked Botes.

'Six,' came the matter-of-fact reply. '*Ons het hulle geroer*' (We shook them).

Blowing up Albie Sachs was the pinnacle of Pieter Botes's military career. He revelled in its horridness and relished the thought of an activist going through life with a stump. Over the ten or so days that I met with him, he repeated his grotesque fantasy several times. At the most inappropriate moment, like when he was showing me his flock of sheep, he would fall silent for a moment, look at me intently, and say again. '*Ek het 'n sousie van Albie se armpie gemaak.*'

In recounting his CCB exploits, Botes sounded like a schoolboy bragging about the Ford Fairmont V8 his dad had just bought. Or a teenager blustering to his mates that he'd smooched the blonde cheerleader they all lusted after. It was as if he had scored an A+ for his maths exam. His tone was one of intense pleasure.

The CCB had to be able to generate its own funds, buy its own weapons and gather its own intelligence. Although part of the SADF's Special Forces, it was a bizarre organisation with a civilian facade. In its final form, the CCB's tentacles stretched from South Africa throughout the subcontinent and as far as Europe. It left a bloody trail in its wake, including the murders of David Webster in Johannesburg and Anton Lubowski in Windhoek, sabotage and bombs in South Africa and neighbouring states, poisonings in Mozambique and grisly 'eliminations' in Namibia.

Although the CCB murdered, planted bombs, conspired to kill, disobeyed military orders and wasted millions in taxpayers' money, the police investigation soon disintegrated and no senior operator was ever successfully prosecuted. The only project files (nothing but death warrants) that entered the public domain were those that Botes showed me on his smallholding outside Pretoria. We spent days sifting through documents that set out the workings and structures of the organisation. Botes also gave me a photograph of Joe Verster, the first and, for several years, the only one to appear in print.

The night before we published his story, Botes had second thoughts about the wisdom of exposing the CCB. He telephoned and said he wanted to talk to Max and me about the implications. In order to persuade him how important it was to come clean, we took him pub-crawling. Our strategy was simple: if we could keep him drunk all night, it would be too late to stop the press. The newspaper would already be on the streets.

We matched him brandy for brandy as he reminisced about his glory days in the CCB and lamented that there was no one left to harass, intimidate or kill. But we had greatly underestimated his capacity for alcohol. By midnight, Max and I were ready to surrender, while Botes was just getting started. He'd agreed that we should publish his story, and with that mission accomplished, all we really wanted was to go home.

Botes was having none of it and took us to his smallholding, where he produced a bottle of pear *mampoer* (potent traditional liquor). We sat at the table gulping down the hellish concoction. After two or three tots, we protested that we could not possibly swallow another drop.

'I'll show you what I do to people who refuse to drink my *mampoer*,' he said menacingly, before disappearing into another room. He returned with a grain sack from which he pulled a Russian-manufactured RPG rocket launcher. Max said afterwards he was sure Botes had loaded a grenade into the launcher and armed the weapon. I was too drunk to notice, but I did remember him pointing it at us and saying: 'Now you will drink my pear *mampoer*.'

We finished the bottle. There was a pot plant standing near me, and from time to time I surreptitiously emptied my glass into it. Max had no such luck and swallowed every drop.

Driving back to Johannesburg in the early hours of the morning, Max was overcome by blindness and stopped the car slap-bang in the middle of the highway. He opened and closed his eyes, but couldn't see a thing. I took the wheel and drove him to my house, where he passed out on the couch. He regained his eyesight only a few hours later.

It was dangerous business to split on cronies. The week after Botes graced the front page of *Vrye Weekblad*, his sheep were poisoned. Another operative was thrown off a building in Pretoria not long after telling me he'd been present when the SADF's Special Forces planned the assassination of activist Dr Fabian Ribeiro and his wife Florence in December 1986.

Six months after Dirk Coetzee had left South Africa, police intelligence traced him to a house in Zambia and gave his address to Eugene de Kock. The men of Vlakplaas assembled at the pub on the farm to decide how they were going to kill him. One of the men volunteered: 'I'll go to Lusaka and do the duck-fucker.'

No, the hit men decided, that would be too dangerous. Another policeman suggested they should send him a bottle of poisoned wine. That plan was rejected because, as a diabetic, Coetzee might not drink it. De Kock gave the order that a bomb should be built.

On 3 October 1990, I was sitting in the international departure hall at the airport in Lusaka, Zambia, waiting for Coetzee and his sons. We were booked on a British Airways flight to London, where the former Vlakplaas commander would spend the next chapter of his life in exile.

After hours of vile coffee and local Mose beer, watching an Ethiopian Airlines Boeing land and an Aeroflot jet take off, I saw Coetzee, his boys and an ANC bodyguard arrive. He was flushed and frenetic. Even before saying hello, he blurted out: 'They've sent me a bomb! Vlakplaas has sent me a bomb.'

I calmed him down and shoved a beer into his hand. On the way to the airport, he said, he had stopped at the post office to collect a parcel from South Africa. When he saw the package, about the size of a shoebox and wrapped in brown paper, he was immediately suspicious and refused to accept it. He told officials to send it back to South Africa. The name of the sender on the parcel was Bheki Mlangeni, Coetzee's lawyer in Johannesburg.

'Why would Bheki send me a parcel without informing me? I think it's a bomb that Vlakplaas and Eugene de Kock posted to me. The parcel is on the way back to Johannesburg. You must warn Bheki. Please warn him.'

I looked at Coetzee, convinced that he'd become totally paranoid. If Vlakplaas knew where he was, I thought, they would send someone to shoot him. I was wrong. As it happened, his former police buddies made three attempts on his life and he had to move house thirty-eight times to stay ahead of them.

Exasperated by my lack of belief, Coetzee turned to his bodyguard, a man named Stanley. 'Warn Bheki! Phone him as soon as you get to the office. Please do it.' By the time we boarded our flight, I had forgotten about Coetzee's warning. Apparently, Stanley forgot as well.

Bheki was an esteemed human rights lawyer and chairman of the ANC's Jabulani branch in Soweto. He was a blithe and tireless man whom I had come to know well while investigating the death squads. A few weeks after we published Coetzee's story, Bheki and I had hunted a killer askari by the name of Jeff Bosigo through the night and all the way to the Botswana border. We had information about where he was hiding and that he might speak to us. As we drove through a dusty village looking for Bosigo, Bheki said to me: 'Hey man, I hope I survive all this to see where it ends.'

He didn't. Some months later, he arrived home with a parcel that he had collected from the post office earlier in the day. One of the apartheid era's many unsolved mysteries is why Bheki, a canny activist who had been detained on three different occasions and received many telephonic death threats, opened the package. Inside was a cassette player and a tape on which was written: 'EVIDENCE, HIT SQUADS.'

Bheki died instantly when the explosives hidden in the Walkman's earphones exploded and blasted his head to smithereens.

Before the news had even reached the media, Coetzee phoned me from exile, feverish as always. 'I told you! I told you!' he shrilled. 'You should have warned Bheki!'

'What are you talking about?' I asked.

'Bheki has just blown himself up with De Kock's bomb.'

I won't even try to express my guilt and remorse about ignoring Coetzee's warning. When Bheki's wife Sepathi later heard how I had failed her husband, she urged me to seek forgiveness before the Truth and Reconciliation Commission.

One of the most bizarre confessions I received was gurgled from the bowels of the maximum-security section at the Weskoppies psychiatric hospital in Pretoria. A patient sent a message asking me to visit him. On a Saturday afternoon, his wife signed me in as his brother, and moments later a frail and fidgety man with bulging eyes joined us in the visitor's lounge.

Ronald Desmond Bezuidenhout, alias Desmond Barkhuizen, Ronnie Daniels and Duncan Smith, was in Weskoppies for repeatedly assaulting his wife. He had gone berserk and threatened to blow up her and the house. A magistrate referred him for mental observation.

Bezuidenhout introduced himself as Tokkie – short for Tokarev, the nickname he'd acquired after being accidentally shot with a Russian-made pistol in an ANC training camp. He had been shot and wounded five times in all and his body was covered in scars. Tokkie had an extraordinary story.

A cough-mixture addict, he had spent more than a decade on the outer fringes of society. He had fought on all sides – for the SADF, the ANC and Vlakplaas. He was one of only two white askaris in the latter unit's history.

After surviving a miserable and abusive childhood, he joined the SADF in 1973 and trained as a reconnaissance soldier. He was parachuted into Angola one night, but, in his own words, 'saw fuck all'. He deserted, but soon went back to the bush as a mercenary. Through the magazine *Soldier of Fortune* he landed himself a job as an instructor for the SADF-supported RENAMO rebel army in Mozambique.

Then Bezuidenhout and a friend crossed the border into Swaziland and joined the ANC. He was sent to Zambia and incarcerated for fourteen months as a suspected spy. He eventually landed up at Vienna, an ANC training camp in Angola, where he underwent guerrilla training. He was arrested on his first mission to South Africa, agreed to cooperate with his captors and became an askari at Vlakplaas.

Bezuidenhout spoke a lot about 'tubing' detainees. Tubing was a favourite security police interrogation/torture technique that required a certain amount of skill. A piece of inner tubing from a car tyre would be stretched taut across the victim's nose and mouth so that he could not breathe. The trick was knowing when to stop and pepper the hapless detainee with questions. Bezuidenhout said his tube had been used so often it was imprinted with the indentations of a human face. 'You wait until you see him wet his pants, then you know he's going through the gates upstairs. Then you leave him, and the moment he inhales, you tube him again,' he explained.

I was interested in what Bezuidenhout had to say not because of his own experiences, but because he was at Vlakplaas when De Kock gave the order for the bomb to be sent to Dirk Coetzee.

Bezuidenhout claimed that he had accompanied the bomb-builder to a butchery to buy a pig's head. A set of deadly earphones was placed on the head and detonated. The device worked exactly as intended.

'There was hardly anything left. Mincemeat. Another Walkman bomb was then constructed and posted to Coetzee,' Bezuidenhout said. 'Hell, we hated that duck-fucker. He was a traitor and had to die.'

Why did I believe a maniac like Bezuidenhout? We knew Eugene de Kock and Vlakplaas had to be behind the bomb that killed Bheki. I established that Bezuidenhout was indeed an askari at Vlakplaas and also a former SADF soldier. He didn't want anything from me – neither money nor an early release from Weskoppies. In any event, shortly after my visit he was declared sane and released.

Bezuidenhout signed an affidavit and we published his story in *Vrye Weekblad*. Police reaction was swift, and this time they had plenty of ammunition to discredit the messenger. He was, after all, in a madhouse.

The day after publication, General Krappies Engelbrecht was on our doorstep. Not surprisingly, he had been appointed to investigate Bezuidenhout's allegations and vowed to get to the truth.

This time, Max told him to his face: 'General, I'm sorry, but we don't believe you.' Unperturbed, he put his arm around Max and said: 'Old Maxie, we are in actual fact on the same side. We both serve the truth.'

Of course, nothing came of his investigation. It took another five years before the full story of the bomb emerged during De Kock's trial in the Pretoria Supreme Court. Every word we had written was true.

When I paged through *Oranje Blanje Blues*, Max's book on *Vrye Weekblad*, I was reminded of a raging debate that had lasted several weeks. Max wrote in a column that he was proud to be an Afrikaner. 'I've never been shy to be called an Afrikaner, or a *Boer* or a *Boereseun*,' he wrote.

I responded angrily the following week. '*Wat? Ek 'n Boer? Die Boere se moere!*' (What? Me a Boer? To hell with the Boers!)

At the time, I had renounced my *Afrikanerskap* and regarded the majority of my people as nothing less than conniving, deceitful and devious. My revolt was rooted in the death squad exposé. When we told Afrikaners what Dirk Coetzee and Eugene de Kock and others had done in their name and with their blessing and their votes and their money, they shunned us and treated us as lepers.

FW de Klerk and the generals denied everything. The churches expressed their shock and abhorrence and said it couldn't be true. Our colleagues at *Beeld* and *Die Burger* and *Rapport* crucified us. My own mother didn't believe me, and responded sadly: '*Ai, my kind, wat het jy nou weer aangevang?*' (Oh my child, what have you done now?)

When De Klerk finally buckled under pressure and appointed a judicial commission of inquiry into death squads, who was tasked to assist the commission with their investigation? Krappies Engelbrecht! And then the president placed the probe in the hands of an angel-faced and frighteningly naive judge who sat week after week lapping up the bullshit that Vlakplaas, Engelbrecht and the CCB dished up to protect themselves. The Harms Commission embodied everything I resented in Afrikaners.

At the earliest possible stage of his testimony in London, Dirk Coetzee was told by the Honourable Mr Justice Louis Harms that he was talking 'crap'. The commission descended into farce when he allowed CCB killers to give evidence in tacky disguise consisting of false beards, Ray-Bans and acrylic wigs. They bluntly denied responsibility for everything they'd been accused of, refused to answer questions on grounds of self-incrimination and hid their project files.

Vlakplaas was murdering people even while the commission was in session. De Kock appeared before Harms with one leg in a plaster cast. Only days before he had broken a knee while leading a killer commando on a raid in Botswana where they mowed down five people, including two deaf children.

Two months later, the Vlakplaas boys emptied an AK-47 magazine into one of their own. Brian Ngqulunga was an askari who had been involved in the murder of Griffiths Mxenge but had become disenchanted. The generals feared that he would spill the beans if called by Harms, thus undoing their careful and convoluted cover-up, so Ngqulunga had to die. And who ordered his murder? Krappies Engelbrecht!

Despite the whitewash, *Vrye Weekblad* and I continued to churn out a weekly diet of death squad exposés. We relentlessly implicated Engelbrecht and published ugly caricatures of the judge.

Nobody listened when we produced evidence that it was business as usual at Vlakplaas. Other journalists covering the commission treated me with scepticism, and officials suggested that I was hindering their valiant search for the truth. 'Yes,' the judge remarked at one juncture, 'he has a lot to explain when he appears in front of the commission.' Thank God I was never subpoenaed to testify.

Harms shamelessly introduced his final report with the Latin expression: *Felix qui potuit verum cognosceere caucus* – Blessed is he who can recognise the truth. One of the biggest tricks the apartheid state ever conjured up was persuading almost everyone that there were no death squads in the South African security forces, and Louis Harms played a crucial role in this subterfuge.

Coetzee had lied, he said. Without a shred of psychological evidence to support his finding, Harms labelled the former security policeman as suffering from psychopathic tendencies.

By contrast, De Kock was an 'impressive' witness. Harms found no evidence to warrant disbandment of the Vlakplaas unit. The only change he recommended was that members should keep diaries and records of all their future actions and operations!

De Klerk revelled in the good judge's findings and said he hoped that the Harms Commission would be the final word in a scurrilous campaign to discredit his fine security forces. He rewarded Harms with an appointment to the Supreme Court of Appeal, then the highest court in the land.

I don't want to linger too long on Vlakplaas and the CCB. Although my image at the time was that of death squad buster, I wasn't permanently submerged in filth and didn't spend all my time at *Vrye Weekblad* scrounging human garbage heaps in search of killer cops and soldiers. There were and are many other stories to tell.

I produced two books about the state-sanctioned killers in our midst and several other people have also written quite extensively on the subject. Max has examined the role of *Vrye Weekblad* in exposing these aberrations in two of his books. It took time and ultimately cost Max his newspaper, but in the end *Vrye Weekblad* was completely vindicated. Every word we had published about death squads proved true. Neither Dirk Coetzee nor the long line of killers who knocked on our door after him had lied. Eugene de Kock did, which is why he was eventually sentenced to 212 years in prison, and so did his commanders and cronies, although they all managed to stay out of jail.

If I erred at all in exposing the death squads, it was by underestimating the extent of apartheid brutality. There were many more killings and many more murderous policemen and soldiers than I ever imagined.

One of the last stories I did at *Vrye Weekblad* concerned Lood van Schalkwyk, a geriatric right-winger with a gun in his hand and hate in his heart. When I first had the idea of writing this book, my offbeat encounter with the political zealot sprang to mind almost immediately. It involved a hold-up and wailing police sirens. The bad guy got nailed and the good guy went home. Readers like being voyeurs of that kind of shit.

In truth, though, I think that night in the godforsaken hellhole of Bronkhorst-spruit crept out of my memory vault because it serves as a reminder that I dare not be too smug about my stint at *Vrye Weekblad* and should guard against over-romanticising the newspaper.

While working there, I became obsessed with the death penalty and embarked on a crusade to have it abolished. I wrote metres of copy arguing against its barbarism and why it has no place in civilised society.

And yet, in one of those ironies that life throws up every once in a while lest we succumb to hubris, I became a witting proponent of the medieval practice of hanging when I helped condemn an old man to death.

CHAPTER 4

A senior citizen's madcap jihad

The most deadly threat the white race faces is the tremendous expansion of the mud (non-white) races led by the arch-enemy: the treacherous Jew. — From the neo-fascist Church of the Creator's *White Man's Bible*

H IS DECISION TO CONTACT ME, SAID OOM LOOD, WAS PROMPTED by prayer: a request to the Almighty to lead him to a messenger worthy of delivering his declaration of war to President FW de Klerk, his liberal government and lapsed Afrikaners who were selling out to the communists and the *Joodse geldmag* (Jewish money-might).

'God showed me the path and it led to you,' he continued. 'So you must listen very carefully. Make notes, because you will not remember everything.'

I wanted to ask him why God would choose me of all people to deliver an avowal of holy war, but being a lapsed Afrikaner myself, I kept quiet and dutifully took out my notebook.

Lood van Schalkwyk (his first name means lead) wanted me to convey a message, and if I did exactly as he said, I reckoned, he would let me go unharmed. 'I already have several dead people on my conscience,' he said in a heavy voice. 'My men are armed to the teeth and are waiting for my order to open a full-scale terror campaign.'

I looked at him. I knew about one man he had killed and a bomb explosion in which he was implicated. 'I am hereby declaring war against State President FW de Klerk. Many people are going to die.'

He called his organisation the Christen-Vryheidsfront (Christian Freedom Front), and said they were organised in two-man cells poised to strike at the heart of the establishment. I had no doubt the poor sod was living a white fairytale, but, at the same time, he was one of South Africa's most wanted fugitives and had already demonstrated his ability to kill. I was not going to argue with him.

I scribbled notes and again glanced at him while he mused over his next pronouncement. I couldn't help but think that Van Schalkwyk looked more like a grandfather who should be cuddling a child on his lap than someone about to embark on a madcap jihad. Bearded and grey-haired, he reminded me of Grumpy in *Snow White and the Seven Dwarfs*. Depicted by Disney as a tough and craggy old boot, Grumpy was one of my childhood heroes.

But on this Monday night in the conservative town of Bronkhorstspruit east of Pretoria, Oom Lood was hardly behaving like an endearing gnome whose eyes filled with tears when Snow White told them about her evil stepmother. When the dwarfs later found the blue-eyed, raven-haired beauty lying lifeless with a poisoned apple by her side, they wept and wept for a long time.

As Van Schalkwyk sat next to me in my Volkswagen Golf, he brandished an Afrikaans Bible with one hand as if swatting invisible liberals to a pulp. In the other was a black revolver that he pointed at me every now and then. At times he was so transported by his own rhetoric that he seemed to forget I was his hostage or that he was supposed to be holding me at gunpoint, and laid the firearm in his lap. At the outset of our encounter he had warned me not to try anything stupid, as he wouldn't hesitate to shoot.

I don't remember being scared, except that the revolver – it looked as rusty as Oom Lood himself – might go off accidentally. I was probably more perplexed and bewildered by this aged and doddering fanatic who believed he could stop FW from negotiating with the ANC.

For the next hour, I scribbled in my notebook while the crackpot spewed his diatribe of racial venom. He seemed to be getting tired, and at one point the revolver was lying on the dashboard. For an instant, I contemplated grabbing it and turning him in, but I wasn't sure how to use the firearm, so decided it was safer just to let him finish talking.

He had almost finished when a vehicle with a flashing blue light pulled up behind us. A policeman bellowed that we should get out of the car. That galvanised the old man into action, and this time the gun pointing at me looked ominous.

It had all started early one Monday morning when the secretary at *Vrye Weekblad* gave me a message. 'Phone this person. He says it's urgent.'

The call went through to a public phone. The voice at the other end said in Afrikaans: 'You have to come to Bronkhorstspruit.'

'Why?'

'I want to tell you something.'

'What?'

'Come and I'll tell you.'

'Who are you?'

'I cannot tell you. Just come.'

'When?'

'Tonight. Meet me at nine o'clock in front of the Bronkhorstspruit Hotel. But come alone.'

Max du Preez said I would be mad to do it. My colleagues agreed. It could have been anyone: a former security force operator bent on revenge or a crackpot right-winger. Or, I countered, it could be someone with invaluable information. I decided to go.

I should have learnt my lesson by then. A few months earlier I had almost died following a clandestine rendezvous with a right-winger that induced a serious case of amnesia.

Some time during November 1991, I met a beefy member of the Afrikaner Weerstandsbeweging (AWB), who claimed to know where his fellow anarchists were stashing arms to be used in a right-wing uprising. He said the caches were on a farm in the Vaal Triangle.

His name was Danie, and I remember him gobbling down six eggs for breakfast. He was some kind of an ex–Special Forces soldier with a moon-shaped face, a mop of dark hair and the ubiquitous Ray-Ban sunglasses. He said he was disillusioned with the AWB and wanted to switch sides. I introduced him to ANC intelligence chief Terror Lekota, a regular visitor to our office. Danie demanded that the ANC relocate him and his girlfriend to Europe and pay for an extended stay. Lekota refused.

Danie decided to show me where the farm was – or so I evidently had told Max the day before we left. I assume he picked me up on the Friday morning. I have no memory of what happened after that.

I woke up five days later in the Garden City Clinic in the most excruciating pain. A doctor was busy administering a lumbar puncture and the procedure must have jolted me back to consciousness. My neck was in a brace.

I was told that I'd been found the previous Friday morning lying unconscious next to a car wreck near Vereeniging. An ambulance rushed me to hospital, where doctors diagnosed a serious neck injury. I was transferred to Garden City Clinic the next day and underwent two hours of neck surgery. I was unconscious for five days and doctors said I was damn lucky not to be paralysed.

My mind was blank, not only about whatever had happened on that Friday, but regarding the two or three days before the incident. I had no idea where Danie was or how to contact him. I didn't know where he had taken me or if he had indeed shown me arms caches on a farm. Police interviewed me in my hospital bed, but I could tell them almost nothing. They couldn't trace the car wreck back to him either.

The Swedish anti-apartheid movement flew me to Stockholm to recuperate. The moment I landed there, I removed the neck brace and spent the next three weeks telling flaxen-haired and wide-eyed Scandinavian students about the dark and forbidden continent from which I came. My neck recovered miraculously quickly.

Over the years, several psychologists had offered to hypnotise and debrief me to try to recover my memory. I always refused. I do not want to know what happened in that car.

Notwithstanding that experience, I drove to Bronkhorstspruit in response to the anonymous telephone call, arriving half an hour before the appointed time. The main street was dark and quiet. Even the hotel was deserted – clearly not the sort of establishment where anyone would choose to spend the night.

A lone light shone from the bar. I ventured in. There were only two people inside – a customer whose face I couldn't see, slumped over a glass of brandy and Coke, and the barman. He turned his bloodshot and befuddled eyes on me. I spoke first. 'A double Klippies and Coke,' I said, not wanting to draw undue attention by ordering anything exotic or outlandish.

'So, where are you from?' the barman asked.

'Johannesburg.'

'And what are you doing in this part of the world?'

'I have to meet someone.'

'Who?'

I didn't know what to say. I mumbled something inaudible, gulped down my drink and got the hell out. It was long past nine o'clock and I was ready to drive back to Johannesburg.

As I reached my car, a tall and elderly man appeared. He was clutching what looked like a Bible in one hand. 'Come on, open the door,' he ordered. 'We have to get out of here.'

As he got into the car, he took a revolver from a holster on his hip and pointed it at me. I froze for a moment, and then he said: 'Van Schalkwyk, Lood van Schalkwyk.'

Oom Lood! A member of the notorious Lunch Bar Brigade!

About a year before, a bomb had exploded at a taxi rank in Pretoria, injuring several black commuters. Two months later, a parcel was delivered to the home of a Durban computer technician. Inside was a computer, and when he switched it on, he detonated a bomb. The man was killed instantly.

Police linked the terror attacks to an extremist right-wing group, the Orde Boerevolk (Order of the Boer Nation). Little was known about these loonies or their cause. At the time, new right-wing splinter groups were springing up like Namaqualand daisies in early spring. The government and the ANC were engaged in 'talks about talks', and every right-winger envisaged an eventual communist victory.

Lood van Schalkwyk, Adriaan Maritz and Henry Martin were arrested and charged with murder and attempted murder. The three men had been told by a sympathiser at the National Intelligence Agency that the Durban man was working for the Communist Party. They manufactured the bomb at Martin's house, put it in a box and addressed it to the technician. Van Schalkwyk took the parcel to a courier service, and his handwriting was found on the box.

Journalist Pearlie Joubert (those acquainted with Pearlie would know that she shamed Koos Coetzee with her use of the dreaded p-word) and I were on the story. We found secret messages the trio had sent one another before the bombs, showing that they were truly abominable human beings.

'Peace on this continent will be when you have to go to a zoo to see what a Negro looks like,' they messaged one another. 'They [blacks] are unintelligent beings that blow up post offices, skin nuns and like to see hospitals and morgues filled with their victims.' The men were followers of the neo-fascist Church of the Creator, which refers in its *White Man's Bible* to black people as the mud races and advocates the killing of Jews.

While in Pretoria Central Prison awaiting trial, the three men embarked on a hunger strike. They threatened to starve themselves to death unless President FW de Klerk granted them political pardon and set them free. They also threatened further violence, although police were convinced that Martin, Maritz and Van Schalkwyk were not just the commanders, but virtually the only members of the Orde Boerevolk.

At first, nobody paid much attention to their plight, but after two or three weeks they were still not eating. Prison authorities confirmed that they were not taking any food. Weak, malnourished and starving, they were transferred to hospital. All three refused intravenous drips. They were under police protection and only their families were allowed to visit them.

For weeks, Van Schalkwyk and two of his henchmen withered away, to the point where they were said to be just skin and bone. As they lay under guard at Pretoria's HF Verwoerd Hospital, their lawyer warned that their conditions were critical; they were slipping in and out of consciousness and hovering at death's door.

The story gripped the nation at a time of great intrigue and turmoil: three fanatical right-wingers on a hunger strike, weak and apparently prepared to pay the ultimate price in their quest to stop their white countrymen from selling out to the ANC.

By day 50 of their hunger strike, South Africans had ugly visions of the ghost of Bobby Sands (the Irish Republican Army guerrilla who starved himself to death) rising on local soil.

By now the story had created a media frenzy, and local and international journalists were camping out at the hospital. Newspapers carried graphic stories of how the human body self-destructed when starved of sustenance, emphasising that it was one of the worst possible ways to die and that a hunger striker eventually lost his mind.

The right-wingers smuggled a tape recording of their ordeal to *Vrye Weekblad*. 'Well, it's nearly half past ten, Tuesday the second or third of September 1991,' one of them said in a hoarse and husky voice. 'After fifty-one days of voluntary total fasting, dates blur, days run into each other. It is not just the not eating that gets you. The thirst never goes away and you keep on wetting your lips. Your tongue is as dry as the outside of your face. Pain becomes a sort of background noise.'

Van Schalkwyk was said to be close to death but bravely clinging to life. Every day the wives of all three emerged from the hospital with tears in their eyes. Karen Maritz said her husband had sustained permanent brain damage and was lame on one side of his body.

'I guess my weight is around fifty kilograms at the moment,' said Adriaan Maritz on the smuggled tape. 'At six foot two I guess you could call it cadaverous. I feel like I've fallen on broken glass and every movement is very painful indeed.'

Nelson Mandela had the grace to visit the hunger strikers in hospital. While Maritz and Martin were visibly surprised to see the ANC leader, Van Schalkwyk reportedly snubbed him, snapping: 'Mandela, what on earth do you want?'

After sixty days without food, journalists were getting suspicious. Why had the three men not lapsed into comas? Rumours started doing the rounds that although skinny and gaunt, the hunger strikers were hardly starving to death. They were getting food from somewhere – probably smuggled in by their wives.

It wasn't long before Pearlie befriended one of the police investigating officers, who slipped her into Maritz's room, where she snapped one or two photographs late one night. The pictures showed him stretched out and asleep on his back. He looked somewhat underfed, to be sure, but nothing like a 'survivor of the Belsen concentration camp' as the trio's lawyer had claimed.

There was no doubt: they were secretly eating! It wasn't long before a nurse revealed the truth: the wives were smuggling scrumptious snacks into their hospital rooms every night – and their favourite nibble was Cadbury's Lunch Bars! The nurse complained that she had to get rid of the empty chocolate bar wrappers every morning. *Vrye Weekblad* duly christened them the Lunch Bar Brigade.

Once exposed, Maritz, Martin and Van Schalkwyk called off their hunger strike, claiming their imminent deaths would have been detrimental to their right-wing cause. They appeared in court and were granted bail of R5 000 each.

Then they disappeared. A massive manhunt was launched. Martin and Maritz were thought to have left the country, while Van Schalkwyk was said to be hiding somewhere on a farm. Nothing was heard from them again, until I got the phone call.

'Are you alone?' Van Schalkwyk asked as he got into my car.

'Of course.'

'Did anyone follow you?'

'No, definitely not.'

'Drive, then,' he ordered.

And so we started driving around Bronkhorstspruit: up one street and down another, past endless rows of face-brick houses with lush and manicured gardens. I didn't say a word, but tried to observe him from the corner of my eye. He had a nervous twitch under his right eye. He spotted me looking at him.

'Why did you write such utter rubbish about us in hospital?'

'It wasn't me,' I retorted, 'it was Pearlie Joubert.' (Sorry, Pearlie!)

'This time you will write the truth, won't you?'

'Of course.'

Van Schalkwyk directed me back to the main street and ordered me to stop on the outskirts of town under a street lamp. He glanced behind him to make sure we weren't being followed.

I stopped the car. By now he was again clutching the gun in his hand.

'Switch off the engine.'

He looked at me ominously.

'I want you to listen carefully. God is about to deliver the enemy into the hands of those he has chosen for salvation. This is war, and this is a declaration of war.'

Rancour rolled off his tongue. 'I have nothing to lose,' he said. 'I'm ready to die. I don't want to live in *kaffirland* any longer. I'll die fighting.'

He alleged that he was the head of a movement that comprised several platoons of right-wingers, armed to the teeth and training for combat on a nearby farm. I immediately thought it was bullshit. There was no way that this lunatic could lead an uprising of any kind.

He continued, quoting verses from the Bible about Satan and the antichrist who were posing as archangels. But he warned about the day of judgment, when true believers, disciples and apostles would be separated from these heathens and infidels.

I was getting bored and wanted to go home. It was a long and tedious drive back to Johannesburg. I tried to interrupt Van Schalkwyk, but he rambled on. I stopped making notes.

And then, from nowhere, the blue light flickered behind us.

Police!

I looked at Oom Lood. Blue fluorescent stripes played across his flabbergasted face, highlighting the deep lines on his cheek. He had fallen silent. I could hear car doors opening and a voice saying in the dark: '*Klim uit, asseblief!*' (Get out, please!)

I found out afterwards that the two policemen had been on their way back to town after investigating a case of stock theft on a nearby farm. They saw the white Golf parked alongside the main road and thought it might be two *moffies* (gays) having a *vry* (necking) in the dark.

I heard a firearm being cocked. *Oom Lood's revolver!*

I tried to pacify him. 'Sit still. I'll get out. I'm sure it's a mistake. I'll tell them we're just talking.'

'No!' he said, panic clearly audible in his voice. 'You're not going anywhere. Drive! Drive!' He pointed the revolver at me.

I had a feeling he was serious. There wasn't time to think. I started the car and sped away, the tyres spinning. In my rear-view mirror I saw the police car take off in pursuit. Van Schalkwyk seemed to be gasping for air. 'Drive! Drive! Left! Right! Go! Go!'

It wasn't just the blue light on our tail now – a police siren was howling as well. 'You planned this! You planned this!' shrieked Oom Lood. 'You set me up! It's all planned!'

'I didn't! I swear I didn't!'

I was astonished by my own driving skills as I sped around corners on screeching tyres and raced up and down the streets. The bizarre chase continued for several minutes, although it felt more like an hour. At one point, Van Schalkwyk leant out of the window, revolver in hand, and took aim at the police car.

'Don't do that!' I screamed at him. 'Don't be fucking stupid!'

'I refuse to be arrested!' he yelled back. What I didn't know was that one of the policemen was also hanging out of a window, his R4 assault rifle primed to fire a burst at the fugitives. His partner told him to hold fire until they had radioed for help.

Van Schalkwyk must suddenly have realised that it was futile to try to escape. As we raced past a park, he yelled: 'Stop! Stop immediately! I say stop!'

'What do you mean?'

'Just stop!' he said, pointing the revolver at me menacingly.

I screeched to a halt. Even before the vehicle came to a proper standstill, Van Schalkwyk tumbled out of the door, picked himself up and started running. He had his gun in his hand but had left his Bible on the seat.

The police car skidded to a stop behind me. One of the policemen ran after Van Schalkwyk, his R4 at the ready, while the other pointed his gun at my car and ordered me out. I emerged with my hands up in the air. Fifty or so metres away, Van Schalkwyk, probably exhausted, threw his gun on the ground and *hensopped* (surrendered). The policeman pinned him to the ground. I was ordered to put my hands on the car's roof.

'I'm a journalist,' I uttered as I was handcuffed and shoved unceremoniously into the back of the police car. Van Schalkwyk joined me a few moments later. We didn't speak on our way to the police station. He glared at me once or twice.

We were taken to separate interrogation rooms and my handcuffs were removed. 'Who are you?' asked a plain-clothes policeman in Afrikaans.

I told him my name. 'I'm a journalist.'

'From what place?'

'*Vrye Weekblad.*'

The policeman looked puzzled, as if he smelt something foul. 'What were you doing with the other man in the car?'

'I was interviewing him.'

'Who is he?'

I despised policemen at the time and decided to be *hardegat* (hard-arsed). 'I can't tell you. I have to protect my sources.'

'Why did you drive away?'

'He forced me to. He said he'd shoot me.'

By then the cops had done a check on Van Schalkwyk's revolver and found it was stolen. They didn't recognise him and he refused to tell them who he was. They knew something serious was wrong, and not long afterwards the station commander arrived. He told me someone from Pretoria was on his way to take control of the case.

At first light a short and slender man with a neat moustache walked into the office. He glanced at me and said: 'Oh ja, I know who he is.'

He stretched his hand: 'Roelf Venter.'

I felt a bit skittish. Not long before I had written about Venter. He was a security policeman who had been implicated in a hit or two. Now I was at his mercy.

He was surprisingly genial and offered me a cup of coffee. It turned out that he had been transferred to a special police unit that was investigating the right wing. He ordered the other policemen to release me.

'Thank you for getting us Van Schalkwyk,' he said to me on my way out. He had identified the right-winger the moment he stepped into the station.

When Lood van Schalkwyk appeared on charges of murder and attempted murder in the Pretoria Supreme Court, it was before one of South Africa's most notorious hanging judges. In a long and what some might even call a distinguished career on the bench, Mr Justice DJ Curlewis had signed Certificate J221A more times than probably any other judge.

Encased in a thick black frame, this document was bluntly headed: WARRANT: DEATH SENTENCE. It ordered a condemned convict to be incarcerated on death row at Pretoria Central Prison until he or she was either executed or reprieved.

Curlewis, a shrivelled and erratic man with untamed white hair, looked old enough to be Van Schalkwyk's father. He sentenced the right-winger to death after just two days of evidence by five state witnesses. I was one of those witnesses, and have always regretted taking the stand and giving credence to an inhumane and discredited judicial system.

I was subpoenaed by the state to testify about Van Schalkwyk's declaration of war. In principle, I had no objection to giving evidence, as I had already written a story in *Vrye Weekblad* and Van Schalkwyk had made it quite clear that he wanted his declaration made public. Little did I know, however, that I would be helping to condemn the old man to death.

I was appalled that I had to appear in front of Curlewis, a judge with a reputation from hell whom we had castigated in *Vrye Weekblad* several times. As I took the stand, I could feel Van Schalkwyk's gaze fixed on me. He and his family believed I had set him up and was responsible for his arrest.

It was difficult to decide who looked most worn and frayed – the judge or the accused. Curlewis was way past retirement age, while Van Schalkwyk hardly presented an image of the military chieftain he so desperately aspired to be. He had fallen seriously ill in prison and was supported by a nurse. He was in a wheelchair and had an intravenous drip in his arm.

His problems began when he refused to accept the jurisdiction of the court or Curlewis to try him. He wanted to be judged by a military tribunal as a combatant and prisoner of war. The judge dismissed his petition with the contempt it deserved.

I testified for an hour or two. I was briefly cross-examined by Van Schalkwyk's advocate and then dismissed by Curlewis. Throughout my testimony, both men glared at me – Curlewis from the bench and Van Schalkwyk from his wheelchair.

Oom Lood called no witnesses to testify on his behalf or present evidence in mitigation. The court heard no evidence about his mental or psychological state of mind or what had motivated him to declare war against blacks and leftists. I had no doubt that he was stark raving mad and should have been sent for mental observation. Not even the state sought the death penalty, arguing that life imprisonment would be an appropriate sentence.

Curlewis didn't agree. He came from an era in South African law where it was compulsory for judges to impose the death penalty in capital cases where there were no extenuating circumstances. He had no hesitation in signing Certificate J221A.

For his part, Van Schalkwyk accepted the judge's verdict without flinching and did not seek leave to appeal. There was a moratorium on hangings at the time, and although there were more than 300 inmates on death row, no one had been executed since 1989. The Constitutional Court finally abolished the death penalty in 1994.

State President FW de Klerk granted Van Schalkwyk a reprieve and his sentence was commuted to life imprisonment. He died four years later in hospital of internal bleeding. According to a statement released by the AWB, the right-winger was screaming in agony as he shuffled towards the Pearly Gates. 'Black hospital staff either ignored him or were not present, and the black prisons service guard lay drunk in a chair in the same room,' said the statement.

In the middle of 1992, reluctantly and with a lump in my throat, I resigned from *Vrye Weekblad*. I deeply cherish my years at the newspaper and the experience remains my fondest memory in journalism. So much has been written about *Vrye Weekblad* that there is little more I could add.

In his book *Beyond the Miracle*, celebrated author Allister Sparks writes that *Vrye Weekblad* (together with the *Weekly Mail*) made history by being among the first to expose death squads. 'Seldom in the history of journalism anywhere can two such small newspapers have played such a large role in the destiny of their country's affairs,' he wrote.

As for Max, he remains the greatest editor for whom I've worked. If it wasn't for his loony brainwave, I might still have been with *Huisgenoot*, churning out stories of premature ageing and people without hands, though I might have been promoted to the Joost and Amor beat by now.

I felt a bit like a traitor leaving the *laager* to join the *Star* and *Sunday Star*. I had just published my first book and felt confident enough to write in English. The stigma attached to Max and me a year or two earlier was gone. Even our fiercest critics had to admit we had been right all along.

Suddenly I was a celebrated journalist and in demand. I was invited to speak at international conferences, lecture at universities and a group of eminent Americans honoured me as one of Africa's most promising young leaders. Several newspapers offered me jobs.

I wanted to get away from death squads and do more 'normal' reporting. It was a futile quest. Apartheid's killers followed me wherever I went. My first *Sunday Star* exposé was about CCB assassin Ferdi Barnard confessing to various people his complicity in David Webster's murder. Next I exposed Eugene de Kock as not just a killer, but also an arms smuggler, and started writing about his role in supplying weapons to the Inkatha Freedom Party. Townships in Natal and around Johannesburg were engulfed in bloody conflict between Inkatha and the ANC. The government conveniently called it 'black-on-black' violence, but in fact, as we all learnt in the fullness of time, its own security forces were covertly stoking the bloodshed.

I spent a relatively happy eighteen months at the *Star* before joining the South African Broadcasting Corporation (SABC). By the end of 1993, this mother of all apartheid propaganda machines was committed to transforming itself into a public broadcaster. The corporation was undergoing radical change and offered me a job as a current affairs television producer. I decided to give it a go.

Not long afterwards, Max also joined the SABC. He had been forced to close *Vrye Weekblad* after the state finally succeeded, through a long and protracted defamation case, in financially crippling the publication. As he wrapped up the newspaper's affairs, he famously said: '*Ons fade nie, ons fokof*' (We're not fading, we're fucking off).

The SABC was a bit of a culture shock. Suddenly our colleagues included journalists we had despised and criticised for many years. One of the current affairs executive producers was the Citizen Force commandant who had commanded the army propaganda unit during my abortive camp in Windhoek. When documents disappeared from my desk while I was working on the story of a South African arms dealer who was implicated in the assassination of ANC activist Dulcie September in Paris, I reminded everyone in the office that there were senior army officers masquerading as journalists at the SABC. The executive producer in question left soon afterwards.

Max and I were back to making mischief. He presented his own current affairs show, and guess who were the guests on one of his first shows? Yours truly and Dirk Coetzee, who had recently returned from exile.

Making television documentaries was thrilling and exciting. My new editors gave me carte blanche and said I could do and go wherever I wanted. I chose to venture into Africa and introduce South Africans to a world hitherto closed and forbidden to them. The end of apartheid had unlocked the door to the rest of the vast continent.

My first assignment took me to the tiny Central African country of Rwanda. Not even my years in the heart of the whore could have prepared me for what I was about to record.

The most abominable act known to man.

Genocide.

CHAPTER 5

The basilica on the hill

*The dead of Rwanda accumulated at nearly three times the rate of
Jewish dead during the Holocaust. It was the most efficient mass killing
since the atomic bombings of Hiroshima and Nagasaki.*
— Philip Gourevitch

THE ROAD TO THE PARISH SNAKED THROUGH TYPICAL RWANDAN
landscape, except that fields lay fallow and villages stood empty. It had rained
the night before and pot-bellied clouds still cuddled the green hills. The pastures
exploded with swarms of butterflies and colourful bursts of daisies, marigolds
and amaryllis. By the time we arrived at Nyarubuye (the name means hard,
stony place), it was afternoon and the red-brick basilica basked in a soft glow.

That morning, our military guide from the Rwandan Patriotic Front (RPF),
Lieutenant Tony Karamba, had told us to get ready because we were going to a
place in the south-east of the country. 'Hurry up,' he said. 'It's a long way.'

'What's at Nyarubuye?' I asked him.

'A church,' he said. 'There's been a massacre. We have permission to go there.'

'How many dead?' I asked Tony.

'Thousands,' he said.

Although I knew that Nyarubuye must be a place throbbing with evil, I was
nonetheless keen to go. I had been in Rwanda for ten days and was eager to get
to a massacre site. I was naive and uninitiated in this kind of journalism and
had no idea that it would take me to the brink of a human abyss.

More than that, I had not yet comprehended the magnitude of what was
going on in Rwanda or the meticulous planning that had gone into the genocide.
I was only just beginning to grasp the level of depravity and the extent of human
suffering. Nyarubuye would change all that and, to a certain extent, strip me of
all incredulity.

The church compound was surrounded by bluegum trees, so that we couldn't
see anything until we were upon it. Tony ordered that we stop at the clinic
dispensary, a few hundred metres from the church. I smelt death long before I
saw it. Thousands of flies took to the humid air when we walked in. Six or seven
or eight female corpses lay on their backs in a neat row. Shreds of colourful
sarongs still clung to their blackened and bloated bodies. Flesh peeled off their
white cheekbones and rib bones poked like chopsticks from their hollowed chest

cavities. Swarms of maggots wriggled around the bodies and pools of black body fluids stained the bare cement floor. Some had their feet chopped off, while others had sharpened sticks forced into their vaginas. Their skirts were hitched around their thighs and they had been raped before they were killed.

The dispensary was a crude preamble of what awaited us at the church. My head was a confused mess and I cannot remember what went through my mind. We drove in silence to the imposing basilica. I was forced to press a cloth in front of my nose as I got out of the car because of the three or four or five or six thousand decomposing bodies that discharged their metallic odour into the sky. Many will have seen pictures of the dead at Nyarubuye. I am incapable of doing justice to the scene, and for years now, words have failed me in trying to depict those unimaginable, nightmare images.

How does one describe the stench, the rotting flesh, ballooned bodies, vacated bowels? Is it really necessary to know all the detail? What do you say about a mother and her two children huddled together where they were clubbed to death? An elderly man still clutching a Bible? What about the cleaved skulls, heads severed from their torsos, hands without fingers, arms without hands, legs without feet, toddlers crushed or hacked almost in half and body parts strewn everywhere? Or the lone figure in front of the altar, cut down, his feet chopped off, as he crawled towards the crucifix?

And yet, the putrefying bodies were the easier to confront. It was the facial expressions of the dead that became engraved on my mind. Imprinted on their faces was the sheer terror with which they had met their end. Their heads were tilted back, their mouths gaping in horror and agony. They died pleading, screaming and in excruciating pain. Scratch marks on the wall bore witness to victims desperately trying to climb up the plaster.

There are big gaps in my memory about the hour or two we spent at the compound. While writing this book, I dug out the two twenty-minute video cassettes we had filmed at the church and watched them again. It was as if every corpse came back to life. Suddenly I recalled individual faces that had stared at me with glassy eyes as vividly as if I had known their names and been familiar with their lives. Every image seemed to be filed somewhere in my mind.

I still find it almost impossible to write about Nyarubuye. I had initially planned an elaborate chapter on the church with a vivid description of what I saw there. The words would simply not come. It is, ultimately, indescribable.

And it wasn't only the fetid mounds of human remains that robbed me of words. It was the unspeakable horror of the way they died. It was the thought of being in that church when the *interahamwe* attacked.

The dead followed me long after I left Rwanda. For more than a year, I couldn't eat meat. The salient smell of death had permeated the pores of my skin and clung to my nostrils. Most journalists who were in Rwanda during the genocide had similar experiences. In *The Zanzibar Chest,* Aidan Hartley writes: 'I can't put my finger on exactly how death smells. The stench of human putrefaction is different from that of all other animals. It moves us as instinctively as the cry of a newly born baby. It lies at one end of the olfactory register. A man who has been dead for seven days reeks of boiling beans, guava fruit, glue, blown handkerchiefs, cloves and vinegar.'

Nyarubuye haunted everyone who went there. The BBC's Fergal Keane described his nightmares in a newspaper article: 'I was lying at the bottom of a pile of bodies. They were thin, reed-like shapes and they squirmed and turned around me, soundless creatures slowly dying, a hand always grasping mine, pulling me back to a land where no sun ever shone, no voices ever laughed. I woke shouting, the figures still present even in my wakefulness; and they have come many times since.'

Journalist Philip Gourevitch says in his meticulous reconstruction of the genocide, *We Wish to Inform You That Tomorrow We Will Be Killed with Our Families,* that the dead will be with him forever. 'There they were, so intimately exposed. I couldn't settle on any meaningful response: revulsion, alarm, sorrow, grief, shame, incomprehension, sure, but nothing meaningful. The horror of it – the sheer idiocy, the waste, the sheer wrongness – remains uncircumscribable.'

I crossed the border from Uganda into Rwanda five weeks after Juvénal Habyarimana's aircraft was shot down. The genocide started as the world held its breath in the run-up to South Africa's first democratic elections. The month of April 1994 was dominated by a last-minute scramble to ensure the participation in the elections of the white right wing and the Zulu-based Inkatha Freedom Party, long lines of voters at polls across the country and Nelson Mandela's subsequent ascent to power. Nothing illustrated the extremes of our continent more than Mandela's gesture of reconciliation to his people's oppressors on the one hand, and, on the other, the unleashing of a campaign in Rwanda to wipe out an entire people.

Most of the Western world's foreign correspondents descended on South Africa in anticipation of violence and bloodshed, but as the right wing got shot up in Bophuthatswana, Inkatha opted for democracy and FW de Klerk accepted defeat at the polls, they turned their attention elsewhere.

There was certainly no shortage of bloodletting in Rwanda. By then, the genocide was in full progress and some of the biggest massacres had already been committed, although they were yet to be uncovered. On a single day in the parish of Karama in the town of Butare, between at least 30 000 and 40 000 people were murdered from ten o'clock in the morning to three-thirty in the afternoon. African Rights, the organization that has produced one of the most comprehensive chronicles of the killings, put the figure as high as 60 000 – more than 200 a minute. At the convent of the Bernadine Sisters at Kansi, 10 000 Tutsis were killed in a single day.

On the hills of Bisero in western Rwanda, 50 000 Tutsis armed with clubs, stones and machetes and an inextinguishable will to live, kept soldiers, *interahamwe*, police and villagers at bay for close on a month. The forces of genocide ultimately overwhelmed them on 13 May, when thousands of killers arrived in buses, vans and trucks, while others came on foot. They were singing, whistling and beating drums, almost as though they were gathering for a village indaba. The organisers wore white shirts and instructed their fighters to wear banana leaves in their hair to distinguish themselves from their prey. That day, 25 000 people died.

As the western resort town of Gisenyi was cleared of Tutsis, *interahamwe* arrived at a boarding school and ordered the pupils to divide into groups of Hutu and Tutsi. The teenage girls refused to do so and said they were simply Rwandans. All seventeen were shot and beaten to death.

'I want to go to Rwanda,' I told an SABC editor a day or two after Nelson Mandela had been sworn in as president. He looked at me pensively and said: 'Are you sure? Do you really want to go?'

'Yes. We have to do the story,' I replied.

The elation surrounding South Africa's transition from apartheid to multi-party democracy had already subsided, and night after night television viewers were bombarded with images of mutilated bodies, *interahamwe* dancing with machetes in their hands and scores of fleeing Rwandans.

Rwanda was uncharted territory, an almost mystical land of mountain gorillas, pygmies and impenetrable rainforest. I was forced to consult a map to find out exactly where it was: squashed between Zaire and Tanzania, with Uganda to its north and Burundi to the south.

A wiry, resolute cameraman by the name of Ivan Oberholzer and I boarded one of the first scheduled Ugandan Airlines flights between Johannesburg and Entebbe. Uganda was another unknown quantity, one that I associated with the brutal antics of Idi Amin and the daring rescue attempt in the 1970s by Israeli paratroopers who shot their way into the airport building at Entebbe to rescue hijacked passengers.

How the devils got to Rwanda was a labyrinthine riddle that took me a long time to untangle. The country's history is replete with bitterness and hatred and everybody seems to blame everybody else. Some point fingers at the sense of superiority of the Tutsis, others at the vengeance of the Hutus, while many fault the greed of Belgian colonialists. There are those who argue that the whole concept of Hutu and Tutsi is of European making. The truth lies somewhere in between.

This is how I understand it. Most African countries are multitribal, and some, such as Nigeria and Congo, for example, are home to more than 200 tribes. Rwanda is inhabited by a single nation, the Banyarwanda, who share a common language, religion and culture. The problem in Rwanda is caste, which, in turn, determines wealth and status. The majority of the population are Hutu, and they are farmers. Only 14 per cent are Tutsi, but they own land and cattle. Hutus were historically their serfs. Tutsis are said to be tall and thin with aristocratic noses, while Hutus are shorter and have less refined features.

Rwanda is a small and populous country, and around the middle of the twentieth century, conflict between the cattle aristocracy and those who cultivated the land flared up. The Belgian colonial rulers, in an effort to delay Tutsi calls for independence, inflamed the Hutus against them, and as a result the peasant revolt of 1959 erupted. After independence in 1962, Rwanda's Hutu leaders embraced an ideology that portrayed Tutsis as advocates of a superior race-based ideology who wanted to enslave Hutus. Many Tutsis fled into exile in neighbouring Uganda and set up the RPF.

Juvénal Habyarimana, a Hutu, staged a coup d'état in 1973 and declared himself president of a one-party state. In his twenty-one years of iron-fisted dictatorship, he ruled Rwanda in line with a Hutu versus Tutsi ideology that required members of each group to carry identity cards stating their ethnic origins. His policies gave rise to the formation of Hutu Power, the group of fanatical intellectuals, military officers and political leaders who plotted and promoted genocide as the only means of survival for the Hutu.

The looming calamity was an open secret. Tutsis listened to the hate messages on radio and knew about the *interahamwe* – Hutu militia trained by the army – and the hit lists. They told of Hutu boys who stared at them and ominously dragged their fingers across their throats. The genocide was preceded by a series of smaller massacres of Tutsis in and around Kigali. If Tutsis knew their extermination was at hand, why didn't they leave the country or organise themselves into self-defence units? Why did they wait to be killed? It's the one question I've never been able to answer. Perhaps the victims had been mentally prepared for death long before the genocide started. People had lost the will to fight. There are instances where the killers told their victims to sit down so that they could be killed. They sat down. People would often plead not for their lives, but for grace from the killers, so that they could pray before dying or be chopped up in the privacy of their homes rather than on the street.

Four hours after Ivan and I had taken off from Johannesburg International Airport, we landed at Entebbe and were welcomed by a customs official with a broad smile (a *smiling* customs official?), who said: 'Welcome to our country.' An hour or so later, we were installed at the Lake Victoria Hotel, a colonial-era relic on the shore of Africa's greatest lake. Waiters in dinner jackets and bow-ties served roasted Nile perch from silver platters while a pitch-black pianist serenaded diners with a Chopin prelude. Uganda was a vibrant country that held an air of promise.

We departed for Rwanda the next day in a rented 4×4 vehicle loaded with extra fuel, tinned food, condensed milk, brandy and water. In the town of Masaka we turned off and drove on a red dirt track through banana groves along the papyrus-lined shore of Lake Victoria. In April, one of the first signs of the horror in Rwanda were the bodies that floated down the Kagera River into the lake. The river is the most remote headstream of the Nile and flows through much of Rwanda before forming a natural border between that country and Tanzania. It eventually flows into Lake Victoria.

Since then a massive clean-up operation had been launched at the river mouth to protect the lake from contamination. Teams of 'body catchers' waited on boats for human corpses bobbing in the water. Some were fresh, others decomposed. Some were clothed, others naked. Some were without heads, feet or hands, others had their hands tied behind their backs. Most were bleached a yellowish white or stripped of all skin. Once the corpses had been 'snared' and pulled to the shore, another crew, decked in gumboots, masks and plastic gloves, stuffed the remains into body bags and tossed them on the back of a truck. Numerous full loads of bodies were dumped a kilometre or two away in a mass grave.

It wasn't just a spectacle of the macabre, but a grisly reminder of what was happening across the border. An overpowering fetor enveloped the shore, where a lone woman stood watching the corpses being pulled from the water. She was searching for her husband.

We entered Rwanda the next day and were met by two RPF soldiers. By then the RPF had captured the east and south-east of Rwanda and had advanced to the outskirts of Kigali. As we left the border post and drove in convoy to the capital, gentle mountain peaks and green valleys stretched to eternity ahead of us. Rwanda was too beautiful to behold, although the hills and valleys were empty and silent. The noises of rural Africa – chirping birds and barking dogs, laughing children and village chatter – were absent. A few weeks earlier, Rwanda had been the most densely populated country in Africa; now it seemed the killers had achieved what they'd intended.

Kigali was a divided city. The government forces, or FAR (Forces Armées Rwandaises), occupied the central precinct, suburbs to the north and south, and most military installations. The RPF had captured the international airport and parliament building and were poised on the eastern and southern fringes of the city. Kigali had stopped functioning and there was no running water or electricity.

We landed up in a deserted house near the Hotel Le Meridien, a mere shadow of its former opulence and on the front line between the warring factions. Minutes after we arrived and were welcomed by Tony Karamba, the two sides lobbed mortars over our heads at one another's positions. We flung ourselves to the ground, but soon got used to projectiles and tracer bullets flying overhead.

Our first days were spent with the RPF on short patrols through the outskirts of the city, where we filmed shot-up houses, dead bodies and shallow graves. 'Come on, you have to take us to the front,' I pestered Karamba. 'We have to film your forces in action.'

He eventually succumbed, and under heavily armed escort we were taken to a military position not far from the airport and next to a bombed-out Coca-Cola factory. A tall, bearded soldier by the name of Major Philbert was in command. The two sides were in a stand-off, with the RPF occupying the high ground on the hill, while across the narrow valley the FAR was dug into a series of factory buildings.

'We shelled one another this morning,' said the major. 'There's supposed to be a ceasefire for an exchange of prisoners, but nobody really obeys it.'

We filmed soldiers lying at their heavy machine-gun posts, mortar units poised to lob projectiles into the air and a sniper aiming at a moving shadow across the valley. Then, in the interest of security, we were ordered to leave. 'No, wait,' I said to the major. 'We need more than this. We need to film some fighting.'

'No,' he said, 'that's not possible. We are not yet ready to fight. And it's very dangerous.'

'I have been told we can film your soldiers in action,' I said. 'Can't you just fire off one mortar or a machine gun and let us film it?'

On that day in Rwanda, I committed an inexcusable blunder, something I have regretted ever since and admitted to very few. I went far beyond my journalistic mandate to record, document and analyse events as they unfolded. I initiated and instigated – and at what price, I will never know.

The major barked orders at his lieutenants and soldiers were told to take up positions. Ivan and I were told to take cover in a building several metres behind the soldiers. No way, I said to the major, we can't see anything from there! We have to get closer. We eventually manoeuvred ourselves to a shot-up ruin next to a machine-gun and mortar post.

'Open fire!' Major Philbert barked. All hell broke loose as heavy machine-gun fire, mortars and RPG rocket launchers pounded the government positions across the valley. Ivan was on his knees, filming. I peeked over the wall and saw smoke rising from one of the factories.

The FAR soldiers responded with fire of equal intensity. And, of course, they were also armed with RPGs, mortars and machine guns. An RPF officer pushed me down and ordered me to keep my head low. Ivan was still filming when a mortar exploded with a tremendous thump some metres to our left. The earth shook and the projectile blasted a cloud of dust and debris into the air. The mortar probably landed further from us than what it felt, but Ivan was thrown from his feet (or knees) and we were covered in dust. The major screamed at his officers to take us away, but we had to cover open ground to reach safety and were trapped in the heavy fighting for several minutes.

The fighting was still raging when we eventually got to the Coca-Cola factory, where we were bundled into a car and driven away. Every time I subsequently visited Rwanda and drove from the airport to the city, I looked at the factory on the hill and pondered the day my misguided zest had ignited a battle.

It is important to understand who the killers were. The architects, engineers and financiers of the Rwandan genocide – they called themselves the *Akazu* (little house) – were among a small band of extremist, wealthy and powerful Hutus who held the real power in the country. These people harboured a simmering malevolence against Tutsis and embarked on a Hitler-like plan – an *endlösung* (final solution) – to preserve their wealth and influence. Their 'permanent solution' was to wipe Rwanda's Tutsi population from the face of the earth. In the process, they spilt more blood than any other living beings on earth. In concocting this plot, they established a network of fanatical and influential Hutus within government, the civil service, the armed forces, the churches and business that came to be known as Hutu Power. They had to oversee, supervise and incite the genocide, and their sphere of operation stretched from national to village level. *Akazu* and Hutu Power were the so-called Category One killers or *génocidaires*.

Preparations for the 'cleansing' of Rwanda began with expansion of the army from 5 000 to 35 000 members. The Presidential Guard was honed to become a strike force and a death squad. The *interahamwe* was formed and trained and thousands of machetes were imported from China. Prefects and deputy prefects were ordered to identify Tutsis and Hutu traitors and draw up lists.

The genocide was a true team effort and, as such, Rwandans had no symbolic figure such as Adolf Hitler or Pol Pot on whom they could pin ultimate and symbolic blame or responsibility. The bloodiest hands in Rwanda were those of Félicien Kabuga – perhaps Rwanda's Goebbels – who financed and organised the genocide, and Théoneste Bagosora – Rwanda's Himmler – a retired army officer and secretary of the cabinet who engineered and managed the genocidal forces. Two years before the killing started, Bagosora openly spoke about the 'apocalypse' that he and others were plotting. Once the president's aircraft was shot down on 6 April, Bagosora took control of the mass killings.

Many thousands, motivated by fear, hatred and profit, joined the ranks of the *génocidaires* and feasted on the blood of their own people. When Hutu Power ordered them to kill, they killed. They were at the forefront of the massacres, the looting and the rapes. They spared no one and were cruel in the extreme. Some seemed to enjoy what they did; others found it repugnant. Some participated in the killings directly, others stood on the sideline and spurred on the murderers. Both groups considered the extermination of the Tutsis an absolute necessity, and their hands were equally bloody.

Then there were those – tens, even hundreds of thousands – who took part in the genocide reluctantly. Some did it under duress or in fear of their own lives. Rwanda is a patriarchal society where the authority of national politicians, prefects, teachers, businessmen, doctors, army officers and mayors is difficult to ignore. So, when those in positions of power called the masses to action, many obeyed.

Never was it truer that evil triumphed because good men did nothing. In January 1994, the force commander of the United Nations Mission to Rwanda (UNAMIR), General Roméo Dallaire, notified his superiors in New York that he had a reliable informant within the senior ranks of the *interahamwe* who assured him that the extermination of the Tutsis was at hand and that Kigali was flooded with weapons. Dallaire warned the UN that genocide was being plotted in the highest echelons of government and emanated directly from Habyarimana's camp. The response from New York? Inform Habyarimana! Dallaire did. His informant disappeared and the preparations for genocide intensified. When Dallaire asked for permission to raid arms caches, he was told it wasn't part of his mandate.

In time, the whole world would come to know about the genocide, but very few understood how it was possible for so many Hutus to become ruthless killers, or how so many Tutsis allowed themselves to be killed. It took me several years to grasp the psychology behind the genocide.

Within hours of the president's death, roving bands of *interahamwe* in Kigali set up roadblocks and hunted and killed Tutsis and burnt their homes. While the *interahamwe* were the storm troopers, the elite Presidential Guard was the main hit squad, and among their first targets were moderate Hutus who supported the power-sharing agreement with the RPF.

Top of their list was Prime Minister Agathe Uwilingiyimana. She was a supporter of the peace agreement with the RPF that would have given the rebel movement a stake in the government and the army. The peace accord was the result of two years of belligerent negotiations in Arusha in Tanzania, and both Habyarimana and the RPF were under international pressure to sign it. It was never established who shot down the president's aircraft, but the strongest likelihood was that his extremist cronies had turned against him and used his assassination as a prelude to genocide.

At daybreak on the morning of 7 April, soldiers surrounded the prime minister's house and killed her as she tried to escape. Several other moderate Hutu politicians were murdered on the same day. The next step was to startle the international community into inaction. Ten Belgian soldiers were seized by the Presidential Guard and taken to an army camp, where they were tortured and killed and their bodies mutilated.

The murder of the Belgians had the exact effect on foreign opinion for which the *génocidaires* had hoped. Belgium withdrew its troops from UNAMIR. Soon afterwards, the UN Security Council, on which the Rwandan government had a seat, debated slashing the UN mission from 3 000 to 270 men.

Two days into the genocide, Roméo Dallaire cabled UN headquarters in New York and warned his superiors that there was a well-organised and deliberate campaign of terror against Tutsis. He said he believed that with just 5 000 well-armed men, he could stop the killing and restore order to Kigali.

A day later, the UN had conclusive evidence of orchestrated and premeditated mass murder. Three senior peacekeeping officers, one of them Dallaire's staff officer, answered a distress call from the Catholic mission at Gikondo, a parish in the heart of Kigali. When they arrived in an armoured vehicle, they found two petrified Polish UN military observers huddled together in the church.

Some 500 Tutsis had sought refuge in the church when the killings erupted on the night the president's aircraft was shot down. On Saturday 9 April, priests held mass for the refugees. The Polish observers were in the compound when there was shooting outside and grenades exploded. Members of the Presidential Guard and the *interahamwe* stormed into the church and began hacking at the arms, legs, genitals, breasts, faces and necks of the asylum seekers. Some were dragged outside and beaten to death. The massacre lasted two hours, after which the killers looted the bodies and finished off those who were still alive.

The UN officials were not only witnesses to the attack, but also took photographs of the victims. Despite this evidence, Dallaire was reminded in no uncertain terms that his priority was to protect his own men, not to save Rwandan lives. UNAMIR watched helplessly as the killings spread.

Confronted with reports that political leaders had been murdered and civilians were being massacred, the United States suggested that UNAMIR should be withdrawn, while Belgium said the Blue Berets should help only foreigners.

'Dallaire need not have bothered to write his cable,' writes journalist Linda Melvern, who exposed the international community's complicity in the genocide in her book, *A People Betrayed*: 'In the first four weeks of genocide, the fact that a systematic and continuing slaughter was taking place in Rwanda was not once discussed at length in [Security] Council meetings.'

The reaction that was most wanting was that of Kofi Annan, then the UN's head of peacekeeping and later Secretary General. An African himself, he reckoned to his eternal shame that sending more troops to Rwanda would be too costly in both time and money. It took the UN six months to brand the killings premeditated genocide.

With foreign embassies closed, their staff evacuated and the UN mere onlookers in the face of extermination, the killers were left to carry out their task unimpeded, and the massacres started in all earnest. Armed with the lists of Tutsis and Hutu traitors, the *interahamwe* had everyone's address and went from house to house with red paint to mark the homes of those under sentence of death. Radio des Milles Collines – Hutu Power's radio station that promoted genocide – reminded its listeners that every living Tutsi was a threat, as were their children and even unborn babies. 'Fight them with the weapons you have at hand. You have arrows, you have spears! Go after them ... blood flows in their veins as it does in yours. They must pay for what they have done!'

The genocide was preceded by a stockpiling of weapons that came mainly from France, but also from Bulgaria, Israel and apartheid South Africa. Throughout the genocide, France continued to support its old ally. Juvénal Habyarimana had been a friend of French president François Mitterand, and the day after his death, Madame Agathe Habyarimana was whisked off to Paris aboard a French military plane.

As the war with the invading RPF intensified, a Rwandan military officer was despatched to French military headquarters in Paris with a list of the arms, ammunition and equipment most needed by the Rwandan army. On 16 and 17 June, arms shipments for the genocide government were landed in the eastern Zairean city of Goma and shuttled over the border to Rwanda.

The French dubbed the RPF the *Khmer Noir* – a reference to Pol Pot's homicidal Khmer Rouge in Cambodia. But it was Paris that delivered arms to the *génocidaires*, lobbied the international community to do nothing and hosted Madame Habyarimana so that she could drown her sorrows in the French capital's haute couture boutiques.

Our request to accompany an RPF convoy to the interior was approved, Tony Karamba announced, but added that the rebels couldn't guarantee our safety, or provide food, transport or shelter. We left early the next morning. Our group included a BBC television team, a Lebanese-born freelance photographer, two Italian journalists and a Ugandan journalist by the name of Sheila Kawamura. She had arrived in Rwanda only four days after the massacres began and had been there ever since. Sheila was famous in Uganda for rescuing twelve Rwandans from a pit latrine. Fifteen Tutsis had jumped into the pit in order to escape the *interahamwe* and were trapped inside for five days before Sheila and a photographer came upon them. Sheila got hold of a rope, lowered herself into the hole and saved twelve people. The other three were already dead.

We travelled for a day in convoy with several hundred soldiers moving westwards along the Burundian border. The RPF had opened a new front in the central part of the country and was advancing on Kigali in a pincer movement from the south and east. The FAR were in retreat, and the government had relocated to Gitarama in central Rwanda. The RPF had gained a reputation as a fierce and disciplined fighting force, and its commander, General Paul Kagame, was known to be a brilliant strategist. Although the RPF permitted its forces to execute people whom they suspected of being *interahamwe* or killers, they succeeded, in the face of international inaction, in stopping the mass murders and drove the *génocidaires* and their henchmen into Zaire.

Travelling with the RPF, we made good progress until we reached the Akanyaru River. The bridge had been blown up. If you wish to continue, said Tony, you will have to leave your vehicles behind and continue on foot. We were rowed across in canoes and greeted on the other side by a hundred or so prisoners in pink clothes carrying boxes of ammunition, food and clothes for the soldiers. An elderly man with thick-rimmed black glasses said the RPF had unlocked the gates of Nyanza prison, enlisted the prisoners as soldiers, and promised them guns and uniforms. This man was a convicted robber and thief. The genocide offered many convicts a new lease on life. In Kigali, prisoners were released and enrolled as militia, while others had to clear the streets of bodies and bury them in mass graves.

We came to a deserted and bombed-out village where Tony said we would spend the night. Two soldiers stood guard as we crept into our sleeping bags. I tossed and turned all night, listening to mortar explosions and gunfire in the distance. When I wandered into a banana plantation at first light to relieve myself, I stumbled over a shallow grave. I looked down, and in the glow of dawn a set of delicate Tutsi fingers poked through the soil. I scurried back to the safety of the soldiers.

This was a journey none of us would ever forget. Several incidents became welded together in my mind. Later that morning, we slowly drove past a deserted marketplace. An RPF soldier who had been shot lay on his back on a canvas sheet. His leg was a bloody pulp. Several people were crouched over him. They were busy sawing off his leg.

'You want to film it?' Tony asked.

'No,' we mumbled as one. We passed in silence.

The town of Nyamata, liberated by the rebels only a day or two before, was practically a ghost town with most of the Hutu population gone, ushered westwards towards the Zairean border by the retreating FAR and *interahamwe*. Tutsi survivors were emerging from their hiding places where some had stayed for more than a month. Whole families, famished, their bodies covered with rags, came out of the forest or down from the hills, wide-eyed and bewildered. Some staggered around numbly on the streets, their houses looted, burnt or bombed, and loved ones tossed into pit latrines, slashed up by machetes or felled by bullets. Some were trying to identify corpses gathered by the rebels and laid out in the empty and looted hospital.

We came to a deserted school, where we spent the night. The building had only just been cleared of bodies and the odour of death permeated the air. There was a tank full of water outside, and for the first time in days we could wash. That night, under candlelight and with soldiers standing guard nearby, each of the journalists dug out a delicacy from their rucksacks. We had condensed milk, tinned fish, chocolate and brandy. The Italians, to our amazement, had sliced Parma ham. The Lebanese had cheese. We chattered about our countries, our families and our loved ones. No one spoke of what we had seen during the day.

Early the next morning, we found an old man sitting like a statue on a broken bench in the school courtyard. His skeletal features were ghostly and his long, thin hands were in a praying position in front of his face. His eyes were vacant and he didn't blink. We offered him food; he didn't respond. When we left an hour or so later, he was still sitting in the same position. His face has never left my mind, and I have always wondered: what had those eyes seen?

Like many survivors, the old man had not suffered a scratch to his body, but he was condemned and sentenced to live his last days with ghouls and bogeymen knocking and ticking and running amok in his head. Wounds can be dressed and a body sewn together again, but once poison and filth are trapped inside a head, a human being finally ceases to exist. That's why the true toll of the Rwandan genocide is far, far higher than what official numbers or statistics can ever reveal.

Soldiers had the grisly task of collecting the bodies of civilians who had been killed as the *interahamwe* and government troops fled. Nyamata's community hall and the surrounding compound had become a refugee camp, with all the usual horror of desolate mortals hunched around smoky cooking fires, snot-nosed kids pulling at your pants begging for a little something, and that all too distinctive reek of squalor, sordidness and human excrement. The inside of the hall had become something of a living morgue. Dying, sick and wounded people were strewn across the bare cement floor. A young boy with an infected machete wound at the back of his neck was crying out in pain. An old man put his shrivelled hand out to me and garbled something in Kinyarwanda. I felt sick and walked out.

The International Red Cross had set up a makeshift hospital in the centre of town the previous day. With the heavy smell of disinfectant pervading the white tent, Sister Maria was preparing to deliver a baby, while at the same time attending to a child with machete slashes in his neck and on his arms. Patients came in with white fat popping out of wounds, gangrene and maggots crawling in gashes. The doctors and nurses did not distinguish between Hutu and Tutsi. They worked twenty-four hours every day, but there was still not enough time to save everyone. They literally had to decide who to treat and who to leave waiting at the back of the line because they were going to die in any case.

Aidan Hartley described it so well: 'The gas gangrene case was taken back outside to die. The disembowelled child went to the operating room. The seven-month pregnant woman with an abdomen wound and in shock got only fluids. A woman with both feet blown to shreds was waiting for a double amputation. A boy had a leg wound heaving with maggots. Bluebottle larvae clean and disinfect wounds by eating away putrid flesh. Thanks to this, there was a chance John could save the leg. He got a dressing.'

One of the Red Cross voluntary workers was Eugene. When the mass killings erupted, he was lying in Nyanza's state hospital with malaria. A group of doctors and sisters compiled lists of their Tutsi patients and gave it to the *interahamwe*. Then the medical staff left. When the *interahamwe* arrived to take the Tutsi patients, Eugene hid in the mortuary. He fetched his wife and only child and fled into the forest. After a few days with no water and nothing to eat, a Hutu farmer scrounging in the woods for wild berries and roots discovered them. He invited them to his house, where he harboured and fed them for three weeks. Whenever the *interahamwe* came to look for survivors, he hid them in the pigsty.

Within this colosseum of misery, we stumbled across the sound of laughing children. It came from an orphanage, where we found a portly and bespectacled French priest with puffy hands and a heart of gold. Throughout the genocide, he had refused to abandon the children, and shielded and protected them from the *interahamwe*. The killers came to the orphanage three times to demand the delivery of Tutsi children for extermination. The priest twice paid them to go away. The third time he hid the children in a cellar and gave the killers most of the food he had. When the *interahamwe* left town, they burst into the orphanage and demanded the pickup truck and its driver to take them to the Zairean border. We don't have a driver any longer, the priest told them, because you killed him. They took the truck and killed more people outside the orphanage gates before they left.

In Kigali, evidence was emerging that UNAMIR was not just understaffed and ill-equipped, but was literally being starved by New York. The Ghanaian contingent had run out of food, drinking water and fuel. Furthermore, they had to deal with a football stadium full of Tutsi refugees. Only a stone's throw from the UN headquarters, children died of dysentery and diarrhoea; cholera had broken out and there were cases of malaria. The soldiers had no medicine to treat anybody.

General Dallaire needed 100 armoured personnel carriers to be effective on the ground. The United States had vast and unused fleets of post–Cold War vehicles. The Pentagon offered fifty, but then changed its mind and came up with a price tag of $4 million, which they insisted had to be prepaid. Then they wanted another $6 million for transportation. The personnel carriers eventually arrived in Uganda stripped of machine guns, radios, tools, spare parts and training manuals. The United Sates, said Dallaire, had supplied him with tons of rusting metal.

Although UNAMIR saved lives and there were examples of soldiers acting with courage and compassion, the mission was a shambles. The UN was not just a bystander to genocide, but abandoned civilians in its care and allowed them to be killed. There is no more devastating indictment against the organisation than the manner in which the Blue Berets, at a school in Kigali, delivered desperate refugees on a tray to the killers.

The Ecole Technique Officielle (ETO) was a UNAMIR base, manned by ninety Belgian soldiers. As mass killings erupted on 7 April in and around Kigali, refugees flocked to the school. By the time they reached the ETO, many were traumatised, injured and exhausted. Three days into the genocide, 2 500 refugees had found refuge at the school. *Interahamwe*, armed with machetes, spears and sticks and poised for attack, surrounded the property.

On 11 April, the commanding officer of the Belgian contingent radioed his men at the school and ordered them to leave the premises and consolidate their position at the airport. Refugees watched the Belgians pack. The *interahamwe*, peering over the school wall, also saw the imminent withdrawal of UNAMIR, and blew their whistles. As the soldiers departed, refugees attempted to stop their convoy by lying on the ground in front of the trucks, while others tried to climb onto the vehicles. The Belgian soldiers pushed the refugees off and fired warning shots over their heads.

The dust of the departing vehicles had not even settled before the *interahamwe* and government troops attacked. They threw hand grenades into the crowd, and hacked, stabbed and shot at the terror-stricken and fleeing refugees. Those who managed to escape the massacre were herded to a nearby hill called Nyanza-Rebero, where they were killed later that day.

When I put it to the UNAMIR spokesperson in Kigali, Major Jean-Guy Plante, that the mission was a disaster and that his men had failed to protect civilians, he responded: 'What? A failure? That's the first time I've heard that. I think in fact what we are doing is very useful.'

A hundred days after the mass killings erupted, the guns fell silent when the RPF declared the war over and swore in a government with a moderate Hutu as president and RPF leader Paul Kagame as his deputy. But by then a new calamity loomed: a million soot-faced outcasts trapped on a volcanic sheet of ragged rock.

In August 1994, a million Hutus, fleeing before the RPF advance and spurred on by *interahamwe* and FAR troops, flooded into neighbouring Zaire with whatever they could carry in their arms, balance on their heads or push in carts. Bureaucrats and businessmen piled household goods, radios, television sets, kitchen equipment, their families and in-laws into their cars and joined mile upon mile of people filing along the road from Kigali to Gisenyi on the Zairean border.

Most Hutus had little choice but to join the throng on the road. Militias went from house to house and ordered people to gather their belongings. The RPF is coming with murder in their hearts and is killing Hutus, blared messages from both Radio des Milles Collines and Radio Rwanda. Even those who had no blood on their hands were convinced that waiting for the arrival of the RPF was nothing less than suicide.

The soldiers and *interahamwe* left in trucks, and in the wake of their departure plundered houses, banks, schools, shops, businesses and hospitals. They destroyed and ravaged electricity stations, water depots and government buildings. Havoc reigned on the winding road to the south-west. Children got separated from their parents, the elderly succumbed to exhaustion and flopped down at the side of the road, and many were crushed in stampedes. Mayors, their deputies and government officials prompted from the front, and soldiers and the *interahamwe* prodded from behind.

The government and its closest cronies left by military helicopter for Goma in Zaire and occupied hotels in and around the city. Nestled between Lake Kivu and a series of volcanoes that straddle Rwanda and Zaire, Goma was once a holiday resort for tourists to the gorilla park. Within a matter of days in the autumn of 1994, it was transformed into the world's biggest refugee camp.

The exodus played beautifully into the hand of the extremists. Not only did the masses provide perfect cover for the *interahamwe* and soldiers to feign the role of desperate refugees and bleed international aid hearts, but the chaos also provided a perfect base for Hutu Power to regroup, recruit new disciples and plot the final phase of Tutsi extermination.

The refugees settled on lava rock that stretched for many miles from Goma along the Rwandan border. Within days, six refugee camps, each bigger than most cities in the region, rose from nothing. It was an almost delusionary image that met international aid workers and journalists. To add to the bewildering sight, the Nyiragongo volcano roared briefly to life and spewed gas and smoke into the air.

The plight of African refugees was nothing new to the outside world, but never before had there been such an exodus. While the international community had met the bloodletting in Rwanda with lethargy and indifference, foreign aid workers descended on Goma in droves to 'save Africans from themselves'. Within days the airspace around the international airport was clogged as cargo planes brought food, plastic sheeting, water pumps, purifying equipment and medical supplies. The UN High Commission for Refugees (UNHCR) took control of what became the biggest single aid operation in the history of humankind. The UNHCR was followed by a horde of aid agencies, each trying to get a finger in the lucrative relief pie. A humanitarian disaster of that magnitude offered golden fund-raising opportunities.

Within days, people started dying. Cholera was unleashed on a million people trapped on an expanse of stone with nowhere to go. Between 30 000 and 40 000 died in the three or four weeks before the disease was contained.

It was around this time that cameraman Ivan and I crossed the Rwandan frontier into Zaire on our second trip to Rwanda. The first had resulted in a forty-five minute documentary and a bout of malaria that landed Ivan in a Johannesburg hospital. While he recovered, I took a short holiday in Zanzibar. It was with a feeling of trepidation that I again boarded the Ugandan Airlines flight to Entebbe in August.

A soldier at the Zairean border gate took one look at our Ugandan driver and arrested him for not having the right papers. I paid him $50. Zaire had succumbed to rampant corruption years before and soldiers and customs officials licked their greedy lips when they spotted us. Your yellow fever certificates are not in order. $20. Visa? South Africans don't need visas to enter Zaire, I protested. Oh yes, you do. Another $20. Where are your import-export papers for the equipment? Ivan gave them to an officer with a red beret who didn't even look at the documents. Another $20.

We pitched our tents at a media enclave near Goma's airport, grabbed a bottle of mineral water and ventured into the human wasteland. It was early morning and the sea of shanties was cloaked in the smog of cooking fires. Those who had died during the night were rolled up in straw mats and left next to the road for collection. The hard rock made it impossible for refugees to bury their dead and bulldozers were brought in to dig mass graves. Sometimes trucks unceremoniously tipped a load of corpses into the holes; at other sites, grave diggers swung bodies one by one into the pits, where they lay in crumpled heaps until they were covered with lime and soil.

Death had become an almost pedestrian event. Next to a waterhole a boy lay motionless while children splashed a few metres away. Ivan told the driver to stop and walked up to the boy. He was dead. We filmed an old man as he staggered along a road, fell, tried to sit up, tipped over and lay still. A Red Cross ambulance drove past. We left as his eyes rolled back and he died with a faint gasp.

In a field hospital, we found Father Vincent preparing a little boy for death. His wailing mother pressed her head to his chest while the priest administered the last rites. 'I did this sixty times yesterday,' he said to me as grave diggers carried the boy away to wrap him up and dump him in a mass grave behind the hospital.

'What do you tell the dying?' I asked the priest.

'All I can tell them is that death is not the end. Even if we are dying, we have to keep hope.'

'Where is God in all of this?'

'This couldn't have been God's will. I am sure he was not responsible for chasing us out of Rwanda.'

By then the genocide was forgotten. Cholera had become the story of the moment, and journalists flocked to the refugee camps from every corner of the globe. Many would fly in on aid planes from Nairobi or Entebbe for the day. Adorned with necklaces of cameras, they would take a short ride into a refugee camp, get a picture of a dying child – *snap, snap, snap* – attend a UNHCR media conference – *scribble, scribble, scribble* – film an introduction (in the case of TV reporters) at a mass grave – *disaster, disaster, disaster* – and fly back to Nairobi with a lead story in the bag and in time for dinner at the Carnivore Restaurant.

Many journalists and aid workers had no concept of the fact that Goma's camps hid the world's single largest congregation of fugitives. The same mayors who had overseen the genocide and the same *interahamwe* who had wielded the machetes during the mass killings were still in charge. Refugees who spoke of returning to Rwanda were branded as traitors, and many were killed.

Although the UNHCR administered the camps, it had absolutely no control over the power exercised by the *interahamwe* and FAR soldiers over the refugees. In terms of its mandate, the UNHCR may provide assistance only to refugees – people who have a well-founded fear of persecution in their homelands. International fugitives are specifically excluded from aid. However, no attempt was ever made to screen the Rwandans in the camps.

The killers owed the success of their extermination campaign to the inaction and apathy of the very international community whose charities were now feeding them and sheltering them from retribution. One or two aid agencies, most notably Médecins Sans Frontières, saw the absurdity of the situation and pulled out. Their places were quickly filled by eager but naive helping hands.

General Dallaire realised the camps had become recruitment centres for further genocide and were organised as replicas of the Hutu Power state. He warned that the presence of the *génocidaires* in the camps could ignite a catastrophe throughout the Great Lakes region that would be even worse than the genocide. He proposed that the UN and international community separate the genuinely displaced from the killers. The refugees should go back to Rwanda and the *génocidaires* be brought to justice. At a meeting with ambassadors to discuss his plan, the French and Americans rejected it as unworkable.

The *interahamwe* dispensed law and order in the camps. Early one morning we came upon a group of four men who were busy killing someone. As we stopped next to them, they got up, holding bloodied machetes in their hands. Ivan and I got out of the car. The leader of the group walked towards us, his machete dangling from his right hand. He had crooked, nicotine-stained teeth and narrow, ghoulish eyes.

'What happened?' I asked him through our translator.

'He's a bandit,' the killer said. 'He took people's stuff last night.'

'Can we film you?' I asked.

'Why not?' he said.

As we walked closer, we could see that the victim was still moving, gurgling on blood gushing from wounds in his neck. The killers posed with their machetes next to the dying man.

We resumed our journey, but minutes later shots rang out and people scuttled in all directions. As we jumped out of the car we saw a Zairean soldier lying on his stomach. Yellow guts oozed out of a gaping abdominal wound. As Ivan started to film, a young man grabbed my arm and said: 'You have to go away! These people are very dangerous. I saw everything. I'll go with you.'

We sped away with the young man, who introduced himself as Jean-Claude. He said Zairean soldiers frequently harassed refugees and confiscated their goods. In this case the soldier had picked on the wrong person, an *interahamwe* leader. His men had turned on the soldier, wrestled his AK from him and shot him dead.

Images like this festered like malignant growths in the back of my head and wouldn't let go. It was my friend Max du Preez who aroused my guilt when he watched our documentary and asked afterwards: 'The old man you filmed dying next to the road ...'

'Yes?'

'You watched and filmed him dying?'

'Yes.'

'How long did it take?'

'Ten, fifteen minutes.'

'Did you try and help him?'

'No.'

'Why not?'

I couldn't answer Max. At the time it never even crossed my mind to try to save a life. Death occurred in the camps every second, minute, hour, day. I could have offered the old man a sip of water. I didn't. I could at least have comforted and supported him in his hour of death. I didn't. I had all the stock arguments and excuses: I was a mere onlooker and observer; it wasn't my job to save lives; a journalist shouldn't get involved. It didn't help.

I started having terrible nightmares about the old man. No matter where my subconscious took me, he was there, like a demon snapping at my heels and always giggling in a frenzied manner. What would start as a pleasant dream soon slipped into torment with the appearance of the shrivelled and wasted face of the old man. He once throttled me, and another time chased me high up the Rwandan volcanoes and into the clouds.

I started mentally reviewing my visits to Rwanda and felt that I was nothing but a peeping Tom, gorging my journalistic appetite on people's misery and suffering. And let's be brutally honest: the more dire the misery and the more gory the suffering, the more sensational the story. Awards are won, viewers drawn and recognition earned by blood and guts, not smiling and contented faces. When Tony Karamba told me during my first trip to Rwanda that we were going to the massacre site at Nyarubuye, I beamed with exhilaration. When I cast my eyes over the multitude of corpses, lying there in rotten and exposed humiliation, I probably realised I had a brilliant opening sequence for my documentary that would shock and horrify my viewers.

I landed up at a psychologist, who told me my emotions were normal and understandable and were a combination of sadness, anger, remorse and guilt. We spoke for a few sessions and then I left it at that and learnt to live with the pictures of Rwanda that were etched into my mind.

One of the most evocative images ever captured by a journalist also contributed to his suicide – because he couldn't reconcile the pictures of death that made him both famous and notorious with his memory of the dying child he had abandoned. South African photographer Kevin Carter won a Pulitzer Prize when he travelled to the desert plains of South Sudan and took a photograph of a starving child crawling towards a feeding centre while being stalked by a vulture. Carter took his pictures, chased the bird away and left the tiny girl to resume her struggle. Afterwards, without knowing her fate, he sat under a tree, lit a cigarette, talked to God and cried.

The acclaim of the Pulitzer was accompanied by criticism of his ethics. The question asked most often by fellow journalists was: Why didn't you help the girl? Wrote the *St Petersburg Times*: 'The man adjusting his lens to take just the right frame of her suffering might just as well be a predator, another vulture on the scene.'

Two months after receiving his Pulitzer, Carter attached a garden hose to his red pickup's exhaust and gassed himself. He described his anguish in a suicide note. 'I am haunted by the vivid memories of killings & corpses & anger & pain ... of starving children, of trigger-happy madmen, often police, of killer executioners.'

After my first visit, I returned to Nyarubuye several times. One year after the massacre, the surrounding fields had been cultivated, there was human life on the terraced slopes and villages, and markets were hives of activity. The air was filled with fragrant breezes and birdsong. As on my initial visit, it had rained the night before, and we drove through mud pools towards the basilica. Nyarubuye was declared a genocide memorial and the bones had been left untouched. But the stench of a year earlier was gone. Rotten flesh had been reduced to white skeletons. Even the tormented faces were nothing more than bleached skulls. In an eerie way, Nyarubuye was more at peace with itself.

Philip Gourevitch was there at the same time and described the scene as follows: 'The skeleton is a beautiful thing. The randomness of the fallen form, the strange tranquillity of their rude exposure, the skull here, the arm bent in some uninterpretable gesture there – these things were beautiful, and their beauty only added to the affront of the place. I just looked, and I took photographs, because I wondered whether I could really see what I was seeing while I saw it, and I wanted also an excuse to look a bit more closely.'

The last time I went back to Nyarubuye was five years after the massacre. By then the church and the compound had been cleaned up and skulls and bones were neatly stacked and packed in adjacent rooms. A priest was on hand to explain what had happened on that day in April 1994.

As the full scale of massacres like Nyarubuye and the extent of the genocide emerged, strings of apologies were heaped on Rwandans. Among the most eloquent and sincere was that of General Roméo Dallaire, the man who had warned the world long before the president's aircraft was shot down that extremists were plotting genocide. He left Rwanda broken, disillusioned, haunted, suicidal and bent on telling the world how he and his mission had been abandoned and betrayed by the international community and UN bureaucrats who refused to give him the men and the means to stop the killings.

'I know there is a God,' Dallaire writes in his book, *Shake Hands with the Devil*, 'because in Rwanda I shook hands with the devil. I have seen him, I have smelled him and I have touched him. I know the devil exists and therefore I know there is a God.'

Dallaire took full responsibility for the failure of UNAMIR to protect civilians. 'The international community, through an inept mandate and what can only be described as indifference, self-interest and racism, aided and abetted these crimes against humanity. We watched as the devil took control of paradise on earth and fed on the blood of the people we were supposed to protect.'

In March 1998, American president Bill Clinton became the first Western head of state to visit Rwanda and apologise for not intervening during the genocide. It was the defining shame of his presidency (as opposed to scandal, epitomised by the Monica Lewinsky affair) that Clinton's administration had not only abandoned Rwanda and its people to genocide, but also encouraged others to do nothing. 'During the ninety days that began on 6 April 1994, Rwanda experienced the most intensive slaughter in this blood-filled century. These events grew from a policy aimed at the systematic destruction of people,' he said.

Clinton listened to the testimony of survivors but never left Kigali's international airport – probably for security reasons. Perhaps he should have done what Archbishop Desmond Tutu did a few years earlier: gone to Nyarubuye and cried for the dead.

CHAPTER 6

A cockroach cannot
give birth to a butterfly

Rwanda is clinically dead as a nation.
— Nigerian Nobel laureate Wole Soyinka (11 May 1994)

ENOSE NSABIMANA WAS FIFTY-SIX YEARS OLD, A FATHER OF FIVE and grandfather of twelve. He had been married for thirty-five years, during which he contentedly tilled his tiny terraced cornfield in the province of Kibungo in eastern Rwanda. He also had a banana plantation and three longhorn zebu cows.

But towards the middle of 1993, he said, things changed when his youngest son, Elizaphan, joined a youth movement called the *interahamwe*. The term means 'Let Us Strike Together'. When Enose asked him what the *interahamwe* stood for, Elizaphan said 'civil defence'.

'Defence against what?' Enose asked.

'The Tutsis,' his son replied.

Enose didn't ask any further questions. Himself a Hutu, he vaguely remembered the killings of 1959 when Rwanda ran red with blood as Hutus rose against Tutsis and set fire to their houses, slit their throats and crushed their skulls. More blood and hate flowed a few years later, and again in 1972 and 1992.

Elizaphan had learnt important things at the *interahamwe* meetings. He told Enose that Tutsis were not even from Rwanda, but a foreign people from somewhere along the Nile River who came to steal the Hutus' land, enslave them and marry their women.

Elizaphan referred to Tutsis as *inyenzis* – cockroaches. 'The *inyenzis* don't belong in Rwanda,' he said. 'They should be sent back with the Nyabarongo River to the land north-east of Rwanda where they came from.'

Enose couldn't read, but Elizaphan told him about *The Hutu Ten Commandments*, compiled by an influential businessman named Hassan Ngeze. He was editor of the newspaper *Kangura* (Wake it up) and a friend of President Juvénal Habyarimana. Enose himself was not involved in politics, but he was a member of the ruling MRND party and revered the president for having done great and important things for Hutus.

Elizaphan explained that the commandments declared every Tutsi dishonest and any Hutu who had financial dealings with Tutsis an enemy of the people. Hutus were commanded to stand together against their Tutsi foes. Hutu men who married Tutsi women were traitors.

This bothered Enose, because his neighbour, Augustine Raturamaruga, was Hutu, but his wife Rose was a Tutsi. Their three children were classified as Hutu. Rwanda was a tiny country in which many people were trying to eke out an existence, and Enose and Augustine had been living a few metres from one another for as long as he could remember. They shared pots of banana beer and their wives had a stall at the market where they sold onions and tomatoes.

When he mentioned to Elizaphan that Augustine was as close to him as a brother, his son told him of the wisdom of Professor Léon Mugesera, a leading figure in the ruling MRND and a close confidant of the president. A few months earlier, Mugesera had made a speech in the western prefecture of Gisenyi. Elizaphan quoted what the professor had said of Tutsis: 'The vermin must be liquidated. Know that the person whose throat you do not cut now will be the one who will cut yours. Wipe out this scum!'

Elizaphan read Enose an article in *Kangura* under the headline 'A cockroach cannot give birth to a butterfly', which said: 'A cockroach gives birth to another cockroach. The malice, the evil is just as we knew them in the history of our country. What if someone brought back the Hutu Revolution of 1959 to finish off these Tutsi cockroaches?'

Like many around him, Enose was anxious about looming war in Rwanda. In 1990, the Tutsi-dominated RPF invaded the country from Uganda and occupied territory in the north-east. It was a long way from Kibungo, but Professor Mugesera warned that the ultimate goal of the RPF was the extermination of all Hutus. Therefore Hutus had to act first, and not let Tutsis get away again like they did in the killings of 1959. 'Destroy them,' he said. 'Drive them out. Long live President Habyarimana!'

Elizaphan also told Enose of the messages of Radio des Milles Collines, an independent radio station funded by powerful ruling party members. It played over and over a song by pop star Simon Bikindi called 'I Hate These Tutsis', which went:

I detest these Tutsis that are here to kill, to kill.
I hate them and I don't apologise for that.
Lucky for us they are few in number
Those who have ears, let them hear!

During the first months of 1994, Elizaphan talked openly about the extermination of every *inyenzi* in the land. By then, his son could lob grenades and shoot with a Kalashnikov. Army instructors had shown them how to hack up dummies with machetes and how to make a *masu* – a wooden club studded with nails. Elizaphan was personally responsible for drawing up lists of names of Tutsis and Hutu traitors in their neighbourhood who were earmarked for extermination.

'And what about Augustine and Rose?' Enose asked his son.

'They are also on the list,' Elizaphan admitted.

'What can Augustine do?'

'He'll have to exterminate his *inyenzi* and cleanse himself,' said Elizaphan.

'And the children?'

'They are *inyenzi* bastards!'

Enose said everyone knew about the *interahamwe* and the lists. Augustine Raturamaruga had also heard rumours of imminent war and killings, and said to him: 'Blood is going to flow in Rwanda. There's hate everywhere. Rose and I are not safe. She's Tutsi.'

It was just before the massacres started that Elizaphan brought his father a *masu*. He himself walked around with a brand new machete. Enose didn't want the studded club, but his son said: 'You will need one, because we will all have to help exterminate the *inyenzis*.'

Enose said he had never killed anyone and didn't intend to use the *masu*. He never told Augustine about his weapon, but advised his friend to leave the country. He told him that he and his family were on the lists. No, his neighbour said, I'm not leaving yet, but I'm sending Rose and the children to family in Burundi.

On 4 April, Elizaphan came home after a long absence. He was dressed in *kitenge*, multicoloured trousers and tunics that would become the trademark of the *interahamwe*. Enose asked Elizaphan what he had been up to. He said the *interahamwe* had been finalising their strategy for crushing the *inyenzis*.

'Their end is near, father. Within the next day or two, you will be hearing a lot of gunshots and grenades exploding,' Elizaphan said. He then wanted to know: 'And where is the traitor next door and his *inyenzi*?'

Enose told him that Rose and the children had gone to Burundi and that Augustine was home alone. It angered Elizaphan that an *inyenzi* had escaped. It scared Enose when his son said: 'His time has come anyway. He's bred with that *inyenzi* and he'll pay for that.'

Elizaphan left again early the next morning without saying goodbye to his father.

By then, Enose knew that killings – so much bloodletting that it would shock even Rwandans – were about to explode around the country. He told Augustine about his fears and advised him to go to Burundi.

'Don't worry,' said Augustine. 'If something happens I will go to Tanzania or Burundi. The borders are not far.'

When Enose woke up on the morning of 7 April, he switched on the radio and tuned to Radio Rwanda. He said he became icy cold when an announcer said that President Juvénal Habyarimana was dead. The radio said the president had been on his way back from Tanzania, where he had signed a peace agreement with the rebels. Missiles shot his aircraft from the sky. The Burundian president and other senior advisors were also on board. There were no survivors.

He knew the day of extermination and bloodshed had dawned. Enose ran next door, where he found Augustine in a sombre mood. He had also heard the news.

'My time has come,' Augustine said.

'No, no, no!' Enose said, pleading with Augustine: 'You must leave. Immediately. Please, go away!'

He helped his neighbour scratch together a few pieces of clothing and packed him some food. 'Where will you go?' he asked.

'I'll hide in the forest and then try and get to the border. I greet you, Enose,' he said.

'And I'll pray for you, Augustine. Go well.'

When Enose got back to his house, Radio des Milles Collines was instructing its listeners: 'Death, death to the *inyenzis*! You must act fast. Force them to come out! Find them at whatever cost!'

When I saw Enose Nsabimana five years later, he appeared unsound of mind and body. A grey beard covered his gaunt face and he gazed with manic eyes straight ahead of him. He was locked up in a fetid makeshift prison near Kibungo, where he had been incarcerated for more than four years. A former army warehouse had been converted into a jail by covering the two windows with iron bars and installing a steel gate. There was no toilet (only buckets) and nowhere to exercise.

I was on my sixth visit to Rwanda to compile a documentary on the fifth anniversary of the genocide. When I first visited this beautiful land of death in the autumn of 1994, hordes of machete-wielding thugs, supported by fanatical Hutu politicians and army officers, had been intent on wiping out the entire Tutsi population. They almost succeeded, and in the space of a hundred days murdered six to seven of every eight Tutsis in the country. Some estimated that 800 000 people were massacred – which computed to 333 murders every hour, or just over five a minute. The Rwandans themselves said the death toll was at least a million – and they ought to know. Of those killed, 300 000 were children. Another 100 000 children were separated from their families, orphaned, lost, abducted or abandoned. A quarter of a million women were widowed. Tens of thousands more Rwandans died in the aftermath of the genocide in cholera-infested refugee camps in neighbouring Zaire and in subsequent raids launched by the killers from their hideouts.

Tutsis were killed simply because they were born Tutsi. Hutus who refused to participate, were married to Tutsis, hid their neighbours or opposed the goal of an ethnically pure state were also murdered. Most of the survivors would go to their graves with pictures of unimaginable horror seared into their minds. In addition to the children who were slain or orphaned, 95 per cent of the country's next generation witnessed or experienced brutality. Many of the survivors were nothing but living dead. Never before had killers used rape as a weapon of war to the same extent as in Rwanda. Four women were raped every minute of every day for the hundred consecutive days of the genocide. Many were raped several times.

I was in Rwanda at virtually every stage of events as they unfolded after the shooting down of Juvénal Habyarimana's aircraft. I traversed the country, small as it is, from north to south and east to west, and in the process produced nine television documentaries. No single happening had a more profound impact on my professional and, perhaps, my personal life than the events of 1994. They filled me at various times with sadness, anger and despondency. I stared into the eyes of countless killers, shook their hands, and even ate pizza and drank wine with a man of the cloth who had delivered his Tutsi parishioners to their killers with a smile on his face. In not a single case could I detect any remorse. I have yet to come across a killer who admits that this was genocide. A 'spontaneous eruption' of anger at the shooting down of the president's aircraft that led to mass killings on both sides, yes. But an orchestrated campaign to expunge every single Tutsi from Rwanda? Not a chance.

It would have been easy to become swamped by the misery. But for every machete-wielding butcher, there was an unsung hero who refused to kill; for every Hutu that succumbed to the message of hate, there was another who resisted the propaganda and pressure and defied a nation. Rwanda showed me the very best and the very worst that mankind has to offer.

I saw Enose Nsabimana only once, and for not more than an hour or two. His story, though, stayed with me as the epitome of the sadness and devilry that engulfed Rwanda in the autumn of 1994 and the embodiment of what happens to an ordinary man when the devil takes control of paradise.

As the guard unbolted the gate to his jail and swung it open, a blanket of pink-clothed prisoners greeted me. More than a hundred men were scrunched together in a space that should have held no more than thirty or forty. Stooped down on stick-thin legs a few feet from the door was a senile-looking man who gaped at me. Clutched tightly in his hands and held closely to his chest was the top half of a human skull.

'This is Enose Nsabimana,' said the guard, as he marched the elderly man out of the cell. He took him to a tiny office and ordered him to sit down. 'You can speak to him,' he said.

'What's your name?' I asked through my Rwandan interpreter.

'Enose Nsabimana,' he answered in Kinyarwanda.

'And whose skull is that?'

'Augustine,' he said.

'And who was Augustine?'

'My neighbour.'

'And what happened to him?'

'I stroked him on his head with a big stick,' Enose said.

'And why are you holding his skull?'

'I want to show it to the court,' he said.

'Where did you get the skull?'

'I got it where we buried him.'

'Why did you kill him?'

'Augustine was an *inyenzi*,' he said.

'And how do you feel about killing him?'

'I've got a big pain. Even my heart doesn't pump well.'

The whole time that I spoke to Enose, he held the skull tightly against his chest and didn't move or blink an eye. As we ended the interview, he asked me if I was going to speak to the state prosecutor.

'Yes, I am,' I said. 'But why?'

'Tell him I'm waiting to show the skull to the judge. He must hurry up because I want to bury Augustine again.'

I called the guard and told him to take Enose back to the cell. Once inside, he slumped down on the cement floor, where he sat cross-legged, the skull still pressed to his chest.

'That's how he sits,' the guard said. 'Day in and day out. He doesn't move. Sometimes he talks to the skull. And if we try and take it away, he fights with us.'

A few hours later I spoke to the state prosecutor in Kibungo. He had Enose's file in front of him. 'He made a full and signed confession that he killed Augustine Raturamaruga,' he said. 'He hit him with a studded stick on his head on 30 April 1994.'

'He seems mad,' I said to the prosecutor.

'He wasn't when he made this confession. We found him with the skull and he admitted to the murder.'

'You don't call a man holding a skull mad?'

'What are we supposed to do? Release him?'

'Put him in a mental asylum,' I said to the prosecutor.

'We don't have asylums. He'll have to wait his turn to stand trial,' he said.

'That could take a hundred years!'

'Then he'll have to wait,' the prosecutor said. He shoved the file across the table to me and said: 'Read his confession. No doubt he's guilty of murder.'

The *génocidaires* had plotted something akin to a team sport exercise. Everybody had to take part. No one was allowed to sit on the sidelines. In arriving at the final solution, there had to be neither witnesses nor accusers or bystanders. Every Hutu was called upon to do his national duty and murder Tutsis.

That was how Enose Nsabimana understood the bloodletting that broke out around Kibungo and its communes within days of Habyarimana's murder. In his own mind, he said, he was convinced that there was no longer space in Rwanda for both Hutus and Tutsis. 'If Tutsis could shoot down the plane of the president,' he said, 'imagine how easy it would be for them to come and kill Hutus like me.'

Hutus from every corner of Rwanda – young and old, peasant and politician, rich and poor, the educated and the illiterate – obeyed the orders to rid their country of Tutsis. That was why most people died not as a result of bullets or bombs or rocket launchers, but of machete cuts, *masu* gashes, hammer blows, and spear and knife wounds. A mighty amount of manual labour went into the genocide.

Neighbour hacked neighbour, husbands clubbed wives, and friends killed friends. Doctors and nurses killed their patients, teachers their pupils, employers their workers, and preachers and nuns delivered their Tutsi congregants into the hands of their murderers.

Early on the evening of about the fourth day of the killings, Enose heard a truck arrive in the village. It screeched to a halt at a house further down the road. He was too scared to go outside, but he knew the *interahamwe* had come for a Tutsi by the name of Frederic Nyilinkwayo and his family. Elizaphan once told him that these *inyenzis* secretly worked for the Patriotic Front. He remembered his son's words: 'Don't worry, father, for the sun is soon to set on them forever.'

There was a commotion at Frederic's house. Men spoke frenziedly, somebody blew a whistle and a single gunshot rang out. A woman screamed and children cried. The whistle blew again, and then it became utterly confusing. Enose heard what sounded like blows. This went on for a minute or two until the cries stopped. He then heard only the exuberant voices of men. They stayed at the house for another few minutes and then got onto the truck. Enose blew out his candle and turned down the radio as he waited for the invaders to leave the village.

The truck stopped in front of his house. Enose jumped up. He wanted to run away, but his feet became heavy with fear. Have they come for me as well? Was my friendship with Augustine a death sentence?

Then he heard Elizaphan's voice. Enose opened the door. Elizaphan and a soldier stood in front of him. They smelt of beer. 'We came for the *inyenzi* Nyilinkwayo,' said Elizaphan. 'He was lucky, we fed him a bullet. But the others were not. We finished them off with our tools.' Enose said some of the *interahamwe* on the back of the truck were clad in attire fashioned from banana leaves and held bloodied machetes aloft.

The next day, Enose ventured out of his house and walked in the direction of the Nyilinkwayo home. Several people stood staring at Frederic's body, which lay a few feet from his front door. The top half of his head had been blown off and he had a gash in his neck. The bodies of his wife and their two children must have been inside. None of the bystanders spoke or entered the house.

By then, full-scale war had broken out. According to Radio Rwanda, the RPF had invaded the country from the north and was killing innocent Hutus in their path. 'I was by then convinced that the violence would only stop once there were no more Tutsis. It seems as if Elizaphan had spoken with great insight about this problem,' Enose said.

Radio des Milles Collines directed the killings. It told the *interahamwe* where the *inyenzis* were hiding, it named people to be exterminated, and spurred the population on to seek out Tutsis and kill them. 'Death! Death! Graves with Tutsi bodies are still only half full. Hurry and fill them to the top!'

General Dallaire asked New York to arrange for the radio station to be shut down, as it was instrumental in promoting and directing the genocide. The UN didn't have the means to jam the signal, and made a formal request to the United States to do so. The issue was studied by the Pentagon, which concluded that the operation would be too costly – $8 500 an hour for a jamming aircraft to fly over the country – and might violate the autonomy of an independent state.

As bodies accumulated next to the roads and the first visuals of the killings reached the outside world, newly appointed president Théodore Sindikubwabo described the violence as a spontaneous outburst of rage sparked by 'sorrow and aggressive feelings of frustration' after the killing of Habyarimana. Prime Minister Jean Kambanda said there was 'a certain frustration among people, a certain vague anger that made it impossible for people to keep control'.

It seemed to strike the right chord and was exactly what the world wanted to hear. The Rwandan genocide happened six months after the humiliation of the United States in Somalia, when eighteen of its soldiers were killed, more than seventy wounded and two Black Hawk helicopters shot down in what became known as the Battle for Mogadishu. The world's most powerful nation withdrew in disgrace. The US didn't want another African adventure that might put its troops at risk, and like the rest of the 'civilised' world, pretended that Rwandans were living out their ancient tribal bloodlust by killing one another.

The world preferred to ignore compelling evidence that the genocide was being orchestrated from the very top. Prime Minister Kambanda was shown on Rwandan television inciting the populace to kill Tutsis. He travelled to the university town of Butare – where killing got off to a slow pace – and urged Hutus to join the campaign to exterminate Tutsis. 'Don't be onlookers when the rest of your brothers are doing their national duty,' he lambasted them as he dished out guns. 'Exterminate the vermin in your midst.'

It was much easier to pretend that this dot on the African continent – where there is nothing that anybody wants – was haunted by a collective madness and incessant hatred. Hutus killing Tutsis and Tutsis killing Hutus was an inevitable and ghoulish national pastime. The international community chose to ignore the fact that the genocide was the result of meticulous planning and indoctrination over years and had been born of the deliberate choice of fanatics to foster hate and fear in order to stay in power.

The killings were more intense and effective than those of Nazi Germany's Holocaust. The machetes and *masus* of the *interahamwe* and the ordinary people they incited produced far more rapid results than Hitler's gas chambers. The genocide was many times as intense as the ethnic cleansing in Serbia, Croatia and Bosnia during the late 1980s and early 1990s, yet Western powers poured more than 50 000 troops, an arsenal of high-tech weapons and billions of dollars into the Balkan conflict.

Less than two weeks after the death of the president, Human Rights Watch labelled the killings genocide and demanded that the UN and the international community meet their legal obligation to intervene. The Genocide Convention of 1946, passed by the UN's General Assembly in the aftermath of the Holocaust, compelled member states to intervene in cases where a population was being annihilated. The United States and others jargoned themselves out of liability. The furthest Washington went was to say that 'acts of genocide may have occurred' in Rwanda. Secretary of State Warren Christopher said in a television interview that there was 'a tremendous civil war' in Rwanda and that America was doing all it could to try to support the UN.

Deputy Assistant Secretary of State Prudence Bushnell was tasked to phone Colonel Théoneste Bagosora, the Rwandan government official in charge of the genocide. He wouldn't speak to her and she delivered her message to army chief General Augustine Bizimungu. She warned that the United States would hold

Rwandan leaders personally responsible if the massacres didn't stop and that they would face charges of violating international law.

'How nice of you to think of me,' Bizimungu responded. The United States then sat back unperturbed and watched the country explode.

Years later, then UN Secretary General Boutros Boutros-Ghali said in an interview that he had had various meetings during the genocide with the American and British ambassadors and urged that action be taken to stop the killings. He described their reaction as: 'Come on, Boutros, relax. Don't put us in a difficult position. The mood is not for intervention, you will obtain nothing. We will not move.'

On the afternoon of 15 April 1994, several thousand men marched towards the red-brick basilica at Nyarubuye in south-east Rwanda. The column consisted for the most part of villagers and peasants from surrounding communes, armed with sticks, machetes and *masus*.

Among them was Enose, carrying the *masu* that Elizaphan had given him a fortnight before. Earlier in the day, Enose and the other villagers had been picked up by an army truck and taken to a spot not far from the church, where soldiers and members of the *interahamwe* addressed them. *Inyenzis* are hiding in the church, the men were told, and we are going to exterminate all of them.

'Why did you go to Nyarubuye?' I asked Enose.

He hung his grey head in thought and said: 'Elizaphan told me to go. He said, father, do you remember the *masu* I gave you? You must take it and come with us because there is an important task at hand. I took it and went, even though I didn't know how to use it.'

The local Hutu mayor, Sylvestre Gacumbitsi, directed the slaughter. He gave orders to police and soldiers to shoot, and then for peasants to move in and hack, slash, club and bludgeon the *inyenzis* to death. 'There must be no survivors and no runaways,' the *bourgmestre* said.

To a peasant like Enose, the mayor was a man of great authority. The villagers were divided into several groups to await their orders. Enose was told to join a group of peasants outside the church to make sure that nobody escaped. In his mind, the atrocity at hand carried the mayor's blessing.

Inside the church and its surrounding compound were several thousand Tutsis and some Hutu 'traitors'. An estimated 3 000 people were crowded into the church, although some put the number as high as 5 000 or even twice as many. Among them was Valentina Izibagiza, a Tutsi who was living with her four brothers and three sisters in Kibungo when the killings started.

As death closed in on Kibungo, a delegation of mainly Tutsis had gone to see Mayor Gacumbitsi, who advised them to seek refuge at the Catholic mission at

Nyarubuye. 'We believed him,' said Valentina, 'because Tutsis found sanctuary there during previous attacks in the fifties, sixties and seventies.' Refugees arrived at the church on 13 April. By then the priests were gone, having left their flock at the mercy of the killers.

By three o'clock on the afternoon of 15 April, the church was completely surrounded by soldiers, police, *interahamwe* and villagers. 'They said that people with money should hand it over and then they would be spared. They took the money and then killed them anyway,' said Valentina.

Bourgmestre Gacumbitsi gave the order to attack. It started with soldiers throwing grenades into the crowd. Gacumbitsi set an example for his men by being one of the first to kill a Tutsi. 'The soldiers and *interahamwe* shot at everyone. One of the leaders said we were snakes and the only way to kill snakes was to smash their heads,' said Valentina. 'Inside the church it was chaos and everyone ran around, screaming and trying to find a place to hide.' According to survivors, Gacumbitsi had a microphone with a loudspeaker, and said: 'We are the *interahamwe* and we are about to eliminate every Tutsi so that in future no one will even know what a Tutsi looked like.'

According to Valentina, Gacumbitsi said: 'If anyone is hiding in this church because of a mistake, because he or she is really a Hutu, they should tell me now.' She said a boy of about eleven stood up and said: 'I am a Hutu.' Everyone knew he wasn't. 'Two *interahamwe* soldiers ran forward and beat him with machetes so fiercely that his body went flying into the air and came down in several pieces.'

Soldiers gunned down people who tried to run away. Militia and villagers waiting with machetes, spears and *masus* intercepted the few that managed to get through the first line of attack. They were hacked and clubbed to death.

'Did you hit anyone with your *masu*?' I asked Enose.

'No,' he said. 'I was too slow.'

As the killers pounced on the thousands in Nyarubuye, Valentina crept into a tiny cubbyhole at the church entrance. She said it was so small that nobody bothered to check if anyone was hiding there. 'Sometimes the killers would just take a child and throw it against the wall. Some fell very close to and almost on top of me. Towards the end of the day more men came and stuck knives in those who lay wounded, to make sure they were dead. By this time I was lying underneath several people, and they thought that I too was dead.'

Killing was much harder work than most anticipated. Victims resisted, crawled away, turned their backs as the blows or machetes rained down on them, held their hands in front of their faces and bodies, or simply refused to die. The feet and hands of many were hacked off in order to 'cut them down to size' (Tutsis are often much taller and thinner than Hutus).

As night fell, only a few hundred had been killed. The killers cut the Achilles tendons of some and left them to wail and cry and maybe die during the night while they retreated to drink beer and barbecue meat from cattle they had looted from their victims.

Enose said he could hear the lamenting of the people inside the church. 'What did you do?' I asked him.

'Nothing,' he said. 'We made jokes and drank beer and ate meat.'

The killers returned to work early the next morning. It took another two days of slashing, hacking and clubbing to finish off all the *inyenzis*. When it seemed that everyone was dead, Valentina said, the *interahamwe* brought dogs, which began eating the corpses.

She knew one of the soldiers, whose name was Fredina. She crept out of her hiding place and begged him: 'Can you find it in your heart to forgive me for being a Tutsi? Will you spare me?' He spat on her and called a man from her village to club her to death.

'Then he began smashing my hands with a club, so that my fingers were broken and my skull was bleeding and the pain was terrible. Soon the pain was so bad that I knew no more. I passed out. They left me for dead.'

Valentina stayed among the rotting corpses for forty-three days. 'I do remember that in the first few days I was in terrible pain. But then I became like a log. It was as if I couldn't feel and I could barely move, except to crawl out to drink rainwater.'

As the killers fled before the lightning-fast advance of the RPF, Valentina and a handful of survivors at Nyarubuye emerged from their holes and hiding places. The stronger ones lit fires and scoured the area for bananas and wild fruit.

'We were just keeping ourselves alive while we waited for death to take us as well,' she said.

Among the RPF soldiers who found the survivors at Nyarubuye was Lieutenant Tony Karamba, a teacher turned soldier who would later become my military escort and guide in Rwanda. He said of Valentina: 'You couldn't tell her age because of the way she looked. She had been tortured, she had been cut with a machete, she had lost her shape. Her one hand had no fingers. But she had a strong heart and she told us what had happened.'

Three weeks into the massacres, Enose Nsabimana saw that Tutsis were extremely hard to come by in Kibungo. Those that had not been massacred in their villages or at the church in Nyarubuye had fled into the mountains and forests, where they were hunted down by Elizaphan and the *interahamwe*.

His own village had been emptied of *inyenzis*. Many of the murdered Tutsis had once been his friends. Frederic Nyilinkwayo and his family were killed in their home. Thérèsa and her children were hacked to death at the market. Ephiphanie Mukakabanda, his wife and five children were intercepted at a roadblock just outside the village, dragged to the side of the road and cut up with machetes. Enose said he watched the *interahamwe*, wearing crowns of banana leaves and spurred on by the screech of a whistle, drag a young man into the village after finding him hiding in the forest. As they surrounded him with their machetes, he was on his knees, begging – not for his life, but for the mercy of a bullet. One of the *interahamwe*, who had a gun, asked him if he had money to pay for the bullet. He didn't. The killers descended on him like a pack of wolves and continued to hack at his body long after he was dead.

With all the Tutsis gone, talk in the village was about the advance of the Rwandan Patriotic Front. According to Radio des Milles Collines, the Tutsi rebels were killing Hutus in the villages and towns they had taken. The radio urged listeners: 'A hundred thousand young men must be rapidly recruited so that they can rise up and kill the Tutsis. We will exterminate them all. So look at a person and see his height and how he looks. Just look at his pretty little nose and then break it!'

The *interahamwe* intensified the hunt for survivors to make sure there would be no witnesses to tell their stories by the time the RPF reached Kibungo. But the perpetrators could not stay in town either, and Elizaphan told Enose they would soon have to retreat south and maybe even cross the river into Tanzania.

'Why?' Enose asked. 'I have not done anything wrong.'

'They will kill you! You're a Hutu and one of us. Remember the church?'

The next morning, as the sun lifted its head over the mountains and cast a mandarin glow down the mist-covered valleys, Enose woke up to a commotion in front of his home. It was a group of men, feverishly babbling all at once. He recognised Elizaphan's voice, and then heard someone pleading, begging and crying. He identified the voice as that of Augustine Raturamaruga, his neighbour! Enose rushed outside.

Augustine was lying in the road with his hands tied behind his back and his face a bloody mess. 'We found the *inyenzi*!' Elizaphan barked triumphantly when he saw his father. Enose said his neighbour's face lit up when he saw him. 'He thought I could help him.'

'What did you do?' I asked.

'There was nothing I could do. He was an *inyenzi* and he was finished,' Enose said.

'But he was your friend. You grew up with him!'

'The war changed everything,' Enose said. 'Augustine was not my friend any longer.'

Augustine had never made it to Burundi or Tanzania. He might have heard the *interahamwe* were waiting for fleeing Tutsis at border crossings, where they cut them down. He probably decided to hide in the forest until the killings subsided. When the *interahamwe* found him, he told them that he had money at home and would pay them to save his life. He didn't have money; he was merely trying to prolong his life for an hour or two.

'He's yours, old man,' a soldier ordered Enose. 'Kill the *inyenzi!*'

Elizaphan also spurred on his father. 'Come on, it's now your turn. Where's your *masu*? Fetch it!'

'I had no choice,' Enose said. 'This was how the war was. Augustine was one of them.'

Enose said he went into his house and fetched his *masu*. All the while, Augustine was crying and pleading for his life. 'My mind didn't think,' said Enose. 'I just knew I had to do it.'

'Did you say anything to him?' I asked.

'Nothing. But he spoke to me.'

'What did he say?'

'He asked me to save his life.'

'And then?'

'I lifted my big stick and stroked him twice over his head. He fell over.'

'What happened next?'

'He might have been dead, but the others finished him off with machetes anyway.'

Young boys who were with the *interahamwe* dug a shallow grave next to Augustine's house. Enose said he watched until his neighbour disappeared into the hole and his body was covered with red soil.

As the RPF reached Kibungo, a quarter of a million Hutus fled across the Rusomo bridge into Tanzania. The refugees were mostly terrified civilians, but among them were also the killers of thousands of Tutsis whose bodies were strewn at the church at Nyarubuye and in communes and prefectures across south-eastern Rwanda. The killers dropped their machetes, knives and sticks on the Rwandan side of the bridge and proceeded into Tanzania, where they were welcomed with food and shelter by the international community. Among the killers were Enose, Elizaphan and Mayor Sylvestre Gacumbitsi.

Enose said it was while he was idling away his days under his blue canvas UN shelter that the death of Augustine started eating into his mind. He couldn't forget the *masu* blows he had aimed at his neighbour and the pain and surprise on Augustine's face when the first one fell on his head. He said he saw the image over and over of Augustine's skull splitting open like a ripe papaya and blood pouring from the wound.

'Augustine was dead and we had killed all the *inyenzis*, but it meant nothing. The Tutsis had won the war and were in power. This is not how it was supposed to be,' he said. 'When I told Elizaphan the killings had been useless, he became angry and said one day we will go back and finish off the rest of the *inyenzis*. I didn't believe him.'

By then the war was over, the RPF had captured power and many refugees were returning to Rwanda. Enose told Elizaphan that he was also going back. 'You're mad!' his son said. 'The *inyenzis* will kill you.'

'I'm old and I don't care,' he said, and left at daybreak the next morning.

Enose said he was surprised to see so many Hutus alive in Rwanda because the Tutsis were supposed to have killed them. Two days after he returned, two RPF soldiers knocked on his door and asked him questions about the massacre at Nyarubuye. He told them he had been there but didn't kill anyone. They also asked him where Elizaphan was. He said his son was in Tanzania.

A few days later, they were back. 'What has happened to your neighbour, Augustine Raturamaruga? We were told that you and your son killed him.'

Enose said he always knew the Tutsis would eventually come for him over Augustine's death. There were many accusations and suspicions of complicity in the killings that led to neighbour indicting neighbour and Hutu accusing Hutu. Enose said RPF soldiers took many people away on the strength of a single finger being pointed. Sometimes it was true, sometimes not. Some used the opportunity to settle old scores or to acquire additional tracts of land.

Enose lied to the soldiers and told them he had heard that the *interahamwe* had killed Augustine. 'You are lying, old man,' the soldiers said as they left. 'We'll be back.'

Enose said he was trapped, but no longer cared. 'I had died with Augustine,' he said. 'My life was useless and my time had come, just as his time had come when the killings started.'

At dawn the next morning, after a disturbed night with monstrous nightmares, Enose took a spade and walked over to Augustine's house. He started digging until he could see his neighbour's skull. The machete and *masu* blows had split his head in two. Enose collected the top half, took it home and waited for the soldiers to come back. When they walked into his house later that day, he sat with the skull in his hands and confessed his complicity in the murder. He was officially charged.

When Enose Nsabimana was incarcerated six months after the genocide, there were 30 000 men, women and children in thirteen red-brick prisons around the country. The prison system was designed to house 12 000 inmates. After six more months, the number of jailed genocide suspects had doubled to 60 000. Prisons were expanded, new ones built, and community centres and other state buildings converted to lock-ups. By the time I saw Enose, there were 125 000 Hutus in custody.

The prisons were human rights calamities, overcrowded to the extent that inmates were so tangled together that it became virtually impossible to determine whose leg belonged to whom and what foot was attached to which body. Inmates had to find a place to sit or stand between the legs of others, take turns to sleep, and wait for friends or family to bring food. Hundreds of prisoners required amputations, as their feet literally rotted in the dampness of the prisons.

Sheer numbers overwhelmed the country's legal system, and some estimated that ordinary courts would take a hundred years to try all those suspected of involvement in the genocide. When the RPF took power in July 1994, there were ten lawyers and six judges in the whole of Rwanda. In an effort to expedite justice, the government in 2001 introduced the so-called *gacaca* system, whereby accused could be tried by traditional village courts and sentenced to community service. *Gacaca* excluded so-called Category One offenders – those alleged to have organised genocide or played a prominent role in killing or sexual crimes. Enose should have qualified for a *gacaca* sentence.

I don't know if he ever made it to a *gacaca* court. On my last visit to Rwanda in 2002, I wanted to do a follow-up on Enose. The makeshift prison near Kibungo had been closed down. He wasn't in the main prison in town either. There was no record that the old man had ever stood trial. The state prosecutor who initially handled his case had been transferred to another part of the country. There was, in fact, no record of Enose at all. 'He might have died,' said a justice official.

Elizaphan also disappeared. As far as I know, Enose never saw him again. His son might have stayed in Tanzania or in one of the neighbouring states, probably plotting the final extermination of the *inyenzis*. Mayor Sylvestre Gacumbitsi was less fortunate. Justice caught up with him in 2001, when he was arrested in Tanzania and handed over to the International Criminal Tribunal for Rwanda (ICTR). The tribunal was set up by the UN in 1996 to trace, arrest and judge the planners, instigators and worst offenders of the genocide.

One of the first witnesses against Gacumbitsi was Ferdinand Rwakayigamba, one of the few survivors of Nyarubuye. Before the genocide, he had had an extended family of 200. He was the only survivor. The bones of his wife and children were somewhere at the church, but he had no way of identifying them.

The court heard that Gacumbitsi had been one of Hutu Power's most efficient *génocidaires* and was instrumental in ensuring that Tutsis in the south-east of Rwanda were almost completely annihilated. He not only incited Hutus all over the area to kill, but also encouraged the *interahamwe* to rape and 'enjoy the *inyenzis* while they could still scream and kick'.

In November 2004, Gacumbitsi was convicted of genocide, rape and crimes against humanity and sentenced to thirty years' imprisonment. He was fortunate. If he had been tried in Rwanda, his sentence would have been death and the method of execution a firing squad.

Valentina Izibagiza survived against all odds. She was admitted to hospital with her hand chopped in half and two deep gashes in her neck. One of the wounds became infected and medical staff thought she would die. She didn't. The physical wounds healed and her emaciated frame eventually swelled and she grew into a healthy young woman. She became the voice of those terrifying seconds, minutes, hours, days and weeks at Nyarubuye.

BBC journalist Fergal Keane was one of the first to show Valentina to the outside world, dubbing her *The Rwandan girl who refused to die*. He said: 'There comes a point in the telling of a story where the existing vocabulary of suffering becomes inadequate, where words wither in the face of an unrelenting darkness. As a reporter I found this the most difficult story of my career to tell. As a parent I listened to Valentina's story with a sense of heartbreak. I marvelled at her courage but felt deep anger that this should happen to any child.'

Valentina continues to be haunted and has recurring dreams of the massacre. She had seen her father and sixteen-year-old brother murdered at Nyarubuye, and when she eventually regained consciousness after being slashed, she crawled to where the body of her mother lay.

Years afterwards, her mother returned to her in dreams. But when she showed her mutilated hand to the woman who gave her life, she slipped away into the darkness.

CHAPTER 7

When Satan wore a collar

There are no more devils left in hell; they are all here in Rwanda.
— A missionary quoted in *Time* magazine, May 1994

WHEN THE SOLDIERS CAME FOR THEM, FULGENCE MUKUNZI AND Lingo Ndizihiwe, both aged twelve, were hiding with their families in a classroom at an Anglican parish in central Rwanda. It was 6 May 1994, and hundreds of thousands of bodies already littered the mist-capped hills and green valleys or were buried in mass graves hidden under layers of red clay and black turf.

One soldier held in his hand an exercise book in which was a list of the names of all the refugees in the Anglican diocese of Shyogwe. Next to each name was written Hutu or Tutsi. He called out the names of twelve Tutsis: 'Mukunzi, Fulgence … come! Ndizihiwe, Lingo … come! Mukunzi, Catherina … come! Mukunzi, Figére … come!' Holding hands and clinging to one another, they moved slowly forward. Although composed, they knew they were damned and that the end was near.

Standing next to the soldier was Pastor Athanase Ngirinshuti, a soft-spoken and fatherly figure who had walked into the classroom a few days earlier with the exercise book and written down the names. The refugees suspected nothing, because the priest was accompanied by their bishop, an eminent and influential churchman who had agreed to protect them against the forces of genocide lurking outside his church gates. As Ngirinshuti scribbled down the names, Bishop Samuel Musabyimana said nothing, but when he left the room, he smiled at the occupants.

The Mukunzi and Ndizihiwe families had fled to the school when the mass killings reached their area. They assumed that the church would be an inalienable sanctuary in a time of madness. Both families belonged to the Anglican Church and attended mass every Sunday at Shyogwe. They had known Bishop Musabyimana for many years and admired him as a compassionate, God-fearing and decent man. When they arrived and asked for sanctuary, the bishop said he didn't want any refugees at his church, which in any event was too small to accommodate asylum seekers. For whatever reason, however, he made an exception in their case and allowed them to stay, along with a few other Tutsi refugees.

They were grateful and had thought they would be safe, but now the soldiers were herding them together outside and Bishop Musabyimana was nowhere to be seen. Please call the bishop, the refugees begged. The soldiers laughed and hit Lingo's father with a rifle butt. Ngirinshuti called a young girl standing a few metres away, watching the commotion. 'Go and call the bishop,' he ordered. 'Run quickly and tell him he must come!'

Minutes later, Samuel Musabyimana strode onto the scene. With him was a dark-skinned man dressed in a suit. He was Elizier Niyitigeka, the recently appointed Minister of Information. By then, government ministers had relocated the seat of genocide from Kigali to Gitarama, about fifteen kilometres south-east of Shyogwe. Niyitigeka was a close friend of the bishop and a frequent guest at the parish. The minister said nothing, but Musabyimana spoke.

'Don't kill them here,' he ordered the soldiers. 'I don't want killings in my parish. Take them away and do it elsewhere.'

The refugees couldn't hear what Musabyimana said to the minister, but both men laughed as the soldiers ordered the boys and their families at gunpoint to get onto a truck. Lingo's father, bleeding from the wound to his head, pleaded with Musabyimana to save him and his family. The bishop pretended not to hear him and didn't look at the refugees. As they were about to leave, Musabyimana pointed at one of the women and said to the soldiers: 'That one, I know her. She's Tutsi but her husband is Hutu. She's okay. Let her go.'

The soldiers set the woman free. Samuel Musabyimana watched as the soldiers drove his other parishioners away to be executed. Then he and Elizier Niyitigeka turned and walked back to his house.

Celestin Hategekimana, a young Tutsi priest at Shyogwe, witnessed the obscenity of the bishop sanctioning the murder of his congregants. He had no doubt that Musabyimana could have saved them if he'd wanted to. When the bishop ordered the soldiers to release the Tutsi woman, they immediately obliged. Musabyimana was a man of immense authority and he was accompanied by a cabinet minister.

'He laughed and walked away because he was happy that they were going to die,' Celestin later told me. 'That was the day that Satan put on a priest's collar.'

Celestin was too scared too intervene because, day after day, Musabyimana had told him with a simmering malevolence: 'The Tutsis are finished! This is the end for them and they have to be killed!'

For several weeks, Celestin had watched in silence as his bishop sent Tutsi refugees to their deaths. As terror-stricken Tutsis knocked on the church gates, Musabyimana refused to let them in. He told them to go to the Catholic parish of Kabgayi in Gitarama, knowing full well that armed *interahamwe* had set up roadblocks all the way from Shyogwe to Kabgayi. Musabyimana regularly travelled between the two places and had seen the bodies lying along the road. 'The Tutsis,' he said to Celestin after one such trip, 'are dying! They're finished!'

When Celestin asked the bishop why they couldn't allow refugees to stay at Shyogwe, Musabyimana said: 'No! This is the end for them. It wouldn't help to hide them. They have to go to Kabgayi because people are getting killed on that road!'

Celestin knew the *interahamwe* had guns, because the bishop had provided them. He had overheard a meeting between Musabyimana, government ministers and army officers where his bishop asked for Kalashnikov rifles. When the guns arrived, Athanase Ngirinshuti was ordered to distribute them among the militia. School pupils and employees from the diocese manned some of the roadblocks to assist the *interahamwe* in identifying those destined for extermination. Many Tutsis were killed at roadblocks just outside Shyogwe, and Musabyimana paid the *interahamwe* handsomely for their handiwork.

A Tutsi man had come to the parish and pleaded with the bishop to grant him and his family sanctuary. They were hiding in a nearby forest. Go and fetch your family and bring them to the church, Musabyimana told him. The bishop then informed the *interahamwe* about the imminent arrival of the refugees. The Tutsi man and his family were killed on their way to Shyogwe.

The bishop's house became a meeting place for government ministers to discuss the progress of their programme of genocide. When the bishop asked for guns, information minister Elizier Niyitigeka and interior minister Edouard Karamera were present. The bishop disappeared at the height of the mass killings for a few days and told Celestin that he was travelling abroad on 'government business'. It later emerged that he had been despatched as an emissary to Europe to convince church leaders that the RPF had started the genocide and was spilling innocent blood.

As a Tutsi, Celestin Hategekimana feared for his own life, but felt he could do nothing. Soldiers once wanted to take him away. Musabyimana and Athanase Ngirinshuti told them to leave him alone and go away. Afterwards, the bishop said to Celestin: 'Don't worry, nothing will happen to you. I'll look after you.'

The complicity of men and women of the cloth in the Rwandan genocide was nothing new. Many became foot soldiers in the extermination campaign or passively accepted its inevitability. They colluded with the *interahamwe*, carried guns and delivered their parishioners for extermination. Others put their own safety first and abandoned their flocks as the killers stood poised to strike. Some told worshippers at mass that they should not trouble their consciences about the Tutsis, as God had determined their fate.

The first priest to be convicted of genocide by the International Criminal

Tribunal for Rwanda, Father Wenceslas Munyeshyaka, had directed mass killings at the parish of St Famille in Kigali. He made no secret of his aversion to Tutsis and referred to them as *inyenzis*. Clad in a flak jacket and armed with a pistol, he shared goat's meat and drank beer with the *interahamwe* outside the church compound. He provided them with lists of Tutsis and allowed them to take *inyenzi* men and boys away to be killed. Girls and women he saved – in return for sexual favours. He kept a room in a nearby hotel.

A mother superior and a nun at a convent in Sovu in southern Rwanda were also convicted of genocide – for setting refugees on fire. Desperate to escape the rampaging killers, 7 000 Rwandans had descended on the church compound. Sister Gertrude Mukangango grew agitated about the presence of so many Tutsis in her convent and enlisted the help of the militia to get rid of them. She had meetings almost daily with militia head Emmanuel Rekeraho, and stood watching when he and his men attacked the compound with grenades and rifles and finished off survivors with machetes and nail-studded sticks. A few hundred refugees fled to a nearby garage and closed and barricaded the doors. Rekeraho and his men surrounded the building and ordered the refugees to come out. They refused. He then announced: 'The nuns are coming to help us. They are bringing gasoline.'

Looking through a hole in the wall, some of the refugees saw Sister Gertrude and her deputy, Sister Julienne Kizito, approaching the garage. They were carrying a petrol can that they gave to the killers. Most of the refugees were burnt alive.

As the RPF overran the country, Sister Gertrude and Sister Julienne were evacuated to an abbey in Belgium. Although denounced by surviving Sovu nuns and deeply implicated in mass murder by Emmanuel Rekeraho at his trial in Rwanda (he was sentenced to death), the Catholic Church rallied behind them and suppressed evidence about their complicity.

The two nuns were eventually arrested under a new law in Belgium that allowed authorities to try genocide suspects in Brussels, regardless of where the crime had been committed. They were both convicted of crimes against humanity and conspiring with the killers and sentenced to fifteen and twelve years in prison respectively.

Father Athanase Seromba not only directed and organised the killings at the parish of Nyange in western Rwanda, he also shot refugees himself. Seromba and the killers developed a strategy of encouraging Tutsis to assemble at the parish, where he assured them they would be safe. When the church grounds were full, Seromba joined the *interahamwe* and militia in their attack. While they shot and hacked people to death, he shot survivors who tried to escape. When the *interahamwe* failed to overwhelm the refugees, Seromba ordered the demolition of the church with them inside. Up to 2500 people were killed in the church, many crushed to death by bulldozers.

Seromba walked away from the bloodstained earth and flattened church at Nyange and, with the help of the Catholic Church, relocated to Florence in Italy. He changed his name to Don Anastasio Sumba Bura and was assigned as parish priest to the Chiesa dell'Immacolata e San Martino a Montughi.

Despite repeated requests by human rights organisations and survivors, the Catholic Church refused to investigate Seromba. When he heard that the Rwandan tribunal had indicted him, he went into hiding. International pressure on Italy and the Vatican led to his arrest, and he was handed over to the tribunal in Arusha, Tanzania, to stand trial. He was convicted of genocide and murder and sentenced to life imprisonment.

The Catholic Church's legacy in Rwanda was abominable. During most of the colonial era it aligned itself with the Belgian overlords and the minority Tutsi elite. After independence, however, the church switched allegiance to the majority Hutus and became deeply compromised by its myriad ties to the Habyarimana regime.

The Catholic archbishop of Kigali, Vincent Nsengiyumva, was chairman of the ruling party's social affairs committee and a de facto member of the cabinet for fourteen years until the Vatican put an end to his political activities in 1990. After years of accepting privileges from the regime and overlooking its injustices in return, church leaders maintained their silence in the face of the genocide.

At the height of the slaughter, Nsengiyumva was living in a compound with army chiefs and cabinet ministers who were directing the genocide. Throughout the worst of it he continued to make weekly broadcasts on Radio Rwanda and blamed the RPF for provoking the bloodshed. RPF soldiers captured him when they overran Kigali in June 1994 and summarily executed him.

No less compromised was the Anglican archbishop, Augustin Nshamihigo. He was a military chaplain before being elevated to the regime's inner circle. Five weeks into the genocide, he refused to even sign an ambivalent and feeble statement by the Catholic and Protestant churches condemning murder on all sides. At the height of the mass killings, Nshamihigo and the Bishop of Kigali, Jonathan Ruhumuliza, held a press conference in Nairobi, Kenya, at which they described the government responsible for orchestrating the genocide as 'peace-loving'. Like many who tried to explain away the slaughter, they blamed the RPF for the killings. Nshamihigo never went back to Rwanda. Asked later if he ever would return, he said: 'Yes, with the army.'

Bishop Samuel Musabyimana was thus in good company. What he didn't count on was the fortitude and resilience of two boys and the conscience of one of his own priests.

Fulgence Mukunzi and Lingo Ndizihiwe didn't die that day at Shyogwe. As the soldiers drove the condemned towards the killing field, they saw a young boy with a hand grenade walking next to the road. They stopped to question him. As the soldiers assembled around the boy, Lingo's father took him by the shoulders and said: 'Jump, boy, jump!' He threw Lingo off the truck, turned to Fulgence and said: 'And you too! Go! Jump and run!' By the time the soldiers realised what was happening, the boys were scurrying like frightened rabbits through the long grass and trees towards a patch of forest in the distance. The soldiers fired several shots and chased them for a while, but then gave up. They probably assumed the boys would die in any case. They drove off with the rest of the refugees to a nearby field, ordered them off the truck and executed them with machine guns.

Fulgence and Lingo stayed in the forest for a week, surviving on wild fruit. Then they found refuge on the farm of Frodouald Karuhije, a Hutu stonemason who hid scores of Tutsis by digging pits. The Tutsi priest at Shyogwe, Celestin Hategekimana, took several parishioners who were turned away by Bishop Musabyimana to Karuhije for protection. He hid them in irrigation ditches that he covered with weeds. Some refugees stayed on his farm for more than a month, and he kept them alive with sweet potatoes and buckets of water he left at their hiding places at night. Twenty-five people owed their lives to him. When the RPF captured Gitarama at the beginning of June, the survivors emerged from their holes to tell their stories.

As the RPF approached Gitarama, Musabyimana was ordered to get ready to leave the country. His government cronies had arranged for him to be airlifted by military helicopter to eastern Zaire – a privilege reserved for senior government officials and army officers, their families and confidants. 'You are coming with,' Musabyimana said to Celestin.

'Why?' asked Celestin.

'I'm not leaving you for the Tutsis,' the bishop said.

'But I'm a Tutsi myself!' Celestin protested.

'It doesn't matter,' Musabyimana said, 'you're coming with me.'

Celestin said he had no choice but to go. Government soldiers surrounded him and the *interahamwe* lurked just outside the parish gates. As they boarded the helicopters, they left behind four Tutsi women, all church employees. As they flew off, the killers entered the church grounds to finish them off.

Celestin had no doubt that the bishop took him with him as a trophy he could display to the outside world as testimony of his compassion towards Tutsis. Should anyone ever accuse him of turning his back on Tutsis, he could always point to Celestin and say, but look at that one, I saved him.

Musabyimana and his wife stayed a short while in Goma before relocating to Nairobi, where he launched a refugee organisation by the name of Hope. Financially supported by the Anglican Church, Hope was ostensibly set up to support and resettle Rwandan refugees driven by war and genocide from their homes and country. It was later exposed as a front for Hutu extremists and *génocidaires* who had regrouped in Zaire to destabilise the new government in Kigali, launch raids into the north-west of Rwanda, kill witnesses and ultimately complete the programme of genocide. Without naming Musabyimana, a United Nations report warned that an Anglican bishop in Nairobi was at the head of an organisation to recruit *interahamwe* for the war effort in eastern Zaire. A host of *génocidaires* settled in Nairobi after 1994 and lived without fear of retribution or extradition, because the Kenyan government refused to act against them.

Celestin Hategekimana returned to Rwanda after the genocide. Despite the fact that Musabyimana had shielded him from the killers, he felt a moral and ecclesiastical duty to unmask his bishop. By then, Fulgence and Lingo had already made statements. Soon afterwards, another bishop and several survivors said they were also willing to testify against Musabyimana. A warrant for his arrest was issued, and his right-hand man, Pastor Athanase Ngirinshuti, was charged with murder and genocide. An army officer implicated in the killings at Shyogwe, Major Anne-Marie Nyirahakizimana, was also detained and charged.

It wasn't long before the human rights organisation African Rights got whiff of the bishop's nefarious legacy and publicly denounced him as a *génocidaire*. It released a report condemning the complicity of clergy in genocide and asked the Anglican Church to investigate the actions of Samuel Musabyimana, whom it said delivered Tutsi parishioners under his care to the killers and acted as an emissary for the government at the height of the genocide. Church leaders refused to take action. The furthest they went was to ask Musabyimana to return to Rwanda, but he declined and said his life would be in danger. He was allowed to partake in services, and it later emerged that he had lived in Anglican quarters throughout the time he was in Nairobi.

Evidence against Musabyimana was mounting. In June 1999, a Rwandan military tribunal convicted Athanase Ngirinshuti and Anne-Marie Nyirahaki-zimana of genocide and murder and condemned them to death. Faced with the testimony of survivors and two Shyogwe clerics, the ICTR launched its own investigation into Musabyimana.

Unperturbed by the evidence against him and denouncing his accusers as liars intent on revenge, Samuel Musabyimana decided in the winter of 2000 to travel south. His destination was Johannesburg, and two bodyguards and another three young Rwandans boarded the Kenya Airways flight with him. The bishop had a pile of false passports and a stack of US dollars in his briefcase. After the group had cleared customs at Johannesburg International Airport, they took a taxi into the city and booked into the Mariston Hotel on the southern rim of Hillbrow.

It turned out to be an ill-fated decision, because at that very moment a Rwandan refugee and I were scouring the Mariston for fugitives and *génocidaires*. Our paths crossed four days later.

I first became aware of the presence of *génocidaires*, fugitives and extremists in South Africa during a visit to Rwanda in March 1999. President Paul Kagame told me in an interview that he was perturbed that so many African countries were harbouring suspects. South Africa, he said, was among them.

'Do you have any examples?' I asked him.

A few days later, an official from the Ministry of Justice gave me a copy of an extradition request served on South Africa. It gave details of a Rwandan doctor, Pierre Mugabo, and his wife, Felicitée Musanganire, living and working in South Africa. Both were wanted for murder and genocide. South Africa didn't have an extradition treaty with Rwanda and was prevented by its Constitution from handing over fugitives to countries where they could be sentenced to death.

In 1998, Rwanda was internationally castigated for the public execution by firing squad of twenty-four condemned killers who had all been found guilty of direct involvement in the genocide. Radio broadcasts called on people to 'come and see the punishment with your own eyes'. One of those who attended was my military escort in 1994, Tony Karamba, who had lost most of his family in the genocide. When I asked him afterwards about the execution, he said: 'I felt relieved. I was happy that justice was beginning to take place.' After that, Rwanda suspended all executions.

African Rights had issued two reports on the alleged complicity of Pierre Mugabo and Felicitée Musanganire in the mass killings. Survivors and former colleagues had accused Mugabo of shooting fellow doctors, overseeing the murder of patients and joining the *interahamwe* as they butchered children.

Professor Mugabo had been a physician at the University Teaching Hospital in the southern town of Butare. Killings were initially slow there until a visit by Prime Minister Jean Kambanda and President Théodore Sindikubwabo, during which they lambasted police, soldiers, civilians and *interahamwe* for failing to deal decisively with the *inyenzis*. As the politicians left town, the Presidential Guard was brought to Butare to kick-start the extermination.

Refugees flocked to churches and the hospital to seek shelter. Survivors and those who refused to participate in the killings said doctors and nurses betrayed their Tutsi patients to the killers. Among them was Pierre Mugabo. His accusers said he ordered Tutsi patients out of his wards, knowing full well they would be killed at the gates. Later, he revealed their hiding places to the *interahamwe*.

The presence of doctors in the ranks of the killers was nothing new. Like priests and teachers, many were enthusiastic participants in the genocide. The presence of armed doctors at roadblocks or on patrol with the *interahamwe* was well documented. President Sindikubwabo was a doctor. Health minister Casimir Bizimungu, another doctor, was sentenced to life imprisonment for his complicity in mass murder.

Mugabo was fingered by survivors for helping the *interahamwe* to cleanse the Buye district of Butare, where he and many other doctors and lecturers lived. Tharcisse Mukasafari saw him kill a colleague: 'They were doctors and therefore used to blood and not afraid to shoot. I saw Mugabo murder a woman doctor. He shot [her] in the head. One shot.'

Survivors also accused Mugabo of being present when soldiers and *interahamwe* raided a convent, where they found the children of a prominent Tutsi doctor who had been murdered a week earlier. Twenty-five children were loaded onto a truck, taken away and executed.

Felicitée Musanganire was a nurse with the university's AIDS project at the time, but according to survivors, she and her husband received so much loot that she opened a shop in town. She made no secret of her support for the genocide, and according to a Tutsi survivor, she accompanied the *interahamwe* to a local hotel, where four Tutsis were abducted and later murdered.

Mugabo and Musanganire fled to Zaire as the RPF overran Butare. From there they went to Nairobi, and then disappeared. They both obtained false Rwandan passports with forged United Nations documents stating that they were refugees who had lived in Algeria since 1989.

When I returned to South Africa in April 1999, I walked into Pierre Mugabo's office at the University of the Western Cape's pharmacology department, where he had been lecturing for two years. A tall, upright man with an open and handsome face, he looked neither surprised nor perturbed. He proclaimed his innocence and claimed he had been victimised by the Rwandan government. 'I will never go back to Rwanda because I know I won't get a fair trial. People are out to get me.'

He refused to do an interview. 'I don't like cameras. I'm not a politician. But I will speak in due time,' he said. He then asked me to leave his office.

The South African departments of Home Affairs and Justice promised to look into the murder charges against Mugabo and Musanganire, as well as allegations that they had obtained work permits with false travel documents. The university said there was nothing but allegations against Mugabo and there was no reason to suspend or act against him. Not long afterwards, the couple left South Africa.

The Mariston Hotel in Johannesburg was something of a global jamboree, with races, nations, colours, clans and tribes from every corner of the globe fusing in its myriad rooms and self-catering apartments. This sky-scraping hostelry had a reputation as a haven for illegal immigrants and outlaws lurking behind steel gates and tight security. 'How on earth are we ever going to find anybody in this place?' I asked my Rwandan investigator as we booked into the hotel.

'If they're Rwandan, I'll find them,' Mugara Godefroid assured me. 'I don't look like a Tutsi and they'll think I'm one of them.'

Mugara had been living in South Africa since the genocide, when *interahamwe* had stopped his family at a roadblock and killed most of them. He managed to escape to Uganda, from where he made his way to South Africa. He did odd jobs as a security guard and infiltrated Hutu extremist cells on behalf of the Rwandan embassy in Pretoria.

Mugara was the antithesis of what Tutsis are supposed to look like. He was short, stocky and dark-skinned. In contrast, Rwandan diplomat Fundi Felix looked like a Tutsi caricature from a Hutu Power manual under the heading *How to spot an inyenzi*. Skinny, with a gangly physique and straight nose, Felix was the diplomat at the Rwandan embassy who kept track of the movements of *génocidaires* and Hutu extremists in South Africa.

According to Felix, a Hutu Power network in South Africa was actively raising money and procuring arms for the war effort in the Congo (Zaire was renamed the Democratic Republic of Congo in 1997), obtaining false passports and visas for Rwandan fugitives and coordinating the movement of extremists around the world. After the mass killings in 1994, the *génocidaires* and former FAR soldiers and officers had regrouped as the Liberation Army of Rwanda (ALIR), and set up bases across eastern Congo. ALIR leaders had openly declared their intention to complete the programme of extermination, vowing that 'not even Tutsi babies or foetuses will be spared'. ALIR launched regular attacks into eastern Rwanda and had killed thousands of civilians. Infiltrators had driven peasant farmers from their land, kidnapped and dragged young men across the border and forced them into military service, and launched a propaganda campaign – similar to the one before and during the genocide – to incite Hutus against Tutsis. One of the pamphlets they distributed read: *Muhutu: Rise Up Before You Die Like an Ant!*

'Go to the Mariston Hotel,' Felix advised me. 'That's where they hide. That's where the extremists meet one another and where they plot the next genocide. They use false passports, but they're out there somewhere.'

I would need help, he said, and phoned Mugara. A day or two later, we booked into a room at the Mariston. It was a long shot. We had no leads or names and didn't even know if there were any Rwandan fugitives or extremists sneaking around in the hotel. I left Mugara to sniff around the bars and hotel for a few days to see if he could pick up anything.

It was less than a week before he called me and we met in his room. 'A group of Rwandans have booked into the hotel,' he said. 'And they're very secretive.'

'Who are they?' I asked him.

'I don't know,' he said. 'I met some in the bar last night and they say they're looking after somebody very important. I don't trust them.'

I gave Mugara a handful of money. 'Buy them beer and find out why they're here.'

'They're protecting somebody they call the bishop,' he said to me the next morning. 'They say they're going to America soon.'

'And who's this bishop?'

'I have no idea.'

'Try and find out what room they are in.'

A day later, Mugara had the information. 'They're in 1009. I drank beer with them last night. The bishop is in the room next door.'

I gave Mugara more money. 'We have to know who the bishop is. Try and find out who is in 1010. If you have to, bribe a hotel worker to get the name.'

We met for breakfast the next morning. Mugara had a piece of paper on which a name was written: Musabyimana, Samuel. The note contained details of his passport, number A0 43889, first issued on 6 July 1956 at Mwendo.

Samuel Musabyimana had committed an inexplicable blunder by booking into the Mariston under his own name. I phoned Rakiya Omaar, the director of African Rights, in London. With an encyclopaedic memory on the genocide, Somali-born Rakiya arguably did more than any other person to lay bare the reality and extent of the mass killings. Since 1994, she and African Rights had painstakingly recorded the testimony of witnesses, tracked down *génocidaires* in their hiding places, and petitioned governments, churches and the United Nations to bring them to book.

'Samuel Musabyimana!' she said. 'Oh my God! We know him very well. He's a big *génocidaire*. I think the UN's Criminal Tribunal wants him as well. You can't let him get away!'

'Have you indicted Samuel Musabyimana?' I asked ICTR senior prosecutor Bernard Muna over the phone the next morning. He kept quiet for a while, and then said: 'Yes, we've just indicted him. We have a very strong case against him.'

'For what?'

'Genocide, conspiracy to commit genocide, crimes against humanity and murder,' he said. It turned out that only days before Musabyimana travelled to South Africa, the ICTR had charged him with the most heinous crime known to man and issued an international warrant for his arrest. The bishop was no longer just a wanted man in Rwanda, but a worldwide fugitive from justice.

Member states of the United Nations are obliged to arrest indicted suspects and hand them over to the ICTR for detention and trial.

Musabyimana was the sixtieth *génocidaire* to be indicted by the tribunal. Although the ICTR, with an annual budget of more than $100 million, had been accused of getting bogged down in incompetence and bureaucratic infighting, it had managed to convict Rwandan Prime Minister Jean Kambanda, the first head of government to be found guilty of genocide and crimes against humanity. Genocide mastermind Théoneste Bagosora and army head General Augustine Bizimungu are standing trial for genocide, though the genocide's financier, businessman Félicien Kabuga, remains at large.

When I met Mugara later that morning, he was smiling from ear to ear. 'I met the bishop last night,' he said.

'And?'

'He fell hook, line and sinker for my story,' he said. Days before, we had concocted an alibi for Mugara. He told the bishop and his bodyguards he was a Hutu from the northern town of Byumba and that invading Tutsi rebels had killed his family. We also decided that he should ask the bishop to help him get a new passport and assist his return to Rwanda.

I decided to arm Mugara with a spy camera concealed in a sling bag. That afternoon, Musabyimana invited Mugara to his room for a beer. As the two stepped out onto the balcony, the bishop looked at the bag and asked him in Kinyarwanda: 'Why does a man walk around with a bag like that all the time?' He stepped forward and started yanking at the bag's zip. Mugara slipped it open. We had anticipated that this might happen and had concealed the camera under a wad of documents, pens, cigarettes and a pile of condoms. Mugara chirped: 'A man has to be prepared. You know how it is these days.' The bishop laughed, slapped him on the back and said: 'Oh yes, I know, I know.' He never asked about the bag again.

The bishop spoke for an hour, until the camera's battery ran flat. 'There are many young Rwandans like you around the world,' he said. 'People like you can help us in our struggle against the new government. I help them to get passports, new identities and can even help them to go to Congo if they want to fight.'

'What do you suggest I do?' Mugara asked.

'I will help you to get a new passport with a visa. You can go to Kenya and from there you can decide what to do.'

'What will it cost?'

'Don't worry, I'll pay for it.'

The next morning, one of the bishop's bodyguards took Mugara to a coffee shop in the immigrant suburb of Yeoville and introduced him to Gratien

Gatarayiha, a former FAR lieutenant who supplied the extremists with false Rwandan passports and South African visas. Mugara gave him copies of his old passport and new identity photos. 'It will be ready in ten days,' said Gatarayiha.

According to intelligence reports that Fundi Felix gave me, Gatarayiha was a core member of ALIR and not only attended meetings in South Africa, but also travelled to Brussels to secure funds for the extremists. ALIR had had a meeting in Cape Town on 14 February 1997, where the following was discussed: 'A need was expressed to select military instructors from ex-FAR in RSA to Equatoria Forest of DRC and Gbadolite. General Bizimungo requested that all soldiers trained in hand combat must be found and go to prepare others for an attack on Ruhengeri, Gisenyi and the volcanoes. Gratien Gatarayiha was selected to get documents and funds.'

Three months after this meeting, between 30 000 and 40 000 ALIR insurgents infiltrated the north-west of Rwanda and attacked several towns and villages. Special units targeted Tutsi survivors and witnesses who could testify against the *génocidaires*. Although the infiltrators were driven back to their hideouts in the Congo, hundreds of civilians were killed.

After meeting with Gratien, Mugara and the bodyguard went off to Park Station in Johannesburg to meet a Rwandan family who had illegally entered South Africa from Mozambique through the Lebombo border post. The father had escaped from prison in Kigali, where he was held for murder and genocide.

Mugara delivered a false Cameroonian passport to a Rwandan woman who was leaving Johannesburg the next day. He showed me spy camera footage of the scantily clad woman sitting up in bed, holding her passport with the South African visa. She then slumped back against the cushions and fell asleep.

'Mugara,' I said to him, 'don't tell me you slept with her! That's not how we do things!'

'Fringe benefits,' he said. 'It comes with the mission.'

A day or two later, Musabyimana told Mugara: 'I'm leaving South Africa. I'm going back to Kenya.'

'I thought you were going to America,' Mugara said.

Alas, the bishop told Mugara, he couldn't get a visa. It turned out that Gratien Gatarayiha had failed to secure American visas for the group and the bishop was too scared to go to the embassy in person and apply for a legal entry permit. He was, after all, an international outlaw travelling on a false passport.

'When does he want to go back?' I asked Mugara when he told me about Musabyimana's travel plans.

'The day after tomorrow,' he said.

The bishop had obviously completed his business in South Africa. A host of people had been brought to his hotel room, including Gratien Gatarayiha and the man who, according to Fundi Felix, was the leader of the extremists in South Africa. His name was Paul Habimana, and he was a former Kigali businessman who had fled to South Africa after the genocide and set up a refugee mission in Pretoria. Although not wanted for murder, he was a close associate of Félicien Kabuga, the organiser and financier of the genocide and Rwanda's most wanted man. Mugara met some of the people downstairs in the hotel lobby and accompanied them to Room 1010. He filmed most of the bishop's visitors, but was always told to leave before meetings commenced.

From a journalistic point of view, my work with Musabyimana was almost done. We had established that the international tribunal wanted him, we had hours of spy camera footage and we had exposed the network of Hutu extremists in South Africa. The plan had always been to go to Rwanda next to look for survivors of Shyogwe – especially the two boys who had escaped – and interview Celestin Hategekimana and death-row inmate Athanase Ngirinshuti. African Rights' Rakiya Omaar was on her way to Kigali to help me conclude the investigation.

But what to do about Samuel Musabyimana? In normal circumstances, I would have waited for him at the airport and confronted him about his complicity in the genocide and the international warrant for his arrest. I was merely telling a story and it should have been none of my concern what happened to him afterwards.

This was different. Musabyimana was a *génocidaire*, one of the most wanted men in the world and implicated in the continued mayhem being sown by his cohorts from their hideouts in the Congo. If he boarded that aircraft and stepped back onto Kenyan soil, he would be gone.

It had also become a deeply personal matter. I had seen the handiwork far too many times of killers such as Samuel Musabyimana to stand aside, fold my hands and plead impartiality. I had lived and breathed the genocide and its aftermath and, although I helped to lay bare its horrors and hopefully contributed to some understanding of Rwanda and its complexity, this was my moment to make a difference. Genocide and those who perpetrate it concern us all, whoever or whatever we might be. Journalist or not, I had no intention of letting the bishop of Shyogwe get away.

'Get the bastard arrested,' said Max du Preez when I discussed my dilemma with him.

'What about journalistic ethics?' I asked him.

'Fuck journalistic ethics,' he said. 'Do it.'

I needed more time to plot the bishop's downfall. I phoned Mugara, who was drinking beer with the bodyguards at the time. Go to Musabyimana, I said to him, and tell him you once did security work for a businessman who frequently travels to America and who has an embassy contact who sells visas. It was a long shot, but an hour later he called me back and said Musabyimana wanted to meet me.

The next day, Bishop Samuel Musabyimana was seated opposite me at a Melville eatery, munching pizza and sipping a gin and tonic. An hour or so earlier, Mugara had arrived with the bishop and introduced me as the South African businessman who might be able to help him and his entourage obtain American visas. It was a rather ridiculous but desperate subterfuge to stop Musabyimana from boarding an aircraft and returning to Kenya.

Evil seldom presents with fixed and staring maniacal eyes. It is far more likely to lurk behind the countenance of a shy and puny man with gold-rimmed glasses, a cross around his neck and puffy, doughy hands. Even when he chased away a fly it was with a slow and gentle gesture. His voice befitted his demeanour and was soft and caring. When our pizzas arrived, he took Mugara's hand and bowed his head in prayer. The bishop was a man of rigid composure.

'I believe, sir,' he said after the formal introductions, 'you can help us to get American visas?'

'Oh yes, I can.'

'And how long will it take?'

'Maybe a few days.'

Journalists are not supposed to fabricate, lie or misrepresent themselves, but this was a rather special case, born of a need to ground the bishop in South Africa.

Apart from the spy camera carried by Mugara, two more cameras in and near the restaurant filmed our meeting. I spoke non-stop for half an hour, pulled visa application forms and documents I had taken off the Internet from a brief-case and prayed that the bishop would fall for my ludicrous and fanciful antics.

He seemed impressed. 'How much will it cost?'

I made up an amount. 'Four hundred dollars each.'

'Do you want the money now?'

'No,' I said, 'but I need your passports. Fill in the forms and I'll collect them from you tonight.'

As he tucked into his pizza, I asked: 'What do you want to go and do in America?'

'Business,' he said.

'What business?'

'Just business.'

The next day, I met with the bishop in the Mariston's lobby, where he handed me a brown envelope containing six passports. 'Tell your contact he's got two days to get the visas,' he said, 'and I'll pay handsomely.'

Hours later, I had a meeting with the Special Operations Unit – the elite Scorpions – who agreed to arrest Musabyimana after confirming that the international tribunal had issued a warrant for his arrest. They didn't want to raid the hotel, as it would take too long to get through the security gates, by which time the bishop might be gone. They told me I had to set him up. I phoned Musabyimana and told him I'd pick him up in front of the Mariston the next morning and we would drive to Pretoria to pick up the passports.

'Are the visas ready?' he asked me.

'Yes,' I lied, 'and don't forget the money to pay for them.'

As the winter sun hoisted itself over the nation's capital, thirty members of the Scorpions gathered at their headquarters for a pre-operation briefing. 'A certain bishop came into South Africa on the fourth of July,' advocate Gerrie Nel told them. 'He's apparently involved in the genocide in Rwanda. The bishop is in the country illegally. We have to act today because the man wants to leave the country tonight.'

I was baffled as to why a platoon of the country's sharpest law enforcement officers was necessary to apprehend the slightly built Samuel Musabyimana, particularly since I was about to deliver him into their clutches.

As the Scorpions moved into position in and around the hotel, Musabyimana stepped out of the building and stood waiting for me on the pavement. I drove up in my aged Mercedes, and as he climbed into the passenger seat, I shook his flaccid hand and limp fingers and realised mine were as damp as his. I drove on for about half a kilometre, steered around a corner and stopped at a predetermined point.

'Why are you stopping?' Musabyimana asked. I didn't answer, but as I got out of the car and slammed the door behind me, the Scorpions pounced. I turned around and glanced at policemen pulling him from the car. There was an expression of stupefaction on his face. Our eyes locked. Hatred spewed from his.

Another group of Scorpions stormed into the hotel, raided his room and found money, false passports and several cellphones. His bodyguards were also arrested and taken to Pretoria, where they and the bishop were locked up.

Mugara could go home. The next morning, I took him to the airport to catch a flight to Kigali. After almost seven years in exile, he was going to search for family members who might have survived the genocide. One sister was alive and living in Uganda. He wasn't sure about anyone else.

'You did brilliantly,' I told him as we shook hands.

'I did it for them,' he said, and walked through customs beaming.

With Musabyimana safely behind bars, I also travelled to Rwanda, to search for survivors of the carnage at Shyogwe. It was my tenth visit to the land of a thousand hills. It was difficult to imagine that the country had lain littered with the remains of a million people only a few years earlier. The physical healing of Rwanda was nothing less than astonishing, with new buildings and businesses mushrooming in the capital, while in the countryside bustling markets and villages, nestling at the foot of neatly terraced fields, were hives of zeal and exuberance.

This sense of normality belied the daily terror that lurked within Rwandan society – a condition brought about by the fear of another genocide; fear of the *génocidaires* lurking in neighbouring Congo; fear of being branded a killer by your neighbour and community and being dragged off to Kigali's Central Prison; and, in certain quarters, fear of Paul Kagame's security apparatus. Activists had disappeared or been jailed, journalists harassed and editors charged for inciting genocide.

Fulgence Mukunzi and Lingo Ndizihiwe, wide-eyed and still traumatised by the events of six years earlier, gave chilling accounts of the horror that had unfolded on that fateful day at Shyogwe. 'Our bishop, a man we loved and trusted, laughed when the soldiers came to take us away to be killed,' said Lingo. 'We can never forget how happy he was.'

Athanase Ngirinshuti, incarcerated on death row at Kigali's dreaded prison, was brought to a musty little room next to the dungeon. He dragged himself slowly in, slumped down in a chair and mumbled something in Kinyarwanda. He looked at me and said: 'I am under sentence of death, but God is my witness that I'm not guilty. My conscience is very, very quiet.'

Dressed in a green prison uniform, the elderly man cut a fatherly and almost piteous figure. He was the pastor at Shyogwe who had compiled lists of Hutus and Tutsis, distributed guns among the *interahamwe* and assisted soldiers in rounding up Tutsis predestined for extermination.

Ngirinshuti and Musabyimana's kinship dated back many years. Ngirinshuti had been the bishop's secondary-school teacher, and years later became his right-hand man at Shyogwe. Throughout our interview, Ngirinshuti scribbled edgily on a piece of paper.

'Did you kill those people?' I asked him.

'No, no, no,' he mumbled. 'There was nothing the bishop or I could do. The soldiers would have killed them anyway. It was very, very, very difficult times.'

'And the bishop? Is he responsible for their deaths?'

'No, no, no. What happened in Rwanda was really tragic. One person could not do anything.'

'Did he tell the soldiers to take the people away and kill them elsewhere?'

'That is a problem,' said Ngirinshuti. 'I didn't hear what the bishop told them.'

'Why didn't he stop them?'

'He didn't have a gun or anything to protect them. It was horrible times.'

'Why did you make a list of who was Tutsi and who was Hutu?' I asked.

'The bishop said he wanted to know who was in his church.'

'What did you do with the list?'

'I gave it to the bishop.'

'And who gave it to the soldiers?'

'I didn't see.'

'And the guns?'

'That was to protect the people in the church,' he said.

'And what about the government ministers in the bishop's house?'

'I don't think it was wrong of him to invite ministers into his house. As a bishop he had to allow everybody into his house.'

Could a learned man be so naive? In trying to protect the bishop with his answers, Athanase Ngirinshuti had instead, albeit unwittingly, implicated Musabyimana in the miscellany of bloodletting at Shyogwe and corroborated the essence of what a host of other witnesses had already testified. Ngirinshuti came across as a bumbling halfwit who probably believed a demon had duped him onto death row. Because he was Musabyimana's serf and disciple and obeyed his bishop's every command, he had become a victim of his master's villainy. At the same time, however, Ngirinshuti embodied the inevitability with which many accepted the extermination programme and thus became accomplices to mass murder. It was precisely because of people like Ngirinshuti that Hutu Power came so close to wiping out the Tutsis.

Rakiya Omaar, who had been investigating Musabyimana since 1995, had no doubt that his house had been one of the most important bases for the forces of genocide. Elizier Niyitigeka had been at the centre of the killing and had not only directed its progress, but as Minister of Information was responsible for the hate and incitement spewed over the radio. Both he and the other minister who frequently visited Shyogwe, Edouard Karamera, were later convicted of genocide by the international tribunal and sentenced to life imprisonment.

Omaar said prosecuting a bishop who had either appeared indifferent to the fate of Tutsis or who actively supported their extermination was critical in changing the minds of the masses. 'Musabyimana gave biblical sanction to genocide by openly appearing with the men who were in charge of the programme, supported the killing of Tutsis and delivered his parishioners to the *interahamwe* to be killed. This was incitement in its purest form.'

As I wrapped up the interview, Ngirinshuti said: 'I know why that Celestin is testifying against the bishop.'

'Why?' I asked him.

'He wants to be bishop. He's jealous.'

'And the two boys?'

'They've been told by Celestin what to say.'

As Ngirinshuti was led away by soldiers, he said: 'Even if they shoot me as they want to, I will die with my conscience white and clear.'

Although the Anglican parish at Shyogwe had long since returned to normal, Samuel Musabyimana's ghost still lurked ominously in his deserted house in the compound. It had been left almost as it was on that winter's day in 1994 when a government helicopter whisked him off to his hideout in Zaire. Some of his furniture, books and pictures were still in the house, almost as if he were coming back. Against one wall hung a portrait of a smiling Musabyimana in his bishop's robes.

In the lounge, where Musabyimana received his eminent government chums and army officers to deliberate the progress of genocide and request guns for the *interahamwe*, hung a framed Bible text. It was from 1 John 4, verse 7:

Beloved, let us love one another; for love is of God,
and he who loves is born of God and knows God.
He who does not love does not know God;
For God is love.

Back in South Africa, I was preparing to air my documentary on Musabyimana. I was under the impression that he had already been transferred to the ICTR in Arusha, Tanzania, and formally charged with genocide and crimes against humanity. Until the tribunal sent an aircraft to fetch him, the Scorpions had to detain him.

From the outset, they had shown a lack of zeal in handling the case. Apart from despatching thirty men to arrest Musabyimana – nothing more than a show of force for our camera – they had no interest in investigating the existence of the Hutu extremist network or the web of criminality surrounding it. Mugara Godefroid was willing to cooperate fully with the Scorpions and could have delivered Gratien Gatarayiha into their hands. They weren't interested.

When I initially decided to involve the Scorpions, I had told Max du Preez that I would feel more comfortable if I captured Musabyimana myself, tied him to the fig tree in my garden and waited for the tribunal to fetch him. That is exactly what I should have done.

I phoned a Scorpions advocate. 'Is the bishop in Arusha?' I asked.

He huffed and puffed for a second or two and then said: 'No.'

'Is he still in South Africa?' I wanted to know.

'No.'

Something was wrong. 'Where's Musabyimana?'

'He's gone.'

'Gone? What do you mean he's gone?'

'He was released.'

'What do you mean he was released?'

'He was accidentally released.'

'By whom?'

'By us.'

'Where is he?'

'Back in Kenya.'

I rushed to Pretoria, where the full story emerged. It wasn't even as if the bishop had broken out of prison and made a dash for his life. Officials had unlocked his cell door, drove him to Johannesburg International Airport and put him on a Kenya Airways flight to Nairobi. As he boarded the aircraft, his briefcase containing his false passports and piles of money was handed back to him. He landed in the Kenyan capital later that afternoon, cleared customs and disappeared.

It turned out that after his arrest, the Scorpions, for some incongruous reason, had handed him to the Department of Home Affairs for detention, pending the arrival of transport sent by the tribunal. But the Scorpions 'forgot' to tell the Home Affairs officials about Musabyimana's status as an international fugitive. He was held as an illegal immigrant and deported back to the country from which he had come, namely Kenya. When the tribunal arrived to pick him up in Pretoria, he was gone. Scorpions head Bulelani Ngcuka accepted full responsibility for the blunder, and said: 'I think the mistake we made is a terrible mistake and I'm sorry for it.'

Was any foul play involved? Did the bishop pay his way out of prison? I don't think so, but there was clearly gross negligence by the Scorpions and an indifference towards what had happened in Rwanda. They simply didn't care enough, if indeed at all.

The broadcast of *The Bishop of Shyogwe* caused huge embarrassment to the South African authorities and made international headlines – to the extent, I was told afterwards, that agents of the National Intelligence Agency's Secret Service were despatched to Kenya to locate Samuel Musabyimana. The Kenyan government was also pressured to seek the bishop and hand him over to the UN tribunal.

On a Thursday in April 2001, more than eight months after his arrest and release by the Scorpions, Musabyimana boarded a chartered aircraft at an airfield in eastern Congo and flew to Nairobi. Since leaving South Africa, the bishop had acquired a new Rwandan passport with which he travelled between Kenya and the Congo to arrange for the transfer of young Hutu men to ALIR bases. As his aircraft touched down in Nairobi, it was surrounded by Kenyan policemen and soldiers, who took Musabyimana into custody. The next day, he was handed over to the International Criminal Tribunal for Rwanda in Arusha.

Wearing episcopal robes at his first court appearance a few days later, he was formally charged with four counts of genocide, conspiracy to commit genocide and crimes against humanity. Asked to plead, he said: 'I am not guilty. There is no blood on my hands. I will prove my innocence.'

Neither Samuel Musabyimana nor his accusers got their day in court. Shortly after his detention, the bishop took ill. He was transferred to hospitals in Arusha and Nairobi. He was also suffering from acute depression, and a psychologist was assigned to help him cope with life behind bars in the company of the world's worst killers.

On 24 January 2003, the International Criminal Tribunal for Rwanda released a short statement. It said: 'Anglican Bishop Samuel Musabyimana passed away after a long illness.'

The Bishop of Shyogwe won two major international awards, one of them the Award for Outstanding International Investigative Reporting in Washington, DC. In their commendation, the judges said: 'Pauw illuminates the tragedy of the Rwandan genocide in the grand tradition of Hannah Arendt's seminal analysis of Adolf Eichmann – by focusing on the banality of evil embodied by a single man. He meticulously tracks the story from the 1994 nightmare in Rwanda to Musabyimana's secret hideout in South Africa. It is a sheer credit to the doggedness of the reporter that we were able to see true evil at work.'

CHAPTER 8

The men that evil do

*Assassination can seldom be employed with a clear conscience. Persons
who are morally squeamish should not attempt it. The assassin should
be determined, courageous, intelligent, resourceful and physically active.*
— CIA assassination manual

THE ANSWER TO ONE OF SOUTH AFRICA'S MOST PUZZLING APART-
heid atrocities lay in a bag at my feet. A few metres away, an elderly woman,
tears rolling down her cheeks and her face in torment, begged Archbishop
Desmond Tutu to help her to find out what had happened to her husband.

At one point, Nqabakazi Godolozi put her hands up in the air, then clutched
her head and sobbed uncontrollably. 'Please help us to find them! They have
been gone now for many years and we are sure they are dead, murdered by the
security police.'

It was 15 April 1996, the first day of South Africa's Truth and Reconciliation
Commission (TRC), charged with unravelling the dirty secrets of apartheid's
darkest hours. Tutu had been appointed head of the TRC and opened what
would be a harrowing session of soul-searching by lighting a candle and saying
a prayer for healing and repentance.

By the end of the first day, people were physically exhausted and mentally
frayed, none more so than the diminutive clergyman who had for so long comforted the oppressed and dispossessed with his hope and humanity. He dropped
his head onto his arms on the table in front of the commissioners and wept
for the man in a wheelchair whose body had been broken by the brutal hands
of his security police interrogators.

Among the first TRC supplicants were the wives of three men who had disappeared from the face of the earth eleven years earlier. On a morning in May
1985, Sipho Hashe, Qwaqwahuli Godolozi and Champion Galela had left their
homes to meet a British diplomat at the airport in Port Elizabeth. They were
never seen again.

The three were leaders of the PE Black Civic Organisation (Pebco), and had
been instrumental in mobilising Eastern Cape activists to embark on a consumer
boycott. According to the security police, the Pebco Three, as they became
known, were largely responsible for making the volatile region 'ungovernable'.

The security police were suspected almost at once – and through all the intervening years – of complicity in their disappearance, but their stock response was that the Pebco Three had left the country and were living in exile somewhere. But after the ANC and other black political organisations were unbanned in 1990, the three men from Port Elizabeth did not return home and no one who had been in neighbouring states or any other country that had harboured activists knew anything about them.

Six years had passed without news of their husbands when Rita Galela, Nothembile Hashe and Nqabakazi Godolozi turned to the TRC for answers. 'I'm asking for assistance. I'm a proud person, I've never liked doing it,' said Hashe, 'but I am also asking the assistance of my enemy. Please tell me what you did to my husband.'

As she spoke, I glanced at Max du Preez. He looked back at me. We both knew that in my bag was a video cassette on which a former security policeman had chronicled the fate of the three men in gruesome detail.

'We have to find their bodies and give them a proper funeral, otherwise their souls can never rest,' said Godolozi.

No one was supposed to see the videotaped confession in my bag. Three months earlier, I had signed an agreement with a former policeman that I wouldn't show it to anyone or broadcast it without his permission.

Days before the TRC hearing, I told Max about the tape and showed it to him. We already knew that the wives of the Pebco Three would be among the first to testify at the inaugural TRC hearing in East London and were desperate to find out what had happened to the missing men.

Max had been commissioned by the SABC to produce a weekly actuality programme called *Special Report on the Truth Commission*. It would be shown on Sunday nights, and over the TRC's lifespan bring the stark reality of a nation's trauma into the homes of millions, black and white.

I was making a two-hour TV documentary on Eugene de Kock. On a Wednesday night in May 1994, exactly a week after South Africans voted Nelson Mandela and the ANC into power, De Kock had been arrested and charged with 121 crimes, including murder, kidnapping, assault, manslaughter, defeating the ends of justice, illegal possession of arms and ammunition, and fraud. As the TRC got under way, he was standing trial in the Pretoria Supreme Court where a long line of Vlakplaas operatives were helping the state build a mountain of evidence against their former commander.

I was back in *Vrye Weekblad* mode, tracking down apartheid's assassins. I had decided to call the documentary *Prime Evil*, one of De Kock's nicknames at Vlakplaas. I worked closely with Max and passed on to him footage and interviews that I couldn't use and that would be more suitable for *Special Report*.

The tape in my bag contained graphic, savage and gut-wrenching stuff.

The policeman was filmed against a stark black backdrop, and with streaks of light dancing across his ebony face, chocolate eyes and fleshy lips, he said: 'The Pebco Three were abducted; they were taken to Cradock, brutalised, savagely assaulted. They were hit with an iron pipe on their heads and they died, yes they died, they died one by one.'

'What was your role in the assault?' I asked him.

The camera zoomed in for an extreme close-up, showing every tiny line on his lips, the sweat pores on his nose and the specks of light in his eyes. 'My role was to choke them, to strangle them. Just to keep them quiet.' He spoke for more than ten minutes about the murders.

'We have to broadcast it,' said Max. 'We have no choice.'

'I can't,' I said. 'I've signed an agreement.'

'Fuck the agreement,' he said.

Max knew it wasn't that simple. An agreement between a journalist and a source or informant is no less sacrosanct than the privilege that attaches to communication between lawyer and client or psychologist and patient. I was honour-bound to stick to my undertaking and, under normal circumstances, would be prepared to go to jail rather than break my word.

But I already knew in my heart that on Sunday night *Special Report* would bring Rita Galela, Nothembile Hashe and Nqabakazi Godolozi the answers they had been denied for eleven years.

Joe Mamasela was a flashy individual, endowed with a set of lips that Mick Jagger would have envied. It was easy to confuse him with an inveterate horse punter or a used-car salesman. Joe was smooth, very smooth. The kind of liar that could sell designer igloos to an Eskimo.

But behind the shiny shoes, three gold chains, florid vocabulary, cocksure demeanour and red BMW with silver mag wheels lurked a habitual killer of mammoth proportions. If there were Olympic Games for assassins, Joe Mamasela would be a sure bet for the gold – provided he didn't nick the medal first.

For more than a decade, Sergeant Joseph Mamasela killed and killed and killed again. The annals of the South African security police were specked with his name in chapter after horrendous chapter. His reputation in the force was that of a perfect and uncompromising killing machine.

By the time he quit the police in 1993, he had been involved in the murder of at least forty anti-apartheid activists, some as young as fifteen. He strangled some, blew up or electrocuted others, and tortured several to death. Then there were those he shot or stabbed. He boasted that he had thrown petrol bombs at the houses of more than 300 activists.

His former commanders had given him glowing references during various court cases, but Dirk Coetzee, under whom Mamasela originally worked at Vlakplaas, would tell the TRC: 'He was ruthless and had the killer instinct. He was always willing to do the job. He was an outstanding criminal and a cruel man.'

Captain Jacques Hechter, Mamasela's commander in the Northern Transvaal security police, concurred. 'He was cruel, more so than any of us. Whenever we had to go and kill, Mamasela was ready and couldn't wait.'

I had known about Mamasela since Coetzee branded him as one of Durban lawyer Griffiths Mxenge's killers. But when Mamasela took the stand to testify against De Kock, his infamy was assured. He told the court how the Vlakplaas commander had plotted the murder of Brian Ngqulunga, one of his most trusted askaris, when the generals feared he might blow the whistle on Mxenge's death. Mamasela also revealed that he had kept a secret notebook detailing killings carried out by Vlakplaas and the security police in which he had taken part.

Asked why he had recorded only some of the victims' names, Mamasela said: 'If I had to write all the names I would be having a Bible. I cannot be writing all the deaths. I mean, I will be a mortuary chap or what? I could not do that.'

De Kock had inherited Mamasela from Coetzee, and the two never saw eye to eye. As Mamasela put it: '*Ek was 'n hardegat kaffer wat niks kak gevat het nie*' (I was a hard-arsed *kaffir* who took no shit). He claimed De Kock had wanted to kill him, but that he escaped late one night and eventually landed up with the Northern Transvaal Security Branch, where he became a master executioner.

When De Kock testified in his own defence, he said that when Coetzee exposed Vlakplaas in 1989, Mamasela had to be paid huge sums of money to keep his mouth shut. 'He received amounts of R18 000, R23 000, R25 000 and R27 000; he got a state vehicle, we had to pay his children's private school fees and install additional security at his house.'

Mamasela demanded that the police erect safety lights and pave the footpath from his garden gate to the garage to prevent anyone from planting a landmine. The police also had to buy him two guard dogs and supply them with food.

'He held the police hostage and it was nothing but blackmail. It is in his nature and he would never have stopped. He's going to suck lots of people dry,' De Kock said.

Mamasela was a phantom-like character. Everyone knew he was a prodigious killer and held the key to many unsolved atrocities, but nobody knew where to find him. When he testified against De Kock, members of a special investigation unit that answered to the Transvaal Attorney-General smuggled him into court and whisked him away to a secret location immediately afterwards.

It turned out that in 1994, just as the ANC assumed power and De Kock was arrested, Mamasela feared that his former masters would make him their sacrificial lamb. He made an affidavit about all the blood that he had spilt,

claimed his life was on the line and was placed in a witness protection programme. Then he demanded money in exchange for his cooperation and was
paid R13 000 a month from the state coffers.

I watched him in court. He was brazen, cocky and eloquent with a spicy
vocabulary. He would make brilliant television. I decided I had to interview
him for *Prime Evil*. I was fascinated by a black man's apparently enthusiastic
role in the 'elimination' of anti-apartheid activists. I could understand what
had motivated Coetzee and De Kock, but why had Mamasela been willing to
maim and murder opponents of oppression?

Mamasela was a prized trophy, and the Attorney-General was not about to
give me access to him. But Dirk Coetzee knew where he was. It turned out that
when he returned to South Africa after three years in exile, Coetzee had looked
up his old Vlakplaas henchman and seen him quite regularly.

A few days after Mamasela gave evidence against De Kock, I met him
in Johannesburg. Nattily dressed in a suit, he arrived in his BMW – for some
reason, the car of choice for gangsters – and confidently strutted into the
restaurant. Within minutes of sitting down and ordering coffee, he told me
he wasn't a natural-born killer, merely a victim of unfortunate circumstance.

He had marched into adulthood with a clenched fist raised in defiance
of Bantu Education during the 1976 Soweto Uprising. He was an executive
member of the South African Students Movement, and left the country the
following year to join the ANC in Botswana, where he was trained as an
intelligence agent. He was sent back to South Africa to mobilise and organise
students in and around Johannesburg.

In 1979, he was arrested when policemen stormed into the house of a fellow
activist and found Mamasela instead. He said he was 'diabolically' and 'satanic-
ally' tortured until 'there was no way I could resist further. So I said no, I will
help you; what do you want?'

When the ANC discovered he had turned, he said, they murdered his brother.
That was when Mamasela told his security police handlers: 'Fine, I will help you
to belt these people.'

He became an askari at Vlakplaas. 'Little did I know that I was jumping
out of the frying pan and into the fire. I was forced to kill my own people, the
people I had devoted my early life to liberating.'

Mamasela was cruel in the extreme and he killed with gusto. He did his job so
well that he was promoted to the status of a regular policeman and given the rank
of sergeant. This is how he described killing Griffiths Mxenge: 'I was grappling
with him. I felt him becoming weak. I felt wet, liquid-like stuff running down
my hands, my arms. When I looked at my hands I saw it was blood.'

Mamasela's speciality was infiltrating groups of young activists who were making their way to the ANC in neighbouring states, just as he had once done. He would present himself as a trained Umkhonto we Sizwe operative and offer to smuggle them across the border. He lured about twenty-five activists to their deaths with this ploy.

In June 1986, Mamasela drove ten young activists to the Botswana border in a minibus. He had met them days earlier and offered to take them safely out of the country. The two youngest members of the group were aged fifteen; the eldest was twenty-two. Mamasela fed them beer and other alcohol throughout the trip and they were drunk by the time he reached the Western Transvaal town of Zeerust, where they turned off the main road towards the village of Nietverdiend (Dutch for 'undeserved'). A kilometre or so further, the journey ended when Mamasela stopped the vehicle and handed the occupants over to a heavily armed security force squad. One by one, the youngsters were taken out of the vehicle and injected with poison. They were then put back in the bus, which was driven close to the Botswana border, packed with explosives and blown up.

When the media reported that 'trained' ANC terrorists had blown themselves up while trying to infiltrate South Africa, Mamasela was paid a handsome bonus.

A year later, nine youngsters were massacred in what Mamasela had told them was a safe house in the homeland of KwaNdebele while they were making their way to Botswana and the ANC. Another activist led to his death by Mamasela was strangled with electrical cord before being 'necklaced' – a tyre placed around his neck, doused with petrol and set alight – to make it appear that he had been murdered by township comrades.

His bloody and barbaric past notwithstanding, two years into democracy, Mamasela was inexplicably calling the shots. Not only did he have the Attorney-General at his mercy, he was also manipulating the TRC. He refused to apply for amnesty because he saw himself as a victim. He said he had been forced to kill. 'I had no alternative. My duty as an askari was to do everything, legal or illegal, that my commanders told me to do. We had no say whatsoever over our lives.'

The ace up Mamasela's sleeve was that he would potentially be the state's star witness in a succession of court cases and, as such, be granted immunity from prosecution.

'The ANC, more than any people, they understand that in every war there are casualties,' Mamasela said in his testimony at the TRC. 'We are the casualties of the revolution; we stood up, we tried to pay our humble contribution to the emancipation of our people.'

From the moment that we met, Mamasela wanted money. How much was I going to pay him for appearing in *Prime Evil*? At that stage he had never given a media interview or been photographed. I had never paid any killer money to get a story and had no intention of rewarding this odious character either, but I was curious about what monetary value he placed on himself. He wanted R100 000, he said, ranting on and on about how much more international broadcasters would pay. Apart from being a thug, he was living in cloud cuckoo land.

We met several more times and his price kept coming down, until eventually he would have been happy to accept less than 10 per cent of his original 'appearance fee'. I once went to his house in a middle-class Pretoria suburb and noticed two certificates on display attesting to Mamasela's fairly recent baptism by some or other turn-or-burn charismatic church. In that sense he was no different from his white puppeteers. He professed to be a born-again Christian and didn't smoke or drink, which made it more difficult to cajole him into an interview.

But Mamasela apparently found the magnetism of television irresistible, and mentioned several times how therapeutic it would be for the families of his victims to see him bring down his security police masters. I persuaded him that publicity could catapult him into the limelight and lead to substantial offers from foreign broadcasters.

He eventually caved in and said he'd do it, but only on condition that his interview was not screened until after De Kock's conviction – which turned out to be several months later – and that he had the ultimate authority to stop the broadcast altogether. He still wanted money and we agreed that we would discuss the amount prior to broadcast.

Mamasela gave a brilliant interview and elaborated in great detail on every killing and the niceties of extracting life from his victims. He had been sent to the Eastern Cape to help the local security police get rid of the Pebco Three. A policeman had phoned them pretending to be a British diplomat on his way to Port Elizabeth to meet them and discuss the possibility of foreign funding for their cause.

Mamasela was in the group of askaris who abducted the trio at the airport and drove them to an abandoned police station near Cradock. This is how he described their last hours:

'[Gideon] Nieuwoudt and the other policemen got angry at Hashe and started hitting and kicking him. He started screaming. We had to keep him quiet while Warrant Officer Beeslaar took a stick and strangled him. Nieuwoudt hit him with an iron pipe over his head. There was blood coming out of his mouth and ears. He lost consciousness.'

Throughout the interview, Mamasela showed no shred of emotion. 'Nieuwoudt quoted passages from the Bible. All the while, there was a braai and drinking. Hashe answered a question in a manner they didn't like and he was kicked in the face. There was foam coming from his mouth. A policeman went to sit on him and strangled him. I stood closer and saw that he was dead. Beeslaar took his watch.'

Then, said Mamasela, Godolozi and Galela were also tortured to death. Throughout the orgy, the braaiing and drinking continued.

When I showed Mamasela a rough cut of the interview, he smiled broadly and said: 'This will shake them to the marrow!'

The day after the wives of the Pebco Three appeared before the TRC, I telephoned Mamasela. Before I could say a word, he said feverishly: 'Did you watch television? Did you see those women pleading? Imagine if they see what we've got!'

I told him I was in East London and had sat through their testimony. 'We're going to broadcast part of your interview on Sunday night,' I informed him.

He kept quiet for a while, then asked: 'How much are you going to pay?'

'Not a cent,' I told him. 'I am not going to pay you at all.'

He launched a torrent of abuse, calling me the lowest white man that God had ever created, and said I would burn for a long time in an excruciatingly hot place. He said we were going to meet again and it wasn't going to be pleasant for me. I'd been threatened many times before and his warning made no impression on me.

I believe Mamasela wanted me to broadcast the interview. He couldn't wait to see himself on television, as the exposure would bear testimony to his benevolence and importance. His only concern was how much money he could make out of public confessions. He eventually agreed to the interview being screened, but by then his minders had got wind of their golden boy's intentions. I received a late-night call from Transvaal Attorney-General Jan D'Oliveira, the man who held Joe Mamasela's strings at the time. He informed me that I couldn't go ahead with the broadcast. I told him he was in no position to dictate what I could or couldn't do. He said I was breaking my signed agreement with Mamasela. I said that was none of his business. He warned me that Mamasela's life would be endangered as a result of our broadcast. I reminded him that the former policeman was in his witness protection programme and that he had two days to beef up security.

D'Oliveira said we would jeopardise future prosecutions if we broadcast the confession. I said that was utter rubbish. If Mamasela was telling the truth, how could we change the course of justice? Ten years later, there had yet to be a successful prosecution emanating from Mamasela's affidavit.

A few hours before the broadcast, the TRC sent counsellors to Rita Galela, Nothembile Hashe and Nqabakazi Godolozi to prepare them for what lay in store. Within minutes of the programme's end, an exuberant Mamasela called.

I passed the phone to Max (we were having a little celebration of our own) so that he could listen. 'It was fantastic!' exclaimed a jubilant Joe. 'Tonight people know who I really am. I'm sure the police are running around like headless chickens!'

Despite all the time I invested in him, Mamasela never managed to satisfy my curiosity about his collusion with the forces of darkness in the ruthless murder of his own people. I could understand that he was tortured to the point where he submitted to becoming an askari and understand his anger when the ANC killed his brother (if that was true). But nothing I learnt from or about him could justify the abandon and pleasure with which he took lives for years afterwards. Perhaps he was simply one of those wretched and wicked mortals that society spews forth from time to time, just as it occasionally gives birth to angels like Desmond Tutu or Beyers Naudé.

Psychiatrist Dr Viktor Frankl, who endured years of unspeakable horror in Nazi death camps, believed that human kindness and cruelty exist among all groups and in all people. Writing about his experience at Auschwitz, he said: 'From this we may learn that there are two races of men in this world: the race of the decent man and the race of the indecent man. Both are found everywhere; they penetrate into all groups of society.'

I believe I know from which race Joe Mamasela emanated. At Auschwitz, he would have been one of the guards who herded camp inmates into the gas chambers with a smirk on his face as he feverishly licked his lips.

On a Sunday afternoon in the Northern Transvaal bushveld, I strolled around the farm Drooglaagte with another member of the indecent race. The bearded and tanned khaki-clad farmer was showing me his prized Brahmans – stout, broad-shouldered and hardy cattle well adapted to the harsh African terrain. But we weren't discussing stock prices or farming conditions. We were having a matter-of-fact conversation about killing. 'I would have killed anybody,' he said. 'If you wanted to be a political activist, you had to be able to take the pain.'

'How did you feel about killing people?'

'It didn't bother me, because it was the enemy. I felt fuck all for life. I would have killed anybody.'

'Did you enjoy what you were doing?'

'Yes, because it was the right thing to do. It was the enemy we were killing. I felt I was busy with big and important things.'

'Do you think it was worthwhile?'

'At the time I was proud of fighting communism, but if I think back about it today, we didn't make any difference. We wasted our time.'

He paused for a moment. 'But it was nonetheless enjoyable while it lasted.'

Paul van Vuuren was one of a trio of police killers who appeared before the

TRC in Pretoria in February 1997 and applied for amnesty for some of South Africa's worst institutionalised atrocities. When Eugene de Kock was asked at his trial if he was the country's most effective assassin, he said: 'I don't know, we never had an assassin's conference. If we look at information I've received about the activities of the Pretoria security police, we may be far back in the line. There were people who were not necessarily more effective at killing people, but maybe more cold-blooded or even sick.'

He was talking about the former head of the Northern Transvaal security police, Brigadier Jac Cronjé, and his two henchmen, Captain Jacques Hechter and Sergeant Paul van Vuuren. Together, they sought amnesty for the deaths of at least sixty people – and acknowledged that their applications did not constitute 'full disclosure' of their guilt. Van Vuuren later told me it would have been impossible for them to document all their crimes; they had simply tortured, bombed and killed too many times.

In a situation not unlike that of De Kock, the three policemen were on their own, abandoned and deserted by the politicians and many of the generals on whose behalf they had acted.

'We have, so to speak, been thrown away in the gutter, where we now have to shoulder the responsibility of dealing with our past, motivating our deeds and presenting our view of the conflict,' they said in their opening statement to the TRC. 'We call upon the previous government and our superiors to explain certain orders given to us. We ask: do not desert us further. Do not turn your backs on us. Help us.' They cited the words of Afrikaans poet C Louis Leipoldt:

> *Give peace and rest to those of us who are tired of roaming,*
> *Courage and patience to those of us who are scared of dying.*

The men were spurred into action not by an awakening of conscience, but by the threat of lengthy prison sentences. They were Mamasela's superiors, and when he defected to the Attorney-General's camp to save his own skin, they realised they might be left out in the cold. They rushed to plead for mercy.

I watched Van Vuuren, a burly and slightly thickset Afrikaner, taking the oath. 'I felt as though I was the one being tortured,' he later said. Staring at him from the public gallery were the families of three of his victims whom he had electrocuted. They were there to find out how and why their loved ones died.

They heard that several hours after mysteriously disappearing from their homes in townships around Pretoria and Witbank, Andrew Makupe, Jackson Maake and Harold Sefola were lying on the ground, bound and gagged, at a deserted stretch of open veld north of Pretoria. All three were members of the

ANC and, according to security police files, trained guerrillas who had been implicated in a wave of unrest sweeping South Africa.

Standing over the activists were Van Vuuren, Hechter and Joe Mamasela. Next to them was a portable power generator that had been used earlier to extract information from the captives.

'We were very good at torturing people,' boasted Van Vuuren. 'We had various methods. We had a gas mask that we would put over someone's face and then close the air supply with a plug. While the activist struggled and gasped for air, we would sit back and have coffee. But that day, we used the generator.'

The three policemen were satisfied that they had broken an ANC cell. Now it was time to execute Maake, Sefola and Makupe. But they were worried that if they shot the men, some trace of forensic evidence might be found. Another method had to be used. The generator.

'We had to kill them,' said Van Vuuren. 'We had to destroy the whole cell.'

'Why didn't you take them to court?' I asked him.

'That would have been dangerous. They were in bad shape. That was not how we operated.'

Maake was the first to be electrocuted. Then it should have been Sefola's turn, but Van Vuuren said there was something different about him. He was stronger than the other two and seemed to believe deeply in his cause.

Sefola asked his executioners if he could say something before he died. They allowed him to stand up. 'You can kill me,' he said, 'but the ANC will rule one day. Apartheid will not survive and democracy will be the end of the Boers.'

He started singing 'Nkosi Sikilel' iAfrika'. As the final notes of the anthem faded away, the policemen attached cables from the generator to Makupe's hands and feet and shocked him until his body went rigid.

'Come on, pray for your friends,' Van Vuuren ordered Sefola. The activist fell to his knees, but instead of praying, he shouted a salute to his fallen comrades in the name of the struggle.

'I thought he was mad,' said Van Vuuren. 'We were winning the war. Where did he think he was coming from?'

Sefola was shocked until foam and blood oozed from his mouth and ears. It was the only killing that ever bothered Van Vuuren. 'It disturbed me,' he said, 'because he wasn't afraid of dying. He died with dignity. The other two I didn't care about.'

The policemen loaded the dead bodies into a minibus and drove to a dirt road, where they blew them apart with explosives. It had to look as if the three guerrillas had died while planting and accidentally detonating a landmine.

'We didn't like what we did,' Van Vuuren said defensively, 'but we had to stop the killing of innocent women and children. I would never have done this under normal circumstances. I did it for my country and my people. I was fighting communism.'

Hechter told the TRC that he suffered from amnesia and couldn't remember the event, but was seeking amnesty all the same. Mamasela was not there. He continued to hide behind the Attorney-General while trying to extort as much money as he could from any source he could exploit.

For some peculiar reason, Van Vuuren warmed to me. 'I know who you are,' he said during a break at one of the TRC hearings, 'but you don't know who I am. I'm not as evil as you think.'

I was working on my second book at the time and trying to fathom killers like Van Vuuren. What distinguished him from his cohorts was that he was brutally honest. He looked me squarely in the eyes and said: 'I had a task, which was to kill activists. I did it well and I'm not sorry.'

We started going for lunch together. Some meetings turned into drinking orgies of note. He could drink any other policeman of my acquaintance under the table. At one lunch appointment, he told me, 'Today I'm going to kill you.'

He almost did. Driving back to Johannesburg on the highway, I realised that, like Max the night we had gone drinking with Pieter Botes, I couldn't see. I pulled the car to the side of the road and fell asleep. I woke up in the early hours of the morning, stiff and cold.

Van Vuuren grew up on a farm near Warmbaths. Like many Afrikaner homes, it was a stable, God-fearing, National Party environment. His mother was once Prime Minister John Vorster's secretary, and the family attended the local Dutch Reformed Church every Sunday. His father had been among the trigger-happy policemen who opened fire on 5 000 peaceful protestors at Sharpeville on 21 March 1960, killing 69 people and wounding 180 more, most of them shot in the back.

'There was always talk of communism and the *swart gevaar* [black peril] and that we had to stand together to combat the onslaught. I didn't really listen, but it must have made an impression on me. In those days, a *kaffir* was a *kaffir*. But we weren't racists. You know what I mean?'

Van Vuuren was an exemplary scholar. He was a prefect, obtained provincial colours for athletics and played centre for his school's first rugby team. He also had a black belt in karate.

He was one of the only apartheid assassins with a university degree. We were more or less the same age, went to the same university and even took some of the same subjects.

He joined the police in 1984 and was assigned to riot control duty in the townships, where strife was rampant and he was exposed to horrific violence on a daily basis. He requested a transfer to the Security Branch and came face to face with Brigadier Jac Cronjé, a seasoned veteran of the 'total onslaught' era. Cronjé had joined the police in 1956 and served in both Rhodesia and the South West African operational area.

'Where do you come from?' the brigadier asked him.

'I grew up on a farm near Warmbaths, Brigadier.'

'So you can work with *kaffirs*?'

'Yes, Brigadier.'

Shortly afterwards, Van Vuuren, Hechter and Mamasela were forged into a death squad. Cronjé gave them unfettered authority to act as prosecutor, judge and executioner against anyone they perceived as a *moeilikheidmaker* (troublemaker) or *opstoker* (agitator).

After several drunken lunches, Van Vuuren invited me to Drooglaagte one Sunday, perhaps to demonstrate how ordinary a man he was. At lunch time, he sat at the head of the table, took his wife Cathryn's hand and bowed his head to say grace. The prayer that rolled off his tongue was of the standard mealtime variety, like those that were said around the lunch and supper table in my own home when I was a child. Oddly, no one ever prayed at breakfast.

The Van Vuurens' guests, sipping on orange juice and semi-sweet boxed wine, tucked into piles of barbecued T-bone steaks and chops. There was nothing unusual about the scene around me. These were true-blue Afrikaners sharing a meal on the Sabbath, talking about rugby and taxes and mutual acquaintances, while the children shrieked and romped on the well-trimmed lawn outside the dining room. A beaten copper plaque of a storming elephant bull adorned the wall behind me. In the study next door hung two university graduation certificates and photographs of prize-winning Brahman bulls.

The conversation shifted to black people who refused to pay their electricity bills. Somebody told a story of a township resident who had tried to 'steal' a power supply and shocked himself to death. People laughed.

'Yes, and now we have our own electrician,' said the woman next to me, looking straight at our host. More laughter. He grinned somewhat awkwardly and demolished another steak. During the TRC hearings, one newspaper had dubbed him *The Electrician*, but he didn't seem to mind the nickname much.

When all that remained of Sunday lunch was a pile of bones, a little boy of about a year tottered into the dining room. Van Vuuren swooped the child into his arms and sat him down on the table. 'Give me a kiss, my beautiful child,' he said, as he hugged his son.

I looked at his hands encircling the child. They were the strong and muscular hands of a farmer. Knobbly hands that had raised award-winning livestock. The hands of a hunter who had felled hundreds of buck. But they were also the hands that had choked the life out of untold people, held guns and pulled triggers in point-blank executions, lobbed petrol bombs into houses and attached electrical wires to human flesh.

As we resumed the conversation we had started earlier while admiring Van Vuuren's cattle, I looked at the man stretched out on the pink couch in the living room and wondered: Is this the face of evil?

'If they used fire, we used fire. We would throw petrol bombs through windows. I suppose people, maybe women and children, could have died in the attacks. In the beginning I was scared, but after a while I couldn't wait to go out at night. I enjoyed it. I'm proud of what we did,' Van Vuuren said.

'How does it feel to shoot a human being?' I asked.

'To shoot a human being or a buck is basically the same.'

I froze. What degradation, what baseness lurked in the psyche of someone who equated the lives he had snuffed out with those of animals? Maybe I had expected him to say killing people had been unspeakably awful. But when I didn't react, he said again: 'There's not a big difference.'

Did he say it just to startle, stun or shock? Was he from the same mould as Pieter Botes of 'little sauce' infamy? Van Vuuren's demeanour was nonchalant, unflappable and dispassionate. He was emotionally bare and empty. How degenerate was a system that could do that to a young man who had entered its fold relatively unscathed, untainted and normal?

Prior to seeking amnesty, Van Vuuren, Hechter and Cronjé were examined by one of South Africa's foremost psychiatrists. Cronjé, said Professor Jan Robbertze, suffered from serious post-traumatic stress disorder. He experienced nightmares, amnesia and flashbacks. Robbertze described him as an 'empty' person. Hechter was equally damaged. Unable to cope with all the murders he had committed, he suffered from 'involuntary memory loss' and simply could not remember many of his operations.

Van Vuuren came from a family with a history of severe aggression, but the psychiatrist could find no evidence of any mental disorder. 'He left the police force, came back from the war and continued a normal life,' concluded Robbertze.

I truly didn't know what normal meant any more.

Van Vuuren continued. 'It was exciting in those days, those years. At times I could not wait to do it. They say to kill is like having sex. It's true.'

I kept silent. 'Do you understand?' he asked me.

I looked at him and didn't answer. There were too many things I was struggling to comprehend, like this man's reaction to taking life and inflicting pain.

Maybe he was a psychopath. Institutions like the security police attracted deviant characters who could live out their debased fantasies in secret interrogation rooms. My limited understanding of a psychopath was someone who felt no guilt, who had no conscience. Unlike some apartheid assassins, Van Vuuren showed no sign of remorse or regret and made it plain that he had nothing to feel guilty about, so maybe he was a psychopath, I thought.

Some weeks later, on a Friday afternoon in a leafy Pretoria suburb, a fourteen-year-old black boy, neatly dressed in his school uniform, walked into a plush law office. Minutes later, Tshidiso Motasi came face to face with the man who had gunned down his parents in cold blood ten years before.

Richard Motasi was a police sergeant who fell out with his white superior officer, who called him a 'stupid *kaffir*' and slapped him so hard against the side of his head that his eardrum burst. He had three operations and instituted a civil claim against the police. By doing so, he signed his own death warrant.

In November 1987, Van Vuuren, Hechter, Mamasela and another policeman stormed into Motasi's house and shot him and his wife, Irene. Their four-year-old son, Tshidiso, was asleep in the next room.

When Gloria Hlabangane, Irene's mother, arrived the next morning, police were carrying her daughter's body out of the house. She found Richard still lying in the lounge with pieces of his brain and skull spread all around the room. She was looking for Tshidiso when she heard him say behind her: 'They have killed them.'

She asked the child whom he meant. 'The police,' he said. 'They have killed father and mother.'

How did he know it was the police?

'They were wearing the same jersey as my father,' the little boy told his grandmother.

Tshidiso was haunted by memories of the killings for years. 'I saw my mother there, she was shot in the head. My father, he was also shot in the head. I just said: Father, wake up! Father, wake up!'

Tshidiso had listened intently as Van Vuuren and Hechter tried to persuade the TRC Amnesty Committee that the killings were politically motivated and that they should thus be pardoned. Afterwards, he said: 'I thought of taking a glass and breaking it and killing him [Van Vuuren]. When they said my father jumped like a tiger, he laughed, that guy. It was very painful to me because they made it like a joke.'

Across a gleaming table in the sanctum of his lawyer's office, Paul van Vuuren extended his hand to the boy he had orphaned. Tshidiso took it and held it for a moment. The former policeman was as unruffled and unperturbed as ever and towered over the boy, who was nervous but remarkably composed.

I felt uncomfortable about this encounter that I had helped arrange. The boy had legitimate questions and wanted to speak to Van Vuuren face to face, but for the latter it was nothing but a public relations exercise. TV cameras were rolling to record the meeting and I had no doubt he saw an opportunity to present a humane face of compassion and benevolence.

Van Vuuren: 'I'm sorry for what happened to your parents and you, because it was a waste of human life. I'm sorry for that. You must remember that in those days there was a war in the country. People were dying on both sides of the struggle.'

Tshidiso: 'You did something very bad. I can't forgive you. I can't. It's very hard for me.'

Van Vuuren: 'I know that you must hate me.'

Tshidiso: 'I don't have parents. My granny can die any day, because she's old now. If she dies, who's going to take care of me?'

Van Vuuren: 'That's a difficult question. You can come and live with me. I'll look after you. If something happens to your granny, you can phone me. I will try and help you.'

The meeting ended shortly afterwards. They shook hands and parted. As the young boy went back to the five-roomed house he shared with his grandparents in Jabulani, Soweto, he said: 'This is my day. A person who killed my parents came to me and said he was sorry. It means something to me.'

'How was I?' Van Vuuren asked me after the meeting.

I told him he was fine, and asked: 'Did you really mean what you said? That you would look after the boy?'

'Of course!' he said. 'He can phone me tomorrow. You know I don't hate these people.'

I kept quiet.

'Don't you?' he asked.

Over a number of years, I spoke to many killers. Most, if not all, said how sorry they were for causing suffering and loss of human life. Most, I suspect, were lying. At least Van Vuuren was honest. The faces and memories of his victims seemed not to haunt him at all. His only regret was that, having lost the war, he was forced into the confessional.

Maybe Van Vuuren didn't show remorse because he didn't need to. The only requirements for amnesty were a political motive and full and frank disclosure, and his submission offered plenty of both. Mamasela didn't show remorse either – probably also because it wasn't necessary. He was under witness protection and wouldn't face criminal charges.

Dirk Coetzee began feeling remorse when he joined the ANC, which did expect to see contrition. When Eugene de Kock was found guilty of mass murder, his reaction was: 'I can't tell you how dirty I feel. I sympathise with the victims as if they were my own children.' Expedient words from a man facing life imprisonment.

I first strolled into Pretoria Central Prison shortly before Christmas 1995. I was producing *Prime Evil* and wanted to meet the spectre and villain of my biggest television production. I arrived unannounced, and when De Kock saw me through the bullet-proof glass, he just stared at me. His face was expressionless, and I remember thinking that the lenses of his spectacles were so thick that it was difficult to make out the colour of his eyes.

'Good morning, Colonel de Kock,' I greeted him. 'How are you?'

'Why do you want to know?' he asked. 'You must be glad to see me sitting here.' He wanted to get up and walk away.

I asked him not to go and told him I'd wanted to speak to him for a long time. He stayed, and for the next hour or so we spoke about his trial, the newly established Truth and Reconciliation Commission, and life behind bars. His court case was in full swing and although he had pleaded not guilty to all the charges, he acknowledged that the evidence against him was overwhelming and that he was facing life imprisonment. I was struck by his politeness, even shyness. He was amiable and, like so many of his co-killers, an unremarkable-looking man. The word 'normal' inevitably sprang to mind.

Before leaving the prison that day I paged through the visitor's book and realised that he'd had very few visitors in recent weeks. I didn't see the name of his brother or any other family member, nor any of the Vlakplaas men. De Kock had been completely abandoned and faced a terribly lonely Christmas in prison.

On my second visit I bumped into a short, chunky chap who was also waiting to see De Kock. It was Peter Casselton, a British-born security police agent and bomber who had lived at Vlakplaas and befriended De Kock.

Casselton visited De Kock every Sunday with a brown paper bag containing a roast chicken. He was down and out at the time and had even sold his watch to get money to provide De Kock with a weekly treat. I took over the task of buying the chicken, extra hot from Nando's, which Casselton said De Kock was particularly fond of.

When I met Casselton he was not just broke, he was heartbroken. He told me how his beloved poodle, Bubas, had been abducted from one of Pretoria's trashy taverns a few weeks earlier. Casselton had got into an argument with a couple of security police outcasts that ended in a fistfight. They grabbed Bubas and disappeared into the night. The loss was almost too much for Casselton to bear.

When Bubas went missing, De Kock pinned a note on the prison notice board offering a R500 reward for information leading to the poodle's recovery.

At one of our meetings, I asked De Kock to nominate three people who could speak on his behalf in my documentary, since it was impossible to interview him on camera. He agreed, provided I undertook not to look for his wife and children, who had gone into hiding abroad. I said fine. He told Casselton to cooperate with me, sent a message to his brother Vossie and asked me to bring a man named Lukas Kalino to see him in prison.

Soon afterwards, the hollow sound of our footsteps echoed down the long, badly lit passage that led to the visitor's section at Pretoria Central. Streaks of sunlight stole through the barricaded windows and the smell of floor polish filled the air. The faint sound of sombre religious music escaped from somewhere deep in the bowels of the stark, yellow-brick complex.

It was Sunday – visiting day – and walking next to me was a big, bulky black man with a square face and a deep voice. It was Lukas Kalino, and in his hand he clutched a Bible inscribed with the words: 'The Lord will decide what is right and what is not.' His other hand held that of his twelve-year-old son.

'This is going to be very difficult for me,' said Kalino. 'It's the first time I've come here.'

We reached the row of visitor's cubicles at the end of the passage and stopped at the first one. Sitting behind the thick bullet-proof glass was De Kock, peering through his black-framed spectacles, his hair slicked across his forehead.

He looked up at his visitor, whose bulk almost filled the booth. Then De Kock's usually expressionless face lit up, he smiled and said: 'My God, Lukas, it's you! How wonderful to see you!'

'Good morning, Colonel. And how is the Colonel?'

Only the glass barrier prevented the two men from embracing.

'I've come to show you my son, Colonel,' said Kalino. 'He's now twelve years old and it's time that he meets his namesake. He's been nagging me to see you.'

The boy shuffled closer to the window. The father put a hand on his son's shoulder and said: 'Colonel, this is my son. His name is also Eugene de Kock. And Eugene, this is the colonel I've been telling you about.'

I was standing a few paces back, witness to one of the most bizarre moments of my career as a journalist. On one side of the window was a political serial killer, a man who had come to personify the most evil face of apartheid. On the other was a black boy who had been named Eugene de Kock Kalino, a tribute from his sire to a man he hero-worshipped for his braveness and chivalry.

Lukas Kalino was a former Angolan rebel who had found refuge in South West Africa and became a fighter for Koevoet, the SA Police counter-insurgency unit. (Koevoet means crowbar.) De Kock had been his platoon commander, and together they were involved in some 350 shoot-outs with SWAPO guerrillas.

Kalino said he owed his life to the man behind bars. They fought and killed side by side, were ambushed and survived landmine explosions. They slept alongside each other in the bush and ate from the same tins of bully-beef. Kalino wept on the day De Kock left Koevoet. 'He is my best friend, that man. I love him.'

'You have probably heard many bad things about me,' De Kock said to the boy. 'You mustn't believe all you hear. You must carry your name with pride. Don't be ashamed of it. I'm not a bad man.'

The young Eugene just stared at his namesake wordlessly, probably not quite understanding what was going on.

I don't know whether Kalino appreciated the implications of sending a township boy into the world with the name of Eugene de Kock, but he said that when his son was born, it was the greatest honour he could bestow on his former commander.

'My son had to see his namesake. When I saw the colonel, my heart had a big shock. I feel very, very sorry for him,' Kalino said. When visiting time was over, he left the Bible for De Kock.

Kalino didn't only pray for the killer every day, but would later travel to northern Mozambique to search earnestly for a magical beetle that he believed would grant De Kock the power to get out of prison.

At the time of our visit, Kalino was one of a few men who had not abandoned and turned against De Kock. Many of the Vlakplaas operatives who had killed and tortured with him and eagerly shared in the booty from the police slush fund were lining up at the Pretoria Supreme Court to testify against their former commander in return for indemnity from prosecution.

During my prison meetings with De Kock we mostly spoke about trivial matters. I didn't presume there was much love lost between us, and he knew that I was going to portray him in *Prime Evil* as the heartless and cold-blooded killer that he was.

He became upset when a fellow journalist told him I was looking for his wife and children in Europe (I wasn't), and sent a message via Casselton that I shouldn't visit him again.

Several months later, De Kock lost his most loyal and ardent supporter when Casselton died in an accident. He was working on a truck when it suddenly started moving and crushed him against a wall. He died a few days later in hospital.

De Kock's conviction for six murders and a litany of other crimes was a mere formality. For eighteen months, the former Vlakplaas commander had sat expressionless and impassive in the dock, making notes and staring straight ahead of him. Many of the state witnesses had been his confidants, co-conspirators and even close friends. The Vlakplaas band had been as close as brothers once, but when they realised De Kock was doomed and that their own freedom was on the line, there was something of a stampede to switch sides and offer their testimony to the state.

Shortly after his conviction, De Kock stepped into the witness box. Facing life imprisonment, he was driven to confession and bent on revenge. For several days he unpicked the web of death and deceit spun on the blood-drenched soil of Vlakplaas.

At one point, senior state advocate Anton Ackermann asked him: 'How would your enemies describe you?'

De Kock: 'Cold-blooded.'

Ackermann: 'Other words you want to use?'

De Kock: 'Determined and persevering.'

Ackermann: 'How do your enemies see you?'

De Kock: 'As merciless.'

Ackermann: 'What else?'

De Kock: 'I haven't seen that many, because most are dead.'

Ackermann: 'Mr de Kock, have you ever tried to establish how many lives you have taken?'

De Kock: 'No, one doesn't do that. It's a terrible thing to think about.'

Shortly after he was found guilty, but before sentence was passed, the SABC screened my documentary. For more than a year I had travelled the length and breadth of the country, tracking down De Kock's co-killers and trying to persuade them to show their faces on national television.

I never understood why some were willing to admit to murder and torture in public. Some, I suspect, did it to justify themselves and their deeds while trying to put forward a face of sanity, while others were either set on revenge against De Kock or singing his praises.

It was a daunting task, but when I finally ventured into the edit suite, I had shot fifty hours of material. I had assembled a remarkable collection of photographs depicting De Kock's early childhood, his stint in the Rhodesian bush war, his operations with Koevoet and his years at Vlakplaas. Although many of his henchmen wouldn't appear on camera, I was astonished by the eagerness of some to slip me photographs: De Kock assaulting a SWAPO captive; De Kock strapping a dead body to the bumper of a Casspir; De Kock interrogating a detainee.

I had traced his life back to early childhood in a typical Afrikaner home on Johannesburg's East Rand, where his father was a senior magistrate. 'He loved his music,' said his brother Vossie. 'He mostly listened to classical music. He was a gentle child who was never violent. He wasn't aggressive at all.'

Staring out from old black-and-white photographs was a *laaitie* (young lad) with slightly crooked teeth, a perky smile and an agonisingly bad short-back-

and-sides haircut. A year or two later, he cut a dapper figure in his Voortrekker uniform. As a teenager, he was pictured shy and bespectacled around a campfire with his first girlfriend.

Eugene de Kock survived more than 300 contacts with SWAPO guerrillas in the thick bush of northern Namibia and southern Angola, as well as two landmine explosions. The first damaged his eardrums, while the second trapped him in an armoured vehicle that had been flung forty metres into the air. His men had to prise him out of the wreck.

By the time he left Koevoet, lunacy glittered in De Kock's eyes and he was suffering from severe post-traumatic stress, which, in the security forces of the time, went both undiagnosed and untreated. 'If you talk to him,' said Vossie, 'don't make a sudden movement or taunt him, because he'll jump over the table and grab you by the throat.'

Without ever being debriefed or receiving psychiatric care, De Kock was transferred from one fighting unit to another. 'I walked from one war to the next. It never stopped,' he said.

After that, Eugene de Kock was not just a highly skilled and professional assassin, but a savage and perverted killer who took great pride and satisfaction in what he did. He not only demanded and got fear and respect, he ultimately decided who would live and who would die. His strategies were based on those of Attila the Hun, who invaded Europe in 350 AD. Attila was renowned for his cruelty because he spared no one. Driven by what he called a 'lust for brutality', the Mongolian would select only the most 'vicious and ferocious-looking warriors' to accompany him on his bloody campaigns.

If De Kock was Attila, his men were his Huns, and the only way they could impress him was by trying to match his debauchery and disdain for life. One of their operations involved the abduction of a young messenger named Japie Maponya. He was not an activist, but his brother was an underground member of the ANC's military wing. In a bid to determine the whereabouts of the 'terrorist', Vlakplaas beat, tortured and mercilessly interrogated Japie. He knew nothing, but his tormentors could not afford to let him go and so he had to die.

Bound hand and foot, Maponya was loaded into a vehicle and driven from Pretoria in the dead of night to a plantation straddling the Swaziland border. De Kock and his men drank heavily along the way and jokingly discussed how they would get rid of their prisoner. Maponya heard every word. At journey's end, he was dragged to a spot between the trees to be shot and buried in a shallow grave. The designated gunman's weapon jammed, so De Kock picked up a shovel and hit Maponya with it, cleaving his skull.

Confronted with these gory details on camera in *Prime Evil*, Peter Casselton laughed. 'Is there a kind way to kill someone? Eugene is a soldier, he's a killer.

If there's a spade handy and you want to kill someone, you better get on with it with a spade.'

And then there were scenes of the Vlakplaas *manne* at play. One of the killers had shoved a stack of photographs into my hand. They showed a 'team-building' exercise on the KwaZulu-Natal North Coast. Pissed out of their skulls, the burly and bearded hit men, their *boepies* (beer bellies) spilling over the tops of their bathing trunks, cavorted in the shallows, wrestled in the sand and playfully pulled one another's swimsuits down. It was, to say the least, suspiciously homoerotic!

I was immensely proud of *Prime Evil*. At that stage of my television career, it was the equivalent of exposing the death squads in *Vrye Weekblad* several years earlier. When the documentary was screened, De Kock and the Vlakplaas squad had not yet made their public debut. The media had reported extensively on the testimony presented at De Kock's trial, but killer cops were still shadowy, face-less figures for the most part. Only when they deluged the TRC with amnesty applications would ordinary South Africans see them confessing to murder, torture and an astonishing array of dirty tricks.

I had an early opportunity to present the reality of death squads as harshly and bluntly as I could. I wanted to horrify and stagger white television viewers in particular with compelling and frightening accounts of a bitter war and a sear-ingly demented past. Never again did I want any of my countrymen to be able to say: 'I am as shocked as you are about these many revelations. I didn't know ...'

Prime Evil was shown in full or in part again and again. With massive publicity preceding its first broadcast, almost two million television sets were tuned to the SABC for the inaugural screening. After that, it was shown around the world and at international television festivals.

'Not only is it easily the finest political documentary yet made in this country,' said the *Star*, 'it also marks the first time that some of De Kock's most notorious underlings, sidekicks, henchmen and acolytes have spoken on camera. Pauw punctured the heart of the whore more than five years ago, but this documentary drives the stake in further.'

Said the *Weekly Mail*: 'The outstanding SABC documentary came straight from the heart of its producer and director. In the admirable tradition of Bram Fischer and Beyers Naudé, Pauw demonstrates that the circumstances of one's birth are not the determinants of the moral quality of one's life.'

On a wintry morning in June 1997 I returned to Pretoria Central Prison to see De Kock one last time. We hadn't met or spoken since the end of his trial, when he was locked up for what would almost certainly be the rest of his natural life. I still don't know why I wanted to see him again. *Prime Evil* had been sent to the archives and I wasn't working on any more programmes about death squads.

At the entrance to the maximum-security section was a blackboard with a text from the Bible scribbled in white chalk: *Peter was sad because Jesus asked him the third time: 'Do you love me?' So he said to him: 'Lord, you know everything; you know that I love you.' Jesus said to him: 'Take care of my sheep.'* (John 21:17)

I wasn't sure why this verse greeted visitors to one of the country's most heavily fortified prisons. Maybe the sheep alluded to the inmates behind the endless rows of steel and barricaded doors that clanged and clattered incessantly.

De Kock was ushered into the putty-coloured waiting room. There were four chairs and one table, all chained to the floor. He was dressed in green prison clothes and looked fit and rested, his face tanned, probably from spending an hour or so every day in the small outdoor courtyard where maximum-security prisoners could relax and exercise. At our previous meetings he had been behind a glass partition. Now, for the first time, I shook his hand – the infamous trigger hand. His handshake was firm, even intimidating.

'It's hard inside,' he said, and told me of fellow inmates who had spat in his food. He had complained that unless they were tested for AIDS, Hepatitis B and other diseases, he wouldn't eat.

A month earlier, De Kock had submitted his 1 200-page amnesty application to the TRC. It contained details of twenty international and eighty-seven local incidents, all of which he was either directly involved in or had knowledge of.

An inmate brought us coffee as rancour and resentment rolled off De Kock's tongue and filled the hollow space around us. When we discussed his amnesty application, he asked me: 'What do you think my chances are?'

It was a question he subsequently asked all his visitors. I told him I didn't think they were very good.

'You must be glad,' he responded curtly.

An inmate called De Kock for lunch. We shook hands again and I watched as he strolled down the dark artery of the prison until a door slammed behind him. He didn't invite me to visit him again and I never entertained the thought of doing so.

Eugene de Kock became the incarnation and human face of evil, the inalienable combatant who rose in defence of an indefensible and unjustifiable system. In that sense, he stood accused on behalf of every white man and woman who grew fat and prosperous under National Party rule – all four and a half million of us.

And then, without preamble, apartheid's ultimate weapon was not just defeated, but denied and shunned. He awakened from his long nightmare alone and forlorn. The politicians who had spawned the hate and funded the killers, the generals who spurred them on, the *dominees* who prayed for their deliverance from enemies, the judges and magistrates who excused their deeds as self-defence, the civil servants in grey shoes who did the paperwork that let the system classify, remove, disinherit and control, clucked their tongues and shook their heads, then gave silent thanks for their personal escape from retribution.

Eugene de Kock's pariahdom was one of the most despicable acts of betrayal in the history of South Africa. The politicians and generals who had pinned medals to his chest and gorged themselves on *potjiekos* and Chivas Regal at Vlakplaas suddenly sprouted wings and sang *Hallelujah, I am saved!* The men in black bowler hats with iron fists and wagging fingers and maleficent ideologies who created the darkness that De Kock and others had to sin their way through – PW Botha, Magnus Malan, Adriaan Vlok and many others – disowned their warriors like a pack of Judas rats. It was nothing new for leaders of base morality to excise conscience from their collective psyche – Nazis had done it in Germany, *génocidaires* in Rwanda and Pinochet's generals in Chile. In this regard, the top echelons of the National Party and its security forces rank among humanity's worst.

In the end, they left us with nothing but burnt bridges, torched fields, the smell of smoke and a false presumption that, like them, we had all been absolved of guilt. When the zephyr of democracy blew away apartheid's detritus, a lone white soul with black-rimmed glasses and a box of their matches in his hand remained trapped in the black-stumped fields.

Sorry, they said, the little wretch stole our fire. He should have kept the matches in his pocket and, anyway, we've never seen him before. In the name of reconciliation, can we please cast him on the heap of yesterday's putrid offal and get on with the business of cultivating a new land?

The archangel himself descended from Abraham's bosom in the person of FW de Klerk. The villainous killers and torturers from Vlakplaas, the security police, the CCB and Military Intelligence were a criminal minority who had acted beyond their orders and the bounds of security force policy.

I had been disillusioned with establishment Afrikaners for a long time, so it came as no surprise when they disowned De Kock and alienated him as a rogue policeman. I expected nothing less from brittle, feeble and morally depraved people. Nor was I surprised when they perjured themselves or lied with one hand on the Bible. I'd seen it too many times before: in court cases, at the Harms Commission, at the TRC.

De Klerk was asked by a TRC commissioner: 'How reasonable is that explanation that a lowly officer, somewhere below these generals, was responsible for this entire aberration that led to all these things?' His disingenuous response? 'There is nothing reasonable in crime.'

TRC: 'Is it possible ... that the commander of Vlakplaas would have been able to sustain, taken all the resources he needed, finances and so on, that situation on his own and keep it secret from everybody higher up?'

De Klerk: 'Yes, I think it is possible. It happens every day with theft.'

Three months after my last visit to Eugene de Kock, he made the first of several appearances before the TRC, explaining his role in the 1988 murder of three black policemen who were blown up because they might have exposed security police atrocities.

On concluding his testimony, De Kock requested a private meeting with the widows to express his remorse and to apologise. One of them, Pearl Faku, said afterwards: 'I was profoundly touched by him. I hope that when he sees our tears, he knows that they are not only tears for our husbands, but tears for him as well. I would like to hold him by the hand, and show him that there is a future, and that he can still change.'

Since then, De Kock had embarked on a remarkable crusade to expose the generals and politicians for whom he killed on the one hand, and on the other to seek forgiveness from the families of his victims.

'We destroyed lives. We ruined the lives of the families of the people we killed,' he repeated time and time again. 'It was a futile exercise. We wasted the most precious thing. Life itself. I would like to tell these families how sorry I am. It's something I can never rectify.'

How ironic that it was ultimately left to Eugene de Kock's victims to restore some dignity to his tattered remains and comfort his shattered soul. It was the people he had deprived of liberty and their loved ones who took his hand and reminded him that he was, after all, a human being just like the rest of us. Maybe something of the true South African miracle is to be found in the story of this killer cop.

For a long time, I resented no one more than Eugene de Kock, and it gave me immense satisfaction when he was condemned to a life behind bars. Humanity demands such punishment for people who are so debased. I could support neither his early release nor a presidential pardon. But I believe it should be up to his victims to decide if he should indeed stay caged for the rest of his days or be allowed to live in the very society he had fought so hard to prevent from becoming a reality.

I would not be able to say whether or when De Kock had changed. Perhaps the prospect of dying behind bars forced him to reflect on how he got there. Maybe his exposure to truth and reconciliation touched a dormant seed of genuine humanity stifled years ago by life in the security police and a death squad.

Psychologist Pumla Gobodo-Madikizela, who served on the TRC's Human Rights Violations Committee, spent almost fifty hours debriefing De Kock in prison before writing *A Human Being Died that Night,* her fascinating study of evil, forgiveness and reconciliation. She concluded that De Kock was a desperate soul seeking to affirm to himself that he was still a member of the human race.

She found two distinct sides to De Kock: the evil killer, and a man capable of caring, feeling and crying. Having watched my documentary, she wrote: 'The image I'd been carrying of a chained De Kock sitting in a small prison chair, trembling and breaking down, was replaced by one of him as the evil one, merciless, lashing out violently at his victims, instilling fear and silencing them. I saw De Kock in my tortured mind's eye in his most vicious state – as *prime evil.* These images were too difficult to take in, too much to comprehend, even if I could imagine them. I had to remind myself that if it was that difficult for me, how much worse it must have been for the people who had faced the evil directly and been destroyed because of it.'

And yet, she said, 'society must embrace those who, like Eugene de Kock, see and even lead on the road of shared humanity ahead. Our capacity for such empathy is a profound gift in this brutal world we have created for one another as people of different races, creeds and political persuasions.'

Not all assassins were as fortunate as Eugene de Kock to receive grace from the families of their victims. Maybe his expression of remorse was more genuine than many of the others.

I never sensed a great deal of regret among the killers. When I once asked Dirk Coetzee about this, he erupted in fury. 'What the fuck do you want me to do? Go on my knees all the time and cry and beg for forgiveness?'

In fact, I encountered only one assassin who showed unadulterated and spontaneous remorse. I was sitting in a Pretoria pub late one night with former security police captain Wouter Mentz when he burst into tears because he was truly haunted by the killings he had participated in. Among his victims were one of his own colleagues and two deaf children. It was an awkward moment and I didn't know how to console him.

According to his psychiatric report, Mentz was seriously disturbed. He was emotional, cried for no apparent reason, and pulled out tufts of his moustache and hair. When he talked about killing, he would giggle one moment and burst into tears the next. Like many of his colleagues, he no longer fitted into society.

Dirk Coetzee told the families of his victims numerous times how sorry he was for what he had done. But forgiveness was not forthcoming.

When he came face to face with the family of slain Durban lawyer Griffiths Mxenge, it was a disaster. Coetzee began: 'Can I first say, I really feel sorry and would just like to apologise for the grief and sorrow I have created as a result of my deeds.'

Dr Churchill Mxenge, brother of the slain lawyer, responded: 'I don't understand why a person like you is walking the streets of South Africa. It doesn't make sense. Dirk Coetzee is not supposed to be where he is today; he should be behind bars.'

Coetzee: 'I understand your point of view, Dr Mxenge.'

Mxenge: 'We would like to see you arrested, charged and sentenced for what you did.'

Coetzee: 'I think it's a question of fellow South Africans appreciating the openness and at least someone that could stand up against the system.'

Mxenge: 'Oh come on, I don't buy that. I think we should stop this interview.'

The mother of activist Sizwe Kondile, Charity Kondile, also found it impossible to forgive Coetzee. Her son had faced a bright future. He had just completed his law studies and fathered his first child. She spent nine years searching for Sizwe until she heard how Coetzee and his men had sated themselves on brandy, rum and meat next to the burning body of her son.

Coetzee had told me that Kondile had to die because he was seriously injured during interrogation by the Eastern Cape security police. Coetzee was summoned to Jeffrey's Bay to take care of the problem. When he walked into the police station, he said, he was taken to a room where the slender, bearded man was handcuffed to a bed. 'Get rid of him,' Coetzee was ordered. The activist was loaded into a car and driven to Komatipoort on the Mozambican border.

After our exposé, Charity Kondile went to the spot where her son's ashes had been thrown into the Komati River. 'As we were nearing that place, I broke down. When we got there, I saluted Sizwe. There were flowers growing next to that place, so I took a stone and put it there and prayed that his soul must rest in peace. I washed my hands and left.'

After the screening of *Prime Evil* I never again attended a TRC hearing and refused to entertain any more apartheid assassins. I had heard enough bloody bravado and gleeful torture talk to last me a lifetime.

The exception was Ferdi Barnard – for a long time one of the most feared men in the country. A menacing-looking desperado decked out in hoodlum garb and flaunting a macho swagger, his path first crossed mine in 1992. Six years later, my last glimpse of him was in the Pretoria Supreme Court.

Barnard controlled a ruthless gang of criminals that held sway over the Johannesburg underworld and plied their lawlessness with complete impunity. Yet, in contrast to many killers who were rather drab and nondescript, Barnard and his henchman were intriguing, swashbuckling characters who lived on the edge and tempted fate.

If ever South Africa had its own mob of *Goodfellas*, this was it.

CHAPTER 9

Hoodlums, hookers and hooligans

What Jimmy really loved to do was steal. I mean he actually enjoyed it.
Jimmy was the kind of guy who rooted for the bad guys in the movies.
— Henry Hill in the gangster movie *Goodfellas*

W E ALL WANT TO GO TO OUR GRAVES IN ONE PIECE. CORRIE
Goosen was not that lucky.

His mangled remains lay encased in an ostentatious white coffin in a brick-faced NG Kerk in the coastal city of Port Elizabeth. A disfigured corpse was all that remained of the chubby hoodlum after he'd crashed his Honda Blackbird at a speed of 300 km/h on a highway outside the city. His face was unrecognisable, and a special police unit had rushed to the Eastern Cape to take his fingerprints to make sure that the remains spread out on a slab in the morgue were indeed those of Johannes Cornelius Goosen. Goosen family members had a reputation for faking their deaths when they were in shit – which was almost always. At the time of his death, Corrie was standing trial in South Africa's biggest diamond robbery.

Hundreds of mourners descended on the church to pay their final homage to the man whose blood had bubbled like champagne at the sight or thought of a flawless diamond. A pink cardboard heart framed by red carnations, with the name 'Corrie' in silver glitter, stood in front of the casket against the pulpit.

A wailing widow added the final touch to this garish tableau. Debbie Goosen sat slumped over the coffin, her bottle-blonde mane stylishly draped across its surface. She had come a long way from the homely *maplotter* (poor white plot dweller) that Goosen had married and chiselled into his personal Barbie doll. In the process he spent a fortune on having her breasts enlarged (though she later apparently had the silicone implants removed) and having buckets of fat vacuum-sucked out of her voluptuous frame.

Every now and then she kissed the coffin while caressing it tenderly with one hand. On her finger the widow flaunted a gargantuan and flawless diamond. Many said the rock originated from a metal box filled with gems that Goosen and his henchmen had looted from a Western Transvaal family of diamond diggers.

Most of the mourners had finished little more than half of their secondary-school education and boasted a hoodlum's sense of style – mullet hairstyles, middle partings with a rat's tail hanging down the back. Among them were thieves, robbers, gangsters, fraudsters, diamond smugglers, a former South African heavyweight boxing champion, a professional kick-boxer, a hot-rod racer and a throng of leather-clad bikers. The gangster tarts accessorising their flanks sported peroxide-blonde hairdos, stiletto heels and pouting red lips; insincere tears rolled down their powdered cheeks.

Goosen had not been a regular churchgoer, and at the outset the preacher, Dominee van Tonder, admitted he hadn't known the deceased well. He none-theless fibbed in trembling voice: 'You are going to miss him. His footsteps will be silent. But his memory is beautiful and you can always take it with you. Corrie was a lovely person and his life was testimony to that.' The mourners rose and burst into song.

Amazing grace
How sweet the sound
That saved a wretch like me!
I once was lost, but now am found;
Was blind, but now I see.

Former boxing champion Jimmy Abbott stayed in his seat. He was too obese to get up. Abbott had once been a mean fighting machine, but since then had ballooned into something resembling an elephantine tick with a mop of curly hair. Abbott, who had become a Pentecostal pastor, grew up with Goosen. So did Ralph Heyns, a mobster buddy who had known Goosen 'since we were too young to smuggle or fuck'. Heyns, a man with an unwieldy poodle coif and a missing limb, was once incarcerated on death row in Pretoria Central. During the funeral service, he sobbed so much he couldn't utter a word.

When I later asked Heyns to describe Goosen, he said: 'About two, three weeks before his death we were in the same Porsche and we spoke about who was going to die first, me or him. We decided we're going out in a hail of bullets. But we lived our lives. Corrie had a saying: live your dreams – and good men die young.'

Absent from the funeral was Corrie's other bosom buddy, Ferdi Barnard. His was a name synonymous with infamy that sent shivers down many a spine. Barnard was a co-accused in the diamond robbery and his bail conditions prevented him from leaving Johannesburg. He later told me he sat crying in his brothel that day, thinking about his chum being buried.

'He said he wanted to die with his boots on,' said Barnard. 'He wanted to die in action. And this is a bad thing to say, but I'd rather see Corrie dead than behind bars.'

As Goosen was lowered into the grave, somebody put a black motorcycle helmet on top of the white coffin. Red and white carnations fell with hollow sounds on the casket, while Scottish pipes bid him farewell. Debbie Goosen stood behind the pink heart. Her wails echoed through Port Elizabeth's cemetery. 'No, no, no!'

If the lives of Ferdi Barnard, Corrie Goosen and Ralph Heyns were a Hollywood movie script, no one would believe it. Their story is stranger than fiction and more fantastic than anything an imaginative writer could dream up. Between them they had been convicted of murder, conspiracy to murder, attempted murder, assault, robbery, theft, fraud, diamond dealing, and illegal possession of firearms and ammunition. Prisons and graveyards are filled with men like them who struck a devil's bargain and ended up paying a high price. One died and another went to prison for life. The third ended up living in an ostentatious *Boere-barok* mansion on a hill in Johannesburg's western suburbs. He had, as he put it to me, 'made it to the top'.

Chronicling the lives of these three gangsters was one of the most enthralling journalistic expeditions I'd ever embarked on. I met Goosen two or three times, Heyns a few times more, but with Barnard I had a much more intimate relationship. It started in 1992 and ended six years later in the Pretoria Supreme Court (now High Court), when I helped condemn him to life imprisonment.

I befriended Barnard because he was a minefield of information and frequently shot his mouth off. He babbled invaluable information about the apartheid government's hit squads, Vlakplaas (and its commander, Eugene de Kock) and the military's CCB. I wrote countless stories based on details he provided and got two great television interviews out of him, both done in his brothels when he was drunk and snorting cocaine. I'm not sure what he got out of it, except that he loved seeing himself on TV and maybe enjoyed the attention he got from a 'leftie' journalist. When he was later questioned in court about his relationship with me, he said he was ordered to foster it in order to discredit me. In the end, he merely engineered his own downfall.

Barnard was one of the most abominable and depraved human beings ever spawned by South Africa. For many years he moved like a spectral ogre between the criminal underworld of drug dealing, prostitution, diamond dealing, robbery and murder, and apartheid South Africa's official death squads and eliminations. He was the ultimate reminder of the years when hoodlums and gangsters had flourished under apartheid by offering their muscle to the state's dirty tricks brigade. In return, they were permitted to cultivate their mafiosi schemes without fear of prosecution, as long as they could further the cause of their political masters. When apartheid ended in 1994, Barnard simply carried on with his nefarious activities as his police contacts were absorbed into the new force.

I spent several evenings with a cocaine-snorting Barnard in his Johannesburg brothels and we got horribly pissed over long lunches in Melville. Sometimes

I met him at a roadhouse in Roodepoort, and he once came to my home uninvited. When he left, he opened the boot of his car and showed me a shotgun. Then he laughed.

Corrie Goosen and Ralph Heyns were more straightforward criminals and thugs, driven by a desire and determination to escape their dismal upbringing and accumulate as much wealth as possible. I eventually produced a seventy-five minute TV documentary, *Death of a Gangster*, on Goosen and the hoodlums and thugs who surrounded and associated with him.

Heyns admitted to me on camera that he had done illegal deals with Goosen to the tune of about R35 million. A hapless policeman with a pile of dockets in front of him in a dismal little office in a Johannesburg police station reckoned that the gang had 'knocked' people for more than R50 million. A knock is simply a robbery or theft. Nothing ever came of the dockets, maybe because Heyns offered the policeman a lucrative job at his new nightclub.

The antics of Barnard, Heyns and Goosen were remarkably reminiscent of those portrayed in Martin Scorsese's masterpiece, *Goodfellas*, the story of three New York mobsters in the 1960s and 1970s. Henry Hill, Tommy DeVito and Jimmy Conway ran some of the biggest hijackings and burglaries the town had ever seen. They killed off all their competition and slowly started climbing the ladder to the top of the mob.

Said Henry Hill, the narrator: 'As far back as I can remember I always wanted to be a gangster. For us to live any other way was nuts. Uh, to us, those goody-goody people who worked shitty jobs for bum pay checks and took the subway to work every day, and worried about their bills, were dead. I mean they were suckers. They had no balls. If we wanted something, we just took it. If anyone complained twice they got hit so bad, believe me, they never complained again. And when the cops – they assigned a whole army to stop Jimmy, what'd he do? He made 'em partners.'

After spending much time with Barnard and his fellow ruffians, I could understand why gangster life is so intoxicating and irresistible. It's the jungle culture, the lion king syndrome, the Tarzan tag; the invincibility, the lure of living on the edge; having not just one woman but a harem on your tail; the shooting irons, the fast cars and the loot. Gangster life cultivates that swagger, that bravado of being untouchable and outsmarting or greasing the coppers. It sets hoods apart from other mortal beings. The battle scars they share, fate they defy and justice they escape forge them into a fraternity that is closer than family.

Randfontein, a bleak and stark town set amid mostly depleted gold mines, is the outback of Greater Johannesburg. Ralph Heyns grew up in the outback of the outback, next to the railway line. He was one of seventeen children, and with a builder father struggling to make ends meet, his early years were hungry and cold. He had to sleep on the dirty laundry and make do with clothes and shoes that were handed down from one sibling to another.

Goosen, the son of a truck driver, grew up on a smallholding on the other side of Randfontein. The two met during a rugby match, when Goosen kicked one of Heyns's teammates' lights out. In that instant, a brotherhood was born.

The boys had to steal to eat. Their preferred target was Uncle Harry's road-house, where they would lurk as waiters carried trays of hamburgers and mixed grills to open car windows. Goosen and Heyns would run forward, grab the food and scuttle away. After a while, Uncle Harry realised they were bad for business and gave them a box of *slaptjips* every day in exchange for abstaining from mischief at his establishment. They broke in at the bakery and stole pies and cakes for their families.

By the time they reached puberty, they were a gang, and violence had become their trademark. 'We were a bunch of hotheads and we didn't have respect for anyone,' said Heyns. 'At night we would patrol the streets, and whether you were black or white, if we got you we'd beat you up so badly you would never be the same again.'

One of their unfortunate victims was Henk Pelser, who in later years became a South African kick-boxing champion. Older than Corrie and the others, he was a fitter on the railways, but, to make ends meet, worked as a male stripper at night. 'As I walked through the bush, they attacked me and beat the holy crap out of me. They thought it was someone else, a black or something. They [the blacks] used to take women into the bush and rape and kill them. It was only when I thought I was going to die and screamed that they realised I was white. It was the beginning of a close friendship.'

Every Saturday the gang, who managed to get hold of a shotgun, went hunting in the area. 'Every Friday we bought about five hundred cartridges. The next day we went to the dams outside town and the mine dumps and killed every bird in front of us. *Bokmakierie, tinktinkie, vink*, whatever it was, we killed it. Sometimes we shot at one another,' said Heyns.

Even at that age, Corrie collected glassy stones and rocks. 'If you had some-thing nice and shiny, he always wanted it,' said Pelser. 'He had a showcase at home full of stones, and he started talking about diamonds when he was still a kid. He said he was going to have lots of them. We just laughed.'

Another Randfonteiner who knew Goosen and Heyns from childhood was Jimmy Abbott, the baby-faced Goliath of South African heavyweight boxers. 'My parents were very poor and there was never food for us. At Christmas there were no presents. It was the same for Ralph and Corrie,' said Abbott. 'I watched the movie *Gone with the Wind*. Scarlett goes to the fields and digs in the ground and pulls out a carrot. It's rotten and she falls on her knees and says, Lord, I will never go hungry in my life again. Even if I have to steal, lie and cheat, I will never go hungry again. And that became our motto in life. Whatever, we will not go hungry.'

None of the boys completed their high school education. 'I said to myself, when I grow up I will never live this way again,' said Heyns. 'At the age of fifteen I told my mother: Do you see this face? Look closely because this is the last time you will see it. I left home. I tried to be a motor mechanic, but it wasn't for me. I then bought cheap cars, fixed them and sold them again. I also started wheeling and dealing.'

At age seventeen, Corrie went to the army. It wasn't long before he was in detention for being absent without leave. During one of his excursions outside camp he impregnated a sixteen year-old Randfontein girl by the name of Debbie Smit. The military police took him under guard to the Magistrate's Court, where he tied the knot. Ralph couldn't attend the ceremony because he was in hospital following a motorcycle accident.

Corrie became an electrician on the railways, but according to another childhood friend, Dawie Lotter, he had already decided that a nine-to-five existence was not for him. 'We all wanted to be on top. If you work for a boss and you earn R2 000 a month, how will you achieve that? He couldn't do it and that's why he started wheeling and dealing.'

Before long, Corrie and Ralph became career criminals. Anything went, from theft to fraud to diamond dealing. Soon they had criminal records, Corrie for diamond smuggling and assault and Ralph for housebreaking and theft. 'We started thinking we were untouchable and could do whatever we wanted,' said Heyns. 'We were the kings of Randfontein.'

Goosen's passions were diamonds, fast cars and motorcycles. 'I remember us getting our first racing bikes. We were travelling at a hell of a speed when I looked over my shoulder to see how Corrie was doing. He was doing a handstand in the traffic! He was up there in the air as though he was pulling off a circus stunt. I told him then that he'd kill himself one day.'

It wasn't long before Heyns moved from petty crime to armed robbery. But that went horribly wrong. Heyns, his brother Barney and Goosen's older brother Mike recruited two black men to pull off an armed heist. A fifty-seven-year-old security guard was shot dead. The gang was arrested, convicted of murder and robbery and sentenced to death. The sentence was overturned on appeal and they each spent eight years in prison.

'When we were pulling robberies we asked Corrie if he wanna be part of it. He walked away. He never was a man for violence because he had a soft heart. He was doing diamond deals,' said Heyns.

When he walked out of prison, Goosen was the one who set him up again.

'Corrie was our Robin Hood, the prince of thieves. He stole from the rich and gave to the poor. He invited me to his house, gave me money and bought me a suit. Then we started doing business together.'

'What kind of business?' I asked Ralph.

'He showed me a couple of stones. By a couple I mean one thousand, two thousand carats.'

'How much were they worth?'

'About seven million rand.'

Prison life breeds new alliances. One of the inmates at Pretoria Central where Ralph was incarcerated was a young policeman convicted of double murder. His name was Ferdinand Barnard.

In December 1984, the twenty-five-year-old Narcotics Bureau sergeant faced Mr Justice Gert Coetzee from the dock at the Johannesburg Supreme Court. The judge, an imposing man with a sergeant major's moustache, had convicted Ferdi Barnard of murder and attempted murder and was about to pronounce sentence.

In contrast to Goosen and Heyns, Barnard had everything going for him. The son of a police colonel, he grew up in a middle-class home in Krugersdorp, about ten to fifteen kilometres from Randfontein. After leaving school he joined the police, excelled during his training and became a detective on the West Rand. According to evidence in his court case, he became disillusioned with policing and the state's inability to deal with crime. He took the law into his own hands and executed two drug dealers who had been set up to rob a Roodepoort pharmacy. He was also found guilty of stealing a car linked to the robbery and of attempting to murder an addict.

Despite the callousness of the crime, the judge decided to be lenient and offer the killer a second chance in the hope that he would rehabilitate himself. As he sentenced Barnard to a meagre six years in prison, he said: 'I will give you a chance. It depends on you what you make of it.'

After serving just more than half his sentence, Barnard was released on parole in 1988 and found a job with an insurance company in Roodepoort. He found his duties as a claims assessor boring, resigned after three months and told his boss he had been offered a job with the security police, where he would be monitoring political activists.

Barnard tendered his services to apartheid's multitude of death squads and counter-insurgency units. PW Botha's regime was in its death throes and desperate to stem the tide of resistance through assassinations, disappearances and dirty tricks. The police had Vlakplaas and various Security Branch units, while the Defence Force had the CCB and the Directorate of Covert Collection (DCC). Barnard worked for both the CCB and DCC, and also had close ties with Vlakplaas. He had found the perfect cover to combine patriotism and profit and conceal his criminal activities as official undercover operations.

His police friends on the West Rand recruited him as a freelance agent for the CCB. He was paid a monthly salary of R5 000 and given a car. Barnard fitted perfectly into this frightening and perverted security force outfit.

The head of his cell was one of South Africa's best-known policemen, Colonel Daniël 'Staal' Burger, whose nickname literally means steel and was taken from a popular radio comedy series about an invincible cop. Also recruited was Lieutenant 'Slang' van Zyl, who earned his pet name from colleagues who thought his eyes were reptilian.

Barnard teamed up with Calla Botha, a cauliflower-eared former Transvaal rugby forward of Herculean proportions. The two had scrummed down together many times on the rugby field, and in the summer of 1988 found themselves on the same side. Barnard and Botha made a bloodcurdling duo, and their schemes were as wacky as their physical appearance.

In one of their schemes, they wanted to bewitch Archbishop Desmond Tutu. They climbed over the wall of his official residence in Cape Town and hung a baboon foetus in a tree. The foetus was inside a bottle and it had to be placed in such a way that, while not overtly visible, it would eventually be found. God knows what they had hoped to achieve.

The CCB then decided that lawyer Dullah Omar – who later became the first post-apartheid Minister of Justice – should be killed for defending 'terrorists'. The plan was to kill him by swapping his heart tablets with similar-looking poison pills. The CCB hired a Cape Town gangster by the name of Peaches Gordon to break into Omar's house and steal the activist's heart medication. Gordon didn't bother. He simply took two pills from his sister-in-law, who also had a heart condition, and handed them to his CCB handler. The CCB then gave Gordon poison pills with the instruction to 'again' break into Omar's house and swap the pills. But instead the gangster pocketed a generous payment, threw his toxic cargo out of the car window, and disappeared.

The initial plot having failed, Barnard was then sent to Cape Town to kill Omar. He stood waiting for him in the garage of the lawyer's house with a silenced Makarov pistol, but when the activist appeared, his wife was with him. Barnard abandoned the operation.

Anti-apartheid activist and university lecturer Dr David Webster was not so lucky. As he opened the back door of his van in front of his home in the Johannesburg suburb of Troyeville on the first day of May 1989, a car pulled up alongside him. Somebody called his name, he swung around and a shotgun was fired at close range. Sixteen coarse-grain pellets entered his body, and as he was dying, the assassin sped away.

In the days, weeks and months that followed, the murder of David Webster became one of the most highly publicised assassinations in the history of South Africa. Few murders in the country's violent past were the subject of so much publicity, investigation, suspicion, false leads and accusations.

Mobsters prefer their broads blonde, buxom and obedient. In turn, stiletto scrubbers just cannot resist the lure of brawn and lap up the danger and excitement of gangland. After the bevies of fluff have swooned into the tattooed arms of smart-arse hoodlums, they join the gold rush, bask in the glory and lavishly squander the loot.

Henry Hill made the point in *Goodfellas* that no self-respecting gangster would be seen playing and partying without a trophy bimbo on his arm. They are as much a trademark of villainy as the BMW, the mansion and the jewellery. Barmaids, strippers, prostitutes and tarts are often not just available for the taking, but gagging for the attention of bad guys with big bankrolls.

Henry Hill, again: 'I suppose that, because I was in a violent world, women thought I would be a violent lover throwing them round the bedroom like Tarzan, having passionate sex up the wardrobes or whatever. I lost count of the number of casual encounters I had. At five foot nine inches tall and built like a brick shithouse, I was no film star. It didn't matter a damn.'

Backscratcher-hookers swamped Barnard the moment he walked into his brothel. They would prance around on their spike heels until he ordered them to pour him another rum and Coke. He once offered me a cute-looking, dark-haired chicky-babe 'on the house'. I declined.

Both Barnard and Goosen kept well-proportioned platinum blondes under wraps at home. Goosen's chums all vouched for his devotion to Debbie, although he had two illegitimate children with other women. This was how Dawie Lotter put it: 'A nice car, jewellery, one or two other women and sometimes a gun. That's the motto of a gangster. Although Corrie would never replace Debbie with anyone else in the world, he believed a gangster must have more than one woman.'

During the time I knew Barnard, he kept his 'permanent' woman under lock and key behind the high walls of his Roodepoort home. Her name was Amor Badenhorst and, predictably, she wasn't just bottle-blonde and well endowed, but also a former prostitute and stripper.

The two had literally fallen into one another's arms next to a pool of blood. On a bitterly cold night in July 1988, Amor's policeman boyfriend was involved in a shootout with a client outside a brothel in downtown Johannesburg. As her boyfriend was taken into custody, Barnard seemingly came out of nowhere and took care of her. Before long, Amor had swapped her killer cop for a ruthless gangster. Not a hell of a difference, according to Henry Hill: 'I think perhaps there may be a parallel attraction of cops and crooks. They are both involved in danger, intrigue, the thrill of the chase, just operating on different sides of the fence. There is a very fine line between a good policeman and a good crook. They think the same. It's the hunter and the hunted. I think women find both a real turn-on.'

When Amor met Ferdi, he'd already worked his way into the heart of the CCB and was dividing his time between the state's official business and the Johannesburg underworld. He told her he was a secret agent and instructed her to ask no questions.

Amor obeyed, at least for a while. But having been self-sufficient from an early age, she soon yearned for the thrill of life on the street. Amor had run away from her home in the East Rand mining town of Nigel when she was only fifteen. In no time she was roaming Johannesburg's streets and selling her body to anyone with the money for a lap dance or a lay.

She became restless as Barnard's *houvrou* (common-law wife), absconded to her hometown and started stripping at the local hotel. Barnard tracked her down. He arrived with eight of his men and waited for her to go to the Nigel Hotel. While she was dancing, he lobbed a stun grenade through the window. He meant it as a warning – I own you and you cannot escape from me. I will find you, wherever you are. Amor got the message.

But Barnard was losing control. He started snorting massive amounts of cocaine and would stay at his brothel in Oxford Road, Rosebank, all night. The more drugs he took, the more he boasted to friends, prostitutes and clients that he was the one who had killed David Webster. During this time, Amor fell pregnant. Ferdi ordered her to stay at home, even though he was never there. She also had to stay away from the brothel and was not to visit her parents in Nigel.

One day, driving to or from the farm in what later became the province of Limpopo where his parents were living in retirement, Barnard pointed to a dam and told Amor that he had thrown the shotgun he'd used to kill Webster into the water. Then he described the 'hit' to her in detail.

Barnard wasn't the only gangster engaging in pillow talk. In the Johannesburg suburb of Brixton, his co-conspirator was also shooting his mouth off. Officially, Eugene Riley was a policeman in the Internal Stability Unit. A knee injury had kept him out of the force for more than three years, although he still received his salary. Unofficially, he had joined Barnard and was selling his services to the CCB and Military Intelligence.

Riley and Barnard had initially planned the murder of David Webster together, but couldn't agree on the method to be used. Barnard wanted to use a shotgun, while the policeman preferred a sniper's rifle with a telescope. Riley's girlfriend was a witness to the planning.

Brunette Julie Wilken was not your typical gangster's moll. Bright, strong-willed and verbose, she seemed an unlikely sweetheart for Riley. On the day Webster was shot, the two were visiting his parents when they heard a radio report about the murder. Riley turned pale and said: 'Baby, there's going to be shit.'

'Why?' she asked.

'There's years of shit coming. That dumb cunt didn't know what he was doing.'

Riley and Barnard had both been Narcotics Bureau detectives in the early eighties. After Barnard's release from prison, they became closer than brothers and formed a gang that included Corrie Goosen among its members.

I first met Barnard in 1992 on the eve of the judicial inquest into Webster's death. A colleague at the now defunct *Sunday Star* and I had discovered that a few days after the murder, Barnard had confessed his complicity to several people. He told, among others, a former employer how he had shot the anti-apartheid activist. We had enough to write a story, but decided to give Barnard a chance to put his side of events.

On the Thursday night before we published the allegations, we drove to Barnard's house in De Wet Street, Roodepoort. The property was enclosed by a high security wall but had no intercom or bell, so I started shouting his name over the barking of a ferocious guard dog.

The next moment, a white car skidded to a halt next to us. A fuming Barnard leapt from the car and made a beeline for me. 'I'm going to send you on fucking sick leave!' he bellowed as he towered over me like an oak tree over an acorn. I was almost paralysed with fear as I slowly retreated to my car, fearful that his trigger-happy, psychotic, pathological temper might be unleashed on me at any second.

'If there is incriminating evidence, they can charge me,' he shouted as he sent us off.

Barnard attended the inquest virtually every day as lawyers representing Webster's partner, Maggie Friedman, tried to pin the murder on him and the CCB. On days when Barnard thought he might be called to testify, his big frame was tightly packed into a brownish double-breasted suit. On other days, he looked more comfortable in jeans, ankle-high white sneakers and a multicoloured short-sleeved shirt. When he finally took the stand, he denied all involvement in the murder.

The inquest found that although Barnard was a prime suspect, it could not be proved beyond reasonable doubt that he had killed Webster.

I had started chatting to him in the court corridors during the proceedings, and eventually he said he wanted to tell me something. A few days later I took him to lunch and he ratted on Eugene de Kock, with whom he had fallen out. The Vlakplaas commander was supplying weapons to the Zulu-based Inkatha Freedom Party in order to destabilise black townships and had formed a company that was importing arms.

Barnard visited me at my home one day and told me he had been ordered to shoot SWAPO activist Anton Lubowski on the eve of the Namibian elections in 1989. He said he twice waited with an AK-47 assault rifle to kill the prominent Windhoek advocate and activist, but couldn't get a clear shot and had to abort the mission. His CCB colleagues then flew to Namibia to finish Lubowski off, four months after Webster was killed.

When he left my house later that afternoon, he said I was never to speak about Lubowski. 'Ask Webster what happened to him,' he said, and laughed.

To rat on Barnard and the gang was to sign your own death warrant. That was exactly what a drug addict and accomplice to robbery had done several months earlier, when he elected to become a state witness against Barnard and Eugene Riley. His body was found in a Hillbrow alley, his face and head battered to a pulp with a baseball bat.

On a Wednesday night in 1991, Barnard, Riley, Corrie Goosen and drug addict Mark Francis loaded Uzi machine guns, got into a couple of fast cars and headed for Taung in the former homeland of Bophuthatswana to rob a diamond dealer. Before they left, Julie Wilken pleaded with Riley: 'Please don't go tonight.'

She felt intuitively that something was going to go wrong, but Riley told her: 'Don't worry, it's a hell of a deal. I'll be back in the morning.'

But Riley didn't come back. Julie Wilken had been right.

When the gang entered the house where the diamonds were, they found two men armed with AK-47s guarding the precious consignment. Shooting broke out and Riley was wounded. Goosen and Barnard thought he was dead. They scrambled out of the house, jumped into a car and sped away. Riley and Francis were arrested and thrown in prison.

By the time Wilken arrived in Taung, Riley was shackled hand and foot, his wound untreated and dirty. 'He was in a bad state and had a wild look in his eyes. He said he had to stand for hours on his toes with his hands against the wall,' Julie told me. It was only later that she discovered he had been assaulted and sodomised.

Francis turned state's evidence and implicated the gang in the abortive robbery. Riley was charged and released on bail. On a Sunday night a few weeks later, he picked up an aluminium baseball bat and left the house. Julie knew Francis was going to die.

'He came back later that night,' she said. 'He took my cigarette lighter, a can of petrol and said he had to go and burn his clothes. When he returned, he took a bath and got into bed without saying a word.'

The next morning, Wilken heard that Francis was dead. Barnard visited them and warned Riley that he was going to be arrested for the killing, but said he shouldn't worry, because a senior police officer had 'everything under control'. A security guard had seen the killers beating Francis with the baseball bat, but couldn't pick out Barnard or Riley at an identity parade. The case collapsed. Mark Francis served as the ultimate post-mortem warning to anyone associated with Barnard and his buddies: you sell us out, you die.

Killing is an unfortunate but accepted element of gangster life – even if it means whacking one of your own. Once an insider breaks the code, weakens the group's invincibility and splits on his cronies, he's as good as dead. Says Henry in *Goodfellas*: 'Murder was the only way that everybody stayed in line. You got out of line, you got whacked. Everybody knew the rules. But sometimes, even if people didn't get out of line, they got whacked. I mean, hits just became a habit for some of the guys. Guys would get into arguments over nothing and before you knew it, one of them was dead. And they were shooting each other all the time.'

How ironic that on a Sunday night in January 1994, Julie Wilken and Eugene Riley were watching the movie *Bugsy* on television. The film ends with the mobster being shot dead by his cronies, who suspect him of cheating them. Wilken didn't see the end of the film, as she went to bed, leaving Riley in the lounge. She was woken around midnight by a shot, and when she stormed into the living room, she froze and screamed. Riley was slumped in a chair, his face covered in blood. His mouth slowly opened and he made a gurgling sound. Next to him was a revolver.

Half an hour later, he lay in hospital, his face covered in bandages. His eyes were half open, but his body was cold. The machine keeping him alive was switched off, and he died without saying a word.

Just after Wilken got home, Barnard and Goosen arrived and demanded to know what had happened to 'certain documents'. Wilken said a month before his death, Riley had started sleeping 'with his hand on a shotgun'. He had, it seemed, turned on his bosom buddy Ferdi Barnard. He was providing Military Intelligence with information about an alleged gun-smuggling scheme run by Barnard. On the Tuesday before he died, Riley told Wilken: 'I will not protect him any longer.'

Despite the mysterious circumstances surrounding his demise, his involvement with the underworld and his connections with covert security force units, police initially treated Riley's death as a suicide. A murder docket was later opened, but no one was ever arrested or charged.

Julie Wilken said a sheaf of Military Intelligence documents that she had typed for Riley disappeared when he died and that she received a string of death threats afterwards. She never doubted that her lover had been murdered or that Barnard was somehow involved.

'He reminded me of a fly,' she said of Barnard. 'Something that had to be crushed to death.'

In a watering hole on the diamond fields of the old Western Transvaal – one of those places where fading rugby jerseys and nylon G-strings hover over the heads of patrons and barflies – a group of diggers were still reminiscing about *that* robbery. It was months since the scoundrels had scurried into a quivering mealie field clutching a metal box full of stones, but riddles and mysteries still abounded over the plunder of the Nel family's fortune. It was a calamitous setback for prudent men who had stashed the diamonds as insurance against an anticipated land grab, civil war and retribution against the white man by the African National Congress.

Wolmaranstad, an outpost of Afrikaner conservatism and home to the Boer prophet Siener van Rensburg, had long since ceased to be the hub of a farming community. The discovery of diamonds had turned struggling maize farmers into millionaires and excavators had replaced tractors and ploughs. One of the first stories I did as a young journalist was about a farmer in the district who had discovered a stone the size of his thumbnail. He put it in a pouch and stuffed it into his underpants. But he blabbed out his secret in a bar, and before long he was the centre of attraction. Not only did a succession of women try to slip a hand into his underwear, but outlaws shot at and attacked him twice before he stowed his treasure in a safer place.

I returned to Wolmaranstad while making the documentary about Corrie Goosen's life. Many people said the pinnacle of his criminal career was a diamond robbery he and Ferdi Barnard had pulled against the Nel family.

Talk in the seedy pub ranged from maize prices (*why do they make it so hard for the Afrikaner farmer to survive?*) and rugby (*transformation is nothing but a plot to kill our national game*) to right-wing politics (*this country is going the same way as the rest of Africa*) and the women's underwear festooning the ceiling (*you should have seen those pink panties when she was in them*). When it came to diamonds, however, the men gulped down their *Klippies en Coke* and shut up. However oiled their throats, they had learnt to keep their diamond secrets close to their chests. The rule was simple: you don't talk and you don't show.

That was precisely what Marius and Deon Nel had not done. When out-of-town ruffians in leather jackets and sporty BMWs came calling with a small arsenal of machine guns to back up their story of being middlemen for foreign diamond buyers, greed overtook common sense. The brothers Nel had no idea that Goosen was South Africa's most notorious diamond thief and Barnard a desperado of Ramboesque proportions. The rest became history.

Old-time diggers with knobbly fingers lovingly wrapped around their tumblers of Klipdrift brandy claimed to have been reliably informed that there were diamonds worth far more than R10 million in the Nel family's legendary metal box. 'Why should they register each and every stone and pay tax? To this government? What for?'

Since the robbery, the Nels had fallen on hard times. Oubaas Nel shut down his diggings and chased Marius off the farm. He was squatting in a prefabricated house in the neighbouring town of Bloemhof. 'Marius is down and out,' said one digger, his face ruddy from copious amounts of brandy and standing for long hours in the sun, sifting through piles of gravel. 'I hear he drinks like a fish and went to Angola to work on a mine.'

'I'm afraid he's going the same way as John Vermeulen,' added an old-timer who had delved and tunnelled into the earth for most of his life looking for *daai moerse een* (the big one). Everybody knew the story of John Walters Vermeulen, once a digger in the small village of Bakerville. He was dead, and on his gravestone were the words: *Alone he suffered, alone he died. There is suffering no more.*

Vermeulen, a successful digger who carried his stones in a small holder around his neck, got a wooden splinter in his thumb. Acid, used to clean diamonds and test their quality, seeped into the wound. First he lost his thumb, then his hand and, finally, his arm. Then his diamonds were stolen. He became an alcoholic recluse in a dilapidated shack and died a pauper.

'Oubaas Nel is not just bitter about the betrayal of his sons,' said a digger, 'but that it was his own people who did it to them.'

'Yes, it's true. Afrikaners did it to Afrikaners. It shocked everybody.'

According to brother Mike Goosen, when Corrie first heard that 829 uncut stones worth almost R11 million were stashed away in the safe of First National Bank in Bloemhof, not only did his mouth water, but his blood sputtered and bubbled like champagne. The Nel family fortune comprised 2 401 carats – too many diamonds for a man to hold in his cupped hands. Among them were a 12-carat rare yellow and an 11.5-carat blue stone the shape of Africa. Marius and Deon Nel had hoarded their best diamonds since they started digging in 1982.

Goosen and Barnard first approached the brothers in 1994, almost a year before they finally laid their hands on the prize. Marius and Deon gave the two ruffians in their fast cars one look and resolved not to do business with them.

'The long hair and the earrings? They were hooligans. I thought, no thank you, I won't do any deals with you,' said Marius, a stern-faced, clean-cut Afrikaner who grew up on the family farm.

The gangsters introduced themselves as agents for an Israeli businessman who was prepared to pay 30 per cent over the market price for the diamonds. The Nel brothers turned them away, but Goosen and Barnard kept coming back, each time with a better offer. 'The said they moved in high circles in the security establishment,' said Deon, a rather scruffy-looking miner with a raspy voice. 'Ferdi opened the boot of his BMW and revealed a false compartment in which there were machine guns and hand grenades. I didn't trust them, but they were clearly powerful people.'

In order to boost their standing with the brothers, Ferdi told them he had assassinated David Webster and recruited Anton Lubowski's killer. 'He said he blasted Webster at short range with a shotgun. I thought it was kind of normal because Webster was a troublemaker who had to be eliminated,' said Deon.

Ferdi gave the brothers an AK-47 of which the serial number had been obliterated. When Marius and Deon visited Johannesburg, Goosen and Barnard introduced them to their favourite policeman: Brixton murder and robbery chief Colonel Charlie Landman. Marius said the colonel had assured them that Corrie and Ferdi were reliable and trustworthy.

Landman owed Barnard a favour. Two years earlier, as democracy dawned across South Africa, Landman's career needed a boost that would propel him to the next rank, so that he could quit the force with a more substantial golden handshake. Barnard obliged by planting a mini-limpet mine under Landman's car and detonated the device early one morning. Landman narrowly escaped death. He had a hangover and had forgotten about the arrangement. A cell-phone call from Barnard had jogged his befuddled memory with seconds to spare. Pan Africanist Congress 'terrorists' were blamed for trying to kill the dutiful policeman. He left the SA Police with the rank of brigadier and a tidy financial package.

It was the lure of an additional three or four million rand that finally seduced the Nel brothers into making a deal with Goosen and Barnard, the hairstyles, garish jewellery and mag-wheeled cars notwithstanding. They gave Ferdi and Corrie – who was a diamond virtuoso, according to the brothers – a list of the stones by colour and carat. The thieves reported back that the Israeli buyer seemed happy with the quality and quantity, but wanted to inspect the diamonds. He was prepared to fly to South Africa.

A meeting was set up at a downmarket resort hotel outside the drab metropolis of Klerksdorp. Goosen and Barnard were booked into one room, the Nels into an adjoining one. The brothers arrived in a pickup armed with revolvers and semi-automatic pistols. Corrie and Ferdi, also armed to the teeth, drove to the hotel in a white BMW M5 with another ruffian by the name of Vivian Beukes. The Nels recognised him as a former digger from the Bloemhof area.

As Deon went to fetch the diamonds, Beukes suddenly fired a shot. Deon, clutching the metal box containing the diamonds, got one helluva fright and stumbled. The box fell to the floor. Corrie, not a small man but darting like a flash, gathered the loot and scurried to his car. 'We are being robbed! They have fucking robbed us!' screamed Marius. As Goosen and Beukes roared off, the Nels opened fire on their car. Goosen hit the barrier lining the exit route, careered over a row of low pylons, and seconds later was speeding down the road to Ventersdorp.

The Nels, realising that the family fortune was about to disappear into thin air, jumped into their pickup. They summoned the police on their *burgerband* (citizen band) radio and called on farmers to set up roadblocks along the way. Hanging out of the window with his LM-6 machine gun, Marius fired forty-eight rounds at the BMW. 'I shot to kill,' he said. 'And I'm a damn good shot. But they just raced on.' Police later found several bullets lodged in the seats of the armour-plated car.

The high-speed chase led by Goosen and Beukes in their BMW, with the Nel brothers in their pickup some distance behind, was joined by wailing police cars and farmers from the district who had answered the call to arms. The pursuers eventually found the BMW abandoned in bushes next to the road. The Nels, the police and farmers scoured the nearest mealie field for the fugitives. They found Beukes hiding behind an anthill about three kilometres from the car. When they found Corrie under a thorn tree, covered with leaves, he was shirtless and had only his revolver and a cellphone. The diamonds were gone.

'If I'd had another bullet, he would've been dead. He didn't deserve to live,' said Marius later.

Barnard, meanwhile, had been arrested at the hotel. He claimed he was there to clinch a legitimate deal and knew nothing about a robbery. 'You think I'm a robber? You must be joking,' he told the police.

Goosen and Beukes were taken to a small police station outside Klerksdorp and locked in the cells. That night, a well-dressed man arrived at the station, introduced himself as Advocate Johan Joubert and demanded to see his clients. A policeman on duty took him to the holding cells.

Of course the visitor wasn't a lawyer at all, or even named Joubert. It was none other than Johan, one of Corrie Goosen's brothers. Also a diamond smuggler (all the Goosen brothers had criminal records), Johan had faked his own death in 1992 to pocket a R172 000 insurance claim. His wife claimed he had drowned off the West Coast of the Cape. Two years later, he was arrested in the Western Transvaal for smuggling diamonds and convicted of fraud. Ironically, not long after visiting Corrie and Beukes in the cells, he really did die, in a motorcycle accident.

After Johan left that night, Corrie offered four policemen R100 000 each to set him and Beukes free. Before sunrise, one of the cops on duty unlocked their cells and drove off with Goosen and Beukes in his car – probably to pick up the box of diamonds they had flung from their car window while fleeing the Nels.

Marius and Deon Nel searched for the diamonds for two days. An army unit with landmine detectors was called in to help. 'It was my future, my security, my savings,' said Deon. 'I was confused for a year. All I thought about was murder. I wanted to kill Ferdi and Corrie.'

The brothers couldn't face their father. Oom Fanie Nel, a dignified and bespectacled maize farmer, had learnt about the robbery from a radio newscast. 'It was like a death in the family,' he said. 'Our sadness was so much more because the thieves were Afrikaners. I really struggled with my Christian duty to forgive them. I couldn't.'

Fanie Nel ordered the closure of his diamond diggings. When I interviewed Marius more than two years later at the abandoned mine, equipment worth millions of rand was rusting away. 'It ruined our family,' said Deon. 'At one point I took my gun and drove to Port Elizabeth to shoot Corrie. I turned around halfway and came back. I knew I would land up in prison. Instead, I went to Angola to work on a diamond mine.'

Although Goosen, Barnard and Beukes were charged with robbery and released on bail, none of them believed they would go to prison. A day or two after the robbery, Corrie arrived at the Randfontein home of childhood friend Dawie Lotter and said: '*Tjomma*, that was a great one. I enjoyed it. Can you believe I did it?'

When I saw Corrie Goosen for the first time, he was standing next to Ralph Heyns in the dock of the Johannesburg Magistrate's Court on charges of stealing yet another parcel of diamonds. Heyns had squeezed his bulk into an ill-fitting cream-coloured suit, while Goosen sported his usual hoodlum attire. They looked like unruly delinquents in dire need of a barber and a tailor. Butter couldn't melt in their mouths as they pleaded not guilty to the charges.

They managed to secure bail of R20 000 each. Investigators found it inconceivable that they were granted bail at all, given their history of previous convictions and the fact that Goosen was already standing trial for the Klerksdorp heist. It later emerged that he had on his payroll a policeman at the Criminal Bureau in Pretoria, who had removed his fingerprints and criminal record from the computer.

After Goosen and Heyns were granted bail, I picked Goosen up at a police station. He thanked the policemen for their hospitality while he was in the cells. We landed up in a Melville bar, where he ordered a double rum and Coke and gulped it down. Before long he was drunk and coming on to the waitress. He took her hand, heaved himself to his feet and warbled: 'Don't you want to meet an honest man?' When she gaped nervously at the greasy ruffian, he vowed: 'I'll put the biggest stone on your finger you've ever seen.'

Goosen made no secret of his diamond deals, and before long the whole dive knew he had buried himself in the Western Transvaal soil before making off with the box of diamonds. Although the South African landscape had changed immeasurably since 1994 and many of Goosen's police contacts had quit the force, he still believed he was untouchable and could bribe, connive and bully himself out of trouble.

His confidence was not unfounded. Not only did he have a cop at the Criminal Bureau cleaning his record, but dockets also disappeared and witnesses were intimidated and paid to change their testimony. Victims were threatened with harm unless they withdrew complaints. Deon Nel got anonymous phone calls promising the annihilation of his family if he pressed charges in the Klerksdorp case. When that didn't work, Goosen negotiated with Marius Nel to return the diamonds and pay him R300 000 in return for dropping the case.

Klerksdorp Gold Squad cop Flip Kruger was investigating fifteen cases of diamond theft and smuggling against Goosen. He couldn't find witnesses who were prepared to face them in court. Equally exasperated was Sergeant Johan Strauss, his shabby office in a Johannesburg police station piled with unsolved dockets. He was investigating eleven cases against the gang, ranging from fraud and theft to assault.

'There's cases where the investigation took three years. When we get to court, the witnesses are not there. They've been threatened. It makes me mad,' said Strauss.

'Corrie offered me R100 000 to make four dockets disappear. I refused,' he said. He had to lock up his dockets at another police station to prevent them from being stolen by his own colleagues. Strauss said he was determined to get the gang behind bars, but the suspects persevered. Heyns was building a multimillion-rand nightclub on a hill outside Krugersdorp at the time. He offered the sergeant the position as head of security at the establishment.

'Are you going to take it?' I asked him.

'I'm not sure,' he said. 'I earn R4 000 a month. And that's before deductions. It's not easy to live on.'

None of Sergeant Strauss's cases were successfully prosecuted.

I received a phone call from the National Prosecuting Authority's special investigation unit – the Scorpions – in Pretoria. 'I have a present for you,' said a contact. An hour or so later, I was in the capital. The gift turned out to be a videotape of Corrie Goosen's tawdry funeral. The Scorpions had just conducted an investigation to confirm that the mutilated body in the Port Elizabeth morgue was indeed that of Goosen.

His death provoked mixed emotions. Good-for-nothings such as Ferdi Barnard lamented his passing, while 200 kilometres away in the Western Transvaal, diamond digger Deon Nel said: 'He should never have been born in the first place. He deserves death.'

Like many others, Nel didn't believe that Goosen was dead. His brother had faked his own demise, and Corrie's accident happened while he was standing trial for the Klerksdorp diamond robbery. His disfigured face added to the suspicion that Goosen had staged his own death to escape justice.

Heyns was at his Roodepoort supermarket when Mike Goosen visited him. 'He told me Corrie was dead. Twenty-six years of friendship was gone. But I suppose that's life. I call it the circle of life.'

Heyns rushed to Port Elizabeth to pay his respects to the widow. Two years earlier, Debbie Goosen had persuaded her husband to move to the Eastern Cape in the hope that he would start leading a crime-free life. It didn't help.

'I made about R35 million with this guy in my time,' said Ralph. 'I spoke to Corrie on the morning before he died and he said he had a business deal for us. He didn't see diamond smuggling as a crime. He always said God put diamonds in the earth and they were there for all to use.'

The speedometer of Goosen's Honda Blackbird froze on impact and showed he was travelling at more than 300 km/h. Sixteen-year-old Corrie junior was on his own Blackbird behind his father and witnessed the accident. Before help arrived, he kneeled next to his father's body and removed an ornate gold chain from around his neck.

Jimmy Abbott, the boxer-turned-pastor, said he tried in vain for six months before Corrie's death to convert the gangster. 'He had his good things,' said Abbott. 'It's just that some people are a little bit gooder than others. In the end it's not how good you are, but how you've led your life: like a candle in the wind.'

Although Jimmy had had the nickname of Jumbo in his heyday, he had since swelled out tremendously. I interviewed him in a hospital bed in Port Elizabeth, where he was being treated for some or other ailment. Slabs of flab hung over the sides of the bed.

'All I can say is that I hope as Corrie hit that pole, he had a second to speak to God. And that he would have said: "Oh God, please forgive me for whatever I have done."'

Snorting smack in his Rosebank brothel, a befuddled Barnard mourned the loss of his friend. He described Goosen as someone with a heart of gold who had once bought a destitute woman a kilogram of mince and a kilogram of boerewors. He played us Goosen's favourite song, 'Ride', by Joe Satriani.

> *I know some people like to take life easy,*
> *That's not my style.*
> *I'm not the type to let this life tease me,*
> *I'm gonna make it wild.*
> *I just wanna ride,*
> *Get on my bike and ride.*

Childhood friend Dawie Lotter, sporting a bad poodle cut, knobs of gold on his fingers and a thin moustache, remembered Corrie for the millions and millions he'd made. 'He would always say he had done a small deal,' he said with a goon's swagger, 'but when he opened the boot of his car, what a sight to see! Ten million, five million at a time. It's nice to touch money like that. It's like a baby's bum.'

Nobody was ever sure what happened to Corrie's money. 'Two months before his death,' said his brother Mike, 'he said he'd generated R25 million with diamonds, but that he had nothing to show for it. It went into Debbie, the in-laws and friends.'

A few weeks after Goosen's death, Heyns opened his new nightclub. Called Bend-the-Rule and built at a cost of more than R8 million, the establishment was his lifelong dream. I was invited to the opening night and spent it in the VIP section of the club with the likes of Calla Botha and Dawie Lotter. Also there was Debbie, her blonde mane rippling in the breeze of the air conditioner, wearing a short black dress and stiletto heels. She refused to speak to me and had eyes only for Ralph.

As he took me on a tour of the club, he beamed with pride and said: 'You know what? I look at this and I know I've made it to the top.'

'And you and Debbie?' I asked him. 'Are the two of you now an item?'

Ralph just laughed and said: 'She's a dream woman.'

Ferdi Barnard was being consumed by an orgy of whoring, drugs and crime. He snorted several grams of cocaine a day and smoked crack non-stop. He would arrive home in the early morning hours and order Amor to cook more crack over a gas flame in the kitchen. He said if she really loved him, she would smoke with him. She did. Their daughter Shania, aged two, watched.

'In the beginning it was only once a month, then it became twice a month,' said Badenhorst when I met her several years later at a hotel in Krugersdorp.

'He would give me cocaine for two days, then keep it from me for two days. He liked to play games with people.'

Afraid of him overdosing, Badenhorst would take Barnard out to pace the streets of Roodepoort at dawn. He would try to work the crack out of his body, holding on to Amor in what he called his 'dance of death'. At the age of thirty-eight, he was grey and gaunt and appeared to be in the twilight of his life.

The crack made Ferdi suspicious, paranoid, greedy. He stopped paying the bills. Amor was barred from shopping, even if Shania went hungry. He imprisoned them in the house. He posted men to guard the entrance. The only visitor Amor was allowed was Julie Wilken, who brought them food from time to time. Amor and Shania lived through the winter of 1996 without electricity or a telephone. Shania soon showed signs of neglect. The child would rarely bath, seldom eat, never play.

'I was his possession and I loved him very much. I was probably the only one who thought there was something good in him. Life with him consisted of four walls. I was the dumb blonde on the side.'

Badenhorst was involved in several of the 'knocks' performed by Barnard and his gang. He once came back from Lesotho with a million rand. When she walked into the kitchen, the money was lying on the floor. She took R80 000 and stuffed it under the bath.

Barnard spent more and more time at his brothels in Johannesburg's northern suburbs. I visited him several times at The Palace and Club 69. Classified ads in the newspapers touted Club 69 as an 'erotic exploration', a place where clients could 'live out your orgasm in our famous fantasy suite' and offered the 'deep throat dome, porn palace and pool room'. Situated on the doorstep of South Africa's most affluent residential area, the 'club' boasted one of the best addresses in the city: 92 Oxford Road, Rosebank.

In the dimly lit parlour, scantily clad women in stiletto heels sucked on cigarettes while waiting for the doorbell to announce the next john. Their nails were painted either a deep burgundy or fire-engine red. There were a few brunettes with small breasts, but blondes and double-Ds vastly outnumbered them.

Drinking rum and snorting cocaine, Barnard lamented the fact that the noose of justice was slowly tightening around him and he could no longer operate with the impunity he had enjoyed during the apartheid years. He was already standing trial in the Klerksdorp robbery, and for once it seemed he couldn't make the case go away.

'They've got fuck all. I'm waiting for them,' he said defiantly. 'I cannot plan my life, because I know they want my blood. There is nothing I can offer any woman. What do I say to her? I have lost two women and two children. I will never get another job.' Every now and then he disappeared to snort another line of coke. 'Just to sober up,' he'd say when he returned.

As Barnard stood there, his 1.9-metre frame rocking back and forth, he said: 'I will go to prison, but I will fight them till the bitter end.'

He often spoke about apartheid, and once told me: 'You know, I've never hated the *kaffir*. That is not the way I was brought up. I fought terrorists and communists, not black people. There was a time when I thought you were a communist, you and that *kaffir* Max du Preez. Both of you were targets, but I've watched you over the years, and you were right. Apartheid was stupid. It wasn't right.'

Barnard was open about his crack and cocaine addiction and said that most of his money had 'gone up in smoke' and that he was struggling financially. He was spending up to R50 000 a month on drugs. He sometimes smoked crack with prostitutes at the brothel, but two girls overdosed and he had to give one mouth-to-mouth resuscitation. The girl bit his lip and he had to have stitches. Amor also overdosed. Her heart stopped beating and Barnard had to rush her to the emergency unit of Ontdekkers Hospital in Roodepoort.

'I once had four television sets in my house, but they are gone, sold to get crack,' he said. 'Some nights I'm too scared to go to sleep in case I overdose. I walk up and down the street at night and can't control the muscles in my face.'

Sitting in Club 69, he told me: 'I have told you many things in the past, and you have never dropped me.'

He kept quiet and then added: 'If you do, I will kill you.'

The morning after my documentary on the life and times of Eugene de Kock was screened, Barnard called me to obtain a videotape of the programme. He was one of the characters I had interviewed for the documentary and we met at a restaurant in Melville.

He was accompanied by a man named Rassie, who didn't speak much and was clearly there to look after Barnard, who excused himself and went to the toilet several times, probably to take another fix of coke.

Rassie was none other than Lieutenant Erasmus of the police Organised Crime Unit. Instead of investigating Barnard for a series of crimes ranging from murder to diamond smuggling, he was acting as his guardian.

At about four o'clock that afternoon, Barnard must have run out of drugs and ordered me to go with him to his car. We got in and he lit a crack pipe, drawing the smoke deep into his lungs.

His head was bouncing and hopping like a rubber ball on his broad shoulders. Clutched between his thumb and forefinger was the thin glass syringe, stuffed with a mixture of tobacco and small cocaine crystals.

'It's true, I killed him,' he suddenly said. He kept quiet for a second or two, then said again: 'It's true. I shot him.'

'Who?' I asked.

'David Webster.'

The tiny orange coal in his crack pipe glowed brightly in the afternoon light as it slowly burnt down the syringe, consuming the crystals and tobacco. He blew a streak of white smoke against the windscreen, where it exploded in a million molecules.

'He flew through the air and landed on the pavement. I saw it, because I shot him. I did it.'

Before he continued, he put the pipe in his mouth again and inhaled deeply. 'I pulled the trigger,' he said. 'I shot him.'

We looked at one another. I didn't say anything, too scared to interrupt him.

'I was paid a R40 000 production bonus after the killing. For a job well done. It was an approved operation and Joe Verster knew about everything.'

Silence again. The coal had burnt almost to the bottom of the pipe.

'Who were the other people in the car with you?'

'There was only one other person.'

'Was it Eugene Riley?'

'No.'

'Chappies Maree?'

'No.'

'Calla Botha?'

He laughed. 'I'm not going to say anything. Maybe he was, maybe he wasn't. Make your own deduction.'

'Why don't you confess and ask for amnesty?'

'I won't. I will never ask for amnesty.'

'And what about Anton Lubowski?'

'No, I didn't kill him.'

'You told me some years ago you tried to shoot him at one stage.'

'Yes, that's true. Everything I told you was true. But I didn't pull the trigger.'

His pipe was finished.

'Come on,' he said, 'let's go back. People are going to think we are two *moffietjies* (gay boys) sitting here in the car.'

Hell hath no fury like a woman scorned. Every man knows it, but for Barnard the realisation came too late. Henry Hill in *Goodfellas* warned against good-time girls who live in the shadows but always lend an ear to the confessions and boasting of the thugs who share their beds. 'Pillow talk is the most dangerous of all romantic activities and it has betrayed many a villain over the years. We'd all like to think it would never happen to us, but look at the number of cases where a police prosecution relies on the word of a disgruntled gangster's moll, spilling the beans to get her revenge. They can really fuck you up.'

In Barnard's case, it wasn't just one woman who spat venom after years of abuse, neglect and humiliation. A trio of lady loves, all infatuated with vengeance, marched to the Pretoria Supreme Court in 1998 to get back at the man they had once loved passionately, but who treated them like dirt and dumped them for crime, whores and drugs.

Twenty-nine year-old Amor Badenhorst, the child prostitute and striptease artist turned gangland tart, fled Barnard's home and found a warm welcome in the camp of Deputy Attorney-General Anton Ackermann, the criminal prosecutor who had put Eugene de Kock in prison for life. Ferdi Barnard had met his match.

Badenhorst and Shania were placed in witness protection and whisked away to the Western Cape. She said in her statement that Barnard had admitted to her that he shot David Webster and committed a host of other crimes.

Former wife Maryna Language said she had read about the Webster murder and spoke to Barnard that night. He said Webster's girlfriend 'screamed like a stuck pig' when he pumped the shot into the anti-apartheid activist. She said she lived in constant fear of Barnard. 'I believed he was going to kill me. He told me that many, many times, and I did not want my child to grow up with him.'

Brenda Milne, who had lived with Barnard for several years, made notes of his devilry out of fear for her life and that of her child. Barnard visited her days after Webster's death and confessed his role. 'He was very excited, he was agitated, he was nervous, he was, I think, scared. Things had happened very unexpectedly.'

After years of striding upwards and onwards in his criminal career without official hindrance, the might of the state was mustered against Barnard. Prosecutors drew up an indictment on thirty-four charges, including murder, conspiracy to murder, fraud, housebreaking, robbery, arson, and illegal possession of firearms and ammunition

But the killer fought back. The state temporarily lost Amor when Barnard traced her to her hideout. He offered her a car, a house and cash. She fell for his ploy and informed Ackermann that she no longer wished to testify against her former lover. There was clearly a leak in the Attorney-General's office, as Barnard had not only found out where Amor was, but knew the exact details of the indictment and investigation against him. However, when Badenhorst arrived back in Johannesburg to claim her hush money from Barnard, he was unable to deliver, and within days she was back in Ackermann's camp.

Since 1992, seven potential state witnesses against Barnard had died. The only eyewitness to Webster's murder, Johannes du Plessis, died of natural causes in the Johannesburg General Hospital in 1994. Corrie Goosen and his brother Johan were both killed in motorcycle accidents. Eugene Riley was murdered.

The most suspicious death was that of Carol-Anne Harris, girlfriend of drug dealer Mark Francis, whose murder was among the charges Barnard faced. Harris was abducted by two men and killed. Days before he was to testify against Barnard, another state witness, Crunchy Johnson, was murdered in his house outside Pretoria.

On the eve of giving evidence, Badenhorst said: 'I want to hurt him like he hurt me.' Then she stepped into the witness box and disgorged a tale of murder, sadism, abuse and depravity.

On a summer's day in February 1998, I took the stand against Ferdi Barnard in the same court and recollected his confession of October 1996.

Months before, I had made an affidavit and informed Ackermann that I was willing to testify. A lot of soul-searching had gone into my decision. Journalists are honour-bound to protect confidential sources and are expected to face prison or a firing squad rather than reveal the names of their informants. But was the conversation I had had with Barnard in his car confidential, off the record and therefore unpublishable? My feeling was that as far as his confession was concerned, there was no agreement between us. He had simply shot his mouth off and I had given no undertaking to never spill the beans. I felt a tremendous citizen's duty to help bring Barnard down, and Ackermann assured me he needed my testimony.

I discussed my dilemma with the likes of friend Max du Preez, former newspaper editor Allister Sparks and colleague Peta Thornycroft. What should I do? Treat his confession as privileged, or do my public duty and stand up against him? They agreed with me and urged me to testify.

I was due to take the stand at a later stage of the case, but on hearing that I was on my way to Algeria to produce a television documentary, Ackermann ushered me into court much sooner than expected. Algeria was a horribly unsafe place for journalists and he wasn't taking any chances.

Beset by a mixture of guilt and fear, I didn't look at the accused once. Sitting only a few metres from me, I could feel his eyes tunnelling a hole through me.

His lawyer, Faan Coetzee, accused me of lying and setting Barnard up. He said I had offered to buy Barnard crack from my entertainment allowance (I wished I had one!). 'If he did say he killed Dr Webster,' said Coetzee, 'it was said in a senseless babble while under the influence of crack. Barnard will say that for days before he met you at the restaurant he continuously used crack.' I responded by saying that although Barnard was using drugs at the time, he definitely appeared to know what he was saying.

After the state closed its case, Barnard took the stand and denied every charge against him. 'Initially, I did not want to know anything about Pauw,' he told the court, 'but after discussing it with my superiors and with Eugene de Kock, we decided to launch an operation that amounted to a smear campaign against him.'

He said that for much of the time in question he had been under the influence of crack and cocaine, which 'makes your head funny'. He spent 90 per cent of his income on cocaine, he said. 'I was so under the influence of crack pipes that I cannot even remember what I discussed with Pauw that day. I can't think that I would have confessed to Webster's murder, because I did not do it.'

Throughout the trial, Barnard still strutted his gangster walk during tea and lunch breaks and attempted to unnerve witnesses by staring at them unflinchingly. But under cross-examination, Ackermann reduced the once baleful and forceful bully to a bumbling halfwit. He turned out to be a hopeless liar. The judge told him so: 'Mr. Barnard, you twist the truth to suit yourself.'

His lawyer admitted that he was unable to find even one witness who was prepared to testify for the killer. As he hunkered down in the dock while his freedom audibly moved out of reach, only his father, doggedly occupying a seat every day of the trial, remained loyal to Barnard. In the end, his deceit and lies stood alone against the detailed testimony of eleven witnesses about Barnard's admissions that he killed David Webster.

Dressed in a double-breasted jacket, sea-green shirt and patterned blue and yellow tie, a solemn-faced Barnard was led into the courtroom on the morning of 1 June 1998. His mother, wearing gold chains around her neck and a glittering purple dress, hugged him. Piet Barnard pressed a couple of R50 notes into his son's hand.

Judge Johan Els convicted Barnard on the strength of witnesses who said he had told them he had murdered Webster. He described my testimony as credible and accepted it in full. He found it 'highly unlikely that the accused could make the statement to eleven different people at eleven different times if it wasn't the truth'.

Barnard was also convicted of murdering Francis, attempting to murder Dullah Omar and of twenty-two additional crimes. He was sentenced to life imprisonment.

'You get used to anything,' Barnard said on being found guilty. 'That is how the human spirit works. I can look after myself.'

One of his first visitors at Pretoria Central Prison's maximum-security section – C-Max – was Amor Badenhorst. She professed her continued love for him. Barnard, however, had the last laugh.

A few days later, a social worker visited Amor. She was told that Ferdi's parents, on behalf of their son, had instituted legal proceedings to get custody

Bloody trail of the SA Police. Coetzee speaks, and
Vrye Weekblad publishes, 17 November 1989

Week after week, we publish more
death squad allegations, 1 December 1989

CCB assassin Pieter Botes speaks out
and tells how he had made 'a little sauce'
out of Albie Sachs's arm, 11 May 1990

Confessions from the bowels of a madhouse.
Ronald Bezuidenhout tells about bombs,
assassinations and torture, 17 May 1991

Martin Welz

Max du Preez and the *Vrye Weekblad* team ... a bunch of
ducktails and anarchists. I'm hiding behind Max

Max du Preez and I leave the Rand Supreme Court with apartheid assassin
Lesley Lesia – a surprise witness – during our court battle with General Lothar Neethling

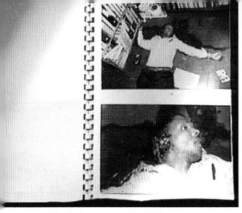

Journal of death. Soweto lawyer Bheki Mlangeni, blown up by a parcel bomb sent by Vlakplaas assassin Eugene de Kock in 1990

The Vlakplaas death squad at a team-building exercise on the KwaZulu-Natal coast

Vlakplaas commander Eugene de Kock in conversation with his men

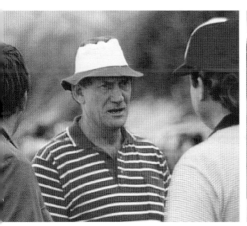

General Krappies Engelbrecht, the policeman who had to cover up the Vlakplaas campaign of death

The Vlakplaas men at play

The scene that confronted me upon our arrival at the Roman Catholic mission of Nyarubuye in south-east Rwanda – thousands upon thousands who had been shot, hacked, clubbed and stabbed to death. Filmed in May 1994

Reporting from the Roman Catholic mission at Nyarubuye in Rwanda. My head was a confused mess and I cannot remember what went through my mind

The day in May 1994 when I ignited a battle in Rwanda. Minutes after doing this stand-upper, all hell broke loose

RPF rebels pounded government positions with heavy machine-gun fire, mortars and RPG rocket launchers. This battle was a result of my misguided zeal

His eyes were vacant and he didn't blink. We offered him food; he didn't respond. When we left an hour or so later, he was still sitting in the same position. Rwanda, May 1994

All that remained from a looted house in Gisenyi, Rwanda, during the genocide. August 1994

Calamity in Zaire following the 1994 Rwandan genocide. Thousands upon thousands died of disease. They fell down next to the road, died in makeshift hospitals and collapsed at waterholes. Filmed in August 1994

Those who died during the night were rolled up in straw mats or cloth and left next to the road for collection

A mass grave in Zaire during the Rwandan refugee crisis following the genocide. Filmed in August 1994

Three months after the start of the genocide: a million people trapped on a bed of lava rock in a refugee camp in Zaire. Filmed in August 1994

One of the refugee camps in Zaire. Filmed in August 1994

Cameraman Ivan Oberholzer and I in a Zairean refugee camp

Zaire's refugee camps hid the world's single largest congregation of fugitives and killers. Interviewing an *interahamwe* leader in a Zairean refugee camp after he had just killed an alleged thief. Filmed in August 1994

Moving with RPF soldiers across the volcanoes in northern Rwanda, March 1999

The Nyarubuye skulls, five years later and neatly stacked in a genocide museum. Filmed in March 1999

Tony Karamba, our rebel guide in 1994, returns to the Roman Catholic mission at Nyarubuye five years later

Genocide accused Enose Nsabimana emerges from a makeshift prison in the south-east of Rwanda. Filmed in March 1999

Enose Nsabimana, clutching the skull of the neighbour he had clubbed to death during the genocide in 1994

Pastor Athanase Ngirinshuti, accusing
his bishop of genocide, August 2000

Spy footage of genocide bishop
Samuel Musabyimana in Melville,
Johannesburg, August 2000

The arrest of Rwandan bishop Samuel Musabyimana
in Hillbrow, Johannesburg, August 2000

Genocide survivors Fulgence Mukunzi (left)
and Lingo Ndizihiwe relive the murder spree of
their bishop, Samuel Musabyimana, in Shyogwe,
Rwanda, in 1994 (interviewed in September 2000)

Trekking through a bamboo forest up a volcano
in northern Rwanda in search of some of Africa's
last remaining mountain gorillas, August 2001

Coming face to face with Africa's greatest apes.
This is a silverback in the Sousa group

Vlakplaas and apartheid death squad commander
Eugene de Kock, photographed at the Pretoria Supreme
Court during his trial that ended in October 1996

Eugene de Kock filmed during an *in loco* inspection of Vlakplaas during his court case

Apartheid assassin Joe Mamasela tells me how he had participated in the killing of the Pebco Three, December 1995

Gangster Corrie Goosen, whom I
interviewed in December 1995

Funeral of a gangster. Corrie Goosen is
laid to rest in Port Elizabeth following
a motorcycle accident in May 1997

Apartheid assassin and gangster Ferdi Barnard, drunk and drugged at his Johannesburg brothel, June 1996

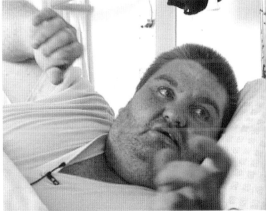

Former heavyweight boxer Jimmy Abbott, interviewed in his hospital bed
about the death of his gangster buddy Corrie Goosen, August 1997

The killing fields of Sudan,
filmed in May 1998

Mass murderer and war criminal Foday Sankoh,
spitting fire at me during our interview
in Freetown, Sierra Leone, October 1999

Captain Cut-Hand, eleven-year-old Sherief Koroma,
pulling faces at the camera during our interview
in Freetown, Sierra Leone, October 1999

Sherief Koroma singing Sierra Leone's
national anthem at school. Saluting is a custom
he learnt at rebel bases deep in the country's jungles

One of the victims of Foday Sankoh's madcap policies: rebels
forced thirteen-year-old Issatu Kargbo's hands
onto the stump of a mango tree. Then they hacked
them off with an axe. Filmed in October 1999

Condemned to a life of begging. Lansana Sessay in
an amputee camp in Freetown, Sierra Leone. After a boy
had hacked off his hands, a rebel smashed out his teeth

Prophet of doom ... Nigerian faith healer TB Joshua praying for South African
pilgrims in the Synagogue in Lagos, in April 2001. None was healed

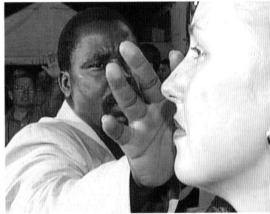

South African Springbok rugby player Wium Basson,
dying of liver cancer. Joshua refused to pray for him

Wium Basson being comforted by his mother after
Nigerian prophet TB Joshua had refused to pray for him

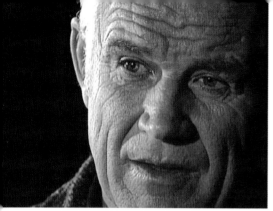

Alex Stellianos … once also known
as Johannes Lodewikus Koekemoer

Inside a Maputo drug house. Sitting with a spy camera
on his lap, Alex Stellianos is offered a plate of crack

Spy camera footage taken inside Maputo's drug houses in May 2003. Heroin addicts 'chasing the dragon'

Spy footage of a heroin dealer in Pemba, Mozambique,
handing Alex Stellianos a capsule of heroin brought from
Pakistan in the stomach of a drug mule, June 2003

Spy camera footage of Tanzanian drug baron
Mangala cutting off a piece of heroin for
Alex Stellianos in Dar es Salaam, June 2003

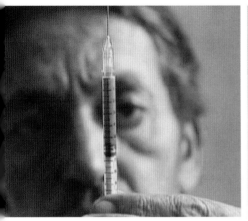

A junky journey through junkie life.
Mozambican veterinary surgeon Carlos Felner
preparing a fix of heroin. Filmed in August 2003

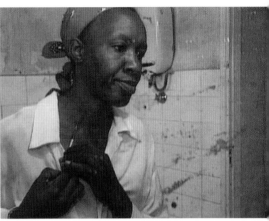

A French kiss in paradise. Heroin addict
Dadinha in Maputo, Mozambique, in
August 2003, injecting herself with heroin

Filming police sergeant Japie Mahidi with a spy
camera inside room 6A of the Booysens police station,
where immigrants had to pay bribes in order
to stay in the country. Filmed in July 2005

Nigerian drug dealer Justin Okyeokwu captured on
spy camera negotiating with a police sergeant
for the release of his cohort. He paid the
policeman R300. Filmed in August 2005

Forced into the role of a Nollywood movie star ... here I am playing the role of a British missionary in a seventeenth-century Igbo epic in a village in rural Nigeria. Filmed in March 2005

Playing a British missionary in a Nollywood epic. This could only have happened in Nigeria

Producer/director/actress/scriptwriter Chinny Ahaneku directing her epic in a rural village in Nigeria

The princess bride, played by Chinny Ahaneku, dances in front of the British missionary – that's me!

Cameraman extraordinaire, friend and travel companion Jan de Klerk

Faring the Congo on board the river boat the *Tshopo* – a stinking, noisy, overheated, overcrowded African market that is part supermarket, part disco, part abattoir and part brothel, June 2004

Oggi Saidi, fisherman, tourist guide and interpreter

Cabine de luxe! Our dark hole on the *Tshopo*. A day after we left harbour, it started filling with water. Oggi Saidi is lowering our luggage into the hole

Destined for lunch. Day 2 of
our journey on the Congo River

Sailing across the equator aboard the *Tshopo*. As Joseph Conrad wrote a
century ago: 'An empty stream, a great silence, an impenetrable forest'

Writing this book in Phnom Penh,
Cambodia, December 2005

Receiving the award for the best television
feature at CNN's African Journalist of
the Year Award, Maputo, July 2006

of Shania. In his affidavit, Ferdi called her an unfit mother. She had, after all, admitted under oath that she had participated in criminal activities and drug abuse.

Some weeks later, the Children's Court awarded custody of Shania to her grandparents.

Two years later, gone were the poodle cut, the swagger and the hopping and bouncing head, but Ferdi Barnard was back on stage, this time intent on avenging himself against those who had abandoned him during his trial.

With an electronic prison-issue 'cattle prodder' shackled to his waist, he took his seat at a TRC hearing and said: 'I'm not here to make anybody happy. I'm doing what I want to do.'

He began by confessing that he had killed Webster. 'He stood with his back to us. I called his name, he turned around and I fired one shot intended to hit him in the heart. He fell and we drove off.' He named fellow operative Calla Botha as the man in the car with him and accused CCB head Joe Verster of giving the order.

Because he had shunned the amnesty process offered by the ANC government to former security force operators, his public confessions came too late to do Barnard any good. He knew he could not be released from prison, but said he wanted to make a clean breast of his political crimes 'for the sake of reconciliation'.

He admitted plotting to kill three South African cabinet ministers, and said the CCB had authorised the Lubowski assassination. Barnard had also been ordered to beat up Finnish diplomat Marti Ahtisaari while he was head of the United Nations mission in pre-independence Namibia.

'I was instructed to fuck him up good but not to kill him,' said Barnard. 'I thought of using a baseball bat, but there was too much traffic in the hotel foyer.' He then asked for brass knuckles. He waited for Ahtisaari, who went on to become president of Finland, at a hotel in Keetmanshoop, but aborted the plan when his target failed to arrive. Barnard also revealed that plans had been hatched to release poisonous snakes at SWAPO political meetings and to wreck the cars of their white supporters.

He also admitted conspiring to kill Dullah Omar. 'I cocked my Makarov pistol with a silencer to shoot Omar, but he came out of the house with a woman. I decided not to shoot,' he said.

The woman at Omar's side was his wife Farieda, and in one of the most gut-wrenching moments of the TRC amnesty hearings, she and Barnard embraced and cried openly together. He said he had been moved when victims of apartheid's dirty tricks greeted him with a smile and showed concern about his well-being.

'As I was led past the gallery, Mrs Omar asked why I had no jacket. She wanted to know who was feeding me and said I must have a good night's sleep and she would pray for me. None of my people worried about me.'

The killer said he deeply regretted his actions and was prepared to spend the rest of his life behind bars. 'I'm not trying to send anyone to prison, though I would love to see Pik Botha and Roelf Meyer in C-Max overalls,' he said. He appealed to those he had harmed 'to find a place in your hearts to forgive me – especially you, Mrs Omar.'

Barnard's lawyer ended his submission with a quotation from American author Mark Twain: 'Forgiveness is the fragrance shed by the violet on the heel that crushes it.'

While writing this book, I had to dig deep into my Oxford thesaurus to find words to describe Ferdi Barnard. Abominable, depraved, offensive, repugnant, repulsive, monstrous, loathsome, odious, execrable, detestable, despicable. He fits all of those, and the list goes on.

I never saw Barnard's outpouring at the TRC and don't know what to make of it. Of course he was sorry for what he'd done. Most killers condemned to a life behind bars are. But I'm not for a moment going to suggest that his torrent of torment was not genuine. Prison changes people.

I'll always think of Ferdi Barnard as a charismatic thug who was as vile as any man can be, yet at the same time funny and strangely likeable. He once said to me: '*Jy dink ek's fokken sleg, né?*' (You think I'm fucking bad, hey?)

I didn't answer him. 'You don't know me,' he babbled (he was as high as a kite). 'But you'll see, one day. I'm not what they make me out to be.'

CHAPTER 10

Welcome to Hotel Mapel

*Long teeth, white tongues, sunken eye sockets, alien heads, ribcages
showing the crocodile-skin ridge of vertebrae poking up through the
back.*   **– Aidan Hartley**

I HAD NO IDEA WHERE WE WERE. THE UNITED NATIONS BUFFALO cargo aircraft was descending over a swampy savannah that, according to a book on my lap, teemed with sixty species of mosquito. The book also said that down below lived herdsmen who composed songs in honour of their cattle, dyed their hair with cow urine and, for the sake of beauty, smashed out their front teeth with fishing spears. This was a land blessed with a multi-tribal plethora of exotic people, the rivers Nile, and a natural beauty that veered between extraordinarily green and the vast bleakness of the Sahara and the Sahel.

But behind it all lurked a reality in which many eked out a scant existence, perpetually on the threshold of death. Life in the Republic of Sudan was difficult enough during times of peace. Malaria was endemic, along with bilharzia, tuberculosis, dysentery, drought, floods and infestations of locusts. Add famine, civil war, drought, human trafficking, ethnic massacres, rebel atrocities, government atrocities, gangs of rampaging militia and erratic boy soldiers and here brooded Africa's largest and longest-festering wound.

And TV cameraman Jan de Klerk and I had been dumped slap-bang in the middle of it. As we disembarked from the aircraft, we crashed headlong into a wall of suffocating heat. The Buffalo had also carried a cargo of emergency food aid for the starving masses in the area. As the bags of maize and boxes of cooking oil hit the ground, a platoon of rag-tag soldiers, some hardly taller than the Kalashnikovs they brandished, surrounded the bounty.

A few metres away stood a throng of stick-like figures. A bearded soldier sporting a red beret, epaulettes on his shoulders and a pistol in his hand, yapped something to them and barked a command at his soldiers. The juvenile riff-raff lifted their guns and curled their fingers around the triggers. The starving horde stopped and stared.

'Who are the people with the guns?' I asked Mac Anyang Yuang, our guide and translator.

'It's rebels. SPLA rebels,' said Mac, an angular young man with a head the shape of a soccer ball, missing front teeth and incisions across his forehead.

Once, he had also been a Dinka herd boy who glorified his father's livestock and smeared himself with cow dung to keep mosquitoes away. But man's aberrations had driven him south across the Sudanese border and into Kenya, where he ended up in a refugee camp. From there he made his way to Nairobi and loitered on the streets of the capital until he found Jan and me and convinced us to appoint him as our guide and translator.

'And what did the soldier say to the people?' I wanted to know.

'He said he'll shoot if they come closer to the food,' said Mac.

It was my first sight of famine, of people starving to death. Their heads looked like those of extraterrestrials and their spindly legs were no thicker than my arm. Hollow-cheeked babies with deep eye sockets and distended bellies clung to their mothers, whose breasts had long since been sucked dry, their nipples reduced to raisins. More twig-like characters squatted with bowed heads under hordes of flies next to motionless bundles that turned out to be babies and children who were too weak to get up.

The aircraft roared down the dirt runway, and within seconds climbed above a cloud of red dust into the sky. We were stranded in a hostile and desperate land, enveloped by a panorama of misery.

We had arrived at an obscure rebel outpost in the province of Bahr al-Ghazal in southern Sudan. There were no roads, taxis, hotels, government buildings, electricity, running water, telephones, cellphones, cold booze or an airport, let alone any form of transport to whisk us back to where we came from. The only remnants of Western civilisation were a makeshift field hospital manned by Médecins Sans Frontières and a small United Nations food centre.

The Buffalo would not return for a week – if the flight wasn't cancelled, the airspace closed or landing rights revoked. We'd been warned earlier that morning before taking off from the Kenyan border town of Lokichokkio that such things happened all the time.

As the aircraft made a wide circle and turned its nose back towards the Kenyan border I sneaked a look at Jan, sweat streaming down his face and body, and knew we were both wishing we were on that Buffalo, and asking ourselves: What the hell are we doing here?

In the winter of 1998, the SABC had commissioned Max du Preez and me to start an investigative current affairs show, which we called *Special Assignment*. Determined to showcase a hard-hitting documentary for our debut that would shock, startle and inform, I chose Sudan.

'Where are you going?' my mother asked me a week or two before my departure.

'Sudan,' I told her.

'And where's that?'

'In Africa,' I told her. 'South of Egypt and north of Ethiopia.'

'And what are you going to do there?'

'I'm doing a story. There's a famine and a war.'

'So?' she said.

Granted, my mother is white, conservative and oblivious to what happens on the greater African continent, but her nonchalant attitude about Sudan was by no means confined to the leafy suburbs of Centurion, a satellite town south-west of Pretoria. If Africa was the world's backwater, then Sudan was the drain. Everyone knew that, didn't they? For many years, one calamity after another had gone unnoticed. Africa's longest civil war had been raging there forever. The southern half of the country had been denuded of all infrastructure and millions had died or been driven across international borders into exile. Sudanese were selling Sudanese into slavery and countrymen were starving their compatriots to death. Everyone knew that, didn't they? So why did no one seem to care?

Sudan is Africa's biggest country, almost twice as large as South Africa and a quarter of the size of the United States. During the colonial era, Britain ruled Sudan as two distinct entities divided by religion and language, but at independence in 1956 artificially glued it together as a single state straddling Muslim and Arab Africa in the north, and black, Christian Africa in the south. It was a recipe for disaster. A long-standing animosity existed between north and south. For centuries Arab slave traders had conducted raids along the Nile and deep into the plains and swamplands of southern Sudan. African villagers were caught, roped together, and walked and shipped great distances to be sold as domestic servants, farm labourers and concubines.

How could these two hostile worlds coexist as a single independent nation, asked the doyen of foreign correspondents, Ryszard Kapuściński, in his book *The Shadow of the Sun*. They could not. 'The Arab lords in Khartoum could not tolerate the shepherds from the south having the same rights as they did. The people from the south could not accept as their rulers, in an independent Sudan, the sons of slave traders. The south demanded secession, their own state. The north decided to destroy the rebels. Massacres began.'

Sudan's history is a litany of coups, wars and famine. The first coup was in 1960. The first war erupted two years later and lasted a decade. Three years on, another coup brought Colonel Jaafar Nimeiri to power. He ruled for sixteen years and survived several more attempted coups. He granted some autonomy to the south, but withdrew it a few years later and imposed Sharia or Islamic law over the whole country, embarking on a process of radical Islamisation.

In 1983, a career colonel, John Garang, organised the Sudan People's Liber-ation Army (SPLA) and went to war against the government army commanded by President Omar Hassan al-Bashir. Although the SPLA took control of most of southern Sudan, a miscellany of armies and warring factions continued to wage war. Various splinter groups broke away from the SPLA and took up arms – against whom was not always clear.

Then there were the *murahaleen*, Arab militiamen on horseback who killed, maimed, raided, looted and burnt down tens of thousands of village homes of non-Arab people, in the process displacing hundreds of thousands. The *murahaleen* were Sudan's *interahamwe*, armed and recruited by Khartoum to carry out their dirty campaign of ethnic cleansing and driving peasants off their land.

Since the outbreak of civil war, government had barely existed in southern Sudan. The region measured more than 500 000 square kilometres but had less than ten kilometres of paved roads. Ninety per cent of the population had no access to health care, and the lack of schools created a generation of illiterate Sudanese.

For many years the regime in Khartoum had availed itself of the weapon of hunger to defeat the rowdy south. It literally created famine and starved the population to death. *Murahaleen* raids didn't just dispossess local inhabitants of their cattle herds, but ensured they couldn't plant or harvest crops. Where the *murahaleen* couldn't go, Antonov aircraft did, spewing bombs from their bellies.

The number of victims in the Sudanese calamity is so shockingly large as to defy comprehension. Between 1983 and 1998, according to human rights organisations, two million people died from war-related causes. One out of five southerners died in this war; four million were forced to flee their homes; 80 per cent of south Sudan's population was displaced at least once, and often repeatedly, from 1983. The death toll in Sudan was higher than the combined fatalities of Bosnia, Kosovo, Algeria, Afghanistan, Chechnya and Somalia.

When starvation took hold in early 1998 and the West and United Nations responded with Operation Lifeline Sudan, Khartoum had another stunt up its sleeve. It restricted the number of flights that ferried food to the hungry. The aircraft were not permitted to land at certain airfields. Sometimes Khartoum suspended relief flights altogether. Warlords, local factions and chieftains plundered many of the aircraft that did manage to reach their destination.

Sudan, especially the south, was a place to avoid. 'Wave after wave of bad news out of Sudan compelled me to travel there eleven times in four years,' wrote *Washington Post* journalist Blaine Harden in *Africa: Dispatches from a Fragile Continent.* 'As tragedy blurred into farce bled into tragedy in Sudan, I dutifully wrote one dreary story after another.'

Sudan does not register on my radar screen as one of the greatest stories I've ever done. One of the most tragic? Certainly. Desperate? Definitely. But poignant, incisive, cutting-edge journalism? Unfortunately not. I came back from Sudan with a fraction of the material I had set out to shoot and produced a rather dull and bland documentary. So why even bother to write about this furnace-hot, mosquito-infested and unruly place that nobody wants to know anything about? Because it was without a doubt the worst trip of my life. Besides being trapped in a Dinka village for days, Jan and I had to undertake a torturous journey across swamps while sitting on crates of ammunition in the back of a Toyota Land Cruiser, only to be stranded yet again, this time in an army base of child soldiers. When we eventually made it back to the airfield, a United Nations pilot refused to pick us up and waved us goodbye as he took off in his Buffalo. And then Jan nearly died.

About a month before our departure I had met a group of gunrunners and self-proclaimed SPLA representatives in Johannesburg. They swore they had a personal relationship with John Garang and could arrange for us to travel to the heart of southern Sudan. They promised to show us the most awful atrocities committed by the *murahaleen* and the Sudanese army – heads on stakes, crucified peasants and mutilated children.

The Sudanese ambassador in South Africa, outraged by the claims, offered me an interview with President Omar al-Bashir. 'Come to Khartoum,' he said. 'You'll like it and you'll hear the true story.'

By then another man-made famine was devastating the southern regions of the country and it seemed the perfect time to embark on an assignment to Sudan. We soon discovered that it was exactly the wrong time to venture into north-east Africa. It was the rainy season – yes, a famine alongside pools of water and lush grassland – and what few dirt tracks existed had been turned into trenches of mud and sludge. It was summer, and hot on the heels of heat waves that rolled through the land came swarms of mosquitoes, relentless and ravenous.

The pledges of neither the gunrunners nor the ambassador materialised. When we got to Nairobi and reported to the SPLA office, they knew nothing about us. When I tried to call the arms merchant, he was in Eastern Europe, probably procuring weapons for the SPLA. We decided to go it alone.

'Where do you wanna go?' asked a lowly SPLA official when I reported to their communications office.

'Bahr al-Ghazal,' I said. It was the only name I knew in southern Sudan because it was the province at the centre of the famine.

'Where in Bahr al-Ghazal?' he asked.

'Wau,' I said. This was the second biggest town in southern Sudan and a theatre of heavy fighting between the SPLA and the Sudanese army.

'You cannot go to Wau. The Arabs hold it,' he said.

'As close to Wau as possible.'

'So you want to go to Mapel?'

'Yes,' I said, not knowing where it was. The official issued us a permit that authorised us to film in and around Mapel.

As we left the SPLA office, Mac Anyang Yuang approached us, introduced himself and asked where we were going. I showed him our permit. 'I come from that area,' he said. 'Take me with and I'll help you.'

Mac was a sweet and endearing fellow desperately trying to eke out an existence as a refugee in a hostile and unhelpful world. Six years earlier, a government Antonov had lobbed a bomb onto his father's hut, killing his parents and most of his eleven brothers and sisters. Mac and a younger brother were a kilometre away herding cattle when they heard the explosion and saw the plume of debris and dust rise in the sky. The *murahaleen* attacked immediately afterwards, raiding their livestock and driving Mac and his brother into a swamp. When they eventually emerged, they found their way back to their village and buried their family's mortal remains. Then they walked to an SPLA camp where they joined the rebels, were herded into a platoon and issued with guns and uniforms. After an instant training course they were, as Mac said, 'killing Arabs'.

After fighting for three years, Mac realised the rebels were outgunned, out-trained and outnumbered. It was a war they could never win. He and his brother deserted the SPLA, walked more than 100 kilometres to the border, slipped into Kenya and applied for refugee status. He went to school, passed Grade 10 in a refugee camp and then made his way to Nairobi, where a church organisation sponsored another two years of education. His dream was to go to university, but meanwhile he was the proud owner of a Grade 12 certificate, which he pulled from his pocket and showed Jan and me.

We enlisted Mac as our translator and guide. I soon found out he had lied about his origins. He wasn't from Wau at all, but a native of Bor, more than 400 kilometres to the south and east. Insisting that we had misunderstood him, he dangled a carrot in front of us: he knew the whereabouts of General Kerubino Kwanyin Bol, who, according to aid agencies, was the creator of the latest Sudanese famine and one of Africa's vilest killers. Less known than the Theoneste Bagosoras, Foday Sankohs, Idi Amins, Mariam Menghistus, Charles Taylors and Jean Bokassas of our continent, he nevertheless ranked right up there with them.

Bol was a former army colonel who in 1983 led the mutiny in the southern town of Bor that sparked the civil war. He was a founder member of the SPLA and became the second most powerful man in the organisation. However, John Garang suspected Bol of plotting a coup and threw him in prison. A few years later he escaped to Uganda and formed his own rebel movement. President Omar al-Bashir, sensing an opportunity to divide the enemy, appointed Bol as deputy president. With a band of well-armed troopers on horseback, attack helicopters on his flanks and tanks to the rear, Bol cut a swathe of mayhem through Bahr al-Ghazal. He looted and pillaged villages, enlisted and coerced boys as soldiers, abducted girls as wives, stole livestock and burnt crops. In drought-prone areas the weather did the rest. Even in areas where rain fell, there was nothing to eat or plant for the next harvest.

But alliances in Sudan were quickly made and broken and an ally today might slit your throat tomorrow. In late 1997, for reasons unknown, Bol decided to 're-defect' to the SPLA. He and his militia turned on their northern masters, hoisted the SPLA flag and attacked villages in government-controlled areas. As punishment for Bol's deception, Khartoum unleashed its *murahaleen* on civilians and banned relief flights for two months.

Aid agencies agreed that Bol's prints were all over successive famines in southern Sudan during the second half of the 1990s. What they couldn't agree on was how many deaths, displacements, rapes and looting sprees should be laid at his personal door. Statistics about mass murder are notoriously inaccurate, and does it really make a difference whether one man is directly responsible for the death of 10 000 or 100 000? Suffice to say that Bol was one of the individuals who wielded and unleashed a weapon of mass destruction on a population, creating famine and displacement in Sudan.

He was an elusive figure, seldom seen, interviewed or filmed. He mostly dwelt in his hideouts at Bahr al-Ghazal, but also had a villa on the outskirts of Nairobi, where his ten wives and about fifty children lived in a walled and protected compound. Mac had a friend who was a bodyguard at the villa, and at that very moment Bol was visiting his family.

We made for the villa. Bodyguards intercepted us before we even got out of the taxi. I wrote a note to Bol, stuffed a couple of dollars into a bodyguard's hands and demanded that my request for an interview be delivered to the great man. A few minutes later, we were in the living room, shaking hands with a chubby, bespectacled man with crooked teeth and an unruly mop of hair. 'Welcome, brothers, welcome,' he said, as he chased a rabble of offspring out of the living room and barked in Dinka a series of commands to his underlings and bodyguards. Set up your camera, he told Jan.

Kerubino Bol was pissed out of his skull, and before long Jan and I were presented with glasses of lukewarm Johnnie Walker whisky and Coke. Behind him the walls were adorned with portraits of a blond and bearded Jesus Christ and a collection of framed Bible verses.

I asked him about the time he had spent with his Muslim brothers from the north. 'It was hell,' he said. 'The north and the south are not the same. I missed my people.'

'Why then did you kill them?' I asked him.

'Because we had arms and we were soldiers,' he said. 'Nobody is blaming me for killing people. In our tradition you fight with your brother today but tomorrow you are together again. Nobody blames me. Nobody!'

I read him an extract from the London *Guardian*: 'If there is any individual who bears immediate responsibility for these stick people – for the mute children with dying eyes who steal into our dreams – it is Major General Kerubino.'

He looked at me for some time, tossed back his whisky and Coke and said: 'Don't blame me for the rains not coming. Never blame me! Never!'

A day later, we drove across Kenya to the border town of Lokichokkio. Our trip took us through forests, past tea plantations and across the arid desert of Turkana, where spear-toting herdsmen in skins were driving their cattle towards watering holes. En route we stopped in a refugee camp to reunite Mac with his brother. We spent a few days in Lokichokkio before bumming a lift on the United Nations Buffalo that dropped us in Mapel.

We were stuck – in a Dinka hamlet two or three kilometres from the airfield. How long we would be there, we had no idea. 'Welcome to Hotel Mapel,' said an elderly man with a grey beard and a big smile as we entered his cluster of mud huts. He introduced himself as Mark Ubong, a shadow prime minister of the SPLA. Jan and I were shown to a bare hut, where we rolled out our sleeping bags and hung our mosquito nets.

Earlier, the yapping SPLA commander with the epaulettes had ordered us into a hut that doubled as his office and said that until he had verified our credentials, we were not permitted to leave the area.

'And where would we go?' I asked.

He didn't answer.

'How long will it take you to make sure we are who we say we are?' I wanted to know. For the second time, he didn't answer. I tried another tack.

'And where do we go then?'

'To the front line,' he said. 'We'll get somebody to pick you up and take you to the front line.'

Until then, we were stuck at Hotel Mapel. We sat there for five days, making the daily trip to the field hospital to charge our camera batteries. The area was littered with starving people. Among the fetid debris and the flies lay children and adults, staring vacantly into space. For many, the food aid had come too late. Starving peasants in the surrounding areas had been drawn to the airfield by news that foreigners were delivering supplies. Mothers carried only their babies and fathers cradled their herding sticks. Many died on the way, while others made it to within sight of the distribution point, but could drag their emaciated frames no further. Running on empty, they simply flopped down in the heat and waited like zombies for the hunger to consume their organs before they died with a faint gasp.

The stories of the living were all the same: *murahaleen* had looted their villages and stolen grain, seed and cattle; unable to plant a crop, they went hungry, the rains failed, they started walking and waiting for food.

We would return to Hotel Mapel at night, take a few swigs of brandy, eat a packet of Chinese noodles each, swallow a sleeping pill and flop down on our sleeping bags. Unlike the memories of Rwanda, the starving people of Sudan never came back to haunt me. I never dreamt about them and didn't think about their situation much. I never figured out why.

Other journalists who saw and reported on famine were consumed by its images. In his book *Zanzibar Chest*, Aidan Hartley wrote of covering the 1992 famine in Somalia for Reuters: 'I'll always have in my mind those children's eyes. As severe hunger took hold of them, their eyeballs turned red and rough. Next, a process the doctors called "melting and wasting" set in. The eyes foamed with mucus. They sagged and formed ulcers that burst in welters of pus. If the kids survived, their sight was scarred for life with blemishes like opals or moonstones on the pupils.'

Within this sea of misery, Hotel Mapel was an island of prosperity. In a land where the Dinkas had been reduced from cattle-rich herdsmen to landless beggars, Mark Ubong was, by all standards, a wealthy man. He had a huge herd of long-horned cattle grazing on the edge of shimmering swamps and water-holes, protected by child soldiers. Clutching a South African–manufactured R1 assault rifle, he took us several times to inspect his livestock.

I asked Mark about the boys in his army. 'You call them boys,' he said, 'but these are our men. They should be carrying a spear or a stick, not a gun! But we have no choice. They are young, but they want to fight.'

The Dinka, sinewy, tall and dark-skinned, were once southern Sudan's proudest and wealthiest people. But war and famine had robbed them of the symbolic heart of their culture and identity: cattle. Cows were worshipped and loved and myths and tales about these animals abounded. Everything Dinka was cow-related, from drinking the blood and milk to using the urine to dye hair and curdle milk. A man identified with one special ox, gave it a name, composed songs and created dances in honour of the animal.

'The lives of the Dinka and the Nuer pass in this immemorial rhythm, this pendulum-like, almost ritualistic wandering between the riverbanks and the pastures on the plateaux of the Upper Nile,' writes Blaine Harden. 'To exist, they must have space, land without boundaries, a wide, open horizon. Hemmed in, they sicken, turn into skeletons, wane, die.'

That night around the fire, Mark announced to my astonishment that he was going to slaughter a cow in the morning. He said SPLA soldiers – probably Kerubino Bol's militia – had returned a few days earlier with a herd of cattle they had captured while raiding government-held areas around Wau. One of the beasts, he said, would be sacrificed in honour of us, his African brothers.

'Indeed, a very great honour,' I mumbled hesitantly. Dinkas almost never slaughtered their animals or ate meat. But I had neither the stomach nor appetite for a feast in the heart of a famine and with people dying all around us.

It was as if Mark read my thoughts. 'We'll take the best parts and give the rest to the hungry,' he said.

As we emerged from our hut after another wretched night of being pounded by heat and mosquitoes, we saw a white cow, slightly underweight but in relatively good condition, tied to a tree next to the huts. It was the beast destined for Mark's pot. A short while later, bloodcurdling bawls echoed through Mapel as Mark's soldiers butchered the animal with machetes. The bowels, gut and intestines were hung in the tree under which the animal was slaughtered, while the rest of the carcass was carried away.

I watched as the intestines ripened in the heat for an hour or two. 'And that?' I asked Mac, pointing to the tree. He confirmed my worst fear: the intestines were being reserved for our eating pleasure!

I called Jan to our hut for an emergency meeting. 'No way in hell can I eat that!' I said.

'You have no choice,' he said. 'You'll have to.'

'I refuse. I can't do it.'

'So what do we do?'

'You'll have to eat on my behalf,' I told him.

By midday, hordes of flies covered the intestines. By late afternoon, several women had arrived to do the cooking. They chopped up the meat and threw it into a huge cauldron. By sunset, the smell of offal hung over the hamlet, reminding me of my childhood when my grandmother stewed the sheep's head, heart and kidneys that she and my father relished, while the rest of the family fled the house.

As night fell, a bull's horn and the thump of a drum announced a dancing ceremony. Young men ran and leapt, their legs splayed, and song filled the air. Mark said this dance was traditionally performed during a dowry ceremony, when the groom's family would present the bride's father with a herd of cattle. But the war and the dissipation of livestock had caused families to settle for promises.

The stew, piles of cooked maize-meal (compliments of Operation Lifeline) and earthen pots of *marissa* beer arrived. A woman heaped two plastic plates and held them out to Jan and me. 'Tuck in,' said Mark. Jan took his plate and slowly started eating. I gave mine back. 'Sorry,' I said, 'but I can't.'

Mark looked perplexed. 'Why not?'

I had been dreading this moment all afternoon. 'It's against my religion,' was the best I could come up with.

Dumbfounded, my fellow diners looked up from their plates. 'What religion?' Mark wanted to know.

'It's a South African religion,' I said, trying desperately to hold my composure. 'I can only eat meat that has been blessed.'

Silent gazes. A notoriously bad liar, I stumbled on: 'It's a bit like the Muslims. A priest must bless the food, otherwise I cannot eat it.'

It was the wrong thing to say. 'Muslims?' Mac asked. 'You mean you're with the Arabs?'

'No, no, no. It's more like the Jews,' I countered.

'But I've seen you eating tins of fish and all sorts of other things,' Mac protested.

'All been blessed, Mac, all been blessed.'

The next day, two Toyota Land Cruisers with sawn-off cabins and ancient Soviet 23-mm anti-aircraft guns mounted on the back came to Mapel to fetch us. In one of the vehicles was SPLA battle commander Daniel Makoi. On hearing that a cow had been slaughtered, he decided to stay for the night. Another stew was cooked. I raised my religious objections and once again Jan had to stand in for me.

Makoi said the SPLA was preparing for an attack on Wau and that his men had moved to within ten kilometres of the town. An enemy garrison, in turn, had manoeuvred to within striking distance of his base and a clash was imminent. 'You are going to witness my men in action,' he boasted after another slug of beer, 'and victory is for sure.' Looking at the rag-tag and mostly barefoot boys and young men surrounding him, I wasn't putting money on the rebels. It was only the guns they carried and their better-fed physiques that distinguished his soldiers from the populace. And in a place like Sudan, a gun was a passport to food.

The two Land Cruisers were loaded early the next morning with cases of ammunition – rocket launchers, mortars and 7.65-mm bullets. Makoi ordered about thirty soldiers, new recruits for the battle of Wau, and Jan, Mac and me to get on top of the crates.

'How far to your camp?' I asked Brigadier Makoi, now dressed in full battle regalia.

'About forty kilometres,' he said.

'And how long will it take to get there?'

'We should be there some time in the afternoon,' he said, adding: 'That's if we don't get attacked on the way.'

Jan and I looked at one another. Our options were limited. Mapel was nothing but a death camp, and we had by then filmed literally every starving man, woman and child and every living cow. Furthermore, Jan couldn't survive another bite of Dinka stew. And we were, after all, in southern Sudan to document the fighting. We clambered on top of the ammunition crates with the soldiers and, minutes later, crawled at snail's pace out of Mapel. I'm not sure which was the scariest scenario: an attack by the *murahaleen* or the real possibility of spontaneous combustion under my backside.

The road to Wau was nothing more than a two-wheeled and almost indistinguishable track that made progress through the swampy terrain excruciatingly slow. Every now and then one of the Land Cruisers would get stuck in a pool of mud and sludge. Sometimes the ammunition had to be offloaded, branches cut and the combined strength of thirty soldiers applied to push a vehicle out of a ditch.

Around us, the land was empty and eerie. The *murahaleen* had clattered into village after village and reduced them to blackened clearings. Some areas were pockmarked with bomb craters. The only comfort in the desolation was that it was improbable for a troop of *murahaleen* to still be roaming the area. They had looted, burnt, killed or driven off everything they could.

Ten kilometres from the SPLA base the gearbox in one of the Land Cruisers disintegrated. The vehicle could go no further – except in reverse! Unperturbed by the temporary setback, the brigadier ordered that we should proceed backwards to the army base. Late that afternoon we limped into the camp, rearwards.

As night fell we were shown to a tiny hut and ordered to be quiet and extinguish all lights. We crept into our sleeping bags, ate tinned sardines, finished our brandy and bombed ourselves out with sleeping tablets, all in the dark. Grimy, rancid and grumpy, we fell asleep with our clothes on.

I was greeted the next morning by a sea of curious gazes from soldiers cleaning their teeth with sticks. Conditions in the camp were appalling. There was no fresh water, and meals consisted of nothing but a grey and grizzly sludge. Most soldiers had no uniform or boots to wear and several were barely in their teens.

Sudan was no different from other African countries where civil war had raged for decades: Angola, Liberia, Sierra Leone or the Democratic Republic of Congo. In all those countries life expectancy was barely forty, leaving scores of youngsters homeless, orphaned and fending for themselves. Many eventually found their way to army camps, where they became 'platoon boys' by cooking, cleaning and carrying ammunition. But before long they were issued with AK-47s and sent into their baptism of fire. Commanders soon discovered that their boys were fierce and bloody fighters who were too young to exhibit the fear that adulthood would evoke.

Said Ryszard Kapuściński: 'Clashes in these children's wars take the form of savagely unmediated collisions, of close, almost physical contact; the children fire at one another separated by just a step. The toll, typically, is frightful. And it is not only those killed then and there who perish. In the conditions under which these wars are fought, the wounded will also die – from loss of blood, from infection, from lack of medicines.'

Battle commander Daniel Makoi was a tense man. A reconnaissance unit had reported movement in the enemy ranks. 'The Arabs have started up their tanks,' he told us that morning, 'and we are expecting an air attack.'

'What about us?' I wanted to ask, but didn't dare. It was a daunting notion that our safety was in the hands of his haphazard army. Soldiers were crouched around the two anti-aircraft guns mounted on the Land Cruisers and units armed with RPG rocket launchers and anti-tank missiles were sent out to meet advancing armour. I couldn't imagine them stopping MiG attack helicopters pouncing on us over treetops or T-72 tanks crushing through the woodlands.

Throughout the day, more SPLA soldiers arrived at the base, including a relatively well-uniformed and booted unit that Makoi proudly introduced to us as his 'special forces'. A few steps away from the base, instructors prepared the new recruits for the battle by demonstrating how to load and dismantle their guns and take aim. Their clumsy hands could hardly cock their Kalashnikovs or fix the bayonets.

When I later spoke to a group of boys, none knew how old they were. Few had ever been to school or enjoyed a semblance of normal childhood. I asked one how old he thought he was. 'He says you must ask the mother,' Mac translated. 'She knows when he was born.'

'And where's the mother?' I asked the boy, no more than a barefoot waif with a Kalashnikov and loaded magazines strapped around his waist.

'The mother is dead,' Mac said. 'And so is the father.'

The boy was called Luk, and he fetched his homemade guitar, made of an old gun butt and fishing gut. His tiny, almost delicate fingers cuddled and plucked the snares while the boys sang:

Our cattle have been captured,
Our children have been captured
And our villages have been burnt down.
We are now clustering under trees like birds.

That night, as we crawled into our hut, Jan and I decided to plot our escape in the event of an enemy attack. We realised that, in fact, there was no way out and that the safest option would be to stay put in the hut with our arms in the air and our passports in our hands. We were miserable. The hut was too small to hang our mosquito nets and we were being eaten alive. Our water was almost finished and our battery power was limited.

It was times like this that forged the working relationship and friendship between Jan and me into camaraderie – something that is born of sharing precarious moments in faraway places with only one another to depend on. Our shared experiences brought a deep understanding of our respective strengths and weaknesses, and although sometimes as *bedônnerd* as *doringdraad* (as grumpy as barbed wire), I could never have hoped for a more perfect travel companion than Jan de Klerk.

Said French writer Antoine de Saint-Exupéry: 'Nothing, in truth, can replace that companionship. Nothing can match the treasure of common memories, of trials endured together, of quarrels and reconciliations and generous emotions.'

The tanks and the MiGs never came. Nor did the SPLA launch an assault on Wau. Later the next morning, Daniel Makoi announced that Khartoum and the SPLA had signed a ceasefire in order to allow more aid to reach the starving masses. Although there would be no fighting in the immediate future, ceasefires were as plentiful in southern Sudan as food was scarce and, like the rest, this one was bound to be broken almost as soon as it had been signed.

By early evening we were back at Mapel. A smiling Mark Ubong greeted us with another 'Welcome to Hotel Mapel!' at the entrance to his kraal. I was delighted to be back and almost hugged our gracious host. News got even better when he told us a UN Buffalo was flying in the next morning with more food. We were upbeat when we crawled into our sleeping bags, drew our mosquito nets over us and fantasised about gorging ourselves on fine food and wine at the Carnivore or Tamarind restaurant in Nairobi within twenty-four hours.

We were packed and ready long before the Buffalo's expected time of arrival at the airstrip. The aircraft landed in a cloud of red dust, made a U-turn at the end of the runway and came to a stop to offload its cargo.

The pilot refused to take us on board, saying he didn't have a 'signal' from the UN permitting him to carry passengers. 'How do you think we got here? Walked?' Jan growled, moving ominously closer to the man. He threatened and I pleaded, all to no avail. The best he could do, the pilot said, was to forward our names to the UN so that they could issue a signal allowing us to leave on the next available flight. As the Buffalo thundered past us a few minutes later, the pilot waved from his cockpit. Jan swore to cut off his balls with a blunt knife if he ever saw him again.

An hour or so later, we were back at Hotel Mapel, where we languished for another four days before boarding a Buffalo back to Kenya.

After gorging ourselves on kudu, buffalo, eland and zebra at the Carnivore, we boarded a Kenya Airways flight for Khartoum, the capital of Sudan. Far below, brown and sluggish, flowed the Nile, slicing like a knife through the desert and almost guiding the aircraft to Khartoum, where the Blue and White Niles converge. As we walked into the airport building, we were intercepted by a group of stark-faced plain-clothes officials. They could have been security police, military intelligence, state intelligence, home affairs, immigration, whatever. The reception was frosty. We had media accreditation and a letter of introduction and recommendation from the Sudanese ambassador in South Africa. It meant nothing.

'Where do you come from?' asked one while leafing through our passports.

'Nairobi,' I said.

'Before that?'

'South Africa,' I lied. I deliberately skipped the Mapel expedition. I'd been warned that the authorities in Khartoum did not allow entry to visitors who had been in southern Sudan. There were no stamps in our passports to indicate that we had been to Mapel.

The questions kept coming for another ten minutes or so. What were you doing in Nairobi? Who did you see and speak to? Were you in southern Sudan?

'No,' I lied again.

Our interrogator kept quiet for a few seconds, letting me stew, before saying gleefully and menacingly: 'We know you were there. You visited the SPLA.'

I protested for another minute or so, but it soon became clear they knew exactly where we had been. I refused to provide them with any further information and asked to see the South African ambassador in Khartoum.

The men wanted to see the tapes we had shot at Bahr al-Ghazal. I said I had left them in Nairobi, which was true. They eventually agreed to allow us into the country for one week, but confiscated our passports. We had to stay in a hotel they provided, report every morning to the Ministry of Information and have an official accompany us everywhere we went. We had to get permission for whatever we wanted to film, whether it was the River Nile, a mosque or traders selling onions in the market.

Khartoum was a typical Arab city: noisy, dusty and choked with traffic and men wearing turbans and djellabas. Whitish-grey and pearly-domed mosques dotted the skyline, while the call to prayer by imams blared across the city. It was a stifling and unfriendly city engulfed in enervating heat and beaten by warm winds sweeping across the Sahara.

On our first night in Khartoum, Jan and I strolled from our hotel down to the Nile and unknowingly into a *Trespassers will be shot* area near the presidential palace. Soldiers cocked their rifles and barked instructions in Arabic. Our minder from the ministry had to come and rescue us, and after that we were restricted to a small area around our hotel.

Khartoum was nervous and jumpy with the United States having declared Sudan a terrorist state. Northern Sudan was a brooding nest and haven of Muslim extremists. One of its most prominent residents in the 1990s was Osama bin Laden, who later became the world's most wanted man. He lived in Khartoum for five years, and according to reports trained Al-Qaeda combatants in the desert and tried to smuggle nuclear material into Sudan.

Sudan implemented Sharia law in its purest form. Adultery was punishable with execution by stoning. The law dictated that 'the stones thrown during the execution should not be so large that the offender dies after a few strikes, nor so small as to fail to cause serious injury'. Human rights organisations repeatedly condemned the regime for sentencing scores of people to amputations and floggings.

It took us days to get permission to venture out of Khartoum to film the endless shantytowns encircling the capital. Southern refugees who had fled the fighting were trapped in featureless and stark slums from where they had to scrounge the desert and the city streets in order to survive. We weren't allowed to interview anybody.

Our promised interview with President Omar al-Bashir dissipated in the thin desert air, and we had to settle for a deputy president by the name of Riek Machar, a former SPLA commander and Upper Nile warlord in the mould of Kerubino Bol, who had also risen to become one of Khartoum's favourite sons.

'And what's life in Khartoum like for a southerner?' I asked him in his sumptuous office at the presidential compound on the Nile.

He looked at me for a while and then displayed a set of perfect white teeth. 'Normal,' he lied with a grin on his orb-shaped face, 'perfectly normal.'

Our visit to Khartoum came to a head in the Red Rose restaurant across the street from our hotel. White-tiled and white-walled with sharp neon lights and barely edible chicken and chips, it became our neighbourhood eatery. As we sat one evening sipping frosty beers – Egyptian brewed and non-alcoholic – a Sudanese family walked in. The man came in first, then a string of children and finally the woman, clad in a black burka that completely covered her body, hands, feet and face. Even her eyes were covered with black mesh.

As the family ordered food, I asked Jan: 'And how do you think she's going to eat it?'

'That is exactly what I have been thinking as well,' he said.

Their food arrived. The woman heaped her fork with food, lifted her burka ever so slightly and craftily popped the utensil into her mouth without showing a square millimetre of skin.

Our prying gazes were simply too much for her husband. Bloated, bearded and greasy, he rose to his feet, strutted to our table and exploded in Arabic. We stared at him, stupefied. I was about to apologise profusely when he pointed his finger at us and spewed: 'Fucking Americano!' That propelled Jan to his feet.

American rap music with lyrics of the *Hey-nigger-motherfucker*-kind blared in the background. Jan took a step closer to the husband, pointed at the loudspeaker and bawled: 'That, you stupid fuck, is Americano!'

When we arrived back in South Africa two days later, Jan was delirious with malaria. A Johannesburg doctor twice misdiagnosed him. Inflamed with fever, Jan collapsed and was rushed to a private clinic, where he was admitted to intensive care. He slipped into a coma, his lungs collapsed and for days he hovered between life and death. Doctors weren't sure he would survive, and then, finally, he opened his eyes, looked around him and asked: 'How's the doccie going?'

Not long after our return from Sudan, warlord Kerubino Bol was shot dead by a member of another rebel faction. The only ones who mourned his passing were his ten wives and four-dozen children.

The civil war continued unabated until 2004, when Khartoum and the SPLA entered into a precarious peace agreement that gave the southerners a stake in government and divided the riches of the oilfields between south and north.

In the meantime, however, a vast tract of land in the west of the country was catapulted into a calamity that overnight became the world's worst humanitarian and refugee crisis. While the government and the SPLA were conniving on how to divvy up the petrodollars, two rebel movements in Darfur took up arms and scored a series of victories against the government. Khartoum unleashed its Arab militiamen not just on the rebels but also on the residents of this blighted region. Estimates varied, but the most conservative spoke of 80 000 dead in addition to almost 200 000 killed by hunger and disease. Two million people were displaced.

In stark contrast to its reluctance to acknowledge genocide in Rwanda, the United States this time fell over its feet in its haste to use the dreaded g-word. The Bush administration, under pressure from the religious right wing, denounced the calamity in Darfur as genocide.

Remember Bill Clinton's visit to Kigali in March 1998 where he apologised for refusing to intervene during the genocide in Rwanda? He also said: 'Never again must we be shy in the face of the evidence of genocide.'

In 1999, when NATO went to war against Slobodan Milošević's ethnic cleansing in Kosovo, British Prime Minister Tony Blair suggested an international commitment never again to tolerate slaughter such as that in the Balkans and Rwanda.

Evidence of cruelty in Darfur piled up in report after report. To swell the militia ranks, the government released Arab criminals from prison and gave them horses, guns, a hundred dollars each and carte blanche to pillage, rape and murder. Human rights organisations exposed rape camps, where captured women and girls as young as eight were incarcerated as sex slaves.

So how did the world react to Clinton and Blair's promises?

The United States and Britain were simply too engaged in imposing Western-style democracy in Iraq and Afghanistan to do anything anywhere else. The United Nations debated genocide in Darfur for five months before deciding the situation didn't meet the g-standard. It did find that war crimes, ethnic cleansing and possible crimes against humanity had been committed.

Officially, there was no obligation on member states to act. The African Union placed a small, inadequate force of 2000 troops on the ground. They were not peacekeepers and had no mandate to stop violations.

More than three years into Darfur, this arid piece of barrenness remains a festering blight on the African map. Nothing unusual. We'd seen it in Rwanda, Congo, Burundi, Liberia and many other trouble spots. Once again, the international community simply didn't care enough.

The turn of the twentieth century saw Africa in turmoil. Across the continent, fires of dispute and quarrel erupted in civil war. It was a time of plenty for a journalist, and following Sudan, I produced documentaries in Eritrea, Ethiopia, Congo, Burundi and, once again, Rwanda.

In the spring of 2000, an energetic and stocky cameraman by the name of Adil Bradlow came to me and suggested a junket to the West African country of Sierra Leone.

It seemed an excellent idea: thousands of people were roaming the country without hands, arms, legs and feet. The United Nations had branded it the worst place on earth, and a raving lunatic was holding the future of the nation in his bloody hands.

Pappy and Captain Cut-Hand

Go and tell the president, Sierra Leone is my home
Go and tell my parents, they may see me no more
When fighting in the battlefield I'm fighting forever
Every Sierra Leonean is fighting for his land
                             – RUF anthem

HARD AS IT MAY BE TO FATHOM, ONE OF MODERN AFRICA'S MOST bloodcurdling mortals had once been a wedding photographer. He was also an illiterate, pot-bellied and bewitching geriatric who chose a former hairdresser and nightclub dancer to command his army of child soldiers, who hacked and mutilated thousands of people in the name of freedom.

The erstwhile photographer and lowly army corporal adopted the title of Chairman Pappy, while the hairstylist chose the *nom de guerre* of General Mosquito. Together they headed a West African rebel movement called the Revolutionary United Front (RUF) and transformed it into a cult. Pappy achieved almost messianic eminence, with followers worshipping him like a god and engaging in occult practices that reportedly included the drinking of blood and eating of human flesh.

When the RUF embarked on a campaign to prevent their Sierra Leonean countrymen from casting ballots in a 1999 election, Mosquito announced on BBC World the commencement of Operation No Living Thing, in which every entity 'down to the last chicken' was to be killed.

Jungle bases spewed forth commanders with names like Colonel Bloodshed and Colonel Doom. At their disposal was an army of mostly abducted teenagers and children, forced at gunpoint to rape or slay loved ones before being dragged into the bush and perverted into killers. The children, emulating their commanders, gave themselves names such as Captain Cut-Hand and Corporal Carnage and formed what became known as Small Boys' Units. Captain Cut-Hand was only eleven years old when he emerged from the bush clutching a Kalashnikov assault rifle in one hand and an axe in the other. As the boys prepared for battle, commanders wired them by rubbing cocaine, amphetamines and gunpowder into incisions on their arms and faces. The RUF's war cry was *Hungry Lion*, and the children threw themselves around shouting *Pappy, our Leader, our Hungry Lion* while clawing at the air. With red bandannas bound around their heads, they were ordered to amputate as many limbs as they humanly could. A message had to be sent. Voters without legs couldn't walk to polling booths and those without hands could not cast ballots.

On a Tuesday morning in January 1999, a Small Boys' Unit and their adult commanders arrived at the home of Lansana Sessay, a fifty-year-old father of five. They wore women's wigs, Ray-Ban sunglasses and necklaces made of machine-gun bullets. Most had guns, while one boy carried an axe. 'Where's your money, Pa?' they asked him. He gave them everything he had. They ordered him and his family to line up in the street outside. As the family prayed and pleaded, the boys laid Lansana and his three-year-old daughter out on their stomachs on the broken tar. A boy lifted a crude axe high into the air and slammed it down through the bones of the child's arm. Her hand seemed to jump away from her body. They hacked off her father's hands as well. With blood gushing from his wounds, Lansana ran after the boys. 'Kill me! Please, gentlemen, kill me! Don't leave me like this!' One of the older boys turned around and smashed his rifle butt into Lansana's face, crashing his front teeth and breaking his jaw.

Unlike the Rwandan genocide, some of the barbarity of Operation No Living Thing took place in the full glare of the international spotlight, due to the presence of incredibly brave journalists and one Sierra Leonean cameraman in particular, who never stopped rolling film amid the mayhem. Thousands of corpses rotted in the streets and rolled in the Atlantic surf that washed Freetown's pristine white beaches. In the countryside, vultures hopped from one body to the next, pecking and tearing at flesh. Thousands of survivors – like Lansana Sessay and his family – were condemned to a life of begging or dumped in an amputee village of white and blue canvas shelters.

As the grotesque acts of violence were briefly elevated to the world's front pages and CNN splashed the bloodshed in Freetown, two new names were added to the list of the worst human beings on earth. The first was that of Foday Saybana Sankoh, the man who called himself Pappy and headed the RUF. The second was that of his army chief of staff, General Sam 'Mosquito' Bockarie, who unleashed the terror of the Small Boys on the civilian population of Sierra Leone.

Profiling Sankoh and Bockarie, the *Washington Post* said: 'Rarely photographed or seen in public, Mosquito moved like a shape-shifting spectral demon around the country's rainforests. Leading a force of more than 10 000 men, he was perhaps the most feared man in Sierra Leone.' By contrast, the *Post* said, Sankoh seemed 'a fuzzy and wizardly man, mild and eccentric'.

Chairman Sankoh might well have been tempted to pinch himself amid the rich harvest that Operation No Living Thing offered. For littering the country with corpses and living spectacles of horror, Pappy was rewarded with the vice-presidency of Sierra Leone, complete with a double-storey mansion on a hill, an entourage of servants and bodyguards, and an official car with wailing sirens.

The broker of the Lomé Peace Accord (so called because it was signed in the Togolese capital) that exalted Foday Sankoh from a rabble-rousing mass murderer to statesman was none other than the Reverend Jesse Jackson, America's most prominent civil rights activist and President Bill Clinton's special envoy to Africa. But it didn't end with the house on the hill. Sankoh had not only terrorised and maimed his people to reach the upper echelons of power, but the accord – one of the most odious pieces of paper produced in the tumultuous history of Africa – also promised him and his men amnesty and immunity from prosecution. If that was not nauseating enough, the RUF was elevated from one of the world's most degenerate fighting forces into a legitimate political party.

The cherry on Jesse's rotten fruitcake was the appointment of Foday Sankoh as chairman of a committee that oversaw Sierra Leone's lucrative diamond fields. It was so-called 'blood diamonds' that had fuelled the conflict in Sierra Leone and financed the RUF's miasmic rebellion. Breaking the RUF's stranglehold on the country's illegal diamond trade was a prerequisite for any attempt to achieve peace. Instead, Sankoh was given control over it.

Suddenly a war criminal rubbed shoulders with world leaders. To his eternal ignominy, Jesse Jackson had the audacity to compare Foday Sankoh to Nelson Mandela. The rebel leader received a phone call from Bill Clinton urging him to accept the Lomé Peace Accord, and US Secretary of State Madeleine Albright visited him in Freetown to convince him to honour its conditions and, for God's sake, refrain from mischief.

General Mosquito, meanwhile, remained in the north-west of the country to guard Pappy's diamond fields and command an army of fighters who were holding on to their arms in case the ceasefire went awry. Mosquito claimed afterwards that the American government, working through Lebanese intermediaries, had offered him two million dollars to leave Sierra Leone and settle peacefully in Nigeria. He said he declined.

By the time I walked into the compound on the hill, Foday Sankoh was deeply entrenched in Sierra Leonean politics and making a bid for the country's presidency. Heavily armed soldiers escorted me past a long row of supporters waiting for an audience with Pappy to the office of his aide-de-camp.

A wiry man with a long neck and a scar on his cheek, he greeted me in Krio, a local dialect loosely based on English but peppered with expressions from other languages.

'How dee boddee (how's the body, how are you)?' he wanted to know.

'Good tank-ee,' I responded with a phrase I had learnt from my translator. 'Dee boddee in dee clothes.'

'Welcome to the confidential office of the leadership,' he said. 'I am the secretary to the chairman.' A picture of Sankoh adorned the wall behind him. He saw me looking at the portrait. 'He's a man of his word. He's dedicated, kind and honest. Just the type of man the country needed.'

I asked him about the possibility of an interview. 'Not impossible,' he said, 'but the chairman doesn't like interviews. All the bad press, you know.' He told me to write an official letter of request, but said we could meanwhile film a meeting between Sankoh and a group of supporters. About a hundred people were waiting for Pappy outside in the garden.

While we waited for Sankoh to emerge from his compound, the aide showed me around the house and garden. Despite Sankoh's vice-presidential status, the house was scantily furnished, the walls grimy and the red carpets frayed. Big pots of beans and rice cooked in the kitchen and scores of women and children (he was the father of thirteen) looked at us with inquisitive gazes, giving the impression that the extended Sankoh family had descended on the free accommodation in Freetown.

Under a tree sat Pappy's personal tailor, hunched over his sewing machine while stitching together a blue robe. A fish pond was empty and cracked. In the back garden a duiker buck with a bell around its neck was tied to a tree. A skinny baboon sat chained in the same tree.

'The chairman is an animal lover,' explained the aide. 'I believe in future we are going to have a zoo. We are going to collect the animals in the jungle and show them to tourists.'

Chairman Sankoh, dressed in a green safari suit and surrounded by heavily armed guards, walked onto the veranda and slumped down in a chair. In one hand was a wad of money, in the other a walking stick with a handle carved in the shape of a crocodile.

A young man wearing a T-shirt with the words *Chairman Sankoh for everlasting peace* stepped forward with a long, silvery fish in his hand. 'This, Pa,' he said, 'is a gift for you.'

'How do you call this fish?' Sankoh asked.

'A barracuda, Pa,' he said.

Another man stepped forward, introduced himself as a soccer coach and requested the intervention of the chairman in order to purchase balls for his team. Sankoh shoved a handful of notes into his hand. 'Go play. Bye bye.' A woman complained about the burden of family members who had recently returned from RUF bases in the bush and had to be fed. Sankoh held out notes to her and said: 'Go eat.' She fell on her knees, mumbled his name and blessed his soul. He looked at her and said: 'Bye bye.'

When the supplications ended, Sankoh rose to his feet, held his hand in the air and said: 'God works in mysterious ways. He called us to war and in war the best sacrifice is blood. But now God wants blood no more. That is why I'm here. With me here, no blood! Without me, blood!'

As his audience broke out in exultation and ululation, Pappy shook and bounced his ample belly through the bevy of colourfully clad admirers to a shiny 4×4 that was waiting to whisk him off to a political gathering somewhere in Freetown.

'A man of the people,' said the aide-de-camp. 'They love him. And he loves them.'

The son of a peasant farmer, Foday Sankoh had received hardly any formal education before enlisting in the army in 1956. He never rose above the rank of corporal. After his resignation, he worked as a wedding photographer and television cameraman for the state broadcaster. One day in 1969 he went to cover a mutiny in the military, but instead of reporting the uprising, he joined it. The coup failed and he was jailed for five years. When he was freed, he was jobless and embittered. In 1987, he joined a group of Sierra Leonean students in Libya, where the mischief-making Muammar Gaddafi was financing and training revolutionary movements from all over West Africa. Sankoh shook hands with Sam Bockarie, and in a guerrilla school in the Sahara Desert, they founded the Revolutionary United Front.

After his training, Sankoh set up base in neighbouring Liberia, where he teamed up with warlord Charles Taylor. Taylor would claw his way to the Liberian presidency eight years later on the backs of thousands of dismembered bodies and crushed skulls. Sankoh assisted Taylor in the early stages of his revolution, and in return the Liberian warlord helped him set up a base across the border in Sierra Leone. It was a baleful alliance that drenched both countries in a welter of blood over the next decade.

Sankoh and the RUF, sponsored by Taylor, launched their first insurrection in 1991. What had started as an idealistic movement to rid Sierra Leone of corruption and poverty soon degenerated into a merciless fighting force whose only quest was to plunder whatever riches they could. Sankoh and Bockarie discovered that they could swell their army's ranks much faster with forceful intimidation than with political persuasion. The RUF adopted a strategy of unparalleled cruelty against defenceless villagers. Young boys were forced at gunpoint to kill parents, relatives and friends. Traumatised and orphaned, the children were then pressed into service with the rebel army. Girls were taken as sex slaves, wives and servants.

When a former United Nations diplomat by the name of Ahmed Tejan Kabbah was elected president in 1996, his slogan was *The future is in your hands.* The RUF wanted nothing but total power and boycotted the ballot. In an attempt to undermine the election, Sankoh employed a logic reserved for madmen: he reasoned he could stop the voting by severing a hand from every potential balloteer. Small Boys' Units went on a brutal rampage and in a cruel mockery of Kabbah's election slogan, relieved voters, non-voters, children, toddlers and the elderly of a limb or two.

Kabbah was overthrown in a military coup. The new leaders invited the RUF to join them in the capital and share in an orgy of bloodletting, looting and raping. It lasted several months and was brought to an end only through a Nigerian-dominated West African peacekeeping force that retook the capital in February 1998 and reinstated Tejan Kabbah. Sankoh was convicted of treason and sentenced to death. It could all have ended there, but in stepped the good Reverend Jesse Jackson, who intervened with Kabbah to have the death sentence against Sankoh lifted.

With a new lease on life, Sankoh ceded the battlefield to Mosquito Bockarie, who regrouped his forces in the jungles of eastern and northern Sierra Leone. In January 1999, with Colonels Bloodshed and Doom at the forefront and Captain Cut-Hand and Corporal Carnage armed with axes in their wake, the rebels again attacked Freetown.

As they captured large parts of the capital, rebels went from house to house seeking out those who had any allegiance to Kabbah or showed any opposition to the RUF. The city's population was trapped in a living nightmare from which there was no escape. An estimated 10 000 were killed or maimed and 150 000 rendered homeless. Entire neighbourhoods were torched, and in many cases families were burnt alive in their homes. As the West African peacekeepers battled to regain control, rebels forced citizens into the streets to serve as human shields. The rebels were driven back but refused to observe a truce unless Sankoh, imprisoned at a secret location, was released.

By then Jesse Jackson was intent on reinventing Foday Sankoh as democrat instead of demagogue. In an interview he compared Sankoh and Charles Taylor to the gang leaders of Chicago, who he thought might have been redeemed by divine intervention – in this case, his.

Jackson's timing was perfect. There was a crisis on Europe's doorstep in Kosovo, Bill Clinton was embroiled in his impeachment hearings and the Nigerian peacekeepers wanted to go home. As Foday Sankoh occupied the vice-presidential villa on the hill, Jackson was mocked in Freetown as not a civil rights leader, but a 'killer's rights' leader.

According to a United Nations report at the time, the RUF continued to acquire weapons. Charles Taylor offered his country as a conduit through which to smuggle guns and money into Sierra Leone. Selling Sierra Leone's diamonds on the international market, Taylor laundered the gem revenue for Sankoh in return for a hefty share of the profits.

When I arrived in Sierra Leone in September 1999, the country was little more than a battered nation populated with mutilated civilians and murderous rebels who had reduced the rural areas to a wasteland.

Freetown, nestled between green hills and the white sands fringing the ocean, was once a beacon of learning and economic prosperity in West Africa. Sierra Leone – Lion Mountain – got its name from early Portuguese explorers who thought the mountainous coastline resembled a sleeping lion. Modern Sierra Leone was established at the end of the eighteenth century, when slaves who had won their freedom by fighting on the British side in the American Revolution were given land along the coast.

It was, according to a recent United Nations Development Programme survey, 'the worst place on earth'. Life expectancy was thirty-eight years, while seventeen out of every hundred babies died in infancy. Seventy per cent of adults could neither read nor write.

It is hard enough for someone in the developed world to lose a limb. In the world's poorest country, amputation meant a life sentence of torment. The streets of Freetown had become a theatre of the macabre. At every corner broken bodies on crutches and throngs of street children swarmed around foreigners for hand-outs. Most were covered in a layer of street grime and missing a hand or arm.

Human rights organisations documented an orgy of sexual abuse in Sierra Leone that is probably unparalleled in the history of Africa. Physicians for Human Rights reported that more than half of all women who came into contact with rebels were sexually abused. A third of them were gang-raped. Family members were often forced to watch the rape of their mothers, wives and daughters as a means of further terrorising and subjugating communities. Woman and girls were sometimes raped so violently that they bled to death, and numerous pregnant women had their bellies slit open. Rebels sexually tortured women with guns, wood and hot oil and forced pepper into their vaginas. Young girls who were abducted to become sex slaves and servants often had the names of their captors carved into their chests.

The victims of Chairman Pappy and General Mosquito were scattered across the capital – and it wasn't just those without legs, feet, arms or hands. We were filming early morning assembly at St Theresa's Primary School in downtown Freetown when I was met with a peculiar sight. The children, dressed in maroon uniforms and standing at attention in neat rows, were singing the national anthem.

That blessing and peace may descend on us all
So may we serve thee ever alone,
Land that we love our Sierra Leone.

One boy towered head and shoulders above his classmates. He was not only older and bigger, but he gave a military salute as he sang the anthem. It was a custom he had learnt as an RUF combatant deep in the jungles of Sierra Leone.

Sherief Koroma was only ten years old when RUF rebels captured him and his father while they were scrounging for food in the forest. The soldiers accused the father of being a government sympathiser and beat him to death. Sherief was dragged into the bush and taken to an RUF base, where he was designated a weapon and ammunition bearer. As the rebels prepared for Operation No Living Thing, the RUF needed more soldiers, and Sherief and a group of youngsters formed a Small Boys' Unit. Sherief was the youngest; the oldest was fifteen. Their commander was called Captain Mad. Training consisted of a crash course in how to shoot with a Kalashnikov and beheading chickens and other animals as a dress rehearsal for amputation. The boys were brainwashed on a diet of political indoctrination and drugs while their commanders made unrealistic promises of pots of gold once they achieved total victory.

As Sherief's unit stood poised to attack a small village not far from Freetown, commanders cut small incisions in his upper arm and cheeks, in which they rubbed a mixture of drugs. It could have been anything from cocaine to amphetamines or, if they ran out of hard drugs, gunpowder. 'Remember the chickens you have killed?' the commanders told the boys. 'Imagine that you are now going to kill chickens. You must spare no one.'

Sherief volunteered to carry the axe. His first victim was a toddler torn from his mother's arms. While adult rebels gang-raped the woman, the screaming child was placed in front of him. Sherief lifted the axe and hacked off the child's arm. His memory was vague about his first taste of battle, but he said another child and an old man were forced to lie down in front of him. Captain Mad stuck a bayonet into the child and ordered Sherief to kill the man. He said he slammed and slammed the axe into his neck until his head was almost severed from his body.

As night fell and the rebels feasted on looted cattle, Captain Mad injected Sherief with drugs and promoted him to corporal for his sterling work earlier in the day. Two battles later, he was a captain. His commanders agreed he had an exceptional talent for amputating limbs, and he adopted the agnomen of Captain Cut-Hand. As an officer he could share in the loot and choose a kidnapped girl as his sex slave. But he had only just turned eleven and picked a girl to merely be his servant.

When Nigerian peacekeepers drove RUF rebels back after their January 1999 invasion of Freetown, Sherief deserted his unit. For days he wandered around on the streets of the capital, and once the effect of the drugs had worn off, he was left with nothing but nightmares. He eventually found his way to a Catholic priest, who reunited him with his older brother. They had been living in a shack in the city ever since. Father Theo Mommo had debriefed almost 500 boy soldiers and said Sherief was one of the worst cases of post-traumatic stress he had ever come across. The boy urgently needed therapy, something that was almost impossible to come by in Sierra Leone.

It was difficult to believe that a boy of ten or eleven could have committed such heinous atrocities. 'Believe me, it's true,' said Father Theo. 'I see cases like this every day.'

Sherief might have emerged from war with a full set of limbs, but he was emotionally and mentally disfigured – probably for life. He was a bully at school, couldn't concentrate and was absent for days on end. His teacher said he was depressed, exhausted and had no friends. Other children were scared of Sherief and avoided him. He lived in constant fear of being recognised, which once happened on his way home from school. A woman without a hand begging on a street corner screamed when she saw him and accused him of being among a group of rebels who had killed her child and amputated her hand. People chased after him and he had to run for his life. When he got home, he hid under his bed.

I wanted Sherief Koroma and Foday Sankoh to be the main characters in my documentary, because they so graphically illuminated the madness and sadness of Sierra Leone. But I had to interview them, and Sankoh despised journalists and ignored my pleas for a meeting, while Sherief was only eleven years old and severely traumatised.

It's an unnerving experience to work with crushed young lives and ultimately put them on camera. Sometimes, as in Sherief's case, adults had deliberately turned guileless children into vicious killers and then abandoned them to their trauma and torment. Other children had often simply seen and endured too much, including the incurable loss of parents and family.

Eighteen or so months before going to Sierra Leone, I produced a television documentary on Algeria's so-called 'triangle of death', a series of villages around the capital of Algiers. This was where most of the massacres had taken place in the decade-long civil war after Muslim extremists, outlawed after winning the general election in 1992, took up arms against the Algerian government. It was an incredibly brutal conflict. On the one hand, there were the sectarian zealots who wiped out villages, and on the other a repressive, brutal regime that deployed death squads and widely used torture and detention without trial.

It was spring and the fields were covered in small, yellow flowers when I arrived at the primary school in Sidi Rais. The village nestled in the shadow of the snow-capped Atlas Mountains and was a picture of rural serenity. When I walked through the school gate, guarded by two heavily armed soldiers, an eight-year-old boy and his teacher were waiting for me. Farook Tarei walked towards me and held out his arms for me to pick him up. He kissed me, Arab fashion, twice on each cheek.

I held him tight for a moment before putting him down. He had an angelic face, framed by a mop of curly brown hair. His eyes were big and brown and should have sparkled with life. Instead, they were bewildered and full of anguish, the eyes of a boy who had seen too much.

Six months earlier, Muslim extremists had surrounded Sidi Rais and butchered 300 people. For several hours that night they rampaged through the village, slashing the throats of women and children and burning people alive. The killers slit the throats of Farook's parents and two brothers. The boy ran away, hid in a forest outside town and found his way to an aunt, who lived nearby.

Since that day, Farook had never spoken again. When his teacher took us into her classroom and showed us his exercise book, it was filled with red drawings, mostly of his brothers and his parents lying on their backs, and smaller, almost phantom-like figures with sticks and guns in their hands. No matter what colour crayons his teacher put in front of him, Farook always picked up the red one and drew the carnage that had destroyed his home and family.

When I left an hour or so later, the little boy pulled at my pants and started crying as I walked away. On the eve of our interview with Sherief, I remembered Farook and pondered the peculiar analogy between the two boys. It might just as well have been Sherief and a Small Boys' Unit rioting through Sidi Rais, but in the end they were both victims and, ultimately, just pre-pubescent boys.

Sherief Koroma was a picture of youthful innocence, his eyes bright and wide as he munched on a chocolate bar and gaped in awe at the television camera Adil Bradlow was setting up on a tripod. An hour earlier, we had bought the boy a new pair of boots in the market – his demand for doing an interview. He said he had always desired boots, and although he was a senior boy soldier, he was never allocated a pair and had to make do with looted shoes he removed from the dead, the captured or the mutilated.

Even before the camera started to roll, the boy pulled faces, wrung his hands and muttered to himself. Our trusted translator and researcher, Allieu Kamara, was sitting next to Sherief, comforting him. 'He's not good,' Allieu said to us. 'He says he gets bad dreams when he speaks about it.'

It had taken days of winning Sherief's trust to get to the point where we thought it was okay to interview him. He told us nightmares haunted him.

'Even now I sometimes get the urge to chop off more arms, to kill more people. I have to fight to keep myself away from people. I try and find a quiet place and lie down and try to sleep.'

Before the interview we had taken Sherief to a human rights organisation working with boy soldiers and requested that they provide him with therapy. They said they were overwhelmed with similar cases and could only assist boys who were in their care. Sherief lived with a family member and therefore didn't qualify.

We eventually met up with Doctor Edward Nazim, Sierra Leone's only psychiatrist, at the Kissy Mental Hospital, sub-Saharan Africa's oldest mental facility and once a functioning hospital. It had been overrun by the RUF during the civil war. The rebels had flung open the steel gates to 300 mental and psychotic patients, some of whom were promptly absorbed into RUF ranks. After the invasion, Nazim reclaimed control of the facility, and since then 150 patients had been incarcerated at Kissy.

'These are the worst cases,' he said. 'They are chronic, psychotic and dangerous. We have no money, no medicine and no staff. This is all we can do.'

Nothing could have prepared us for the level of depravity that lurked behind the grey-black stone walls. I could smell the bowels of the hospital as we entered the building. It was a mixture of shit, piss and disinfectant. The odour grew stronger as we walked down a gloomy and grimy passage where electricity had died long ago and every tile begged for a mop or a rag soaked in soapy water.

An old man lay in a pool of urine next to an iron bed with no mattress. His pants were wet and filthy and he was oblivious to the world around him. One of his arms was missing, the other chained to the bed. A blind boy heard Nazim's voice and crept across the floor towards him. He grabbed the doctor's hand and clung to it, begging him to take him home to his village in northern Sierra Leone. Chained to a bed across the passage, a half-naked woman sat cross-legged, laughing deliriously. She held a small baby in her arms. We decided that therapy at Kissy was not an option for Sherief. In the end we could do nothing more than ask Allieu to take the boy once or twice a week for counselling to a Catholic mission that cared for orphans and children affected by war.

With Allieu translating, Sherief recounted how Captain Mad and the Small Boys' Unit had swaggered into a village and rounded up the horror-stricken residents. Two of the men, he said, while pulling faces at the camera and sniggering at the most inappropriate moments, were accused of being government spies and promptly executed. A handful of young boys and girls, destined to become soldiers, servants, wives and sex slaves, were ordered to stand aside.

One of the village boys, eager to impress his vanquishers, accused a young man of being a government collaborator. The man was hauled in front of the soldiers. He wore a watch that the boy claimed was payment for spying on the RUF. Several boy soldiers pinned the man to the ground while Captain Mad removed the watch and stepped on his hand. He told Sherief to give his axe to the village informer. 'Cut it off,' he ordered the boy, who eagerly took hold of the axe, swung it through the air and slammed it down on the man's hand.

That left the rebels with a young and heavily pregnant woman and her five-year-old child. She was on her knees sobbing and begging the rebels to save her, her child and her unborn baby. 'Sometimes we saved people and even gave them food,' said Sherief. 'But that day Captain Mad was in a hurry and we were moving fast.'

The woman's fate was sealed and it was up to Captain Mad to decide how she was going to die and what would happen to the toddler. He ordered Sherief and another boy soldier to stand closer and pointed at a machete the rebels had found in the village.

'The soldiers made bets,' Sherief said, wringing his hands together and scratching his face. Then he looked at the camera, grinned and said: 'Was it a boy or was it a girl?'

He sat quiet for a moment, pulled another face and said: 'Then Captain Mad ordered me to open up her belly. She screamed, but I did it. When I was finished he pulled the baby out and held it in the air. I cannot remember if it was a girl or a boy. I didn't have money, so I didn't care.'

Sherief again kept quiet, made another face and said: 'Then I cut her into pieces.'

'And what happened to the child?' I asked him.

'Oh yes,' he said, with a grimace on his face. 'One of the other boys cut off his hands and then he died.'

'Why did they do it?'

'It's hands that vote!' he shrilled and burst out laughing.

RUF commanders promised their soldiers great wealth when the war was over. Chairman Pappy was going to give them diamonds, they could take lots of wives and live like kings. 'We were fearless,' said Sherief. 'Whenever there was a battle, we were in front. All the time they gave us cocaine. It made us very brave. All we had to do was kill, kill, kill. Cut, cut, cut. Every day. It never stopped.'

At night in the base, the boys were fed with a final concoction of drugs, washed down with a dose of Pappy's political doctrine. It usually included readings from his political manifesto: 'It is our right and duty to change the present political system in the name of national salvation and liberation. This task is the responsibility of every patriot. We must be prepared to struggle until the decadent, backward and oppressive regime is thrown into the dustbin of history.'

A day usually dawned with the singing of the RUF anthem:

RUF is fighting to save Sierra Leone
RUF is fighting to save our people
RUF is fighting to save our country

'Are you proud of your soldiers?' I finally got to ask Foday Saybana Sankoh.

It was at times like this that both his vanity and megalomania surfaced. Glancing at the camera to make sure that the lens was fixed on his face, he held for a second or two an expression that veered somewhere between surprise and disdain. Then his face lit up and he exclaimed: 'Of course! They are not soldiers. These are fre-e-e-dom fighters!'

But he quickly got back to his usual sneering when I asked: 'Why did your forces amputate the limbs of people?'

He leant forward, his face no more than twelve or fifteen inches from mine, and spat out in a high-pitched voice: 'No! They did no such thing!'

'Who did it then?'

'Not them! We fought with guns, not machetes! How can an AK-47 cut off an arm? Huh?'

'Do you want to say that all the people without hands in the amputee camp are lying when they say your forces committed these atrocities?'

His face moved even closer to mine. 'What is your name?' he shrieked. I was taken aback for a moment. Then he continued: 'This is Africa! People are not honest! People are not sincere! There is no love!'

'Why would people lie?'

'To tarnish the reputation of the RUF!' he ranted, his finger in the air. 'Pure fabrication! All this is fabrication to tarnish and destroy the image of the RUF!'

'The evidence against your forces is overwhelming,' I put it to him.

'They are being sp-o-o-o-n-fed by the enemy! Anything to tarnish our name!' Probably content for the moment that he had forcefully made his point, he sat back in his chair, folded his puffy hands and sneaked a look at the camera before continuing in a calm, almost rational manner: 'I condemn all such atrocities. Everybody who took part in this war is responsible. So there is no need to talk about atrocities. There is no war where you don't experience this.'

It was through sheer perseverance that we had finally got Sankoh in front of our lens. Every morning, lunch time and late afternoon for about a week, cameraman Adil Bradlow and I made the trek up the hill to the vice-presidential compound to enquire about the well-being of the chairman, his family and the animals in his garden. It was during one of these visits that Sankoh's aide-de-camp emerged from the 'confidential office of the leadership' and said: 'Good news! The chairman has agreed to talk to you.'

Minutes later, Sankoh nodded his head at us and flopped down in his armchair on the veranda. 'Here I am sitting just like Mandela or any other leader,' he began. 'The people of this country have been crying for war and their cry has been answered by the God Almighty.'

'Do you see yourself as the Nelson Mandela of Sierra Leone?' I asked him.

'The people are to decide,' he said warmly. 'I'm just one of them. A photographer, a corporal in the army. People call me Pa, Papa, Pappy. I am Pappy of Sierra Leone.'

Sankoh's lunacy shone as brightly as one of his blood diamonds. After a moment of contemplation, he said: 'In future people will not call me Chairman Sankoh but Chairman Peace. That is what I am: a peacemaker!'

Cameraman Adil Bradlow was brilliant. No wonder he became one of CNN's top cameramen. Throughout the interview he kept Sankoh's bearded face fully in frame, accentuating his lunatic and shifty eyes and the permanent frown on his forehead.

When Madeleine Albright visited Foday Sankoh in Freetown to convince him to honour the Lomé Peace Accord, he reportedly said to her: 'I've started this and I will finish this.' Since then he had repeatedly warned his countrymen that unless they voted for him in the upcoming election, he would return to the bush and butcher his country back into the abyss.

'Do you want to be president of Sierra Leone?' I asked him.

'I want to be a l-e-e-a-der for the people of Sierra Leone. I'm going to be the l-e-e-a-der of the revolution!'

'What if you do not win?'

'Ha!' Sankoh screeched and shifted to the front of his seat. 'We are going to win. We have already won. As long as we are in Freetown, people shouldn't worry. There's peace.'

'And if you're not in Freetown?'

He kept quiet for a moment, leant further forward, and said softly and ominously: 'There is war.'

It was unconscionable to envisage Sankoh as the future president of Sierra Leone, and even more so to entertain the notion of the international community that he could be rehabilitated and trusted with the fate of his people. When he clearly ought to have been languishing in prison, or at the very least have been chained to a bed in Doctor Nazim's madhouse in Kissy, Sankoh had no illusion about his greater mission. 'I'm just an instrument for the God Almighty. He told me to serve the people of Sierra Leone. So we are the winners. We've already won.'

I mentioned to Sankoh that I had interviewed Sherief Koroma, alias Captain Cut-Hand, the day before and that Freetown was littered with his boy soldiers and their victims.

'They lie!' he shrieked. 'No boy can stand before me and say he fought for the RUF. We rescued them and we fed them. Were we to kill them? Huh! No!'

'Why would these children lie?'

'They are being sp-o-o-o-n-fed by the enemy! I have children myself. I have thirteen children in this country. Would I let them fight? No!'

On the other side of town, near a busy road in the suburb of Aberdeen, was a patchwork of makeshift homes that was a living monument to the handiwork of Foday Sankoh, Mosquito Bockarie, Charles Taylor and the RUF. It was a place as grisly as its name implied: *Médicins Sans Frontières Amputee and War Wounded Camp*. It had become the number-one stop for international dignitaries, diplomats and journalists. UN Secretary General Kofi Annan visited and so did Madeleine Albright and UN Human Rights Commissioner Mary Robinson.

The camp was also a sure stop on our journey, and we spent days listening to stories identical in their barbarity and deprivation. The amputees told of bands of young boys, accompanied by a few adult soldiers, wearing red bandannas around their heads with adhesive strips covering their cheeks. They were armed to the teeth and there was always a boy carrying an axe or a machete.

Send your hands to President Tejan Kabbah and ask him to sew them on again, RUF rebels told thirteen-year-old Issatu Kargbo as they forced her hands onto the stump of a mango tree. She told them she was a schoolgoing girl and knew nothing about politics. It didn't matter, they said, as they amputated both hands. Family members and neighbours were forced to sing and clap hands while six people had their hands lopped off.

Condemned to a life as a cripple in the world's poorest country, Issatu, a pretty girl with braids in her hair and a coy smile, expressed what every other amputee in the camp told us: I will forgive. I will not forget, but for now, I will forgive.

The craving for peace ran so deep through Sierra Leone that it seemed to have smothered any desire for revenge or retribution. A woman whose legs had been forced open by grimy rebel hands before she was repeatedly gang-raped and locked in a small cage for months, said she and those around her had suffered enough. They wanted a new future for their country. The voices of the maimed echoed a desire for peace, even if it meant sacrificing justice for the criminals of the RUF.

'What about Foday Sankoh?' I asked Lansana Sessay, the fifty-year-old father of five who had both hands chopped off and his teeth smashed with a rifle butt.

He was sitting in front of his canvas shack, nothing more than a room behind a flap that he shared with his wife and five children.

'What about him?' he asked me. Standing next to him was his youngest child holding a cigarette that he from time to time put in his father's toothless mouth. Lansana gave a wry smile and said: 'There's nothing I can do. I can't kill him.' He held his stumps in the air.

'How do you feel now that he's back in Freetown?'

'If it's for peace, it's okay. I forgive him. For now, I forgive him. For now.'

When I interviewed Foday Sankoh, I asked him: 'Are you willing to go to the amputee camp and ask for forgiveness?'

He leant forward, glared ominously at me and said: 'Forgiveness for wh-a-a-t? For making a revolution?'

'Surely a revolution does not include the maiming of people?'

'I challenge anyone to prove that the RUF committed these atrocities!'

'Are you willing to go to the amputee camp and say to the people they are lying?'

'Listen,' he said as he waved his finger, 'those people know the truth and the truth will come out. Don't incite me or intimidate me or provoke me to war!'

A day or two after the Sankoh interview, Adil and I boarded an elderly Ghana Airways Boeing 727 to fly to the Ghanaian capital of Accra. I left Sierra Leone despondent and without much hope or faith. Peace was on a knife's edge and in the hands of madmen. With Sankoh in Freetown, Bockarie in the bush and Taylor in power in Liberia, it was easy to see Sierra Leone sliding back into yet another cycle of anarchy and slaughter.

Not long after our return to Johannesburg, the first cracks appeared in RUF hegemony and unity. General Sam 'Mosquito' Bockarie was forced to flee his northern Sierra Leone stronghold of Buedu after he had executed eight senior commanders whom he accused of conspiring against him. He fled to Liberia, from where he threatened to launch a new insurgency that would ensure continued access by the RUF – and its Liberian backers – to the diamond fields. Foday Sankoh, visibly shaken by the absconding of his decorated field commander, held a press conference in Freetown and announced that Mosquito had been fired.

At the dawn of the millennium, 6 000 United Nations peacekeepers were deployed throughout Sierra Leone. In the months that followed, their ranks more than doubled, making it the biggest peacekeeping operation in the world. The Blue Berets had a mandate from the Security Council to help enforce the Lomé Accord and oversee the disarmament of the rebels. But several months later, only a handful of rebels had handed in their guns and the RUF continued to control large areas in the north and east of the country. In an ominous warning, Sankoh said the UN had no place in Sierra Leone.

In April 2000, RUF rebels captured 500 United Nations peacekeepers and detained them at their bases in the north of the country. Several Blue Berets were murdered. Britain sent 900 paratroopers to evacuate its nationals and secure the international airport and routes into the capital. Before long they were engaged in battle with the RUF.

Nine months after it was signed, the Lomé Peace Accord was nothing but scrap paper in Sankoh's rubbish bin. Believe it or not, the nimble Jesse Jackson once more entered the fray. He tried in vain to wheedle 'Brother' Charles Taylor – widely seen as the godfather of the RUF and Sankoh's arms and diamond broker – to negotiate an end to the hostage crisis. Jackson then announced that he would personally travel to Sierra Leone to bring an end to the crisis. The US State Department urged him to stay away as angry citizens could physically assault him. Sierra Leone's foreign minister, Sama Banya, went on state radio and said Jackson was not welcome in the country. Shortly afterwards, Jackson was fired as Bill Clinton's special envoy for Africa.

A month after the capture of the UN soldiers, thousands of women took to the streets of Freetown to protest against RUF ceasefire violations. After a rally at the national stadium, they proceeded towards Sankoh's compound on the hill to hand over a petition to him. In what became known as Black Friday, RUF rebels guarding Sankoh's house opened fire on the protestors. Nineteen people were killed, many shot in the back.

For once the Sierra Leonean government had had enough of Sankoh's shenanigans and issued a warrant for his arrest. He disappeared before the police could get to him, raising fear and suspicion that Pappy might be on his way back to his rebel stronghold of Makeni in northern Sierra Leone.

Ten days later, a thirty-six-year-old stonecutter by the name of Kabbah Sessay was on his way to morning prayers when he spotted none other than the rebel leader just outside his compound, by then deserted and trashed by angry protestors. Sankoh was wearing a green and white knitted hat and had a colourful beach towel draped around his shoulders. He asked Sessay to get him a taxi to take him to the Nigerian embassy, where he probably wanted to ask for political asylum. Sessay told him to hide in his ransacked house while he went to get transport. Instead, he alerted a soldier who lived nearby.

The soldier got together five friends and returned to the compound. When Sankoh emerged from the house, expecting to hop into a taxi, he walked straight into a trap. His bodyguard pulled a gun, but the soldier shot him dead. The bullet passed through the bodyguard and hit Pappy in the leg. By then, an angry crowd had assembled. They grabbed hold of Sankoh, hit him and tore at his clothes. He was stripped naked before soldiers arrived, hustled him into a car and drove him to an army base. A British helicopter whisked him away to a secure location, where he was incarcerated. For almost two years, Sankoh disappeared.

With Pappy in custody, the UN announced the formation of the Special Court for Sierra Leone. A hybrid war crimes tribunal that blended local and international law, the Special Court was given $60 million and a mandate to strike at the main players and bring justice to Sierra Leone. Sankoh and Bockarie were among the first to be indicted for crimes against humanity, murder, rape, sexual slavery, extermination, abduction, looting, burning, acts of terror and conscripting children into an armed force. Charles Taylor was later indicted for war crimes in that he supplied guns and ammunition to the RUF in return for diamonds. The accused, said chief prosecutor David Crane, 'criminally gutted an entire nation'.

In January 2002, with the RUF defeated, 47 000 rebels and soldiers disarmed and 14 000 UN peacekeepers deployed in the country, the civil war was finally declared over. On a summer's day five months later, the gods at last shone their grace on the war-torn nation when nearly 2.5 million voters out of Sierra Leone's population of five million went to the polls. Many were amputees who used their feet to make crosses.

Tejan Kabbah won by a landslide, taking 70 per cent of the vote. Foday Sankoh's RUF collapsed, winning less than 2 per cent of the vote and not a single seat in parliament.

When Foday Sankoh finally emerged after twenty-two months in custody to appear before the Special Court, the once ebullient rebel leader was a shadow of his former self and of unsound mind and body. His barking madness had finally caught up with him. He was slouched in a wheelchair, his hair in matted white dreadlocks, and he appeared dishevelled.

His comments were rambling. 'I'm a god,' the handcuffed Sankoh told court officials. 'I'm the inner god. I'm surprised that I'm being tried because I'm the leader of the world.' He made no reply when Judge Benjamin Itoe from Cameroon asked him to confirm his identity. The judge ruled that he should undergo psychiatric evaluation to determine whether he was fit to stand trial.

Sam 'Mosquito' Bockarie never got to court. Wanted for war crimes, the Special Court announced in April 2003 that it had information Bockarie was in Liberia. Liberian authorities denied this, but a week later announced that he had been shot dead. Two months later, his body was flown to Freetown and handed over to the Special Court for confirmation of his identity. According to newspaper reports in the Liberian capital of Monrovia, Taylor had executed his former confidant to prevent him from ever testifying against him.

As Sankoh's sanity continued to wither away, the United Nations lifted his international travel ban in order to send him abroad for further treatment. No country was prepared to accept the rebel leader for even short-term treatment. By June 2003, doctors treating him said he was in a catatonic, stuporous state – incapable of walking, talking or feeding himself and unable to recognise his immediate surroundings.

At 22h40 on Tuesday 30 July 2003, Foday Saybana Sankoh died. Said David Crane in a statement: 'Sankoh's death from natural causes granted him a peaceful end that he denied to so many others.'

With Sankoh and Bockarie dead, the most wanted man in Sierra Leone was Charles Taylor. Less than a month after Sankoh's death, with rebels advancing on the Liberian capital of Monrovia, Taylor abandoned his presidency and fled to Nigeria, where President Olusegun Obasanjo gave him asylum and protection and refused to hand him over to the Special Court. As the trial of three former RUF commanders got under way in July 2004, David Crane said Taylor should be sitting next to them in the dock. As for Bockarie and Sankoh, he said: 'Throughout this war crimes trial the phantoms of Foday Sankoh and Sam Bockarie will be ever present in this hall of justice.'

The first witness was a man from the north-eastern town of Koidu, who saw twenty-five men and women burn to death in a house. He and his children were then forced to watch his wife being raped by eight different rebels before the last one stabbed her to death with a bayonet.

'How come you recall the exact number of rapists?' the prosecutor asked him.

'I had to count out loud the number as they went into her,' he said.

The year 2006 dawned with new hope for Liberia as the tattered and war-ravaged nation voted into power Africa's first female president, Ellen Johnson Sirleaf. Nigeria's President Olusegun Obasanjo finally bowed to African and international pressure and extradited Charles Taylor to the Special Court that had indicted him to stand trial for war crimes.

Taylor was a self-professed reborn Christian and lay preacher in the Baptist tradition and was known for clothing himself from head to foot in angelic white. He was also given to murmuring Bible verses at public appearances, and when a journalist once put it to him that many regarded him as nothing but a murderer, he responded: 'Jesus Christ was also once accused of being a murderer.'

CHAPTER 12

Profit of doom

Prophet TB Joshua is a channel of shining light, putting an end to the
darkness in the lives of those held captive by Satan.
— **The Synagogue, Church of All Nations website**

THERE IS A COMMON SAYING, WITH SLIGHT REGIONAL VARIATIONS,
in Nigeria. It goes something like this: No matter how tired, beaten,
oppressed and downtrodden you are, no matter how deplorable your lot, you'll
soon find a way out of misery.

Nigerians are among the most optimistic people on earth, even though
their country constantly appears to be falling apart, hovers on the brink of
political turmoil or financial collapse, is torn apart by religious fervour and
infested with endemic corruption. Life in Africa's most populous nation seems an
endless battle not to drown in its daily tub of greed, political rot and economic
decay.

Religion plays a pivotal role in the nation's quest for a better tomorrow. In
a country where it feels as if the state has abandoned its citizens, and where
decent education, health care and housing are the privilege of the elite, the God
business is booming.

Down and out, insolvent, bankrupt? Sick, afflicted, lame? A wandering spouse
or a barren womb? A worm in your stomach or a frog in your head?

Easy. Pray it right. Nigerians have little other choice. Diseases such as polio,
long eradicated in other parts of the world, persist there. Hospitals and clinics
regularly run out of medicine or bed space. Many cancer cases go untreated.
AIDS is rampant and the vast majority of victims cannot afford antiretrovirals.
So they turn to faith.

There are thousands of Nigerian pastors, preachers and prophets who claim
to have a hotline to heaven and can convince the Almighty to heal, mend and
restore any human condition. Some say there are 2 000 churches in Lagos – the
African continent's largest metropolis with a population of around twenty
million – while others say it is closer to 6 000. Every street corner in Lagos
is home to a Pentecostal church, and on Sunday mornings the city explodes in
a blaze of colour as residents don splendiferous robes and flock to places of
worship.

Pentecostal preachers have acquired the same celebrity status as national soccer players or Nollywood (as the flourishing local film industry is dubbed) film stars. Not only do they attract vast audiences and godlike admiration, but the more eminent have also been blessed with divine prosperity and fortune. Although they guarantee free healing and delivery, the flock is encouraged to give till it hurts.

In the first decade of the third millennium, one of the rising stars of the Nigerian Pentecostal movement was a fortysomething evangelist by the name of Tenitope Bolegun Joshua, universally known as TB Joshua or The Prophet. Very little was known about him, but apparently he was anointed at birth by Nigeria's water god. He started The Synagogue, Church of All Nations, during the 1990s with a handful of acolytes. Ten years later, his religious empire stretched across international borders with branches in several countries and a compound in Lagos with seating for 20 000 and accommodation for pilgrims from around the world.

Presidents and kings had made the trek to the Synagogue, among them former Zambian president Frederick Chiluba and Zulu king Goodwill Zwelethini and his daughter, Princess Sibusiso. According to the church website, the princess suffered from epilepsy, which not even Nelson Mandela could do anything about. The king arranged for the best doctors in the world to help her, but to no avail, so she turned to TB Joshua.

'The Prophet began to pray in his own way over her. She immediately stopped using her medicine for the seizures,' the website trumpeted. 'Many people around her began to notice the princess was back to her normal self again.'

Around the year 2000, South Africans started journeying to Lagos in droves to find salvation and healing at TB's Synagogue. Most were from good Afrikaner stock but had abandoned the stoical NG Kerk in exchange for a Nigerian 'turn-or-burn' approach to redemption. The fact that the new messiah was black and his church in the ghetto of Africa's biggest and maddest metropolis added to an almost masochistic enchantment.

People returned from Lagos with gripping testimony of disabled rising from their wheelchairs, AIDS viruses banished, terminally ill restored to former health and festering sores healed before their very eyes.

The Synagogue's website and videos, distributed around the world, resembled a freak show. A woman was shown giving birth – close-up and in the most intimate detail. She came to the church because she was due to deliver, but her baby was in the wrong position. 'As soon as the man of God stretched his hand in the power of the Holy Spirit, God Almighty took control of Mrs Olaitan Olomo's situation,' the website said. 'Prophet TB Joshua declared that the baby had turned and was now in the right position. The baby was delivered the moment the Man of God spoke those words.'

The drinking water in the Synagogue – ordinary tap water – was sanctified and turned into 'the blood of Christ'. Videos showed crowds scrambling forward in an attempt to touch the 'blood', which caused them to writhe on the floor as if in pain, grab their genitals, vomit and pee.

The water was said to contain divine powers. This was proven by a maniacal geriatric who had been rabid for decades. His exasperated family took him to the Synagogue, where a prophet told him to pour TB's magical water into his ear. That was on a Sunday. On Monday a bullfrog crept out of his head. Needless to say, he had been of sound mind ever since.

The website claimed a host of miraculous healings, including (close-ups again) severely diseased and afflicted male and female genitalia. After TB's prayers, to prove they were healed, people pulled down their pants or lifted their skirts. The same happened with cancer of the anus, infested sores and open wounds.

The visit of two Springbok rugby players to the Synagogue opened the floodgates to Lagos. Former Blue Bulls and Springbok loose forward Ruben Kruger was the first to arrive, with a brain tumour. TB prayed and declared him healed. Although Ruben refused to undergo medical tests on his return to South Africa, he was convinced the tumour had vanished.

Shortly afterwards, Blue Bulls fullback Jaco van der Westhuyzen returned triumphant from Nigeria. He had a serious knee injury and doctors had declared his rugby career doomed. After the Prophet's prayer, he removed his knee brace, jumped up and down and ran around in the church complex. He never again had a problem with his knee and continued to play rugby at international level.

Suddenly, the regular South African Airways flights to Lagos were packed with the sick, the dying and the curious. On one of those flights was another Springbok rugby player and Blue Bulls lock by the name of Wium Basson. At the tender age of twenty-five he had been diagnosed with liver cancer and given only weeks to live. When news of Wium's imminent death reached Lagos, TB Joshua invited him to the Synagogue and promised to pray him back to health.

I was also on that flight after being invited by the organisers of the pilgrimage to witness the anticipated miracle for myself. With me were cameraman Dudley Saunders and soundman Mandla Mlambo.

'Are you a believer?' organiser Jannie Pelser asked me before our departure. With blond hair falling over his forehead, he looked more like a surfer boy than a pastor and gospel singer. It was only his drooping moustache that gave him away.

'No, I'm not,' I said.

'And Dudley and Mandla?'

'I don't think so.'

'After this you will be,' he assured me.

Jannie told me we would stay with the pilgrims in dormitory-style accommodation. No smoking or drinking was allowed in the compound and we would not be permitted to leave the church, as that part of Lagos was too dangerous.

The prospect of being incarcerated with the sick, the dying, the diseased and often the raving and fanatical for more than ten days was horrid. Mandla, Dudley and I sat in the rear of the Boeing 747, gulping our way through a bottle of Jack Daniel's like true infidels. We behaved like heroin addicts indulging in a last fix before checking into a rehabilitation centre. Jaundiced eyes were already being cast in our direction.

Landing at Murtala Muhammed International Airport brought us back to reality soon enough. After a squabble of probably an hour with customs officials about our television equipment, we hit the traffic of Lagos – reputed to be the worst in the world. Countless words have been written to capture the image of the miles upon miles of cars, trucks and battered taxis crawling through a toxic mist that hangs like a blanket over the city.

As we slithered along sewer-lined and rotting roads, the South Africans gaped wide-eyed at hawkers and vendors conducting frantic business in the exhaust and slum-fire smog of Lagos. Women had set up stalls at the busy intersections, where they sold yams and forest rats, goat meat and dried fish, cola nuts and warm beer. An army of street traders offered clothes, batteries, hangers, plastic bags, screwdrivers, pain pills, movies, shoes, socks, puppies, rat poison and CDs.

As the traffic ground to a halt – as it does all the time – legless beggars on skateboards propelled themselves off the sidewalks and attached themselves to vehicles. They held on until an exasperated driver or passenger tossed a coin through the window or managed to shake them off.

Said Hennie Traut, a thickset pilgrim with a middle path and a moustache: 'It's another world! A completely different world. Seeing all these dilapidated houses and business being conducted on the streets. Amazing!'

'Yes,' agreed his wife Moira, her hair sculpted into a beehive, 'we're not used to this in South Africa.'

'Definitely not,' said Hennie. 'We're used to everything being gold and silver.'

Lagos was indeed light years away from Hennie and Moira's forlorn hometown of Brakpan, where gold had long since been mined out, leaving residents impoverished and the town's economy in ruins.

'Man, when I saw that first video of Joshua and heard about the miracles in the church, I had to get to Lagos,' said Hennie.

Like their forefathers, Hennie and Moira had embarked on a Great Trek to the north, but instead of rolling farmland and the right to govern themselves, their quest would end with a black saviour of the soul.

The sleeping arrangements at the church compound realised my worst fears. Single beds were pushed tightly against one another and there were only two toilets for thirty or forty males – and some almost immediately got diarrhoea from the food!

Dudley, Mandla and I scrambled for a corner and settled into our miserable little space. On the bed next to mine a slightly built man was stretched out, reading his Bible. When he saw me, he looked up and held out his hand.

'I'm John,' he said.

I introduced myself and tried to make small talk. 'Were you on the same flight as us?'

'Oh no,' he said, 'I've been in the church for a week. I'm here to give testimony of my healing. I first came here more than a month ago.'

'And what was wrong with you?'

'I had full-blown AIDS,' he said.

'And now?'

'I'm completely healed,' John said.

'And how do you know that?'

'The Prophet prayed for me and told me so.'

John Rindel had been diagnosed with HIV/AIDS sixteen years before. He said he was gay and promiscuous but had only been sick for the past year. Although he was on antiretrovirals, his weight had dropped from sixty-five to forty-eight kilograms. He also went blind. Despite the fact that he had never been religious, he went on his knees and prayed.

'And I said to God: Lord, I know I'm dying. But please have mercy on me. If you give me more time, I will change my life and dedicate it to you. When I woke up the next morning, I could see again,' he told me.

He was still sick and his condition deteriorated even more. His doctor put him on a course of different medication, but said he could only hope to keep the virus at bay, as AIDS was incurable.

John started losing his mind. He had a medical certificate from a specialist stating that he had full-blown AIDS and suffered from dementia. Dying, dejected and manic, he bought an air ticket to Lagos.

'I was the only white person in a row of 400 HIV victims. When Joshua reached me, he stopped and held out his hand. A thunderbolt hit me as the demon left my chest. Joshua had to jump out of the way to make sure he wasn't affected,' said John. He said he knew he was healed, and that AIDS was a demonic disease and God's punishment for homosexual sinners like him.

'How do you know the AIDS virus is gone?' I asked him.

'I have no doubt that I'm healed. I should have been dead by now.'

'Why?'

'After my healing, church people took my medicine. They said I didn't need it any longer. I said without it I would die. They said no, you're healed, give it to us. I did, and have never taken any pills again.'

When he left the church to fly back to South Africa, Joshua gave John money for another air ticket and told him to return in a month to testify in public about the miracle.

'Have you gone for an AIDS test?' I asked him.

'It's not necessary. It's been seven weeks since I've taken any medicine. I've never felt better. Even my doctor said what happened was a miracle.' Since his first visit to Lagos, John had gained weight, the dementia had receded and he looked relatively healthy.

I warmed to John during our stay of almost two weeks. He was quiet, reserved and never partook in the follies of the other South Africans. He kept to himself and read his Bible all day long.

'I have not only been cured of AIDS,' he told me.

'Oh yes?'

'After my healing I went on my knees and asked God to also deliver me from homosexuality.'

'Why?'

'It's a sin. It is not how God wants us to be.'

'And what happened.'

'I was cured. I have no more desire for men,' he said with a grin on his face. 'In fact, when I see a pretty woman go by, I can only say: Wow, what have I missed all these years!'

'Remarkable,' was all I could say.

'Oh yes,' he continued. 'I look at my past life and think *sies man*! How could you have been a poofter for so long. *Sies*!'

Although I'm not religious, I understand the desperation of terminally ill people and why they grasp at final straws. It was completely human for John Rindel to have fallen on his knees and turn to prayer, despite a lifetime of religious apathy. It was an entirely natural progression for him then to have bought an air ticket to Lagos, stand for hours in a queue in the stifling heat and renounce his sexuality.

My father died of lung cancer, and as he withered away, he went through similar emotions. He turned to a well-known faith healer in KwaZulu-Natal who drove the demons out of his body. It didn't help, and he died a short while later. If someone like Joshua had been on the radar screen at the time, my father might well have trekked to Lagos.

Jannie Pelser addressed the 130 South African pilgrims on their arrival at the church. 'Nothing is going to happen to you except that God will touch you. God will not pass you by. He will touch you in a very special way when you stand in the prayer line on Sunday. What do you say to that?'

'*Die Here is groot!*' (The Lord is great!) The roar came from Hennie Traut. The rest of the group burst into spontaneous song.

> *Lord I love to feel your praises,*
> *I'm so glad you came to save us,*
> *You came from heaven to earth to show us the way.*

Hennie and Moira were in Lagos for healing and spiritual enrichment. She suffered from breast cancer, back pain and crooked teeth. Hennie said he was in fine fettle but wanted the Prophet to save the sinful souls of all South Africans.

Several of the pilgrims were dying, while others were seriously ill. Maxie Claassen had breast, liver and brain cancer. Veronica Oosthuizen had crippled feet, a stiff neck, osteoporosis, arthritis and a degenerative spinal disease. Nine-year-old Muller Starke was born with an incurable heart disease and had already had two operations. He was due to have a third, but his father took him to the Prophet in the belief that he would be healed. Medical doctor Jacobus Opperman was HIV-positive, while Louis Badenhorst had cystic fibrosis and a respiratory disease.

Two sets of parents trekked to Lagos with photographs of their terminally ill children who were too weak to undertake the journey. Six-year-old Alessandro had kidney and lung cancer. One-year-old Kyle had brain damage.

Victor Wilken suffered from 'smoking and lust', Pastor Robert Sheppard had a shrill voice and Linmarie Olivier stuttered.

The morning's activities kicked off with testimony from about forty HIV/ AIDS patients who claimed the Prophet had healed them. They wore T-shirts that said: *HIV/AIDS is real and it kills. Are you a victim? A divine solution at last!*

Jannie Pelser introduced the session: 'It was medically confirmed that they had this disease in their blood. Some had already started preparing for death. Then they came to the Synagogue, where they received prayer. They went back to hospital and everyone has documented proof that he or she was healed. That virus is not in their bloodstream any longer.'

The patients held up their 'before' and 'after' certificates. I took the two pieces of paper from a woman in the first row. They were both from the Federal Ministry of Health in Lagos. The first said: 'This is to certify that Abiola Abayomi has been confirmed for HIV anti-body, using Western blot technique and was found positive on 16/04/99.' The medical laboratory scientist and the assistant director of primary health care had signed the certificate. The signature for both was the same. The same official had also signed the 'after' certificate, again on behalf of both people, dated 22/01/2001, which stated that Abiola was HIV-negative.

The certificates were ominously suspect and not worth the paper they were written on. Other 'written proof' followed a similar pattern and none would pass the scrutiny of proper examination. Nowhere in the world has it been proved that anyone has ever been cured of HIV/AIDS.

But the South Africans were in awe.

By then word had spread that Dudley, Mandla and I were non-believers and *Special Assignment* was a 'negative' programme (I doubt that many pilgrims were regular viewers). After a tedious session of testimony by the 'cured' HIV patients, a woman walked up to me and demanded: 'So, what do you say now? How are you going to get past this one?'

'We'll just have to wait and see what happens to Wium,' I said.

She continued: 'I know why *Special Assignment* sent you to Lagos.'

'Why?' I asked.

'Because Satan is using you to undermine God's work,' she spewed in disdain as I turned and walked away.

But I did wonder: was I the right person to be in Lagos? Wasn't it a bit like a vegetarian doing a story on big-game hunting? I'm not religious and cringe at the antics and frivolity of many Pentecostal churches.

I had done enough research to know that TB Joshua was nothing less than an insatiable tick feasting on the blood of the gullible and the desperate. There was no way that Wium Basson or John Rindel was going to emerge healed and healthy from the Synagogue. AIDS is incurable, and if Wium's liver cancer was indeed spreading like wildfire through his body, his end was near.

Dudley did nothing to redeem our image. He was a chain-smoker and was caught several times taking a puff around a corner or sneaking outside the compound. One of the church officials spotted a tattooed lizard – a symbol of wizardry – on his foot and he became a target of prayer.

And then there was Linmarie Olivier, a twenty-year-old blonde and blue-eyed Barbie *pop* from Pietersburg in Limpopo. She had travelled to Lagos to be cured of stuttering. The moment Dudley laid eyes on her, he mumbled: 'Oh my God, this is going to be interesting.'

Bald-headed Dudley has a devastating reputation with women. He got hold of a key to unlock a gate to the roof of the church in order to film the traffic outside. At some point, Linmarie ventured onto the roof with him. I don't know what sin the two committed, but suffice to say the poor girl's stutter was more pronounced than ever when she left the church, despite the Prophet's prayers. Pilgrims were warned beforehand that should they sin again after being healed, their original affliction would return and be even stronger than before.

Linmarie's case exposed the sinister side of Joshua's serene and saintly composure. One of his assistants showed Dudley a confession Linmarie had been ordered to write about her sinful life. She had had a private audience with Joshua, who ordered her to admit when she had lost her virginity and how many men she had slept with. The poor girl wrote several pages, and all this was blabbed to Dudley.

By day two the pilgrims were in a religious stupor after being bombarded non-stop by confessions, healing videos and promises. One of the videos showed a middle-aged and moustached South African confessing his sins. He began by saying: 'I'm a serial killer.'

Standing a few feet away was TB Joshua. 'What is the evil you have done to your fellow human beings?'

'I destroyed a lot of women with this power in my penis.' The camera moved down to focus on his crotch. 'I destroyed a lot of children. I used to urinate on people and used the urine to wash their cups.'

'You have done a lot of evil,' Joshua said as he struck the man down with a flick of his foot. The serial killer writhed in agony in the dirt. When he rose from the ground, it was with a smile on his face. He had been cleansed of his sins and all seemed fine and forgotten.

Then there was a video of what was alleged to have been a stillborn birth. In graphic detail, the mother was shown delivering a dead baby. She rushed the corpse to the church and demanded to see the Prophet. By then the child had been dead for two hours. Joshua was busy and couldn't see the mother. However, he sent a prayer on a piece of paper with the instruction that the mother should press it against the baby's chest. The video showed the mother doing just that. The baby came to life and started crying.

It was on the second day of our visit that Joshua appeared to the pilgrims. He appeared soft-spoken, gentle and caring, and I suppose if Jesus Christ did exist and was black, he might have looked like TB Joshua.

'God will heal you,' he promised. 'All of you. In His name and the glory for Him.' The South Africans broke into spontaneous song:

You came from heaven to earth
To show the way from the earth to the cross
From the cross to the grave.

People had started arriving at the church long before sunrise for the Sunday healing service. By nine the church was packed with white-robed male worshippers and women in their Sunday best, while hundreds, maybe thousands, of the sick, lame and infected lined up to await the arrival of their saviour. They held up placards that named their ailments and waited for hours under the spinning ceiling fans for the Prophet to arrive.

There was a long queue of HIV-positive victims, each one armed with a 'before' medical certificate. One of the church workers who registered the sick and wrote their afflictions on placards was a petite blonde South African by the name of Marsha du Preez. She had gone to Lagos a few months earlier, claimed she was cured of her heroin addiction and stayed on to dedicate her life to the Prophet.

'I was a complete junkie and a walking skeleton and my mother didn't know what to do with me,' she told me. 'One day she said, let's go to Nigeria on holiday. I thought, oh my God, that's so cool. Nigeria! My dealer was a Nigerian. There must be lots of drugs.'

Instead of dropping them in downtown Lagos, the taxi driver took them to the Synagogue. 'By then I was craving a fix and was going into withdrawal. But the amazing thing is, from the moment I walked in here, I never again missed heroin. The Prophet prayed for me and I never suffered from withdrawal. He's the most awesome man you'll ever meet. He's lovely, caring and passionate. My mother left me in Nigeria and went back home.'

Every possible illness, mishap and setback was written on the placards: Family Curse; Dull Brain; Business Failure; Leg Cancer; Fruit of the Womb; Irregular Breathing; Shortage of Blood; Severe Heart Breaking.

The healing service started with a woman identified as Mary Salifu, who was lifted out of a car and lowered into a wheelchair. Mary, who claimed to have been the wife of the former Nigerian ambassador to China, said she had suffered a stroke seven years ago and been paralysed ever since.

The South Africans surrounded her. Jannie Pelser gave running commentary. 'She is full of anxiety and fear. She fears that she will die if God doesn't touch her today and help her to walk.'

Joshua arrived on the scene. 'I am not the healer, but I know the healer and his name is Jesus Christ.' The woman started crying. 'Tears cannot save the soul,' Joshua said. He held a shaking hand out to her in what was known as his 'remote control'. The South Africans started singing again:

> *This is my story*
> *This is my song*
> *This is my saviour*
> *All the day long …*

Mary's toes started to move, then her feet and finally her legs. A church worker helped her as she shakily stood up from the wheelchair. She gave a few tentative steps and declared: 'I can walk now. I am strong now.'

Everybody cheered, some cried and others began to pray. The tone had been set for the rest of the day and there was a festive, even joyous atmosphere as churchgoers sang, danced and clapped. The South Africans soon joined in the festivities and it wasn't long before Hennie Traut was jiving a kind of Boere-polka with one of the female singers.

It was time to cast out evil spirits. In front of a round altar stood a young woman holding a microphone. She said: 'I've sinned against humanity and God. I wanted to woo my boyfriend and make him love me forever. A herbalist prepared a white substance. I had to rub it onto my private parts. I've called TB Joshua a magician. Please cleanse me and deliver me, oh man of God.'

Joshua stood a few feet away. 'You have sinned against God Almighty,' he said, stretching out his hand but never touching her. The woman dropped to the ground and as she snaked in the dirt, her eyes rolled back and she mumbled in tongues. A voice over the microphone declared: 'The holy spirit is casting out all the negative spirits.'

Next in line was Amina. She had a chilling story. 'I'm a sinner and I'm a murderer. I killed my baby of one year and six months old. The baby was sick and there was no solution. My sister gave me medicine to give to the child. The baby died.'

Her words were hardly cold before she, too, was writhing on the ground. She vomited as Joshua rid her body of the spirits. Churchgoers cheered.

Now the healing ceremony started in earnest. A group of people with suppurating leg ulcers was first. Joshua prayed for a soldier, who threw his crutches in the air, jumped up and down, fell to the ground and did push-ups.

'Praise God! I'm healed! I'm healed! No more pain! Hallelujah!'

A woman yelled as she leapt to her feet and ran around in circles. 'Pastor, my hands are heavy! God is touching me! In the name of Jesus Christ!'

Jacobus Opperman stood in the row of HIV sufferers. Before Joshua prayed for him, Jacobus said: 'As a doctor I know that HIV is real. AIDS will kill you and there is nothing that can cure you.'

He broke out in sweat and his knees buckled as the Prophet prayed for him. 'It's the disease coming from your body,' Joshua said as he moved on to the next person. There were too many HIV patients and Joshua couldn't pray for everyone. South African pastors – there were about fifteen of them – seized the moment and started praying and healing on his behalf. It was a mortifying spectacle: sweating, panting men in a trance-like state flapping and waving their hands in an effort to imitate Joshua. The HIV/AIDS patients were somewhat perplexed. They had come from near and far expecting to receive Joshua's personal minis-trations, but instead these white men were murmuring and grunting in a language they didn't understand. Nonetheless, they were all declared healed!

'What do you think of this?' sound technician Mandla asked me.

'Frightening,' I said.

'Why?' he wanted to know.

'There were about 200 HIV patients in the church. He didn't even pray for everyone,' I said. 'Yet they all think they've been healed. Do you know what that means?'

'What?'

'That they're going back to their husbands and wives and boyfriends and girlfriends and having sex without condoms. Do you know what that makes TB Joshua?'

'What?'

'Guilty of culpable homicide.'

'How do we prove it?'

It was difficult. The Synagogue's propaganda machine feasted on people's ignorance and the difficulty of verifying the 'before' and 'after' status of people in the HIV line. There simply wasn't time to have someone independently tested, wait for Joshua to perform a 'healing' and repeat the test a week or two later.

The only solution was to have a post-Lagos test done on one of the South African HIV patients. There were two: Jacobus Opperman and John Rindel.

Despite having testified that he was HIV-positive in the full glare of the church's extensive closed-circuit television system, in front of thousands of fellow pilgrims and our camera, Opperman suddenly decided that he did not want his status revealed or questioned by an SABC documentary. John Rindel, however, would be the perfect candidate. There was irrefutable proof that he had AIDS before his first trip to Lagos, but had been assured by Joshua that the virus was gone and ordered to return to the church to confess his miraculous healing.

John wasn't eager to be tested, though. 'I know I'm healed,' he said. 'I can feel it.'

'It's not good enough, John,' I told him.

'Why not?' he wanted to know. 'Can't you see for yourself?'

'I'm a journalist,' I said. 'I need proof. Something on paper.'

'Okay,' he said, 'I'll do it. But not for you. For TB Joshua.'

Tears cascaded down Hennie Traut's baby-pink cheeks as he lined up to receive the Prophet's grace and salvation. On his placard was written: 'Sin no more in South Africa. Win more souls for Christ in SA.'

Moira was sitting next to him, her eyes also wet, asking for healing from breast cancer, back pain and crooked teeth. A few seats away were lustful smoker Victor Wilken, terminally ill Maxie Claassen and the young Muller Starke, with his father Aubrey standing behind him. The stuttering Linmarie Oliver was also in line.

Absent, though, was Wium Basson. Since our arrival there had been no news of him. Wium and his mother were in a guestroom somewhere in the sprawling complex.

'Where's Wium?' I asked Jannie Pelser.

'He might come out later,' Pelser said.

Moira Traut was one of the first South Africans to receive prayer. As her hands shook and she convulsed in her chair, she mumbled: 'Thank you, Lord Jesus, thank you. I will never, never sin again.' She sat upright, looked at Joshua and yelped: 'Emmanuel! The Lord is alive inside me! Emmanuel!'

Moira had no doubt that she had been healed. Weak-kneed, she said afterwards: 'I feel terrific. I have no pain at all. I used to have this burning sensation, but it's all gone. He's a great guy. Cool and calm. And that's the way the Lord is. Cool and calm.'

Hennie Traut carried the burden of his people on his shoulders as he rose to his feet and stared Joshua in the face. He sobbed uncontrollably as the Prophet prayed for South Africa's salvation and redemption. Hennie stumbled around on his feet, pirouetted like a ballet dancer on one leg and afterwards declared: 'There is no doubt in my mind that the word of God is going to spread through South Africa like wildfire.'

Victor Wilken also tottered around on jellied legs before crashing to the ground. He said that after the prayer he had no desire to smoke and that his lust was gone.

'Not much to lust after in the Synagogue, Victor,' I pointed out.

'True, true. But I feel different,' he said.

Halfway through the service a beefy and bearded fellow took the microphone and introduced himself as Stefan Vosloo from Pretoria. He said: 'I have a confession to make that I want the whole world to hear. In the past I've always hated blacks, really hated them. But here I saw and felt love from black people. And I saw the love of Prophet Joshua and the way he treated people. With this sort of love we can heal our country.' His countrymen sang joyously:

Lord I give you my heart
And I give you my soul
I live for you alone.

As TB Joshua reached Maxie Claassen, she removed her headscarf with trembling hands. She had lost all her hair as a result of chemotherapy. Her daughter stood behind her, crying, as Joshua held his hand inches from Maxie's head.

'Is she healed?' her daughter asked.

'Yes,' Joshua said, 'the cancer is gone. She won't need any more medicine.' Maxie clasped her hands together, thanked him in a whimpering voice and wept.

Louis Badenhorst, suffering from cystic fibrosis, had brought three bottles of pills and an asthma pump to the prayer line. After Joshua had said his magical words and pronounced him healed, he threw his medicine on the ground and said: 'I will not need this rubbish any longer.'

The service was interrupted when more evil spirit-carriers (called *ogbanjes* in Nigeria), wizards and witches were pinpointed in the crowd. One by one they fell to the ground as Joshua floored them with his 'remote control'. They mumbled in unintelligible tongues, some had their feet 'clamped' by the man of God, they peed in their pants and one vomited out a worm.

The South Africans were perplexed. 'What do you think of all of this?' Hennie Traut asked me after yet another *ogbanje* bit the dust.

Careful not to get involved in a debate, I merely said: 'Interesting.'

'Hey man, we have to remember this is Africa,' he said, as he shook his head. 'Things work differently here.'

The crowd was fired up and sang, prayed, danced and exulted over the marvels in their midst. Churchgoers followed the events on closed-circuit television sets in and around the compound. Every now and then baskets were passed down the rows from hand to hand. They emerged stuffed with cash offerings.

Dudley and Mandla were brilliant. It was steaming hot in Lagos and the church compound was covered with corrugated iron. Sweat poured from both my colleagues as they tracked Joshua, ran around in the church to film yet another evil spirit being cast out or the South Africans symbolically washing themselves of sin. Dudley's camera lingered for a long time on Linmarie Olivier as her hands stroked her lithe body.

'His eyes are very soft and full of love,' Linmarie stammered after Joshua had attended to her. 'I had this warm feeling when he prayed for me. I believe I'll go home and speak normally.'

Pastor Robert Sheppard, who had a voice problem, shuddered in his chair as Joshua's hand trembled close to his throat. Afterwards he jumped up and shrieked in a high-pitched voice: 'Thank you, Jesus! Hallelujah! I couldn't speak loud and now I can! Praise the Lord!' I don't know how Robert sounded before, so maybe there was an improvement.

Muller Starke looked wide-eyed at the Prophet and said in a tiny voice: 'Lord Jesus has made me healthy again. I won't need any more operations.' Aubrey Starke was also convinced his son had been healed. 'It's been very emotional to see my son being prayed back to health and to know he won't need an operation. It has really touched my heart.'

Muller had an appointment with a medical specialist a week after their return to South Africa. Aubrey said he'd have the boy examined – just to make sure everything was fine.

'Can I phone you and get the results?' I asked him.

'Of course. But I already know what the answer will be.'

TB Joshua had not received a message from God to pray for Wium Basson. That was the official explanation of why the terminally ill rugby player had not emerged from his room to join the pilgrims in the prayer line.

'You mean he got a message to pray for smoking and lust and crooked teeth but not for Wium?' I asked Pelser, who said that he was sure the Prophet would pray for Wium at the next service. This meant we were stuck at the church for another four or five days.

It was our fourth day at the Synagogue and we were desperate to get out. The bottle of bourbon we had smuggled in was depleted and the sleeping arrangements and rabid atmosphere were getting to us. More and more pilgrims were praying for us, and at night there were pieces of paper with Bible verses tucked under my pillow.

I couldn't spend another night there. I had lain awake every night listening to the coughs, pants and gasps of the ill and diseased. The sounds somehow fused with the snores and spontaneous prayers, mumbling and even hymns of the religiously inflamed. The only way to escape the congested toilets was to get up at five every morning.

Pelser assured the pilgrims the next morning that Wium was well and had slept all night. It was a lie. It emerged later that he was in excruciating pain, near death and had been abandoned by TB Joshua.

Months later, I spoke to his mother, Cloeté Geldenhuys, at her home in Paarl in the Western Cape about the ten days her son had spent at the Synagogue. She said when Wium left for Lagos, he was already on his deathbed. He undertook the harrowing journey because he truly believed he was going to return a healthy man.

As soon as they had settled in, junior prophets demanded that she hand over Wium's morphine and other medication. She refused. Wium was by then in such agony that he couldn't possibly have done without painkillers. You are not allowed to give him any medicine, they instructed Cloeté, because this is the House of God and here we depend on Him for healing and salvation. She had to administer morphine to her son in secret.

Cloeté and Wium waited. They were told the Prophet had not yet received a message to pray for him. Only once during their stay did Joshua pop in to see Wium. He glanced at the dying man and said: 'Praise the Lord,' and walked out again.

I interviewed Joshua at his sacred hideaway where he prayed, meditated and prepared for his sermons. The place is known as Prayer Mountain, but to my astonishment it wasn't on a hill but in a mosquito-infested swamp slap-bang in the middle of Lagos! It consisted of a maze of stilted wooden alleyways with interlocking rooms.

I asked him about his refusal to pray for Wium. He said: 'I have not heard from God. Any moment now I can hear from Jesus. And when I hear from him, I will go and pray. There's never a sickness that Jesus cannot heal. This is a minor case. This is just a sore on the liver.'

'Why don't you go to his room and attend to his spiritual needs?' I asked him.

'My brother, I cannot look at you when you are in pain. If I don't have a solution, I will not come to you. I first want to hear from God. I cannot look at you. I cannot say I'm sorry,' he said.

Cloeté and Wium decided to stay and wait for the Wednesday healing service. Although some of the South African pilgrims and other journalists had gone home, we stayed, too. And Wium Basson clung to both life and hope. At one point he crawled on the floor in unspeakable pain and said to his mother: 'Mom, I'm dying. I cannot go on any longer.'

As the antics in the church continued unabated during the Wednesday service, Wium waited for Joshua. Just after two that afternoon, a junior prophet called the Bassons. 'The Prophet's ready,' he said, 'come to the prayer line.'

Wium looked like a corpse. Supported by Cloeté and a church worker, he slowly shuffled towards the prayer line. It was the first time any of the South Africans or I had seen him. He was ashen, gaunt and very thin. His skin had taken on a grey, cadaverous tinge and his eyes were sunken in their sockets. Pilgrims burst out in tears and I had a lump in my throat.

Wium slumped down in an armchair while Joshua prayed his way down the South African line. It was hot and sticky and sweat streamed off Wium. His mother cooled him down with a wet cloth. From time to time he threw his head back as his eyes rolled over.

Joshua reached Wium and glanced at him. Wium forced a brave smile and stuck his thumb in the air. Joshua moved on. About half an hour later he passed the dying man again. He didn't even look at him.

TB Joshua had prayed for every single South African who had come to Lagos – except for the one person who needed him most. God had instructed him to pray for lust, bad teeth, stuttering, a shrill voice and smoking, but not for a young man near to death. It was a desolate and broken Wium who was helped back to his room.

At breakfast the next morning, Pelser announced that Wium and his mother had decided to leave the Synagogue and were on their way back to South Africa.

I didn't know at the time under what circumstances they had packed their bags.

'Why did they leave?' I asked him.

'They wanted to go back,' he said. It was another lie. I discovered the truth only months later, when Cloeté confided in me. Wium and his mother had literally been kicked out of the church.

Cloeté said her son was evidently crushed after Joshua's failure to pray for him. Wium knew death was imminent, although junior prophets urged him to hang on and wait for God's message. Cloeté could do nothing but inject him with morphine, read from the Bible and pray until late into the night.

At four the next morning, mother and son were woken by church workers. Get dressed and pack your bags, they were told. The Prophet wants you to leave the church. A taxi is waiting to take you to the airport.

When I learnt that Wium and Cloeté had left, I said to Dudley and Mandla: 'That's it. Let's pack and get the hell out of here. There's nothing more to do.' While they gathered their equipment, I made a booking for the night in the five-star Hotel Le Meridién in downtown Lagos. We had been in the midst of crackpots and zealots for far too long and craved comfort, good food and booze.

As I said goodbye to John Rindel and confirmed that he would go for an AIDS test (he was due to fly back the next morning), he said to me: 'You don't believe any of this, do you?'

'No, I don't,' I said.

'You still don't believe in Jesus Christ?'

'I don't think so,' I admitted.

'And what about all the healings that have taken place?'

'You'll have to prove to me it's real,' I said, and shook his hand.

As we were about to get into a taxi, a church worker stopped us. 'The Prophet wants to see you before you leave.'

We walked into his stuffy office and sat down. For a moment an uncomfortable silence filled the air. 'We have finished our work and we are leaving. Thank you for your hospitality,' I told him.

'Well, gentlemen,' he said, 'I would like to give you some gifts before our ways part.'

We said nothing. Joshua took out three stacks of church tapes, T-shirts and religious books and put them down in front of us. We mumbled a thank you, but as we were about to get up and leave, he added: 'But I also have here a gift from God.'

He pulled three white envelopes from his drawer and put one in front of each of us. By then I already had a premonition of what the envelopes contained. I was right: wads of money! TB Joshua was trying to bribe us, to buy our good-will after his feeble performance with Wium.

Each envelope was stacked with hundred-dollar notes. There could have been one or two thousand dollars or even more in my envelope. I pushed it across the table to Joshua.

'I'm sorry,' I said, 'but I cannot accept a gift from you.'

'It's not from me,' he said, 'it's from God.'

'Doesn't matter from whom, but I cannot accept it.'

Mandla and Dudley were already counting the notes in their envelopes. 'Dudley, Mandla,' I said firmly, 'give it back. We cannot take it.'

Both stared at me in disbelief. Dudley later told me he was doing renovations to his house and could have done with a few extra grand. 'Give it back,' I said again. The two slowly pushed the envelopes towards Joshua.

We were not the first journalists TB Joshua had tried to buy. In February 2004, a British production company visited the Synagogue while making a programme on Christianity in Nigeria. Director Robert Beckford said Joshua gave him $1 000 as he was leaving the compound. The church's website did not deny giving money to Beckford. 'We felt he needed our help so we invited him and gave him free accommodation. We feel we could still help him further so we gave him $1 000. We are surprised that he can use this money against us.'

As we drove away from the church, I said to the taxi driver: 'Hotel Le Meridién. And please try and get there as quickly as possible.' He was a member of the Synagogue and not only delighted in driving us around, but spoke non-stop about the divine powers of the Man of God. As we ground to a halt in an inevitable go-slow (traffic jam), he put on gospel music. We arrived at the hotel with song and praise blaring.

If we had behaved badly on the aircraft taking us to Lagos, we now ran amok. We checked into the hotel but didn't go to our rooms. We headed straight for the Sunset Bar. Mandla and Dudley didn't order double or triple Jack Daniel's, they each got a bottle. I ordered French chardonnay. Suffice to say, the carousing lasted all day and well into the night. By the time we had to leave for the airport at four or five the next morning, we hadn't slept at all – and our bill was R13 000!

Wium Basson died within days of returning to South Africa.

TB Joshua called Cloeté just after the funeral to say he had made contact with Wium in heaven. Her boy sent his regards from 'the other side' and didn't want the family to mourn his departure from earth.

Maxie Claassen, suffering from brain, liver and breast cancer but declared healed by TB Joshua, also died shortly after returning home.

Specialists who examined nine-year-old Muller Starke found no improvement in his condition. He had to undergo further heart surgery.

John Rindel went for an AIDS test at a private clinic in Johannesburg. He called me minutes after he had received the results. 'I'm still HIV-positive,' he said. 'I'm sure it's a mistake. They make mistakes with these tests, you know?'

'I hope they did, John,' were the only words of consolation I could think of.

'I might go back to Lagos,' he said. 'I want the Prophet to pray for me again.'

John Rindel never made it back to Lagos. He died a few months later.

More than a million television sets were tuned to *Journey of Faith* in which I chronicled Wium's ill-fated trip to Lagos and Joshua's failure to heal him or anybody else I could find. After the programme, viewers phoned in with more evidence of unfulfilled promises of healing, religious fraud and even sexual abuse.

For a while South African pilgrimages slowed down to a trickle, and even the Prophet's subservient houseboy, Jannie Pelser, stopped trekking to Lagos. Churches warned their members not to seek instant and cheap solutions in Lagos, and TB Joshua became the subject of endless radio and newspaper debates.

But the Synagogue and the Prophet hit back with a vengeance. They put my name and photograph on their website under the headline 'International Journalists Swarm The Synagogue'. I was quoted as having said: 'In my whole life, I have never seen an avalanche of miracles such as the ones that take place here.'

And then Joshua regurgitated a spectacle that would not only restore faith in his ability to heal but gain him the reputation of possessing the divine power to bring the dead back to life. Such an attribute was worth a pot of gold, as it could attract thousands more to his church – especially from the miracle-hungry, religiously naive and dollar-swaggering American market.

A year after our visit, newspapers reported that the Prophet had resurrected a seventy-six-year-old man by the name of Moses. He was among a group of South African pilgrims in Lagos when he suffered a heart attack in the dining room. Thousands of church videos were distributed around the world showing three pilgrims, including a medical doctor from Bloemfontein, trying to resuscitate Moses. According to the video, the resuscitators failed and the 'dead' man was carried to a room in the church. TB Joshua walked into the room, bent over Moses and ordered him: 'In the name of Jesus, rise! Rise now!' Moses opened his eyes and with a gasp of breath 'came back to life'.

The video was exposed as fraud when it emerged that Moses had been both alive and breathing when he was carried from the dining hall. His awakening was a simple matter of resuscitation, not resurrection. Joshua calling on the 'dead man' to rise was cheap and nasty deceit and the video the result of manipulative editing.

TB Joshua and his disciples and followers remained defiant and unashamed. The church continued to grow, and Joshua subsequently set up congregations in Germany, Korea, Austria, Australia and South Africa with familiar claims of wonders, miracles and salvation.

I suppose desperation spawns ignorance, and South Africans once again began flocking to Lagos. What in the Afrikaner psyche found TB so irresistible? Why did so many fall hook, line and sinker for his buffoonery and pranks?

Perhaps it was because Afrikaners had so recently awakened from centuries of repressive and agonising Christian National Education, which fostered the belief that heaven was white and hell was black, with something in between for Indians and Coloureds.

Suddenly, with the dawn of a new South Africa, a messiah emerged from darkest Africa and extended to them a hand of forgiveness and redemption. The blackness of his face and the 'Africanness' of his church made him simply irresistible.

But it went deeper than that. TB Joshua not only promised to absolve them of their white guilt, but liberated them from the chains and shackles of Calvinism, which had for generations instilled a sense of suffering, remorse and fear into virtually every Afrikaner heart. TB allowed them to worship with gusto and a fervour previously thought unseemly.

The result of this newfound unholy brotherhood?

A religious hodgepodge concocted in cloud cuckoo land.

CHAPTER 13

A wife for the baas, tontonto for the native

I smile when I'm angry.
I cheat and I lie.
I do what I have to do
To get by.
But I know what is wrong,
And I know what is right.
And I'd die for the truth
In my secret life.
– Leonard Cohen, 'In My Secret Life'

THERE WAS A SOFT KNOCK, A MOMENT OF SILENCE AND ANOTHER knock. I looked up to see an elderly and dark-skinned man standing in the doorway. He was squat and stocky and held a file in his hand.

He nodded his head. 'Good morning, sir,' he said softly. 'I hope I am not disturbing your peace, but I am here to make your acquaintance.'

'Sure, come in.'

He continued in an almost subservient tone. 'My name is Alpheus Siebane, sir. We spoke on the phone yesterday in connection with body parts.'

We shook hands and I showed him a chair. He sat upright on the edge of the seat and said: 'This is my file, which I would like to draw your attention to. I think once you have studied it you will agree that we should proceed to do a story on body parts.'

The file contained *Sunday Times* clippings of articles he had written about the trade in human body parts. He had exposed a muti (traditional medicine) shop in downtown Johannesburg that had sold a baby's liver and heart. The owner was arrested and appeared in court, but the case fell apart when the state prosecutor died in a mysterious car accident. There was also a letter of reference from a *Sunday Times* editor, who described Alpheus as diligent, hard-working and resourceful.

'I am aware of several *inyangas* (black witchdoctors) in Johannesburg and Venda who sell human body parts or make muti from them,' he said. 'In some cases the parts come from up north, from Mozambique, Malawi and Tanzania. I think we can solve this riddle.'

'It's a great story,' I said. 'Tell me about it.'

His face lit up and he leant forward. For the next half-hour he poured forth a freakish tale of *inyangas* who concocted muti from human flesh – eyes, ears, genitals, intestines, organs and whatever else they could lay their hands on.

'How do you propose we go about it?'

'Sir, I'll buy an eye or a heart and you can film it! If they don't have any in stock, we can order,' he said.

'No way!' I said. 'We can't become part of the trade! Somebody might get killed for the part you want. What then?'

Alpheus said a substantial part of the trade originated from workers in hospital and state morgues who removed body parts from pauper corpses and sold them to *inyangas*.

'Nobody gets killed, sir,' he said. 'So I would suggest that we proceed on this basis.'

Alpheus was an amicable, open-faced fellow and I immediately warmed to him. He'd had an illustrious career as a journalist in the former homeland of Venda and was renowned for his exposés on body parts, wizardry and witchcraft in this almost mystical region of South Africa's northernmost province. One of his two wives still lived in Venda and was a member of the royal household.

I gave him a contract, a spy camera and a stern warning: Don't buy or order any body parts. Merely enquire if the trader has anything in stock. If so, say you want to see the parts and try to film them.

I assigned producer Anna-Maria Lombard to work with Alpheus, and before long the duo had produced remarkable results. In the gloom of a decrepit and makeshift shack somewhere under a bridge in Johannesburg's central business district, an obese man by the name of Pretty Vukutu pulled a human eye from a glass bottle. Fatty blood vessels dangled from the ball that he held triumphantly in his pudgy fingers for Alpheus to see.

'There are many where this comes from. Nice hey?' Alpheus sat with a grey sling bag on his lap and captured the macabre incident perfectly on spy camera.

Alpheus and Anna-Maria went off to Venda, his home turf and the centre of the trade in body parts. It was among the green valleys and sacred lakes that a new side of Alpheus emerged: his obsession with musician Leonard Cohen and with his song, 'In My Secret Life'. He would get into the car in the morning and not say a word until he had listened to *his* song. He was a notoriously bad driver but detested the fact that a woman was driving him around. While Anna-Maria had to navigate her way through valleys and around herds of goats, he would lustily sing along:

I'll be marching through the morning,
Marching through the night,
Moving cross the borders
Of my secret life.

In a remote village, he found Sara (not her real name), a young woman ostracised by her community after she had killed her baby. Her boyfriend had had a dream that he would find a cure for AIDS, but he needed fresh human blood. He persuaded Sara to murder her infant. They dismembered the child and strained its blood into a bottle. The baby's remains were stuffed into a bag and buried. They were both arrested and charged with murder, but Sara turned state witness and was pardoned. Her boyfriend was sentenced to life imprisonment.

Sara, who was relatively well educated and could speak English, was desperate to get out of Venda. She agreed to be interviewed, but wanted Alpheus and Anna-Maria to help her find a job in Johannesburg. They did – at a chicken take-away in Melville!

I discovered only later that Alpheus also had an affair with Sara, which of course would have been off-limits, as she was both a case study and severely traumatised. She was haunted by nightmares, couldn't sleep and cried incessantly.

Back in Johannesburg, Alpheus made contact with a laboratory assistant at the mortuary of the Medical University of South Africa (Medunsa) in Garankuwa, west of Pretoria. Levi Masebe boasted that he was selling body parts and that there was a cadaver in the morgue that was 'ready to go'. He offered to sell two hands for R3 000.

'Let me go and show you,' Levi said to Alpheus.

Alpheus couldn't believe his luck. 'You will?'

'Oh yes, there's nobody in the lab but me.'

While Alpheus waited in the laboratory for Levi to fetch the corpse from a refrigerator, he switched the camera on. Levi pushed a trolley into the room, lifted the white sheet and revealed the yellow, bloodless and bloated cadaver of a young man. It was covered in roughly sutured incisions and scars where medical students had practised their surgical skills.

'We're finished with it. It's ready to go,' Levi said, and continued to explain in detail how and where he was going to cut the hands off.

The two agreed to meet again the next day. It was an elated Alpheus who strode into my office an hour or two later. 'Got him!' he said, as he lifted the camera, entangled in a mesh of cables, from his bag.

'Watch this,' he said, as the screen flickered to life. There was a brief glimpse of the laboratory before the camera blinked once or twice and went black. Nothing else. Alpheus stared in disbelief at the dead screen.

'It didn't work,' he said.

It wasn't the first time that the spy camera had let us down at a crucial time. In fact, the results were seldom perfect. There was often a loose connection, the light was too bright or low, or the pin-eyed lens simply faced in the wrong direction.

'Now we're fucked,' said a dejected Alpheus.

The plan had been to confront Levi the next morning with a full camera team at the laboratory with our spy camera footage as evidence. Now we had nothing. Alpheus couldn't go back and ask Levi to show him the body again.

There was only one solution: buy a hand! It was a decision I would afterwards deeply regret. It took me weeks and piles of memorandums and meetings with the SABC's financial manager to explain why we had found it necessary to invest thousands of rand in a venture of that nature. The hand followed another unorthodox purchase a few months earlier: a fighting dog. A former dogfight gambler had told us that if we bought a puppy from a trainer, we could infiltrate the blood sport's inner circle and expose it. We paid R3 000 for the puppy, but the whole story fell apart when our source got cold feet and pulled out. We gave the bull terrier puppy to friends who offered to look after it. This acquisition was discussed at the highest management level of the broadcasting corporation. Eventually the top brass said they wanted proof: where was the dog? They wanted to see it. A short while later, an external auditing house descended on *Special Assignment* to probe our financial affairs. The dog and the hand were at the top of their list.

In buying the hand we were complicit in committing a crime, but I was convinced we could justify it in that we were exposing a crime and that it was in the public interest.

We left for the university the next morning armed with a plastic bag full of money and a cooler box of ice. Anna-Maria and I waited in the cafeteria while Alpheus smooth-talked his way past security guards into the laboratory.

He emerged an hour later with a smirk on his face. The amputated hand was in the box, packed in ice. By the time we got back to our office, after an hour's drive on a sweltering late summer's morning, the ice had almost melted and the severed limb – which we took out to film – was grey and yellow and fast becoming disconcertingly rubbery.

What to do with the hand? It eventually found its way to a bar fridge in Anna-Maria's garage. Needless to say, the fridge was retired soon after.

About a week later, Anna-Maria and Alpheus returned the frozen hand to the cooler box and went to Medunsa to confront Levi and interview the head of the anatomy department. They left the cooler box in the laboratory. The cameraman and Alpheus stepped outside for a smoke. Anna-Maria, in her usual frantic fashion, paced the passage outside the lab while negotiating with the professor on her cellphone. When the professor finally declined an interview and informed the team that the police were en route, they returned to the laboratory. The hand was gone! It was never found again.

Levi Masebe was arrested, charged and convicted, but the story had an almost catastrophic aftermath when angry residents in Soweto pounced on Pretty Vukutu, the trader who had shown Alpheus the eye. The mob accused Pretty of being a witch. He narrowly escaped with his life, but his house was burnt down. The police took Pretty into protective custody, and he promptly held a press conference at Johannesburg Central Police Station to protest his innocence.

'They didn't get anything right,' Pretty protested. 'They even said I'm a man. Well, I'm not a man, I'm a woman!'

You could have floored Alpheus and Anna-Maria with a feather! Pretty was a hermaphrodite and officially registered as a female, although he/she looked, spoke and had the demeanour of a man.

The story made headlines, and Anna-Maria and Alpheus were nominated as finalists for South Africa's Journalist of the Year award. The morning before the award ceremony I took Alpheus to Rosebank in Johannesburg and hired him a tuxedo. He admired himself for quite some time in the mirror and said: 'I've never worn anything this beautiful.'

They won the award, and I have never seen a prouder man than Alpheus, his round face wreathed in a broad smile as he posed for photographers. In one hand was his award certificate and in the other a cheque for R50 000.

Not only could Alpheus now afford a car, but the award also elevated him to celebrity status. His Soweto neighbours threw him a street bash, a provincial cabinet minister held a tea party in his honour, and women, he told me with a twinkle in his eye, phoned and harassed him non-stop.

Not long afterwards, Alpheus and Anna-Maria produced another award-winner when they infiltrated and exposed so-called sweatshops in the Johannesburg suburb of Fordsburg. Unscrupulous businessmen operated illegal clothing, textile and food factories in dilapidated buildings. None of the sweatshops met any safety standards, and in many cases labourers – mostly illegal immigrants from neighbouring states – were enslaved, abused and locked up.

Alpheus pretended to be a Zimbabwean job seeker and managed to spend a few nights in sweatshops. On the morning before broadcast, the Department of Labour raided several of the buildings, arrested owners and shut down one illegal operation.

But Alpheus's newfound fame had a downside – there was a warrant for his arrest and the cops were onto him! It turned out that he had stolen a computer from his previous employer. He had a completely different version of events, but had signed a confession admitting to unlawful 'borrowing'. The employer was willing to withdraw the charge if Alpheus paid for the computer. He undertook to do so.

Alpheus's next assignment was in the Mozambican capital of Maputo, where desperate poverty and civil unrest had given birth to a secret sex trade – human trafficking. For as little as R1 000, one could buy a Mozambican girl and have her delivered to your doorstep in South Africa. She was yours to do with as you wished.

A human rights organisation contacted *Special Assignment* with information about a syndicate that recruited Mozambican girls by offering them jobs as waitresses and shop attendants in Johannesburg. The racketeers then smuggled their gullible victims across the border into South Africa, where they incarcerated them in transit houses for a day or two.

By then, the girls were confused and disorientated. They didn't know where they were, and their captors had seized any identity documentation or papers and money they'd had. They were in South Africa illegally, and therefore at the mercy of their abductors.

As dusk fell, it was what the syndicates called payback time. They told the girls they had transported them at great risk and expense across the border and deserved a reward. Their captors were blunt: you *will* fuck tonight. Those who refused or resisted were raped. Their ordeal often lasted the whole night.

The next day they were bundled into taxis and driven to Johannesburg. Once in the City of Gold, they were sold to the highest bidders – either low-class brothels on the seedy side of town or mineworkers living in hostels and compounds around the city.

Up to four million women and children are trafficked around the world every year, and the United Nations has branded this one of the biggest and fastest-growing organised crimes. South Africa has become a regional centre for human trafficking, with local and international syndicates smuggling women and children into the country from across the subcontinent and from as far away as China, Bulgaria and Russia. The Eastern European, Thai and Chinese girls usually end up in upper-class bordellos in Johannesburg's northern suburbs, while the Malawians, Zimbabweans and Mozambicans are sold to downmarket brothels.

South Africa is a signatory to the UN Protocol on Trafficking in Persons and has drafted legislation to outlaw the practice. Mozambique, however, has not ratified the protocol and trafficking isn't a crime in that country.

I despatched Alpheus to Maputo to scrounge the city's markets, clubs and dives in search of traffickers and their girls. It was his first trip 'abroad'. Although he had grown up virtually right next door to Mozambique, he had never been there.

Despite Maputo's exotic and tropical veneer, there is no disguising the devastation of almost two decades of civil war. Snot-nosed orphans clutching glue bottles, destitute mothers with babies and legless beggars on crutches litter the streets – the result of economic destruction, a lack of the most basic social services and some of the world's most lethal minefields. Despite a post-war business boom and one of the highest economic growth rates in the world, two-thirds of the population live in dire poverty and average life expectancy is only thirty-seven. Almost half of the population is younger than eighteen and cannot find jobs upon leaving school.

The result is a desperation that forces many young women onto the streets – and into the claws of slippery and sneaky thugs like Mazet, a human trafficker whose acquaintance Alpheus made in a Maputo market. Mazet sold girls and young women to low-class brothels and Mozambican mineworkers in South Africa.

Alpheus told Mazet that he worked for a white brothel owner who wanted *fresh* girls. No problem, said Mazet. I'm in Johannesburg next week. Tell your boss to meet me and we can discuss a deal.

A few days later, Alpheus gave Mazet and his girlfriend, Hercillia, a lift to Johannesburg. They first stopped at Mazet's house in a village near Komatipoort on the border between South Africa and Mozambique. While they had lunch, Mazet told Alpheus that this was where the girls stayed for their first night in South Africa and where he and his henchmen 'initiated' them.

As they approached Johannesburg, Mazet asked Alpheus to drop him and Hercillia at an old farmhouse on the outskirts of Soweto. He said he kept the girls there before despatching them to the mines and brothels.

We met Mazet the next morning at an Angolan bar. He was flashily dressed in a cheap yellow suit, a collection of gold chains adorned his neck and two cellphones rang non-stop. He walked with a swagger and spoke with the glibness of a bordello tycoon. He was clearly trying to impress me.

'I've got three girls,' he said. 'All pretty. One is seventeen, another nineteen and the last one twenty-two. But she's the nicest. Very pretty.'

The owner filled our glasses with acidic Portuguese red wine from a five-litre plastic container and topped them up with Coke. Several foreigners were glued to a television set screwed to steel brackets in a corner, blaring out a mixture of Angolan government propaganda and cheap Brazilian soap operas.

Mazet made no secret of being a human trafficker who acted with impunity and without fear of prosecution. He crossed the border weekly without a passport and smuggled six to eight girls to Johannesburg every month. He didn't regard this as a crime, although what he was involved in amounted to nothing less than kidnapping and rape.

'Policemen? Ha, they're nothing. I pay them,' he boasted.

Mazet showed me his forged South African identity document. It was in the name of Joseph Khoza. His real name, he said, was Joshia Lubisi. Mazet was just a nickname.

Alpheus was sitting next to me as quiet as a mouse, the grey sling bag resting on his lap. The lens was aimed a little low and sometimes cut Mazet's face in half, but the conversation was clearly audible, even against the background of an Angolan military band on the TV set.

'The girls all think they're going to work in a restaurant?' I asked Mazet.

'Ja, that is what I have told them.'

'And when do you tell them the real story?'

'I tell them in my house.'

'Which house?'

'The one in Komatipoort.'

'And how do you tell them?'

'Ha, you don't worry. When they come from there, they are ready to fuck.'

'And then you sell them on the mines?'

'Ja, I sell them at the mines. The men need wives,' he said.

'She becomes a prostitute?'

'Sometimes. Other times she's just a wife.'

A few days later, Alpheus and I set off for Maputo to meet up with Mazet again. Before we reached the border and while he was telling me about his daughter at university and his recent holiday in the Eastern Cape, my cellphone rang. It was Alpheus's previous employer, who told me he hadn't yet paid for the computer. He knew we were on our way to Mozambique and threatened to alert the border police. Alpheus was facing arrest. Before I had finished the call, the elderly man sitting next to me burst into tears. An asthma sufferer, he was also short of breath.

'What now?' I asked him.

'I'll sort it out. Drop me at the border post. You go through. I'll see you in Maputo later today or tomorrow.'

Alpheus arrived in Maputo the next day looking scraggy and exhausted. It turned out he had paid a 'guide' at the border post to smuggle him into Mozambique. He said he had had to plod over a mountain and through thorn bushes, scale a razor-wire fence and bribe both Mozambican and South African border patrols. When they got to the national road, a minibus picked him up and took him to Maputo. Ironically, he had travelled by the same route that Mazet used to traffic his girls.

We picked Mazet up on a Friday afternoon and drove to a bar to meet the girls. 'Don't say anything about a club,' Mazet said. 'They think you have a restaurant and that you are looking for Mozambican waitresses because you serve Portuguese food.'

'Where do they come from?'

'They work in the market.'

'And how much do you want?'

'R3 000 a girl.'

'And what if they get to Johannesburg and they don't want to be prostitutes?'

'Don't worry. I've told you they'll be ready to fuck.'

The three girls arrived with Hercillia, who it seemed was Mazet's recruiter. The two younger girls were sisters, slightly thickset and rather ordinary looking. The oldest was called Anita, and she was delicately built with big brown eyes and thick dreadlocks. They greeted me in Portuguese and shyly shook my hand. As they ordered Fanta Orange, Mazet explained something about a restaurant and pointed at me. They smiled and nodded their heads.

'They all want to go to South Africa,' Mazet said. 'They are happy to work for you.'

On the way back to our hotel, Mazet said he wanted to leave for Johannesburg the following Wednesday. Alpheus and I decided that night that we had to find the girls and warn them about Mazet's plans. We went to the market the next morning and found Anita behind her stall of green peppers, onions and tomatoes. She didn't understand English, but she could speak to Alpheus in Shangaan. He told her we had to see her, and we made an appointment to meet at her parents' home on Sunday afternoon.

The family had a pig farm next to the main road between Maputo and Xai-Xai. We were clearly expected. Anita's brother greeted us at the car and showed us to a neatly set table under a big tree. I was ushered to a chair at the head of the table. Then I was introduced to the rest of the family. Her father was pissed out of his skull and could barely stand. To my astonishment, her mother, a sturdy woman wearing a bright red headscarf, kissed me heartily on both cheeks before saying something to Alpheus in Shangaan.

Alpheus chuckled liké an awkward teenager and said: 'She's very happy to see you.'

Something was wrong. 'What's going on, Alpheus?' I asked him.

'I'm not sure yet, but I'll find out.'

Next in line were the grandmother and grandfather and a long line of brothers and sisters. All greeted me like a long-lost son. Anita finally arrived, clad in her Sunday best. She greeted me coyly and sat down on the chair next to me. A brother brought beer, while the father quaffed Mozambican whisky. He stared at me with bloodshot eyes and a smirk on his face. The mother brought plates of spicy roast pork and sweet custard pastries.

'So when do we tell her about Mazet?' I asked Alpheus.

'Definitely not now. We can't.'

'What's going on here?'

'I'll tell you later.'

One of the brothers invited us to inspect the family's pigsty. I was happy to get away from the intense gazes. The brother pointed at a big, black boar and said something in Shangaan to Alpheus. He burst out laughing so heartily that he spilt his beer.

'What, Alpheus?' I demanded.

'That one,' he sniggered, pointing to the animal, 'is for the wedding. And whether you like it or not, I'm your best man!'

It slowly dawned on me. Anita thought I wanted to take her to South Africa to marry her! And the family was obviously delighted with their future son-in-law. Their daughter was, after all, twenty-two years old, divorced and a single mother. Not exactly marriage material in Mozambique.

We sat for another excruciating hour under the tree until Anita's father fell over and was carried away by two of his sons. Alpheus and Anita's mother were babbling away, discussing the wedding.

'Over there,' said Alpheus, pointing into the darkness, 'is going to be a church tent. The family is big and they will come all the way from Bilene.'

He was clearly deriving great pleasure from my predicament. 'She wants to know if you're a Christian?'

I mumbled something inaudible. He told her I was a devout Christian. When I finally wrenched Alpheus from the table, Anita's mother bid me farewell as though I was her soldier boy going off to war in Iraq. Anita, who hadn't spoken throughout the visit, again held out her hand. This time, however, she looked up at me.

As we got into the car, I got a take-away of pork and custard pies and Alpheus a bottle with a whitish liquid for the road. 'What's that?' I asked him.

'*Tontonto,*' he said.

'What's that?'

'Homemade booze,' he said. 'It burns your lips white!'

A while later, he chirped: 'That's how Mozambique works. A wife for the white *baas* and *tontonto* for the native!'

Alpheus said Anita didn't like the idea of being a waitress. Mazet had concocted a story that I was looking for a wife and fancied her. In turn, Anita wanted a husband who could care for her and the baby.

We went to the market the next day to break the news to my 'betrothed'. She looked truly humiliated and devastated, and just shook her head when we told her about Mazet's true intentions. Everything had sounded just too good to be true, she lamented, and promised to warn the other two not to go.

'I've been thinking a lot,' Alpheus said on our way back. 'Maybe I should take Anita to Johannesburg and take care of her. Poor girl.'

'Oh please! Keep your dirty paws off her,' I told him. 'Pay your computer debt first.'

Alpheus and I had had a squabble earlier that morning. The hotel manager had complained to me at breakfast that there was another person sleeping in Alpheus's room, and we were only paying single rates. I knocked on his door. In his room was a young girl – wide-eyed and trying to cover her face. She couldn't have been older than fourteen or fifteen.

Two days earlier I had dragged Alpheus from the beach, where he was frolicking with the same girl in the shallow waves. I told him then: 'She's not just young enough to be your daughter; you could have been her grand-father!'

Alpheus had succumbed to the carnal pleasures of Maputo. With its steamy and tropical climate, hot and spicy food, and buoyant and playful people, the city holds a sensual and seductive promise. The best time in Maputo is on a balmy Sunday when the beaches along Avenida Marginal swarm with a throng of black and brown bodies and the air is permeated with the smell of barbecued chicken and peri-peri prawns. Teenage boys in baggy beach shorts play volley-ball, while girls in itsy-bitsy bikinis adorn the shoreline.

The Portuguese had left an exotic legacy in Mozambique. Besides the brilliant art deco houses and buildings that line the *avenidas* named for Samora Machel, Julius Nyerere and Mao Tse-tung, the colonial masters had no qualms about marrying or sleeping with locals. In the wake of their sudden departure from the country in 1975, they left a generation of mixed-blood and olive-skinned Mozambicans. The result was some of the most vivacious and buxom women on the African continent.

'These *mulattos* drive me mad,' Alpheus once said to me. 'Something happens to me in this place. I don't know what it is.'

I told Alpheus it wasn't him the girls found attractive, but his money and his comfortable room at the three-star Hotel Terminus. He promised to keep his libido in check and avoid Maputo's late-night clubs, yet, two days later, there was another girl in his room – Anita's eighteen-year-old friend, whom Mazet wanted to traffic!

The woman had barely escaped being a victim of sexual exploitation, I bawled at him, and now you take advantage of her! I told Alpheus he had to go back to Johannesburg to face a disciplinary hearing. First the computer theft, then the warrant for his arrest, then the fourteen-year-old – and now this woman in his room!

He burst into tears and offered his resignation. I accepted. He wrote it on a piece of paper. It was the second time that I had a run-in with a *Special Assignment* spy camera operator. The first had left after extorting CDs from a record company. He threatened to expose their appalling labour practices if they didn't supplement his CD collection. At the time he was also up for murder for allegedly executing a hijacker who had wanted to take his car. After quitting our team, he became a traffic cop!

But before Alpheus could leave, Mazet phoned. Come and see me, he said, because I've got new girls. His call extended Alpheus's professional life at *Special Assignment* for another few days.

Mazet directed us to a house in a suburb near Maputo's international airport. Hercillia was waiting for us with two girls. Amelia Lazaro was twenty-one years old and one of seven children. She had a baby of eight months and had to find a job in order to look after the infant. She had been a waitress at an ice-cream parlour called Ponto Final, but they had laid off staff and she was out on the street. Etelvinah Nkuna was eighteen, olive-skinned and exotically beautiful. She had trained as a hairdresser in Maputo, but had also lost her job.

Hercillia turned out to be Etelvinah's aunt. I was astounded to think that Mazet's girlfriend was trafficking her own family, but according to various international studies, this was not unique. Human traffickers often recruit their relatives. It's easy, because the victims trust them.

We never had a private moment with either girl to get their telephone numbers or find a way of contacting them. Three of Mazet's hoodlums were always lurking nearby. Mazet himself wouldn't let anything slip about where the women lived. Maybe he was suspicious after the failure of his previous operation.

Mazet said he was leaving for South Africa within the next day or two. He wanted R3 000 for each girl. 'Prime meat,' he said, as he pointed at Etelvinah and Amelia and fixed a price. I tried to delay their departure by telling him I had spent all my money when the first deal fell through and it would take some time to get money again. 'Tough,' he said, 'they're going in any case.'

We met him again the next day to renegotiate the price. He came down to R5 000 for the pair. 'I can make more than that on the mines. Take it or leave it,' he said.

I was faced with a terrible dilemma. How far do you go as a journalist? Do you remain a mere reporter, recorder and onlooker in the face of death, suffering and human tribulation? Or do you intervene, save, shelter and shield? What was I supposed to do? Watch the women being carted off to Johannesburg, knowing they would have to walk for miles through bushes, scale the border fence and probably be forced to have sex with Mazet and his cronies? And know that they would then be sold to mineworkers who might infect them with AIDS? Did I play any part in their recruitment and trafficking? Alpheus was adamant: no, Mazet would in any case have recruited and smuggled them across the border.

We considered our options. We didn't know where the women lived and couldn't warn them. We went to Ponto Final the next day to find out if anyone knew where Amelia was. They couldn't help us. It would have been worthless to go to the Mozambican police. Not only do they have a terrible record of corruption and bribery, but the only accusation I could level against Mazet was a conspiracy to commit trafficking. And that wasn't even a crime in Mozambique. In addition, Alpheus was in the country illegally. We didn't think it was a good idea to confront Mazet on camera and reveal our true identities to him. Not with his henchmen prowling around.

However, once the women were in South Africa, we could help them. Mazet would be on foreign soil, and illegally too. I could involve the police and ask them to raid his house or intercept the minibus on its way to Johannesburg. We knew what route he took. We did not know, though, if we could prevent the girls from spending their first night with Mazet and his men in the house near Komatipoort.

It was an issue I never resolved, because the very next day I received a phone call from Mazet.

'We are leaving this afternoon. The girls will be in Johannesburg tomorrow afternoon,' he said.

We rushed to his house. A minibus was already waiting to transport the girls to the footpath from where they would walk several kilometres to the border fence.

'Why are you going now?'

'I know a South African soldier who's on patrol this afternoon. He says he can unlock the gate for us. Then we don't have to climb the fence.'

Amelia and Etelvinah were both clad in frippery, complete with new high-heeled sandals. They had no idea what lay ahead for them. Etelvinah and her boyfriend were sitting on a bench in the backyard holding hands. Amelia, her mother and baby were sitting under a tree talking to Hercillia.

Mazet ordered the girls to board the minibus. They both carried small bags. Etelvinah kissed and hugged her boyfriend; Amelia embraced her tearful mother and screaming baby.

And then, as the taxi door slammed shut, from nowhere and from all directions, heavily armed policemen and soldiers swooped on us. I was too dumbfounded to move. A soldier shakily pointed an AK-47 at me and barked something in Portuguese. I didn't know what he said, but I understood perfectly that he was toting an automatic rifle capable of shredding me to pieces. I thought it appropriate to drop my sling bag and stick my hands in the air. Alpheus followed suit. Within seconds, Alpheus, Mazet, his henchmen and I were bundled onto the back of an army truck and driven away.

It later emerged that one of the neighbours had become suspicious of the presence of so many men – especially a white one – and young girls at the house. She contacted the police, and the security branch launched a full investigation. We had been under surveillance for several days.

We stopped a few minutes later at a police station and were marched into an office. Mazet and his men were taken to another section of the station. A tall, sinewy man in a purple shirt and a black tie introduced himself in English. His ID card showed he was a brigadier in the police special branch. With him were four or five plainclothes policemen.

He looked at me and said: 'You are under arrest.'

'For what?' I asked him.

'Kidnapping. Maybe more. We're still investigating.'

'Kidnapping of whom?'

'The women. We know everything.'

'Nonsense,' I said.

His demeanour became icy cold. 'Who do you think you are? Do you realise in how much trouble you are?'

It was Friday afternoon and there was a real prospect of spending the weekend behind bars in a rotten and decrepit Mozambican prison, charged with God alone knew what. For all I knew, the police might have decided we were spies. I reckoned confession was the best defence. 'We are journalists, sir. We are investigating the trafficking of women to South Africa.'

The policemen looked at me incredulously. 'You can tell that to the judge next week when we take you to court.'

'We have to go to court, sir?'

'Yes. Next week.'

'And until then, sir?'

'You stay in prison.'

Because we were working undercover, we had left our press cards and a letter from an SABC editor stating the purpose of our visit to Mozambique at the hotel. It was a silly mistake.

I'd had altercations with authorities in foreign countries before and had always been able to talk (or bribe) my way out of trouble. But things looked bleak. 'If you allow us to go back to our hotel rooms, sir, we can prove that we are journalists.'

The brigadier wouldn't budge. 'Tell that to the judge next week.'

We were ordered to empty our pockets and take off our shoes, belts and jewellery. I had a wad of American dollars.

'Ha! Obviously to pay for the girls,' sniggered the brigadier.

One of the policemen inspected our passports. 'Where's your visa?' he asked, pointing at Alpheus, who seemed paralysed in the face of calamity and stared straight ahead of him. I tried to explain he had entered the country illegally in order to uncover the route used by Mazet.

The brigadier gave a sardonic smile and said to one of his underlings: 'Add illegal entry to the charge sheet.'

A policeman pulled the spy camera from Alpheus's bag. A flickering red light indicated that it was still running, as Alpheus had been filming the departure of the girls. The cop frantically pulled at the wires to try to get the device to stop. This was too much for Alpheus, who up to now had been numb. He leapt from his chair and snatched the camera from the cop's hands.

'Don't do this! You'll break it!' For a moment pandemonium broke loose as the cops jumped on Alpheus and wrestled him back to his chair. The brigadier bellowed something in Portuguese, and we were marched off to the cells at the back of the police station.

We were pushed into a communal cell with about eight other inmates. It was even worse than I had imagined. There was a layer of grime on the floor and an odour of piss enveloped the space. Alpheus and I sat down on a grass mat in a corner and for a long time didn't say a word. I swore to myself there and then that if they kept us inside I would embark on a devastating hunger strike – to avoid using the single toilet that stood out like a sore thumb in the darkest corner of the cell!

Time ticked by. I knew the cops were going to knock off at four or five and leave us in that stinking hole for the weekend. The other inmates looked like juvenile gangsters and were sitting in an opposite corner of the cell. One tried to speak to Alpheus, but he brushed him off.

'What did he want?'

'Cigarettes. He said he heard that we've got lots of money.'

'And what did you say to him?'

'The police have taken everything.'

At four thirty, the cell door swung open and a guard ordered us to follow him. He escorted us to the brigadier's office, where our possessions were spread out on his desk. Among them were camera tapes, batteries and our press cards. The brigadier must have realised that we were journalists, after all. He seemed more amicable.

'So you are journalists?'

'We are indeed, sir.'

'I am not sure that it changes anything.'

I took a long shot. 'I beg of you, sir, is there no possibility that I can make just one phone call? I'm sure we can then sort this out.'

'Who do you want to phone?'

'My embassy, sir. I beg you.'

He spoke in Portuguese to his colleagues and said: 'I'm sorry, but we don't have airtime on our phones.'

I spotted a ray of hope. 'I'm sure I can help, sir. I have no objection against buying you airtime.'

A policeman unlocked a safe and took out our money. Accompanied by the brigadier and two guards, we rushed to a spaza shop behind the police station to buy a pay-as-you-go card. I also bought cigarettes, cold drinks and chocolates for everyone. One of the guards wanted a packet of chips and biscuits. He got them. It was just before five when I got through to the *Special Assignment* office in Johannesburg.

Anna-Maria Lombard answered the phone. 'Phone the South African embassy in Maputo,' I told her, 'and tell them we're in prison. They must come immediately.' I gave her the brigadier's telephone number.

A few minutes later, she phoned back. 'I spoke to the embassy. They're on their way.' Not long afterwards a diplomatic delegation in a Mercedes-Benz and a 4×4 screeched to a halt in front of the police station. The driver opened the door for Her Excellency the High Commissioner, who strutted with great purpose into the station, took one look at me and said to the brigadier: 'I know him. He is a journalist. He has to be released.'

I wanted to kiss her. Alpheus and I waited in the office while a meeting commenced behind closed doors between the High Commissioner and the brigadier. When the two parties emerged fifteen minutes later, the brigadier's bravado had dissipated.

'Gentlemen, you are released,' he announced. 'I am sorry if we caused you any inconvenience.'

The brigadier personally counted our money and gave it back to us. It must have been the first time that anybody left Mozambican police cells with the same amount of money as when he was incarcerated.

He thanked us for the contribution we had made to justice and ensuring the safety of the girls. 'Mister Mazet will spend a long time in prison. Be sure of that. We have very strong evidence against him.'

As we left and shook hands like old buddies, the brigadier wanted to know: 'So how were we? How would you describe our investigation?'

'Very professional, sir. Brilliant.'

Alpheus and I booked into the sumptuous five-star Cardoza Hotel, perched high on a hill and overlooking the Bay of Maputo, for the night. As we tucked into tiger prawns drenched in olive oil and garlic we joked about the black pig, the besmeared prison toilet and the earnest brigadier. We toasted our freedom with two bottles of vinho verde.

We returned to Johannesburg the next morning, which was a Saturday. I had to reassess the story's progress and Alpheus had to clear his desk. I didn't give Mazet another thought. He was, after all, safely behind bars.

The next day started out as just another Sunday in April – an early morning stroll in the park with the dogs, the newspapers, strong Italian coffee and freshly baked croissants. Later that day, however, Alpheus phoned.

'You won't believe it!'

'Believe what?'

'Mazet phoned me.'

'You're joking! He's in prison.'

'No he's not. He's out. He's in Johannesburg.'

'What?'

'Yes, and what's more, he's got the two girls with him.'

I rushed to the office to meet Alpheus. I called Mazet. He seemed frisky and cheerful. 'They're here! You must come and fetch them tomorrow and bring my money.'

'How did you get out?'

'Hey man, that was nothing. I paid them one hundred dollars. They let me out yesterday morning. We left in the afternoon.'

'And the girls?'

'They still wanted to come. So they left with me.'

'Where are they?'

'With my girlfriend. But I'm not going to keep them for long. They are not happy and I don't want them to run.'

We agreed to speak again the next morning to arrange where to meet. Alpheus was sure the two women were on the farm where he had dropped Mazet and Hercillia when he drove back from Mozambique with them.

We started making plans to get the girls back. I was sure Mazet would give them to me only once I'd handed over the money. And there was no way I could pay R5 000 for the girls. We needed muscle, and lots of it.

I turned for help to the man known as the Pretoria Godfather. Mike Bolhuis was a debt collector and bouncer boss who was both loathed and feared. With his Nazi-style haircut and watery blue eyes, he cut a frightful figure. A year or so earlier I had done a television documentary on a bouncer war in Pretoria. I portrayed Bolhuis as a maniacal zealot who had literally bashed his bouncer

rival to a pulp with a baseball bat. I thought I had done a deft character assassination and portrayed him and his ruffians as the sleazy debt collectors they were
– but no! After the programme aired, his bouncers were more in demand than
ever and his debt-collecting business boomed.

Bolhuis lived on a smallholding outside Pretoria with his Burmese pythons,
anacondas and blue crane birds. A glass wall separated the dining room from the
snake pit, and one evening I had dinner there while an anaconda was devouring
one of his children's rabbits! I drank too much and later that night stumbled
into the pit. The cameraman stood outside with his camera. I was astonished to
see the footage the next morning of me posing happily with a python curling
around my neck!

We called Bolhuis: 'Mike, can you help?'

'Of course I can.'

'What do you suggest?

'I'll get the men together. Don't worry, they'll have guns and shotguns. And
just to make sure that he doesn't get away, we'll take the police with us. They'll
make the arrest.'

By eight the next morning, I'd met up with the Bolhuis troops at a filling
station in Johannesburg. They were a combination of bouncers and off-duty
policemen earning an extra buck. They were armed to the teeth. We waited for
several hours for Mazet to call. He didn't. At noon, we decided to raid the farm.
We met a Soweto police contingent near the farm and a few minutes later the
men stormed the house. Anna-Maria, Alpheus, a cameraman and I were a few
metres behind them.

Pandemonium broke loose as people emerged from every nook and cranny,
hole and pit in and around the house. The police gave chase. 'Here, here! Hurry
up! *Jissus fok*! Watch out! There's a bloke behind that door!'

A young woman scurried into a dry mealie field. Others tried to climb over
a high fence at the back of the house, but the policemen pulled them back. A
young man who protested too much was pinned to the ground and handcuffed.
Others, in an act of desperation, yelled and screamed, but surrendered without
a struggle.

A policeman checked for passports and visas.

'No visa!'

'No visa!

'Nothing!'

We followed the police as they moved through the house from room to room.
Foam mattresses, clothes and blankets were strewn around the bare cement
floor. An elderly woman squatted next to a paraffin stove while stirring a pot.
She looked up, shook her head and continued cooking.

The farm was a transit camp for Mozambicans who had entered the country illegally in the hope of finding a job and a better life. For now, their dreams had been dashed. The police commander radioed Protea police station to send a bigger truck to take them away.

A young man told us he had left Maputo with Etelvinah and Amelia on Saturday afternoon, but a few kilometres before the border post, Mazet told the taxi driver to stop, got out and ordered the trio to join him. The man said they were taken aback as they had each paid R500 for passage across the border. Mazet made them believe he had arranged for them to simply walk through the border post. Now they had to plod uphill through thorn bushes for two hours to where the border fence sliced the Lebombo Mountains in two. En route, Mozambican soldiers stopped the group and took their money and food. They were exhausted, and one of the women started crying. Her new dress had been torn to shreds and her high-heeled shoes broken. At the fence, a South African soldier unlocked a gate and waved them through. Mazet gave him a handful of notes.

Another minibus awaited them on the national road and took them to Mazet's transit house near Komatipoort. He gave them water, bread and a few tins of fish and told them they would spend the night there. Most of the group slept in a shed at the back of the house, while Etelvinah and Amelia slept in the house with the men who had guided them across the border.

Mazet had brought them to Johannesburg on Sunday morning. Etelvinah and Amelia had spent the night on the farm, but were taken away early that morning. We were just too late.

A member of the Bolhuis group, a thin, hawkish man with a double-barrel shotgun, ordered a woman to phone Mazet. He took the phone from her and spoke to him. In the vilest language possible, he ordered Mazet to bring the women back to the farm.

'And believe me brother, if you're not here within a fucking hour, I will personally hunt you down and fuck you up! I know about this farm and I know where your houses in Komatipoort and Maputo are. Nothing will be left of them or you.'

Mazet asked to speak to me. His boastfulness was gone. 'What's up?' he asked. I told him things had turned ugly and I had no doubt the policeman would carry out his threats. 'Cut your losses and give the girls up,' I advised him. He called back a few minutes later and said he was too scared to come to the farm. He offered to leave the women with his girlfriend in a squatter camp on the outskirts of Soweto. He gave me directions.

We found Amelia and Etelvinah soon afterwards. They were startled when the police and bouncers with shotguns pounced on them, dragged them out of the shack and loaded them into our car. We took them to a pizzeria, where we fed them and told them who we were and what Mazet had planned to do with them.

Hercillia claimed she was unaware that Amelia and Etelvinah had been recruited as prostitutes and said she never wanted to see Mazet again. At first I didn't believe her, but I changed my mind after Etelvinah and Amelia told us about their night of anguish at Mazet's house near Komatipoort.

Before they left Maputo, they had each handed him R500 as payment for the journey. They had a few thousand Mozambican meticais (M3 000 is R1) left, but the soldiers who stopped them near the border fence took the money and all their food.

The group arrived at Mazet's place at dusk. Said Etelvinah: 'We got scared because nothing was as Mazet had told us. He said at some point we should repay him for the policemen he had to bribe. We said we had nothing. He said tonight you sleep hungry.'

Amelia: 'Later he brought us food and called me aside. He said I should thank him by loving him tonight. I asked him what about Hercillia, and he said she's nothing, she just cooks.'

Etelvinah: 'They ordered us to sleep in the house. There were two men. One was big and black and told us we will sleep in the one bedroom. Mazet and Hercillia were sleeping in the other room. I asked them where they were going to sleep and they said in the bedroom with us.'

Amelia: 'The dark one said we were going to make lots of money and should thank him for that. I said we wanted to sleep outside with the others, but he said no, you will sleep on this bed.'

Etelvinah: 'I got onto the bed and slept against the wall. Amelia was close to me so that we could protect one another.'

Amelia: 'The dark one liked Vinah. He jumped onto the bed and tried to pull her away. He was strong and we were losing our grip.'

Etelvinah: 'I screamed and screamed. At one point he hit me in my face and told me to shut up or he would kill me. I didn't mind and knew that he would never have me. I screamed.'

Amelia: 'It was then that Hercillia came from the next room and tried to push the man away. She told him to stop, but he hit her with his hand. She fell but stood up and fought him.'

Etelvinah: 'We were all crying and screaming. Hercillia said she was going to phone the police. The black one said he'd kill her. She said do that, but I'm not leaving this room tonight.'

Amelia: 'The other man was now holding Hercillia while the black man jumped on us. He said tonight we'll pay. We were fighting and hitting and kicking.'

Etelvinah: 'Mazet came into the room and the men stopped. He told Hercillia to come back to their room, as this was none of her business. She was crying and said no, this is my sister and I stay here.'

Amelia: 'We stayed together the whole night. They didn't speak to us the next morning and we didn't get food.'

We told the women we would take them back to Maputo. To our astonishment, they said they didn't want to go. There were families and a baby back in Mozambique depending on them to make money in Johannesburg. They said if they went back so soon, they would be regarded as failures.

'We'll stay with Hercillia and find a job,' they said.

'You probably won't,' I said. 'You have no qualifications. You'll land up on the streets.'

Mike Bolhuis had a guesthouse on his fortified property and offered to shelter the women until we could take them back to Maputo. They lived there for a week, guarded by bouncers and dogs and pythons, while we arranged official papers for their extradition back to Mozambique.

Alpheus and I took them back to Maputo. He told me on the way that he had finally settled his computer debt and landed a plush job at a medical investigation firm. 'At least they pay more than you.'

A few days after we had returned the women to their families, Etelvinah was gone again. She told Amelia she was going back to Johannesburg to make money. I have no doubt she landed up in a sleazy Johannesburg brothel.

Alpheus and I had one last meal at the Café Costa del Sol on Maputo's beachfront. We ordered a kilogram of prawns and a big *jarra* of cheap Portuguese wine.

We went back to Johannesburg the next day.

Alpheus left *Special Assignment* as quietly as he had joined.

I never saw him again.

He died at the beginning of 2005.

He had a lung infection.

CHAPTER 14

Koekemoer, aka Stellianos

I wouldn't recommend sex, drugs or insanity for everyone, but they've always worked for me. — **Hunter S Thompson**

ALEX STELLIANOS WAS SOLD TO ME AS A GRUBBY AND MANGY character who mingled with the underworld and was embroiled in the whore business. He'd been a confidential police informant at some stage, was some kind of private eye and spoke Portuguese, which made him the ideal operator for Mozambique.

A friend suggested that I should meet Alex and find out if he could help me finish the story about human trafficking in Mozambique. Alpheus was gone and only half the programme had been done.

'He sounds perfect,' I said.

'And by the way,' my friend added, 'the little finger on his right hand is missing.'

'What happened to the finger?' I wanted to know.

'Rumour has it that it was cut off by a drug cartel in South America in order to test his allegiance,' said the friend.

'What was he doing in South America?'

'Infiltrating cartels for the Americans,' she said. 'He was apparently very good.'

A day later, I shook hands with Alex at a Melville coffee shop. It was an uncanny feeling as I felt only three of his fingers folding around my hand. When I looked down, I noticed the little stump on his right hand.

Square-jawed with deep lines etched on his face, Alex Stellianos was an engaging and likeable character. He had lived in Mozambique as an undercover drug agent in order to infiltrate a Mandrax-smuggling network as part of a joint South African–Mozambican police operation. Although the house where the Mandrax was made had been raided and several dealers and distributors arrested, the suspects disappeared when they were released from prison before sentencing.

'And what do you do now?' I asked him.

'Ah, just business.'

His cellphone rang and he bickered for several minutes with someone over a set of papers before telling the person to piss off. I couldn't help asking: 'And what was that all about?'

'A girl. A Russian,' he said, and then his eyes lit up. 'Gorgeous bitches, all of them. Tall, blonde and blue-eyed.'

'What did she want?'

'She's waiting for her papers from Home Affairs.'

I didn't push the subject further and asked Alex if he could help me find Mozambican girls who had been trafficked to South Africa and forced into prostitution. No problem, he said, I know a girl who was kidnapped from Maputo, thrown onto a minibus, smuggled across the border and sold to a Johannesburg brothel.

'She would tell you her whole story on camera. No problem,' he promised.

'How do you know?'

'Trust me. I know her.'

'Let's go to Maputo,' I suggested.

'Oh, I love that place,' he agreed, and held out his hand. When I shook it, I couldn't help asking him about his finger.

'Oh that? It was an accident. When I was a child.'

When I later asked him if a Colombian or Brazilian cocaine cartel had sliced off his finger, he just laughed and said it was an urban legend. I was puzzled that a man with an exotic surname like Stellianos spoke English with an Afrikaans accent. Are you Greek or something, I wanted to know?

'No, I'm South African. That's my surname.'

'Tonight we're going to Luso,' Alex announced during our first day in Maputo.

'What's that?' I asked him.

'It's a club.'

'What kind of club?'

'It will blow your mind.'

'Why?'

'The girls.'

'What about the girls?'

'You've never seen bodies like that.'

Alex seemed to have picked up where Alpheus left off. We were sitting at the Café Costa do Sol on Avenida Marginal dipping pieces of Portuguese bread into a bowl of *ameijoas* (clams). He openly flirted in Portuguese with one of the waitresses.

'You know, I don't know where the women in Mozambique come from,' he said, 'but I think they manufacture them somewhere in a factory.'

After dinner Alex and I headed down the coastal boulevard to downtown Maputo. My mother used to visit colonial Lourenço Marques (as Maputo was previously called) as a young woman and told me the palm-fringed boulevard had then been a hive of activity, lined with fishermen, lovers holding hands and vendors selling bowls of fried *camarões* (prawns).

Although the area had recently been restored and the yacht club returned to its former colonial glory, the dimly lit roads were potholed and the only life on the crumbling pavements were a skinny dog and two or three forlorn prostitutes. Under a bridge a homeless man was hunched over chicken or fish innards sizzling on a fire.

Luso wasn't far from the harbour and just around the corner from Maputo's glorious art deco train station with its bold and delineated motifs. The city was dark and ominously empty, but as we turned into Avenida Bogamoio, it exploded into life. A collection of bars and 1970s-style discos lined the street, and the distorted sounds of Shakira, Mariah Carey and Britney Spears burst through doors and spilt onto the streets. Comely girls with violet Day-Glo lipstick and chemically straightened hair, wearing tight-fitting jeans and miniskirts, milled around on the pavements, ready to vamp potential clients. An odour of cheap perfume and a promise of sex permeated the humid Mozambican air.

Entering Luso was like walking into an inferno of a thousand lecherous, wanton and sex-crazed nubiles. Tender female flesh lined the bar, the heads all turned towards the entrance, the legs crossed seductively. They were young – many still at school – and ripe for the plucking. Where else in the world, Alex commented, could a man select fresh teenage fluff and pay as little as 300 000 meticais (R100) to have them spend an entire night with you?

The girls seemed to know Alex and descended on him as he swaggered into Luso. There were cries of: 'Alex! Alex! Alex!' and some threw their arms around his neck or pushed his head between their breasts.

'How come you know so many girls?' I asked him.

'Oh, I come to Maputo from time to time.'

As we sat down at the bar, three or four girls surrounded us. Alex slapped a plump bottom, fondled a luscious breast and asked a girl to lift her skirt. She promptly showed him her breasts as well. A white client like Alex was a passport to liberation from Maputo's sprawling and poverty-stricken *zonas* (suburbs), peasantry and teenage marriage.

'I'm telling you,' Alex shouted above the distorted music, 'in Mozambique they manufacture them in factories. And they turn them out by the thousand.'

There was a blur of groping young hands and the competition was fierce and relentless to lure a potential customer into a night of passion or a moment of lust in one of the rooms upstairs. 'No man is safe here. You must watch your wickets,' Alex said.

'Where do you come from?' was one of four English sentences most of the girls could utter, along with 'How are you?' 'Buy me a beer' and the inevitable: 'Do you want to fuck?'

Once the girls had landed a client, they dragged him off to a dance floor with flashing strobe lights. It was a peculiar sight: among the bobbing heads were Filipino seamen, Chinese contract workers, Indian businessmen, white aid workers, United Nations officials and South Africans who had crossed the border (only a hundred kilometres away) for a night of illicit passion.

The girls had naturally lithe hips that rhythmically moved from side to side. Not so the men. One of the dancers looked like a cattle farmer from the Mpumalanga bushveld and was clad in short pants and a pair of boots. He had no rhythm, but it didn't matter. Huddled close to him was a teenybopper hip-hopping to the pulsating beat. Her erect nipples brushed his bloated torso and there was an expression of utter bliss on his face.

I don't know if the girls enjoyed what they did, although most were laughing, dancing, drinking bottles of Laurentina beer and ambushing and wooing the *brancos* (whites) coming through the door. Alex was convinced Mozambican women had the same sexual bent as their Brazilian counterparts. 'They like to fuck,' he said, 'and they start when they're very young.' Brazilians had 'the best female body in the world' he reckoned, 'but Mozambicans are a close second'.

In all the years I knew Alex, I never saw him happier or more elated than that night at Luso. His eyes sparkled, his face lit up and there was a permanent smirk plastered across his face. No matter how old Alex Stellianos might be, the girls at Luso would always be eighteen and only a handful of meticais away.

I once told him that Luso reeked of AIDS. Mozambique had one of the highest infection rates in the world and the clubs on Avenida Bogamoio were a fertile breeding ground for the virus. The girls must have known about AIDS, but could not afford to let even a deadly disease stand in the way of paying school fees, buying new clothes or feeding their babies. Alex said the majority of girls asked clients to use condoms, but could make more money with a so-called 'de luxe fuck' – a 'skin-on-skin' experience without protection.

There was a high turnover of faces in Luso. When Alex and I visited the club again a few months later, there were scores of new girls. Alex said there was a permanent influx of girls from the rural areas looking for work in Maputo. When they couldn't find a job, they landed up at the club. Some worked there for a few months and then made their way to Johannesburg or Durban, where they could earn much more. Others were recruited by traffickers and smuggled across the border to be sold to brothels or mineworkers in South Africa. Some undoubtedly also fell victim to AIDS.

During our second visit, a tall girl with straight black hair, a wide red mouth and green eyes walked up to Alex.

'Buy me a beer,' she demanded. Alex bought her a Laurentina.

'Do you want to fuck?'

Alex said he didn't want to, but spoke to her in Portuguese. A few minutes later, he said she was a trafficking victim and had spent a year on a South African gold mine near Carletonville on the West Rand.

Lucrencia Shimene was twenty years old and could have been beautiful, but too many nights at Luso and a year on a mine had rendered her eyes empty and her mouth harsh. She was at first aloof and detached and warmed to us only after several Laurentinas.

Lucrencia was seventeen and still at school when a human trafficker recruited her to work in a Johannesburg bar. She left school and embarked on what she thought would be an adventure of a lifetime. She arrived on the mine a few days later. By then several men had raped her and she was hungry, destitute and without any documents or money. A Mozambican mineworker bought her as his wife and kept her incarcerated in a hostel for more than a year. He battered, abused and raped her and locked her up in a tiny room. Police found her when they raided the hostel and arrested several mineworkers – including her husband – for a gold-racketeering scheme. She was deported back to Mozambique and had worked at Luso ever since.

A day or two later, Alex arrived at our hotel with a bubbly and vivacious woman. He introduced her as Noemia Americo and said we should interview her.

'Why?' I asked.

'She's the girl I told you about. She worked at the Summit Club. A lot of trafficked girls work there.'

The Summit was one Johannesburg's oldest and seediest stripper joints. Situated in the heart of the high-rise and crime-ridden suburb of Hillbrow, it was frequented by well-to-do clients from the northern suburbs who parked their Mercs and BMWs behind razor wire before feasting on exotic girls from Mozambique, Malawi, Zambia, Thailand and China.

'How come you know this woman?' I asked Alex.

'I was the manager at the Summit. She worked for me!'

I couldn't say I was in the least surprised that Alex had had an innings in a brothel. There was a dark side to him, and the Summit was just part of it.

Noemia, who spoke English, told us she was eighteen when she visited her sister in Johannesburg. 'She worked at the Summit. I said to her: Is this your job? She said yes. I said: But me also, I want to work here. It's not difficult work.'

'Could you speak any English at the time?' I asked her.

'No, I was just saying, let's go upstairs. Because they teach me to say, let's go upstairs. That's all you need to say.'

I had visions of Alex pulling an Alpheus on me when I saw him with Noemia several times after the interview. 'You're not trying to get into her, are you Alex?' I asked him.

'No, no, no. We're just friends.'

'Keep it like that.'

It was at the Ressano Garcia border post upon our return to South Africa that I realised Alex was not who he purported to be. I handed our passports to the Mozambican immigration official while Alex got the car papers stamped at the customs counter. I opened his passport. His photograph stared back at me, but the name in the document was Johannes Lodewikus Koekemoer!

'How come your surname is Koekemoer?' I asked him later in the car.

He seemed discomfited, but said: 'That's who I used to be. But I changed my name officially.'

Alex spent his first years in an orphanage, but was adopted by the Koekemoer family of Port Elizabeth. He said he was abused and neglected and was forced to sleep in the maid's quarters. He was a young child when his father, who worked on the railways, beat him with his fists and left him bleeding on the ground. He swore he would leave home as soon as he could and never return. At the age of seventeen, he turned his back on his adopted family and never saw his father or mother again. He didn't even attend their funerals.

He joined the air force and adopted a new persona when he became engaged to a Greek woman. Although the relationship didn't end in marriage, Johannes Lodewikus Koekemoer found a new identity: Alex Stellianos. He never spoke Afrikaans again, changed his name and adopted the Greek Orthodox religion. Alex not only spoke Greek, but also Portuguese, Spanish, Zulu and, of course, English. I never heard a word of Afrikaans tumble over his lips and he pretended not to understand the language at all.

Alex moved to Johannesburg and opened a series of clubs and bars in and around Hillbrow – places where, in the midst of apartheid, he said, 'White guys could meet black chicks.' The establishments had names like Babylon, L'Afrique and Harlem Shuffle.

But his clubs went bust and he opened a grocery store in Turffontein, one of Johannesburg's southern suburbs and an area of growing concern in terms of drug trafficking. It wasn't long before he was a registered informant for the police Narcotics Bureau, not least because he needed the money to get his new business off the ground.

His handler was none other than police death squad operative Chappies Klopper, in later years one of the main state witnesses against Vlakplaas commander Eugene de Kock. Alex was a regular guest at Vlakplaas and said he remembered braaiing huge steaks and drinking brandy and Coke while the men trumpeted about 'taking care of the terrorists'. Chappies carried a briefcase full of money, from which he paid Alex.

Tales about Alex and his Narcotics Bureau handlers siphoning off police money became legendary. A former narcotics cop told me about suitcases of money that had disappeared in a Brazilian drug operation. The story was that the police had wanted to infiltrate Brazilian drug cartels that used South Africa as a transit to smuggle cocaine to Europe. Alex was given R1 million and sent to Rio de Janeiro to infiltrate the networks. After only a few weeks, he disappeared and cut communication with his handlers. The South Africans, concerned he had been killed or kidnapped, asked their Brazilian counterparts to investigate. They found Alex living in a palatial villa at a coastal resort outside Rio de Janeiro with an army of servants, an array of sports cars and a clutch of bikini babes.

When I asked him about the alleged theft, he said angrily: 'And where's that money? Do I live like a rich man? It's bullshit.'

It was true, however, that he worked for the American Drug Enforcement Administration (DEA) for four years in the late nineties and was registered as a narcotics informant in fourteen countries in South and Central America, the Caribbean and Pakistan. He was, by all accounts, very successful. He was credited with bringing down Nigerian drug baron Sande Oladele by infiltrating the inner circle of his cartel. He played tennis on Sundays at Oladele's grand mansion in Rio where the champagne was Dom Perignon and the prostitutes were young, gorgeous and very expensive. And best of all, said Alex, he didn't dare refuse the carnal offerings Sande showered on him!

The cartel eventually entrusted Alex with seven kilograms of cocaine in a suitcase that had to be smuggled out of Brazil to Europe. The DEA and the Brazilian drug police set a trap for Oladele, and when Alex picked up the suitcase, the Nigerian and his cohorts were nabbed.

Alex returned to South Africa at the end of 2000. By then the Narcotics Bureau had been disbanded and most of its members transferred to the Crime Intelligence Unit. It wasn't long before Alex was again on the payroll and tasked with infiltrating a Nigerian drug syndicate that smuggled compressed dagga to London, where it was exchanged for heroin and trafficked back to South Africa.

The syndicate bought Alex an air ticket to London and packed a suitcase with seventeen one-kilogram bricks of dagga. The operation went awry when the police failed to arrest the kingpins and compromised Alex in the process. He was assaulted and beaten with an iron bar and landed up in hospital.

There was a miscellany of accusations and counter-accusations between Alex and his handlers about the failure of the operation. Most of the dagga and many thousands of rands vanished and many said Alex was the prime suspect.

'Once again: where's the money?' Alex said. 'I have nothing, but I can tell you who lives in double-storey houses and drives top-of-the-range BMWs. The cops who ran the drug operations!'

There had been bad blood between Alex and the cops ever since. I'd been warned on numerous occasions to watch out for him. At one stage a rumour was doing the rounds that the only reason I had employed Alex was because he had taken spy camera footage of an underage prostitute in my hotel room in Maputo and was blackmailing me.

Shortly before we broadcast the human-trafficking documentary, I headed to Pretoria to interview a senior Home Affairs official about the extent of the problem. When I mentioned that Alex had conducted research for us in Mozambique, he nearly tumbled off his chair.

'How well do you know that Stellianos?' he asked me.

'I'm not sure,' I said.

'Do you know who he is? He calls himself Stellianos but his real name is Koekemoer.'

'Yes, I know.'

The official had a voluminous file on Alex. There were several police intelligence reports, photographs and photocopies of identity documents, marriage certificates and passports. There were also identity document photographs of young white women.

'Russians,' the official said. 'Alex makes them legal. A syndicate smuggles them into the country and he gets them papers. Do you know that Alex is a trafficker himself? We are investigating him and he is going to be arrested soon. And do you know that he has been married three times?'

'No, but so what?'

'He's still married to all three of them!'

His last wife was a Mozambican by the name of Noemia Americo – the prostitute we had interviewed in Maputo! Alex had produced his own spouse to reveal her seediest sex secrets on national television.

How could you, I asked him later. He said Noemia meant nothing to him, as the marriage was part of his undercover operation in Mozambique so that he could infiltrate the Mandrax-smuggling ring. 'Crime Intelligence said I needed a cover. I brought her back from the Summit and married her. She's merely an acquaintance.'

He did, however, stay with Noemia and her family for the duration of the operation and, according to one intelligence report, later tried to get an egg import business in Maputo off the ground in order to be with her. Alex admitted that he'd been married three times, but said that he had divorced the first two wives.

When I first met Alex he was penniless and desperate for a job. I knew he had been involved in the seedy underbelly of Johannesburg's sex industry. He knew several brothel bosses, had an intimate knowledge of sex-for-sale operations, and knew at which clubs Russian, Thai and Bulgarian prostitutes worked. He assured me he had broken all ties with the industry and the promised warrant for his arrest never materialised.

I could never understand why anyone questioned my relationship with Alex. He was loyal, dedicated and provided an invaluable service in that he could infiltrate syndicates and fraternise with criminals, villains and prostitutes. He had in many ways become a secret weapon in *Special Assignment*'s quest for scoops, viewers and credibility.

As Alex himself said: 'I blend in.'

Alex's next assignment took him yet again into the sewers of society when he followed a trail of whoremongers who kept Thai prostitutes captive as sex slaves in their brothels. There are two categories of Thai sex workers: those who practise vice in their own country but travel to South Africa to earn more money, and those – not unlike Mozambicans – who are lured with false promises of employment and a better life and then forced into prostitution.

A syndicate pays their airfares and upon arrival picks them up at Johannesburg's international airport. They are bundled into a car and taken to a house, where their benevolent benefactors turn ugly. They are told they owe the syndicate an astronomical fee for bringing them to South Africa and will have to repay their debt by screwing morning, noon and night. The girls often work for a year or longer with nothing more than food to eat and a place to sleep.

Anna-Maria Lombard stumbled upon a syndicate that rotated their girls between brothels in Johannesburg, Durban and the conservative outpost of Ladysmith in the KwaZulu-Natal Midlands. The syndicate moved the girls between the three brothels in order to entice their customers with 'new' and 'fresh' prostitutes.

We traced the Ladysmith brothel to a farm just outside the town. It was called Stables, but became known as the Varkpaleis (Pig Palace), and was owned by Vuilpiet (Dirty Piet) Delport, a burly *boer* with khaki pants and a short-sleeved shirt strained tightly over his *bierpens* (beer belly). Vuilpiet took pride in the fact that he ran an old-fashioned bordello where hospitality, satisfaction and customer service were still highly prized.

The conservative townsfolk of Ladysmith had fought and lost a long battle against Vuilpiet and his Varkpaleis. The police seemed paralysed to act against the unholy joint, despite the fact that the police station was just across the road from the Varkpaleis! Needless to say, several policemen were valued guests of the establishment.

Alex was tasked with capturing the tale of a Thai prostitute on spy camera. We wanted to know how she was recruited, got to the brothel and how much money she had to repay the syndicate.

'That's not difficult. I can do that,' he said.

'How?' I asked him.

'I'll have to hire a girl. She'll talk to me and I'll film her.'

'You know that you can't touch her?' I told him.

'Of course,' he said.

He returned a day or two later, walked into the office and handed the tape nonchalantly to Anna-Maria. 'It's all there. Her whole story,' he said.

Minutes later, shrieks and screams echoed from the viewing booth. Anna-Maria – brilliant but perpetually on the verge of a nervous breakdown – burst into my office.

'You have to come and watch!'

We rushed into the booth. She rewound the tape and pushed the 'play' button. It showed Alex and the prostitute – a tiny Thai woman looking rather worn – walking into a cubicle. She stood on one side of the bed and Alex on the other. She told him to undress.

'This is where it starts getting interesting,' grimaced Anna-Maria.

Alex put the sling bag, with the hidden camera rolling, on a bedside table and took off his shirt. He probably underestimated how wide the angle of the lens was and didn't realise he was also in the picture! The prostitute chatted away while shedding her clothes. She told Alex she owed the syndicate R100 000. They took every cent she earned and she saw nothing of the fruits of her labour. But nobody in the viewing booth was listening to what she was saying. By now the little room was rather crowded. All eyes were fixed on Alex.

'Now watch this,' Anna-Maria said, as his pants came down.

'It can't be true!' somebody said.

Alex lay down naked on the bed on his back. 'He's a bit worked up!' Anna-Maria shrieked.

'*Punt in die wind!*' someone else added.

The prostitute seemed perplexed by a customer who was clearly ready for action but refused to let her touch him. 'I just want to talk,' he repeatedly said to her.

When I saw Alex later, I asked him: 'How on earth could you take your clothes off? You were not supposed to do that!'

'But you said I wasn't allowed to touch her. And I didn't!'

'God Alex, how on earth are we supposed to use footage of two naked people?'

'How else do you get a prostitute talking?'

'What do we do now?'

'Blur my face,' he said.

'We'll have to blur much more than your face!'

Vuilpiet caused us many moments of mirth, not least when Anna-Maria drove to Ladysmith to doorstop him. The team had all the evidence they needed. It was the moment of truth.

'Would you consider yourself a trafficker?' Anna-Maria asked. Vuilpiet stared at her, slightly perplexed, for a moment or two, smiled and said: 'Yes. Yes, I would say so.'

Vuilpiet was arrested after broadcast of the documentary and his bordello closed down. Another brothel in Johannesburg was raided and the owner taken into custody. Several prostitutes were deported back to Thailand.

Alex's finest hour took us thousands of kilometres up the African east coast in search of some of the subcontinent's most notorious heroin dealers. It all started while we were investigating human trafficking in Mozambique.

'I want to show you Little Colombia,' Alex said to me one day.

'Oh my God, is it another club?'

'No, this is serious stuff.'

'What's Little Columbia?'

'Maputo's drug suburb. You won't believe it.'

'Where is it?'

'Not far from here. Just down Avenida Julius Nyerere.'

As we drove past the American, Brazilian and Nigerian embassies, Alex explained that when he was in Maputo in 2000 to uncover the Mandrax factory, he stumbled upon *Zona Militar* – or Little Columbia as everybody in the city called it. It consisted of about forty houses that had once been part of the main military barracks. When the civil war with RENAMO ended in 1992, the houses were allocated to FRELIMO war veterans. Many were soon destitute and jobless and turned to drug smuggling as a means of survival. It wasn't long before there was a narcotics enclave slap-bang in the heart of the city.

'And what's the main drug in Little Colombia?' I asked Alex.

'Heroin. But you can find anything else as well.'

'Why heroin?'

'It comes from Tanzania up north.'

'And how does it get to Tanzania?'

'From Pakistan. By boat or drug mules.'

Little Columbia had only one entrance and a single exit, both guarded by policemen in drab and threadbare grey uniforms. As Alex rolled down his window to wave at them, he said: 'Don't worry. They're not here to catch criminals but to extort bribes from dealers and addicts.'

My first impression of Little Colombia was that it didn't look different from any other Maputo suburb. In the street children played soccer with plastic shopping bags rolled and tied into balls while women grilled *sardinhas* and fried *sabusas* on the corner. A bearded man with a knitted Rastafarian cap was fast asleep next to a pushcart selling lottery tickets.

'He's fucked,' said Alex.

People stopped whatever they were doing and stared at us. A group of young men yelled something at us in Portuguese. Alex stuck his head out of the window.

'*Vá-se foder!*'

'What did you say?'

'Fuck off.'

We slowly passed a couple of ramshackle houses, and when we turned a corner, we were confronted by an almost delusional spectacle. 'This is the heart of Little Colombia. Every house you see is a drug house,' Alex said.

Several addicts milled aimlessly about in the street, stumbled out of houses or lay slumped on the pavements. Alex pointed at a man sitting on the side of the street, his eyes fixed and saliva drooling from his half-open mouth. A young boy was trying to pull him up.

When we stopped the car, merchants clutching drugs in their hands swamped us. They elbowed one another out of the way as they jostled for position to get as close to us as possible. They banged their fists on the roof and shouted prices in Portuguese. We were *brancos* and the dealers assumed we would be willing to pay higher prices for drugs.

'Brown sugar!'

'White Thai!'

'Brown sugar!'

'Cocca!'

'Speed!'

I felt like a sardine trapped in a shark feeding frenzy.

'Welcome to Little Colombia,' said Alex.

CHAPTER 15

An African drug safari

I had a stash like you wouldn't believe. I hid it in the jungle; the wealth of the Orient: marijuana, hashish, opium, cocaine, uncut heroin, the gold of the Golden Triangle. And acid. I make Koolaid that makes purple Owsley come on like piss.

– Moonby in the movie Apocalypse Now!

IT WAS A GLEEFUL ALEX STELLIANOS WHO PULLED THE SMALL SONY camcorder from his grey sling bag and disentangled the mesh of red, black and white wires, his nine fingers trembling.

'You will not believe it! Un-fucking-believable!' he crowed. A flame illuminated his lined face as he lit a cigarette.

'Believe what?'

'Fucking watch this,' he said, as he pushed the 'play' button and the black screen flickered to life.

A pair of denim-clad legs and white sneakers walked in front of Alex up a flight of grimy and dimly lit stairs. I knew by then it was Jimmy, a young drug addict and housebreaker we had hired in order to gain access to the notorious crack and heroin houses of Maputo's Little Colombia.

He knocked on the door. It slowly creaked open. The unkempt and spotted face of a white woman peeked through the bars of a steel gate. '*Hi lá, Mamma!*' said Jimmy. She recognised him, unlocked the gate and embraced him. He was clearly a regular client.

'*Bom dias*, Jimmy!'

Alex said the woman was sloppy and he felt repelled when she embraced him, too. She pressed her thickset frame against his body and the hidden camera was momentarily blinded as she blocked the lens.

She beckoned them inside. It was like entering the set of *Apocalypse Now!* The sense of complete despair and debauchery in Francis Ford Coppola's epic movie echoed eerily in Alex's wobbly and slightly underexposed black-and-white footage. Both casts were intoxicated – the American GIs drunk and stoned, the outcasts captured by Alex's lens comatose and, for the moment, oblivious to their dysfunctional existence. But where the American troops in the movie had incinerated villages with napalm in a brilliant display of orange and red, the junkies in Maputo's Little Columbia were shooting heroin into their veins.

The mayhem, gunfire and explosions in the jungle of Vietnam were replaced by a blaring television set, standing on a knitted Portuguese doily. Coppola's soundtrack, courtesy of Wagner and Jim Morrison, had made way for a distorted version of 'The Lion Sleeps Tonight', anthem of another jungle, this one in Africa.

There were four addicts in the lounge. Alex stopped in front of each and surreptitiously turned the bag containing the spy camera in their direction. One had a needle dangling from his arm, while another was boiling heroin in a teaspoon over a flame. The other two were slumped on a worn-out couch. None of them paid any attention to Alex.

He and Jimmy sat down in a corner on plastic drums. Mamma sauntered through the lounge and into a bedroom, where she fetched a dose of heroin for Jimmy.

While many addicts prefer to spike – inject the narcotic into their veins – Jimmy chased the dragon, as addicts call the art of smoking heroin. He sprinkled the brown powder on a piece of tinfoil and lit a coil of tightly rolled toilet paper. He held this underneath the foil until wisps of smoke began drifting upwards.

As he sucked the analgesic vapour into his lungs through a straw, a couple who had just entered the flat took their seats on a single bed opposite Alex and Jimmy. The man was white, the woman black. They were both gaunt and withered and the heat of crack pipes had burnt away their front teeth. They looked irritable and almost frenetic as they waited for Mamma to bring the life-saving heroin. They were clearly in desperate need of a fix.

The man looked at Alex and introduced himself in Portuguese: '*Eu sou Carlos. Este é Dadinha. É minha esposa.*'

'Can you believe they're husband and wife? Husband and wife!' said Alex.

Carlos was in a sorrier state than Dadinha. Even on Alex's black-and-white film his skin appeared ashen and his eyes were deeply sunk in their cavernous sockets.

'He looks like a corpse,' Alex said.

Mamma brought them two doses of heroin wrapped in tinfoil. As Carlos liquefied the brown powder over a flame, Dadinha fixed her hungry eyes on the boiling concoction. For the moment, neither paid any further attention to Alex, sitting opposite them with the grey bag on his lap.

Carlos squeezed a drop of lemon juice into the spoon and drew it into a syringe through a tiny piece of cotton wool. Dadinha turned towards him and bent her head to bare the arteries in her neck. Carlos stabbed the needle into a protruding vein. Dadinha closed her eyes for a few seconds, waiting for the heroin to catapult through her tiny frame and bring that sense of contentment, warmth and repose her body craved so much. She relaxed, took the syringe from

Carlos and jabbed it into his neck. It had the same effect on him, except that after a minute or so, he wanted more and started to boil another batch.

With his upper capillaries too perforated to endure any further penetration, Carlos stuck the needle into his forearm, then into his leg, and a few minutes later, into the other leg as well. His hand was steady and he found his sunken blood vessels with precision, as if he possessed some medical expertise.

Dadinha handed Mamma a thick wad of dirty metical notes, which she stuffed into a bulging plastic bag. It was a Saturday morning and business was brisk.

Carlos opened a brown packet and sandwiched two samoosas between slices of stale bread. As he stuffed the food into his mouth, he looked at Alex and said: 'This is a spectacle. I am sorry.'

And then, for no particular reason, the couple started talking to Alex. They asked him where he came from. When he said South Africa, they switched to English. 'We are educated,' Carlos said. 'We don't want to live like this.'

Said Dadinha: 'Carlos is a veterinary surgeon. I don't work any more, but I was an auditor at the United Nations.'

'And now we have nothing left. Everything is gone,' Carlos added.

'Everything,' said Dadinha. Their speech was garbled as the heroin numbed and anaesthetised their senses.

Their surname was Felner, and it turned out that Carlos had championed and been at the forefront of colonial Mozambique's struggle for independence from Portugal. He told Alex he was once a professor of veterinary science and an agricultural advisor to Mozambican independence hero and the first post-colonial president, Samora Machel.

Carlos and Dadinha ranted non-stop for the next twenty minutes until the spy camera's battery ran flat and brought their self-inflicted confession to a merciful end. The screen blinked once or twice and went black.

By now cigarette number four or five was burning in Alex's fingers. 'Can you fucking believe this?'

'Unbelievable,' I had to admit.

'Now we know why he spikes so well. He's a kind of a doctor.'

It was difficult to imagine that a few years earlier, Carlos could have used this performance as a demonstration for his university students of how to locate an artery and pierce it with one decisive jab. I'm sure they would have agreed that their professor was an extremely skilled and gifted man.

Later that day, he might have attended a *partie de cocktail* at the French embassy in Avenida Julius Nyerere, where the *Ambassadeur français* announced that Paris had just approved a new emergency relief package for Mozambique. Nibbling on hors d'oeuvres and sipping chilled chablis, everyone would have agreed that the aid was long overdue, even though the package was yet another example of the civilised world's benevolence towards the globe's poorest and least developed continent.

Maybe *Excelência o Presidente* was there as well, and he would without a doubt have excused himself to stroll over, shake the esteemed professor's hand and enquire warmly: '*Camarada Carlos. Como são você?*' He was, after all, one of the president's most gifted and dedicated civil servants.

As always, his elegant wife Dadinha would be moving from one group of guests to the next, hugging wives and turning her head to accept pecks from emissaries. Being an accountant at the United Nations, she was widely respected and impeccably informed. Not only was her English much better than his, but she was also a student of philosophy and a writer of poetry and could easily switch a conversation from the new HIV/AIDS project in the northern province of Cabo Delgado to the works of Sartre and Rousseau.

When Carlos finally managed to drag Dadinha away, it would be back to their art deco–style double-storey house, not far from the French embassy and just around the corner from the palatial Hotel Polana.

His two daughters from a previous marriage were both in private schools, the eldest just reaching puberty. When she was born, he called her Katia. Carlos adored her, a beautiful gift who was an almost perfect blend of his Portuguese ancestry and her mother's African heritage.

But all that had been almost a decade earlier. Since then, Carlos and Dadinha had become shadows of their former selves. The house, cars and all their possessions were gone. The children had been taken away as well. When former friends, comrades or colleagues spotted them on the streets, they turned their heads away in disgust and pretended not to recognise them.

Their one-bedroom flat in one of Maputo's shabbiest *zonas* had no furniture and they slept on a thin mattress on the floor. The books on poetry, politics and philosophy that had once adorned their bedside table had been replaced by a basket with syringes, crack pipes and crumpled scraps of tinfoil. Where they once drove 4×4s, their aged sedan parked in the street, below was immobile and standing on bricks. They had pawned the wheels for a fix of heroin.

Carlos and Dadinha Felner had literally shot their lives into their veins.

Our drug investigation had started two weeks earlier, when I asked Alex: 'How are we going to get into Little Colombia?'

'Jimmy. We're going to use Jimmy.'

'Who's he?'

'A criminal. A housebreaker. Also uses drugs. Smokes anything. Knows Little Colombia well.'

Jimmy was a Mozambican criminal who lived and burgled in Johannesburg. When he partially lost the use of his right hand after a rival gangster shot him in the shoulder, he couldn't steal with the same acumen as before and wanted to go back to Maputo to undergo surgery on his crippled limb. Alex wanted Jimmy to take him into the drug houses and introduce him as a South African dealer looking to buy heroin to take back to Johannesburg.

'And then there's Chico,' Alex said.

'And who's Chico?'

'A drug dealer I met when I was in Maputo looking for the Mandrax factory. He lives in Little Colombia. I'll go and look him up.'

'But you're white. You'll stand out like a sore thumb!' I said.

'There are white addicts in Maputo. And I can speak Portuguese.'

We told Jimmy we would take him back to Mozambique, where he could stay with us. We would feed him and pay him a researcher's fee in return for taking Alex into Little Colombia. Although it was naive to think that Jimmy wouldn't use the money for drugs, he was an adult and responsible for his own actions.

We set up base in an apartment just around the corner from the Hotel Cardoza in one of Maputo's middle-class suburbs. Our aim was not just to get into Little Colombia, but to expose the whole heroin route from Pakistan to South Africa via Mozambique and East Africa.

A 2002 study by South Africa's Institute for Security Studies (ISS) concluded that Mozambique was very close to becoming a criminal state. The country had become a hub of international drug smuggling, with traffickers using their government connections to buy immunity from investigation and prosecution. There was evidence that drug trafficking had become the single biggest commercial enterprise in Mozambique.

At the time of our investigation, no significant heroin or cocaine dealer had been successfully prosecuted or convicted in Mozambique. A glaring example of the ineptitude of the authorities was the Mandrax case that Alex had been involved in. Known as the Trevo case, the Pakistani businessmen who were arrested and charged were inexplicably released on the orders of the Attorney-General before sentencing. They disappeared and were still at large.

Chico lived in the first house as Alex turned into *Zona Militar*. His father was a FRELIMO war veteran and the house had been allocated to him after he was demobilised when the civil war ended in 1992. Chico was the sole breadwinner in the family. Their only income was drug trafficking, but there was a problem: Chico was a junkie and their profits went up in smoke!

His mother opened the door and said Chico was sick, but she'd call him. It was a ghost of a man that dragged himself around the corner and gazed for a moment at Alex before he recognised him. He uttered something inaudible and shook his hand. He had spent his boyhood with his father in exile in Tanzania and could speak some English.

We sat down in the garden. Chico opened a big brown envelope, pulled out a set of X-rays and held them up to the light for us to see. They were images of his lungs. He spoke with a hoarse voice and said: 'It's fucking bad. It's no good. It's very bad.'

Chico was dying. He had just come back from the military hospital, where doctors told him that unless he stopped smoking heroin, he wouldn't live long.

'I smoke too much,' he said.

'Brown sugar?' Alex asked.

'Yes, brown sugar. I'm fucked.'

'How much do you smoke?'

'Too much. Here in *Zona Militar*, business is drugs. You wake up in the mornings, drugs. Afternoon, drugs. Evening, drugs. Every day.'

Three weeks later, when we told Chico that we were, in fact, journalists, he agreed to be interviewed on camera in exchange for a bottle of cough syrup and a lift to the military hospital, where he was going to admit himself. His condition had deteriorated considerably by then.

A day or two after Alex's first meeting with Chico, he loaded his spy camera and met him at his house in Little Colombia. Their first stop was a drug dealer by the name of Martha. She was a plump and jovial woman who pulled a small bag of heroin from her ample bosom and dangled it in front of Alex.

'So how much do you want, hey?'

'No, that's not enough,' he said. 'I want much more.'

'How much more?'

'I was thinking about a kilo,' he said.

'Oh my God,' she laughed. 'For that quantity you'll have to go to Tanzania.'

'Why Tanzania?'

'That's where it comes from.'

'How does the stuff get to Maputo?'

'Via Pemba.'

'And where's Pemba?' Alex asked.

Martha again roared with laughter, her well-upholstered frame rounded even more by the wide-angle lens of the hidden camera. The footage was underexposed and her face was nothing more than a black blob.

'Up north,' she said. 'Not far from the Tanzanian border.'

'I might just go there,' Alex said.

'Maybe you don't have to,' she said. 'I know a dealer in Maputo who can help you. He's one of the biggest.'

'What's his name?'

'Mario.'

'Will you introduce me?'

'Yes.'

That night, Alex and Jimmy ventured into Little Colombia. They returned a few hours later with Jimmy as high as a kite and Alex sullen. We set the camera up on the dining-room table.

'It's Alfonso's house,' Alex said.

'And what did they say about your white face?' I asked him.

'At first they were a bit puzzled. Later on they didn't care.'

I was astonished that Alex could sit unhindered with the grey bag on his lap without ordering any drugs. 'How come?' I wanted to know.

'They're not worried about the police and don't think about journalists. They've never been bothered except to pay bribes. They thought I was a dealer who wanted to buy,' he said.

The heroin house was bare, dirty and dark. Alfonso ushered Jimmy and Alex to a room where eight addicts were hunched around a dinner plate of crack rocks. They were shown two crates to sit on.

'The worst was the smell,' Alex said. 'Everybody smokes. Crack, heroin, whatever else.'

He pointed the camera at a lone figure sitting in a corner smoking heroin. It was a middle-aged Rastafarian whose long dreadlocks and full beard perfectly framed his lean and handsome face. In his one hand was a burning coil of rolled toilet paper that he held underneath a sheet of tinfoil. He sucked the smoke that rose up from the foil into his lungs with a straw drooping from his mouth. It was an almost perfect picture, beautifully framed, with the addict's face partially lit by the single bulb dangling from the ceiling. The flame from the coil cast playful figures on the wall behind him.

When he had finished, he handed his burning coil to Jimmy, who was about to smoke his own dose. The Rasta man sat back and looked straight into the camera as if he knew there was something in the bag. His facial expression was one of utter contentment and I always felt that we had somehow intruded on a very intimate and private moment, however depraved the deed might have been.

The following day was Alex's forty-ninth birthday, and he chose to celebrate at Luso, being pawed by a troupe of teenage fluff. Holding a girl in each arm, he said he needed a drink.

'And make it hellishly strong,' he said to Luso's Portuguese owner, a pale-skinned and sun-phobic fellow with a droopy moustache.

He handed us a bottle of *bugasera*. 'What's that?' Alex wanted to know.

'Firewater,' the man told him.

Alex was not normally a drinker and it wasn't long before I had to drag him back to the apartment.

The next morning, his eyes bloodshot and his hands trembling more than usual, he walked into Mamma's house and filmed Carlos and Dadinha's drug spectacle.

Mario was like most drug dealers – glib. He arrived at Bar Strelia in a flashy Volkswagen Jetta with a South African number plate – we later discovered it had been hijacked in Johannesburg – and bodyguard. He flopped into the seat opposite Alex, stretched out and said: 'Hey man, I had too much last night.'

'Ag, so what? Have another one,' Alex said.

'If I drink another one I'll be drunk again.'

'Let me order you a beer. You'll feel better,' Alex said.

'I drink whisky,' said Mario, 'and if you insist, I'll have a double.'

He barked an order to a waiter in a white shirt and a bowtie who scurried off and returned with a tray holding a glass, a bottle of single-malt whisky and a bucket of ice. He carefully measured two tots. Mario lifted his bangle-adorned arm and toasted: 'To life.'

Around his neck was a further collection of gold chains, and on his other wrist a Michel Herbelin watch. Mario clearly wasn't a Luso kind of guy. In fact, he mentioned that he frequented the swanky Shake disco opposite the Hotel Polana and took *platter da lagosta* at Sagres along the coastal boulevard.

'How's Shake?' Alex asked him.

'Good bitches there, man! Whisky is 75 a tot.'

Alex complimented him on his car.

'Ah, it's almost new,' he said.

'Do you have papers for it?' Alex asked.

'Oh yes,' he said, 'the police can check, they will find nothing.'

Mario asked Alex why he wanted the meeting. 'I want to buy brown sugar,' Alex said. 'Lots and lots of it. I want a kilo of heroin and 500 grams of cocaine.'

'No problem,' said Mario. 'Do you want to take it here in Maputo or do you want me to bring it to South Africa?'

'Do you deliver as well?'

'Oh yes, it's no problem. I come to Johannesburg all the time.'

'And the cops?'

'Ah, that's no problem. Don't worry.'

Over the next two or three days Alex and Mario had several meetings to discuss his order. They met at either Bar Strelia or at Pizza Branco just around the corner from Little Colombia. Every time the grey sling bag was left inconspicuously on the corner of the table or resting on Alex's lap. Like most criminals in Mozambique, Mario seemed to conduct his business with no regard for the law or any fear of prosecution. Every meeting started with whisky and he was always nurturing a mother of a *tantaranta* (hangover).

'Double whisky. Today I need a double whisky.'

It freaked Alex out that Mario ordered aged and single malt, and after a meeting he would return to the apartment and complain. 'The bastard doesn't come cheap, does he?'

It turned out Mario had a team of so-called drug mules that smuggled heroin in suitcases or in their stomachs from Pakistan to Tanzania. He had a brother who lived in Pemba in northern Mozambique. He fetched the drugs in Dar es Salaam and flew them to Maputo.

'I don't sell small. I only sell in half or full kilos,' Mario said.

'That's exactly why I came to you,' Alex said.

'And I don't sell half-kick. I only sell full-kick.'

'And I don't buy half-kick.'

Alex and I couldn't buy any drugs. But we had to establish if Mario was indeed the big dealer he claimed to be. Alex asked him for a sample of heroin, which he duly provided. I carried it across the border in my pocket and had it tested in a forensic laboratory in Pretoria. It was pure brown heroin from northern Afghanistan.

Alex and Mario settled on a price: just over R200 000 for a kilo of heroin and R106 000 for half a kilo of cocaine. Mario introduced him to Charles, his drug courier, who would stash the drugs in the door panels of his Volkswagen Golf and smuggle them across the border.

'How long will it take you to prepare?' Alex asked him.

'My brother, the stuff is with me. As soon as you bring the deposit, we pack the car and we go,' said Mario.

'Tomorrow morning at nine,' said Alex.

'Nine is fine,' said Mario.

The next day, Alex, Mario, his bodyguard and Charles were sitting around a table at Peri-Peri restaurant on Avenida 24 de Julho. Cameraman Jan de Klerk and I watched as the four rose and shook hands. We got out of the car. As Mario and his henchman crossed the street, we walked towards them with the camera rolling on Jan's shoulder. We stopped Mario in the middle of Maputo's busiest thoroughfare. Traffic came to a standstill. Mario froze, while the bodyguard scurried away.

'Are you Mario?' I asked him.

He shrugged his shoulders and mumbled something in Portuguese.

'Are you Mario?' I asked him again.

'*Eu não compreendo,*' he said, his eyes glancing around, searching for a way out.

'Don't pretend you cannot speak English,' I said. 'You've just made a drug deal with Alex over there. In English!'

He stuck with: '*Eu não compreendo.*' Cars hooted. He started walking towards the pavement.

'You are a drug dealer. We have filmed you.'

'*Eu não compreendo.*'

'You sell heroin and cocaine and you drive a stolen car.'

Mario started running. He was young, strong and fast.

I was galvanised into action. 'Run, Jan, run!' I screamed. 'Fucking run! Get the bastard!'

By then Mario was way ahead of us. He had crossed the street and was scuttling through the pedestrian throng like a rabbit.

We were late getting out of our blocks – and then the sound boom's wire snagged on a bench! It stopped us in our tracks and we nearly fell down. People laughed at us.

By then Mario was gone. Later that night over dinner, Jan summed it up: 'We're getting too damn old to chase drug dealers through the streets of Maputo.'

A few days later, we were travelling north by truck towards Pemba, capital of the province of Cabo Delgado and an area celebrated for its sandy white beaches. It was a journey of more than 2000 kilometres through pristine and almost unspoilt countryside, past the resort towns of Xai-Xai and Inhambane, the decayed harbour city of Beira and into the Gorongoza Mountains, former head-quarters of the RENAMO rebel movement. The charred wrecks of Russian T-54 tanks, rusted skeletons of armoured personnel carriers and strips of crumpled metal bore testimony to some of the fiercest fighting of the civil war.

It was a captivating landscape of waving palm trees, green marshlands and the lukewarm water of the Indian Ocean lurking in the distance. In traditional *mercados* next to the road, villagers sold piles of gleaming red tomatoes and green peppers, fiery red chillies and tropical pineapples. We passed fishermen holding whole barracuda aloft and village boys on bicycles with bleating goats tied to the back. In makeshift bars men played *bao* (an East African version of backgammon) while sipping on *tontonto* and *barril* – cheap red Portuguese wine in plastic bottles.

Parts of the country were caught in an almost complete time warp, and none more so than Ilha de Mocambique, a tiny island a few kilometres off the coast in the province of Nampula. The Portuguese first arrived there in the late fifteenth century, set up a trading enclave and built a fort to act as a collection point for gold, ivory and slaves brought from the interior. The island is an evocative monument to Mozambique's history and a captivating place with mildewed seventeenth-century mosques, churches, palaces and Portuguese colonial buildings.

As we booked into a historical *pensão* and bought a bag of lobsters from young boys, Jan asked me: 'So how do we justify staying here?'

'We'll film the old Portuguese fort,' I told him.

Jan and I had left Maputo a few days after Alex, who insisted on travelling in a small Toyota Corolla. He reckoned it would be less conspicuous, despite the fact that long stretches of road north of Beira disintegrated into rubble and the potholes were as wide and deep as the Toyota itself. On the way, another car had rammed into the back of the Toyota and Alex had hit a goat.

It took him six days to reach Pemba, almost three of them spent at the ferry station on the bank of the mighty Zambezi River. One of Africa's greatest waterways, the Zambezi literally cuts Mozambique in two. Despite repeated undertakings by the government to build a bridge across the river, the battered ferry was the only way of crossing the wide expanse of water. The reason was simple, a Mozambican journalist who travelled with us explained. 'The ferry belongs to a cabinet minister. No way they are going to build the bridge soon.'

The ferry frequently broke down – in Alex's case, it sank and took two nights and three days to refloat! He had to sleep in the car, eat goat stew at makeshift restaurants on the riverbank and relieve himself in the bush.

We reached the ferry early one morning after a torturous night in a mosquito-infested *pensão* not far from the Zambezi. My heart sank when I saw mechanics working on the two diesel engines. There was nothing we could do but wait. We had oily omelettes and instant coffee at one of the bars. By midday, the engines roared into life and spewed black smoke from their rusty exhausts. We bribed an official and were the first to drive our truck aboard.

Pemba's idyllic facade of palm-fringed beaches belied its reputation as a haven for illicit drug dealing. One of the biggest hashish busts ever was made on one of its virgin beaches in 1995, when a fisherman stumbled upon several tonnes of hashish that had been offloaded by an Asian ship. The drugs were destined for the European market. The startled fisherman alerted the police, who pounced on the bounty and promptly arrested the smugglers, who were bringing the crates ashore. The trail led to a cashew nut export business in the city of Nampula and a businessman with high connections in the ruling FRELIMO party. He and two of his associates were arrested but released without standing trial. They fled to Portugal. The case disintegrated when the provincial Attorney-General mysteriously died of poisoning.

Shortly after arriving in Pemba, Alex asked for directions to the central market. He approached a group of young men manning a bicycle repair shop and enquired about dagga. No problem, they said, dagga is plentiful. We can even score you a joint or two.

'And brown sugar?' Alex asked.

'There is brown sugar in town,' they said, 'but for that you must speak to the Tanzanians.'

'Do you know where I can find them?'

A young boy took him to Obie and Abdullah. At first wide-eyed and skittish at the sight of a white man on their doorstep asking about heroin, the two smugglers were soon seduced by the lure of a big-time buyer from Johannesburg. Small talk about the condition of the roads and the rainy weather turned to drugs.

'You are looking for brown sugar?' Obie asked.

'Yes, and I want a lot,' said Alex.

'We have *ovos* (eggs). One ovo is five grams.'

'How much for an egg?'

'Two hundred and fifty US,' said Obie.

'And how many eggs do you have?'

'About twenty.'

Alex had never heard about heroin eggs before. 'I want to see one of your ovos,' he said to Obie.

The two drug dealers disappeared into another room, where they probably discussed Alex's bona fides. What was the *branco* doing in Pemba? They knew it was highly unlikely that he was linked to the police. And it never crossed their minds that there was a spy camera in his sling bag.

They walked back into the room. Dusk had fallen and a soft light fell through the single window. With a wry smile on his face, Obie took an egg from his pocket and held it in front of Alex. It was covered in tinfoil and wrapped in plastic.

'Straight from Dar,' Obie said.

'And how did it get there?' Alex said.

'Someone carried it in his stomach.'

'Where did he swallow it?'

'Karachi.'

'Now open it,' Alex said.

'Are you going to buy it?' asked Obie.

'I first want to see.'

Obie slowly unwrapped the plastic and tore away the tinfoil. In his hand was a capsule of pure brown heroin. Alex took it and held it in front of the lens.

'How many do you have?' he asked.

'Twenty,' said Obie.

'That's not enough. I want a kilo. I can't take this.'

The mood in the room changed. A sullen Obie demanded: 'Why did you make me open the egg? What for?'

'I want you to take me to Dar and introduce me to the wholesaler. A place where I can buy one or two kilos. This is not enough.'

The two went back into the other room. They were in much better spirits when they came back. 'Three hundred dollars,' said Obie.

'Three hundred for what?' asked Alex.

'Then Abdullah will take you to Dar.'

'And what do we do when we get there?'

'He'll take you to Mangala.'

'Who's Mangala?'

'A big dealer. He can give you whatever you want. One kilo, two kilos, three kilos, twenty kilos.'

'How do we get there?'

'You go from here with a car to the river,' said Obie. 'We cross the river and go straight to Dar.'

'How are the roads? Sand or tar?'

'Some are tar, some are sand.'

'How many kilometres?'

'I don't know.'

'How many days?'

'Three.'

You are completely and utterly insane, I said to Alex that night. We were sitting at a beach bar on Praia di Wimbi just outside Pemba, devouring a plate of *camarao nacional* (prawns in beer) and freshly caught dorado. 'Three days! With a drug dealer? Heaven knows what can happen to you!'

'There's no option. I've done things like this many times before in South America. I'll be fine.'

'It's still a long, long way to Dar.'

'I know. It's fine.'

I felt both apprehension and slight guilt. I would fly into Dar while Alex would have to sit in a bus or on a truck for three days. It was to a large extent *my* story for which he was taking the risks and I was paying him a pittance.

'Don't worry,' said the cameraman, Jan. 'He loves it. This is what he lives for. He works for you. So if the story bombs out, you're in shit, not Alex. The story is your responsibility.'

Alex left at four o'clock the next morning with Abdullah on a bus for a town by the name of Vila de Macímboa. 'The bus had no shocks or windows,' he told me later. 'My back was blue by the time we got there. And God knows why this town exists, because there's nothing there.'

After a sleepless night in a grimy *pensão* he was on the road again – this time on the back of a Land Rover. 'There were fifteen people and six bags of beans. There was virtually no road and I had to hold on so as not to fall off. And all the time I had an excruciating headache.'

They finally reached the border town of Namoto, where Alex had to pass through customs to exit Mozambique. His visa had expired and the official demanded a bribe. Exhausted and feverish, Alex told him to fuck off. Threatened with arrest, he paid a bribe of six million meticais.

They crossed the Rovuma River in a dugout canoe, went through customs on the Tanzanian side and took a taxi to the harbour town of Mtwara, where they hoped to board a boat to Dar. The next vessel was not due for two days, so they boarded a bus again for the final leg of the journey to Dar es Salaam.

Cheerful but distorted music blared through the bus and *Safari njema* (Swahili for 'Have a safe journey') was painted in bright yellow on the side. Alex described the bus as a 'death trap'. He said afterwards: 'The axle was probably bent from all the potholes it had hit and it crawled like a crab across the road.'

When Alex got to Dar es Salaam (the name means Haven of Peace), he was delirious with fever. He had contracted malaria. I had to force him to go to a doctor, who pumped him full of chloroquine and ordered him to stay in bed and look after himself.

Of course he didn't. The next morning he loaded the camera, threw the grey bag over his shoulder and ventured into the suburbs with Abdullah to look for Mangala.

They found the tiny, weasel-faced and bespectacled drug dealer in a bar, drinking whisky. He invited Alex back to his house. He lived in a Muslim neighbourhood not far from a nineteenth-century mosque. From the outside his house was unassuming, except for a Mercedes-Benz and a BMW parked on the pavement. A woman covered in a black burka opened the carved wooden door and invited Alex in. The interior was spacious, airy and furnished in the customary Zanzibari style. Five veiled women sat on a woven carpet dipping *chapatis* (Indian bread) into a spicy *nyana* (tomato) sauce while sipping on small cups of *chai* (tea).

'Hi!' they greeted Alex.

Mangala sat in a corner of the lounge behind a desk with a ball of *qat* in his cheek. *Qat* is a mildly sedative leaf that men in the Horn of Africa and the Arabian peninsula chew. I don't know if *qat* makes people talkative, but Mangala spoke non-stop for the next hour until the camera battery ran flat.

'I need to know the type of something you are looking for,' Mangala said as he stuffed more leaves into his mouth. He spoke with a high, shrill voice.

'Can I speak in front of these ladies?' Alex asked.

'No problem. They are with me.'

'You know I'm here for brown sugar. Abdullah told you.'

'Anything you want, I'm the right person. Maybe you look at me and think I'm nothing because I'm a little man. But I'm the big one here.'

'How much do you have for me?'

'It depends on how much you want.'

'Three kilos?'

'No problem.'

'And the price?'

'Fifteen thousand US for a kilo. If you take three, the price comes down to thirteen thousand,' Mangala said.

He called the black-veiled woman who had opened the door and barked an order in Swahili. She returned with an *ovo*, similar to the one Obie and Abdullah had shown Alex in Pemba.

As he unwrapped the egg, Alex complimented Mangala on the beautiful vehicles parked outside. 'I have five cars,' the drug dealer said, 'all from South Africa. They steal them there, bring them here and I pay them.'

'That is fantastic,' Alex said.

'I have a BMW M5. And a Mitsubishi 4×4 and a Mercedes and a Camry and a minibus.'

'And Mangala,' said Alex, 'I have to say that you've got a beautiful house with beautiful ladies.'

He laughed, held the egg up in the air and said: 'Oh yes. They are the ones who take the eggs in Pakistan.' He pointed at the women and continued: 'That one is Rati. And that one is Annie. And that one is Halimi. And that one is Dida. They travel for me.'

'You mean they bring the heroin to Tanzania?'

'Yes, they are the ones!'

'How do they bring the drugs?'

'They swallow!' Mangala said, and laughed again. 'You will not believe when I tell you that each of them can swallow a hundred or a hundred and twenty of these eggs.'

'These women are your mules?' asked Alex.

'Oh yes! Every time they travel, they carry something for me,' Mangala said, as he spat out a wad of *qat* and stuffed a new bunch of leaves into his mouth. He explained to Alex that a man could swallow up to a kilo and a half of heroin eggs and a woman about a kilogram.

'These sure are special ladies,' Alex said.

'Each and every one of them!'

'I must admit, Mangala, women like this make me weak!'

The two shared a bonding moment as Mangala leant forward and slapped Alex on the back. 'And me too!' He burst out in more frenzied laughter.

As soon as he had calmed down and manoeuvred the ball of *qat* into his other cheek, he snarled an order at the group of women. One got up and returned a few moments later with a pack of photographs.

'Dubai airport,' Mangala said, as he handed Alex a photo. 'This is Halimi and me. We're on our way back from Pakistan.'

'Has she swallowed?'

'As she is standing there!' Mangala said and gave another shrill laugh.

'And she too!' He passed Alex another photograph. 'Karachi.'

More snapshots of Mangala and his mules followed. Singapore, Thailand, London, Lisbon. Mangala said in order to avoid detection, his mules would never fly directly from Pakistan to East Africa. They would swallow in Pakistan and fly to a destination like Dubai and go in transit to a hotel near the airport, where they would pass their valuable cargo to another mule.

'And how do they do that?' asked Alex.

'Oh, it's just a matter of a good shit!' Mangala shrieked.

He cut a small piece of heroin from the egg lying in front of him. 'I now want you to go and test this,' he said, as he handed it to Alex. 'You see the colour of this? It is hundred per cent pure.'

Shortly afterwards, with Mangala still ranting on about his mules, the camera battery died and Alex made an excuse to leave.

A veiled woman draped in colourful garb opened the door for Alex and escorted him to his car parked outside the house.

'And what is your name?' he asked her.

'Dida,' she answered softly.

George Timbuka was the quintessential civil servant: neat, earnest and diligent. Sitting behind his well-organised and polished desk, he admitted: 'Yes, drugs are killing our youth. There are so many drugs in Tanzania. It's a porous country and it is streaming in.'

Timbuka, dressed in a greenish safari suit, was Tanzania's anti-drug commissioner. The courteous, bald-headed policeman was candid about the problem. 'When somebody is poor, you can use him. So our youth have been recruited to travel to Pakistan, India and Colombia to fetch heroin and cocaine.'

Tanzania had been far more successful than Mozambique in the war against drugs. The international airport at Dar was equipped with modern drug-detecting equipment, and the week before our arrival a mule was arrested with 120 heroin eggs in his stomach. Not long before that, a South African couple was nabbed with a suitcase full of heroin.

Timbuka advised us to travel to the central Tanzanian town of Dodoma, where one of the country's most notorious drug dealers was incarcerated in a mental asylum. Othman Dede became maniacal after injecting himself with a so-called speedball – a mixture of cocaine and heroin. He attacked his family, who in turn called the police and gave him up. The judge found Dede was mentally disturbed and unfit to stand trial.

Dodoma had been the official capital of Tanzania since the founding father of the modern republic, Julius Nyerere, decided in the 1980s to relocate the seat of government to the centre of the country in order to unite his people. Although parliament convened in Dodama for several months a year, not even the national airline flew to the capital. We had no option but to hire a car and drive.

The road gleamed in the heat as we left the palm-fringed boulevards and mangroves of Dar es Salaam and climbed up to African savannah, with its vast rolling plains of thorn trees and scrub. We travelled past Morogoro, an attractive town trapped between two huge verdant walls of mountains that had once concealed the ANC's secret military training camps.

The closer we got to Dodoma, the more severe the landscape became. We were on the southernmost boundary of the Masai grazing land, which stretches north into Kenya. Goats feasted on thorn bushes and a spear-waving herdsman wearing a red kikoi wrapped around his taut body burst from the arid landscape.

Within this wasteland lay Dodoma – nothing more than a dreary African town held hostage by the heat. It boasted an East German–designed parliament, a presidential palace donated by the North Koreans and a hotel near the train station. It was the last place in the world where one would expect a wine industry, yet Dodoma is the centre of Tanzanian viniculture and houses one of the only vineyards north of South Africa and south of the Sahara. We washed the African dust down with two bottles of Tanganyika Vineyards Makutupora Red – aptly described by South African wine master John Platter as being blessed with 'robust goat flavours'.

Othman Dede was an affable fellow with a permanent smile plastered across his face. He was kept in the high-security section of the mental institution, but looked completely sane compared to some of those locked up with him. But the hospital superintendent warned me: be careful, his mood could change and turn volatile.

But Dede was as sweet as honey and eager to tell his story to a journalist. 'Heroin and cocaine, ja, brown and white, I was using like my sugar.'

'And how much did you use?' I asked him.

'I used like five grams a day. I was a big addict. That is why I am in this hospital.'

He then described how he chased the dragon. 'I used to take something like a foil and put a bit of sugar on that. Then I start to smoke. We call it chase. Draw that sweet smoke. That is what you chase. The sweet smoke.'

As a drug mule, Dede regularly travelled between the Pakistani city of Peshawar and Tanzania. He could at one time swallow 150 ten-gram eggs. 'We make the heroin into a ball. After that we take foil and solution tape and we tie it nice. And then I swallow.'

'And if it leaks?'

'You are sure to die.'

Back in Dar es Salaam, drug merchant Mangala was chewing *qat* and shooting his mouth off in full view of Alex's spy camera. Four of his female mules were sitting in the lounge softly twittering, while in the mosque around the corner an imam summoned the faithful to prayer.

'And how was that sample I gave you?' Mangala asked Alex.

'Perfect.'

'So are you ready to buy?'

'Yes, we can talk business,' Alex said.

'If you take one or two kilos now, I can give you connection with friends of mine who are dealing with huge amounts. If you need ten or twenty and up to a hundred kilos, they can bring you.'

'And what about the police?'

'The police? They know what I'm doing. They come here and take my money and then leave me alone. As long as you are not a politician and not going for politics you are safe.'

The druglord – an ever-present ball of *qat* in his cheek – cackled on for the next hour about his fleet of cars, his female mules and his growing drug empire. 'My friend,' he said in his shrill voice as he slapped Alex on the back, 'God has brought you to my house and together we can achieve great things!'

After only a week in Dar, Alex had not only won Mangala's trust, but Abdullah had also introduced him to various other drug dealers. He was generating more spy tapes than I could look at. 'You have to stop now, Alex,' I told him. 'We cannot possibly use all of this.'

'One more meeting,' he would say. It was this one more rendezvous with the Tanzanian underworld that almost proved fatal. Alex received a phone call from two drug dealers called McGee and Mac who wanted to meet. He waited for them outside his hotel with the grey sling bag over his shoulder. They pulled up in a white minibus and told him to get in. There were two more men in the vehicle.

They drove down Upanga Road past a series of whitewashed and red-tiled colonial buildings before turning into Sikukuu Street. They passed the Karaikoo market and continued into one of the suburbs. Nobody said a word. Alex clung to the bag on his lap, aware of several pairs of eyes fixed on him. The minibus stopped at a nondescript house and McGee – a burly fellow with a flat nose and a shaven head – ordered Alex to get out.

With the spy camera rolling, they escorted him into the house, where McGee told Alex to sit down. One of McGee's henchmen blocked the front door while the other took up a position at the exit to the kitchen.

'I've been in situations like this in South America before,' Alex told me afterwards. 'If you show them you're scared, you're fucked.'

McGee took up a menacing position in front of Alex and bent over him. Their faces were centimetres apart. 'So, my brother,' the drug dealer said in a hoarse voice, 'I need to know why you came all this way to see us.'

Alex looked him straight in the eye. 'I am here for sugar. Brown sugar. And I want full-kick. Two or three kilos.'

'And why do you think I have the sugar you need?'

'Abdullah said you're the best. He said I should deal with you.'

'I don't trust Abdullah,' he said, as he tapped Alex on the shoulder. 'I don't deal with him.'

'Or with any of his friends,' said Mac, an older man with a slight limp and a soft voice. He stood up and waddled towards Alex. 'That's why, Mister Alex, you should leave Dar as quickly as you came.'

'Yes,' said McGee, 'or you might not leave at all.'

Alex said it was at this point that he decided attack was the best form of defence. He got to his feet and stared McGee squarely in the face. His voice lifted an octave. 'Do you want to tell me that I drove all the way from Johannesburg to listen to bullshit like this? Oh, fuck you!'

He then exploded into a fury. I don't know if it was real or not, but his face reddened and a diatribe of abuse poured from his mouth. His finger was virtually up McGee's nose.

I'd witnessed a similar tirade once before in Maputo when a grey-uniformed cop had jumped out from behind a bus stop shelter and pulled Alex over for an alleged traffic offence. As Alex got out of the car, the constable garbled something about skipping traffic lanes and slammed a fine of a few hundred thousand meticais on him. Alex blew his top, took a few steps forward, pointed his finger at the policeman and ranted and raved him into complete submission. The man feebly apologised and waved his hands in desperation to try to get Alex on his way again. Alex continued to hurl abuse at the policeman until we were out of hearing range.

He used the same tactics at McGee's house to wriggle out of a potentially perilous situation. McGee and Mac were stunned into silence by Alex's barrage. He threw the grey bag over his shoulder, pushed McGee out of the way and said: 'I never ever want to see you in my life again! How the hell can you do business like this?' He walked up to the man at the door and barked: 'Open this fucking door or I will break it down!' In the background McGee and Mac muttered something about a misunderstanding and said they should talk again.

The henchman unlocked the door and Alex was out. He briskly walked to the nearest road, stopped a local *matatu* (taxi) and drove back to the hotel.

'You're finished in Dar, Alex,' I said to him that night. 'It's getting too dangerous. You got them good, but it is time to leave.'

Early the next morning, McGee phoned Alex to say they were ready to do business with him. His face lit up. 'One more time,' he pleaded.

'Forget about it,' I said. 'Get the hell out of here while you can.'

Alex flew back to Pemba, where he had to pick up the Toyota and start the journey back to Maputo.

He gave me the Tanzanian SIM card of his cellphone when he left. An hour or two after I had slid it into my own phone, it rang. I answered.

'Alex!' said a woman's voice softly.

'No, this is not Alex.'

'Where's Mister Alex?'

'Who are you and what do you want?'

'This is Dida and I want to speak to Mister Alex.'

Dida was one of Mangala's drug mules. Alex had shown me footage of the veiled women he referred to as Mangala's ninjas. He had spoken with great affection of Dida and said she had even invited him for dinner at her house.

'Watch out, Alex,' I had warned him. 'This time you might lose more than just a finger!'

I told Dida that Alex had left Dar.

'Where is Mister Alex?'

'Back to Maputo.'

'When is he coming back?'

'I don't think he is,' I told her.

'And who are you?' she asked.

'His friend,' I said.

'Mister Alex said he will be back,' she said in a pleading, almost desperate voice before hanging up.

Dida called again the next day and said she had a letter for Alex she wanted me to deliver to him in Johannesburg. A short while later a veiled woman with big brown eyes arrived at my hotel. She was delicately built and it was astonishing to think she could stuff a kilogram of heroin into her tiny body.

'This is for Mister Alex,' she said, as she handed me an envelope.

'I'll give it to him,' I told her.

'I'm waiting for Mister Alex to come back to Dar,' she said.

'Why?' I asked her.

'That is what he promised me. Mister Mangala is also waiting for Mister Alex.'

'I'm sure he is,' I said.

Dida, clearly disheartened by the news that Alex might not be back soon, excused herself. She waved down a taxi, got in without a word and drove away.

Back in Maputo, I asked Alex: 'What's up with Dida?'

He was taken aback. 'What do you mean?'

'She's waiting for you. What did you promise her?'

'How do you know?'

'She came to my hotel in Dar to deliver a letter for you.'

He looked uncomfortable. 'You will not believe what happened.'

'Tell me.'

Alex said Dida had escorted him out of Mangala's house after each visit. The first time she simply asked him what his name was and introduced herself. The second time she engaged in small talk. Where do you come from? Do you like Dar? How long are you staying?

'She wanted to know if I was married. I said no, and she said she wasn't either. I think she was coming on to me.'

Dida told Alex she had been married but her husband divorced her and left her with a small child. 'I told her I had always been intrigued by Muslim women and their way of living. It was then that she invited me for dinner.'

'And then?' I asked him.

'I said I would love to have dinner with her, but why didn't she come and visit me at my hotel.'

'And did she?'

'Oh yes, the following day.'

'And?'

'She arrived in her veil. Just her eyes were showing. We sat in the lobby drinking tea. I said I would love to know what she looked like under that mask.'

'And then?'

'She said she could not take her veil off in public.'

'Ja?'

'I asked her if she would show me in my room.'

'And?

'She said we should go to my room.'

'And?'

'We went to my room.'

'And then?'

'She took her veil off. Dida was a beautiful woman.'

CHAPTER 16

A French kiss in paradise

I chose not to choose life. I chose somethin' else. And the reasons? There are no reasons. Who needs reasons when you've got heroin?
— Renton in the movie *Trainspotting*

'I'VE FOUND THEM!' ALEX ANNOUNCED TRIUMPHANTLY. 'AND THEY are willing to see us. But we have to leave right away.'

It was a Sunday morning at the Café Costa do Sol in Maputo. Across Avenida Marginal, craftsmen displayed their wooden carvings on the pavement, beach boys erected volleyball nets on the beach and a fisherman with a basket of coral fish strapped to his bicycle pedalled his way to the market. Further down the road, vendors set up stalls for the day while street chefs lit charcoal fires to roast flattened chickens that had been soaking for hours in a fiery marinade of olive oil, chilli, garlic and lemon juice.

We had returned from Tanzania the day before to start the final leg of our drug investigation. So far, we had achieved virtually everything we had set out to do two months earlier when we set up camp in a Maputo apartment. Alex had made contact with twelve drug dealers in Maputo, Pemba and Dar es Salaam. He had filmed them, their merchandise, homes and women. We had countless pieces of paper on which they had scribbled prices and quantities and descriptions of the drugs they had on offer.

Each time Alex returned from a rendezvous and pulled the Sony camcorder from his grey sling bag, there were some anxious moments. On several occasions our apprehension turned to despair when he pushed the 'play' button and we saw either an overexposed white screen or an underexposed black picture in which nothing and no one was discernible. Sometimes the batteries went flat or the tape ran out before Alex could capture crucial moments. At one point a loose connection stalled the operation for days while I rushed back to Johannesburg to have it repaired. Mostly, though, thanks to his remarkable skill and courage, Alex had captured amazing footage with his spy camera.

The most daunting missions were those when, long after dark, Alex threw the grey bag over his shoulder and disappeared with housebreaker Jimmy into Little Colombia to try to infiltrate one of the crack and heroin houses. Once the doors or iron gates were bolted behind him, he was a lone and abandoned figure in surreal capsules of perversion where blankets hung in front of windows blocked out any air or light.

'That's the worst; there's no air,' he once said to me. 'I must have inhaled a hundred rocks and ten grams of heroin.'

Alex had shot twenty-five hours of secret film and in the process had contracted malaria, been held captive by drug dealers and must have driven about 5 000 kilometres through harsh African terrain in a small Toyota. When the sedan could go no further, he made his way on buses and trucks and boats.

The last part of our quest was to find Carlos and Dadinha Felner again. Of all the footage Alex had shot, the most harrowing was without a doubt the images of Carlos and Dadinha jabbing needles into each other's necks. They haunted me, and I told Alex often that we had to track them down. They were perfect case studies: a mixed-race couple, educated and with distinguished careers and revolutionary credentials, eloquent in English, down and out and totally addicted to heroin.

Early that Sunday morning, Alex had ventured into Little Colombia in search of Carlos and Dadinha. He eventually found himself back at Mamma's heroin parlour and had to endure another embrace from her in order to find out where they lived. Minutes later, he knocked on their front door. Carlos opened it, and after a brief conversation Alex rushed back to Costa do Sol to fetch cameraman Jan de Klerk and me.

The couple lived on the second floor of a decrepit apartment building in downtown Maputo, conveniently situated just a few blocks from Little Colombia. The area was awfully rundown, with piles of rubbish in front of buildings and lines of washing stretching from window to window. Residents loitered aimlessly on the crumbling pavements as two boys rolled a tyre down the pot-holed street. A broken-down Peugeot stood on bricks outside the building.

We climbed the gloomy stairs to the second floor and Alex knocked on a dark-blue door. Carlos opened and stared at us with a blank expression on his emaciated face. He was a pitiful and forlorn figure. He waved us in without a word. Dadinha was standing behind him. They both looked far worse in the flesh than on film. His skin was pasty and pallid; she had dark spots on her face, probably the result of excessive scratching in order to temper the skin irritation caused by heroin.

She spoke first. 'Well, as you can see, gentlemen, there's no furniture in the lounge.' Her voice was slurred, clearly the result of an early morning fix, and the heat of thousands of crack pipes had burnt her front teeth away. 'So let's move through to the bedroom.'

That was equally bare, except for a thin mattress on the floor, a basket with drug paraphernalia next to it, a rail with clothes, and one or two dilapidated chairs. A torn sheet covered the window. '

'What you see around you is not who we are. We have education and culture. We don't want to live like this,' Dadinha said.

We sat down on the mattress. Alex cleared his throat. 'I told Carlos and Dadinha you wanted to see them and tell them something. So go ahead.'

I didn't know who Carlos and Dadinha thought we were, but they looked dumbfounded when I said we were journalists. I explained that Alex had carried a concealed camera in his bag at Mamma's house with which he had surreptitiously filmed them. They didn't seem to grasp the implications of my words.

Carlos spoke for the first time. His front teeth were also missing. 'And what do you want from us?'

'I want to interview you about your heroin addiction.'

Silence permeated the room. Dadinha spoke: 'We are honoured, gentlemen, but that is absolutely impossible.'

'Why?' I asked.

'We are too well known in this city,' she said. 'And what about our children? We don't want them to see us like this.'

'No, we don't,' said Carlos. 'And besides, I don't have time. I have to fly to Beira later this afternoon.'

By some miracle, Carlos had managed to hold on to his partnership in a veterinary concern. He told us he had landed a substantial government contract.

'I have to get my computer back before I leave. It has very important information I need in Beira and I can't leave without it,' he said.

'Where's the computer?' I asked.

'With the drug dealer,' he said. 'I left it with him for drugs and now we don't have money to buy it back.'

'How much do you owe?'

'A hundred dollars,' he said.

I saw a small window of opportunity opening. 'And if I get you the computer, will you speak to us?'

'And how would you do that?'

'I'll pay the drug dealer.'

They looked at one another. 'It's not enough,' said Dadinha. 'You have to pay much more.'

'I can't,' I said. 'I don't pay for stories. I'll get your computer back and that's it.'

'And then you do the interview and you leave Maputo and what becomes of us?' Dadinha wanted to know.

I promised we would not broadcast the documentary in Mozambique. And then I had a sudden inspiration. 'What if we can find you a rehab in South Africa? You've said you don't want to live like this. I agree. What if we can find a place that is willing to take you in and get you off drugs?'

'It's very expensive. Where will you find the money?'

'We'll ask them to sponsor your treatment. In return we film your recovery and broadcast it.'

'How can we trust you?' Dadinha asked.

'When I get back to Johannesburg tomorrow morning I'll start working on it. I promise.'

Dadinha looked at Carlos, mumbled a few words in Portuguese and said: 'Fine, we'll do it. Carlos needs that computer.'

A hundred-dollar note in hand, Alex and Carlos rushed off to get the computer. Dadinha excused herself to put on make-up. Jan and I fetched his camera equipment from our vehicle.

When Alex and Carlos returned with the computer, we placed the couple on the mattress, Jan set up his camera and started rolling. For the next two hours, Carlos and Dadinha spoke. They were initially hesitant and even shy, but as we got to the heart of their story they opened up, pouring out a torturous account of addiction, depravity and desperation. They no longer put up a veneer of decency or shame; they were simply too tired and depleted to pretend anything. They had hit rock bottom.

Dadinha said they had taken a dose of heroin just before we arrived. She took a syringe from the woven basket next to the mattress and said: 'If we don't take this, we can't speak to you. We'll just be lying on the bed.'

'It's become like medicine,' Carlos added. 'If we don't take it, we can't walk.'

'It doesn't make us drunk or high any more,' said Dadinha. 'If we don't take it, we have pain. Terrible pain. We get stomach and muscle cramps, we vomit, we feel cold, we have diarrhoea.'

Carlos must have taken a much larger hit than Dadinha. I had hardly asked the first question when his eyes rolled back and he passed out. Dadinha elbowed him and slapped him against the head. He woke up with a sheepish grin on his face. She snapped something at him in Portuguese.

'I always have this struggle in my mind about heroin,' Carlos said. 'Yesterday I needed lots of it.'

'Last night we washed and cooked and got into bed,' said Dadinha. 'I wrote my diary and thought we would sleep without a shot. Suddenly, Carlos said, let's go and get a dose.'

'I was anxious and depressed. My heart was pounding and I knew I wouldn't sleep,' he said.

'Carlos was like a lion. Nothing was going to stop him.'
'I got up and went to buy a dose. This morning I took another one.'

Carlos Felner was born halfway through the twentieth century in a country and on a continent at the peak of colonial rule. The mandarins in Lisbon argued that Portuguese seafarers had made landfall in Africa almost five centuries before and therefore Mozambique and Angola were not colonies at all – they were 'overseas provinces', part of the indomitable Portuguese empire.

His father worked on a tea plantation in the Zambezia province of northern Mozambique. Carlos remembered his first years as uneventful and relatively happy, but when he was six years old he was sent to boarding school in Lourenço Marques. 'I was not yet seven and already living on my own. The teachers were violent; they beat us and maybe I already then developed an instability in my life,' he said.

His secondary education was at an agricultural school in Portugal, and over a period of seven years, he saw his father only twice. 'By fifteen I was living like a full-grown man. I paid the school, I rented my own room and bought my own clothes and food,' he said. That was when he started drinking and took the first steps towards a life of addiction and dependency. His addictive personality seemed to have genetic roots. Back in Mozambique, his father was drinking himself to death and beating his mother to a pulp. The Felner family had a terrible legacy of alcoholism. His mother, father and sister all died of liver failure caused by alcohol abuse.

Dadinha was fifteen years younger than Carlos and came into the world on the wrong side of the tracks. Her father was a gardener, her mother a maid. They were both employed by a wealthy Portuguese family and lived in an outside room on the property owned by a woman doctor and her husband, a civil engineer.

Dadinha's earliest memory was of extreme violence, when her father would go into an alcohol-induced frenzy and beat up his whole family. 'I still have this picture in my head. He hit my mother cruelly, so much that she would lie on the ground and cry. He once smashed my little brother's hand with a meat hammer,' she said.

Finally, her mother could take the beatings no more and ran away, abandoning her children. The beatings from their father grew worse and more frequent. His Portuguese employer sometimes intervened and took the children into the house, bathed them and put them to bed.

The woman eventually fired Dadinha's father and told him to leave. He did, but Dadinha and her brother stayed with the Portuguese doctor, who later adopted them. Suddenly Dadinha was a pupil at the best schools and basked in the attention she received from her foster mother. Her brother never recovered from his childhood trauma. He became addicted to drugs and committed suicide.

When Carlos left school, he trained as a veterinary surgeon. By then, Mozambique had changed immeasurably and was in the grip of civil war. The Mozambican Liberation Front (FRELIMO), founded in Dar es Salaam in 1962 to oppose colonial rule, was attacking the Portuguese armed forces throughout the northern provinces of Cabo Delgado, Niassa and Tete.

By 1970, the writing was on the wall and Portuguese families, among them the Felners, were abandoning the colony and returning to the motherland. However, Carlos regarded himself as Mozambican, supported FRELIMO and joined a Marxist youth movement.

'I was a true communist and worked for the defeat of the Portuguese. I was in prison several times. But I didn't care. We were young, drank a lot, smoked dope and dreamt of a new country,' he said.

The turning point in Mozambique's struggle for independence came in 1974 when Portuguese army officers, tired of fighting three futile colonial wars in Mozambique, Angola and Guinea-Bissau, staged a lightning coup d'état in Lisbon. Within hours the oldest dictatorship in Europe disintegrated and made way for the socialist regime of António de Spínola. At the time, FRELIMO held the military initiative in Mozambique and was striking deep into the heart of the country. For all practical purposes, Portugal had lost the war.

The exodus of Portuguese from Mozambique accelerated, and within eighteen months 90 per cent of the *brancos* had left the country. Few were prepared to live under a socialist regime in one of the poorest countries in the world. When Mozambique became independent in June 1975 and Samora Machel was sworn in as its first president, Carlos was the only veterinary surgeon in the entire country. There were only forty qualified doctors and a handful of other professionals in the new republic.

Shortly after independence, Machel – one of Africa's greatest revolutionary leaders and a man of exceptional charisma – called Carlos to his office. Son, the president said, you are young and I am sorry to do this to you, but I want to appoint you to a very important position. Carlos, who was only twenty-five, idolised Machel. Of course, *Presidente*, he said, whatever you and the revolution require of me.

Vast tracts of land and farms had been abandoned by the Portuguese and nationalised by the new government. The nation had to be fed, but farming had virtually ground to a halt. Carlos was given the task of establishing cooperative farms and making them productive. Before long, he was the second most power-ful civil servant in the department of agriculture.

Carlos said he tackled his presidential mission with great devotion and soon realised that he was an addict: a work addict. He was drinking a lot, but felt it was under control. He was married, but it wasn't long before his wife left him.

By 1977, Mozambican independence and stability were under threat. Rhodesian military intelligence had given birth to the Mozambican National Resistance (RENAMO), a combination of former members of Portuguese army units, defectors from the Mozambican army and peasants press-ganged into service in areas near the Rhodesian border. Although RENAMO was initially dismissed by FRELIMO as nothing but a gang of armed bandits, military units soon filtered into the Gaza and Inhambane provinces and evidence emerged of villages being razed, women raped, men killed and boys forced to join the rebel army. Mozambique found itself in the grip of full-scale civil war.

By the late seventies, Samora Machel had given Carlos a new task: help to feed our troops! He was reassigned to the northern Manica province to kick-start state farms that had to produce meat, milk and maize.

'FRELIMO taught me that service to my country and the revolution came first. My family came second and I came last. So I knew I was going to a war situation and that I would see terrible things. But I still had this dream of a great Mozambique, and I accepted.'

Carlos had remarried and fathered two daughters, Katia and Yara. 'This was when I really started to drink. It was a terrible war and every morning when the soldiers came to fetch me at my house, I looked at my two daughters and knew I might die in an ambush and never see them again. There was so much stress. I drank and drank,' he said.

Back in Maputo, Dadinha was a teenager and in love. One day, she and her boyfriend went for a stroll on the beach. Three fishermen attacked them. The boy ran away and the men repeatedly raped Dadinha. The boy and rescuers who later came to help found her unconscious.

Nevertheless, Dadinha excelled at school, passed with flying colours and eventually found a job as an accountant with the United Nations in Maputo. She married and had a daughter, Debbie, but divorced soon afterwards. Her former husband became a senior civil servant in Maputo.

RENAMO was grinding ever southwards and, by the middle of the 1980s, its mortars and bombs were exploding around the capital. Dadinha lived on the outskirts of Maputo and an army convoy had to escort her daily to the UN offices in the city. One day, the convoy drove into a RENAMO ambush. Several FRELIMO soldiers were mowed down. A dying soldier gave her his pistol and told her to fight back. Dadinha did, and she and one soldier kept the RENAMO insurgents at bay until help arrived.

After seven years in the thick of war in northern Mozambique, Carlos and his family returned to Maputo in 1986. He resigned from his government job, became a director of an Italian company, set up his own veterinary concern and was at one stage also a university professor.

'I felt my life was good and that I was a winner, but really, that is not how it was. I was destroying myself. It was just work, work, work. My wife left me because of that. I had no self-esteem,' he said.

A mutual friend introduced Carlos and Dadinha to one another and it was love at first sight. It seemed like an odd romance. Apart from the age gap, they came from totally different backgrounds.

'He bowled me over. He was so strong,' she said.

'Ja, and she too,' he said. 'She understood me.'

Before long, with Katia, Debbie and Yara as witnesses, Carlos and Dadinha were married in a simple ceremony performed by a justice of the peace in Maputo. She had known immeasurable trauma at a tender age, and he had been exposed to the savagery of one of Africa's worst civil wars, so it was a fresh start for both of them. In many ways, their union embodied the hopes, dreams and tribulations of Mozambique and its people.

'We never thought anything could go wrong,' she said.

But within two years, their relationship had become so calamitous that it would ultimately destroy their lives and bring them face to face with death.

The house, oh the house was so beautiful, Dadinha said. And I had furnished and decorated it myself, she added. She was sitting upright on the mattress with a smile on her face. Carlos had done most of the initial talking and was exhausted. He was slumped against the wall and was dozing off again.

'I don't know if it was classic or Victorian, but we had everything renovated and refurbished. The interior was very colonial. Very comfortable, with three living rooms and a veranda,' Dadinha said as she once again elbowed Carlos out of his heroin stupor.

'The children were growing up and going to school. On weekends we would take the Nissan and ask ourselves: Where shall we go this time? Bilene or Xai-Xai, or maybe Ponto do Oura? We would pack everything and take the kids,' Dadinha said.

'We were both earning in dollars and we had lots of money,' Carlos added, having regained consciousness. 'We were invited to all the parties and drank lots of alcohol, but everybody around us was also drinking. So it was kind of normal.'

'In 1990 Carlos was getting very frustrated with the war. There was no end to it,' Dadinha said.

'All my dreams were destroyed,' he added.

'Everything he had worked for was falling apart,' Dadinha said. 'And so when drugs came, we took them.'

It started with cocaine. 'First I felt energy,' Dadinha said. 'In the house and in life. I could be at the office at eight, work the whole day, arrive home at seven or eight, take care of the children, work all night long and go back to work in the morning.'

Ironically, although drugs had always been available in Mozambique, it was the end of the civil war and the birth of democracy that unlocked the narcotic floodgates. President Joaquim Chissano and RENAMO's Afonso Dhlakama signed the General Peace Agreement in Rome in October 1992 and contested the first democratic election a year later. The economy was liberated and the country's borders opened up. International investment, tourism and trade poured in – and so did drugs.

Said Carlos: 'I would be drunk at a party and it would be difficult to drive home. When I changed from alcohol to drugs, I suddenly wasn't drunk any more. I thought, hmmm, that's very nice. I didn't realise I was out of control.'

They were soon on heroin. 'I would smoke all weekend. When I stopped to go to work, I felt sick. I had cramps in my body and pain in my bones and was infected with diarrhoea. I said to Dadinha, I think I have malaria, but she told me, no, you have withdrawal from heroin. I was addicted,' said Carlos.

There was a cynical twist to their heroin addiction. For some time, Carlos had been beating Dadinha during outbursts of anger and aggression. Cocaine, known as an 'upper' by addicts, made him frantic and even more violent. Heroin, a so-called 'downer', pacified and calmed him. When Carlos spiked or smoked heroin, he didn't thrash his wife.

Dadinha lost her job in 1994 when the United Nations discovered she was a drug addict. She was unstable, depressed and had mood swings. 'I was always a good worker, but when they discovered the drugs, they told me to leave,' she said.

The couple tried several times to kick their habit and once went for rehabilitation at an exclusive resort outside Johannesburg. When they went back to Maputo, one of their first visitors was their Nigerian drug dealer – to congratulate them on their sobriety! When he left, he 'forgot' a gram of heroin on the coffee table. Carlos ran after him to return the drug. Don't worry, he told Carlos, keep it. He did, and placed it in a jar in the living room. A few days later, Carlos was stressed from work and Dadinha had run out of anti-depressants. They opened the jar. They were back on drugs.

'Ah, that feeling,' said Dadinha, 'was something else. Like a French kiss in paradise.'

They started spiking heroin in the morning, afternoon and evening and smoked crack throughout the day. The veins in their arms soon collapsed and they had to inject themselves in their necks, legs and armpits.

Dadinha scratched around in the basket and pulled out a long, slim sliver of tinfoil. 'This is a dose of heroin,' she said. 'It cost 80 000 meticais (about R30) and is a tenth of a gram. We need this every day.'

She unfolded the foil and showed us the tiny strip of fine brown powder. Then she took a crack pipe – a thin glass syringe – and held it in the air. 'Crack is for a short time, but heroin is for all time. The feeling of crack lasts only fifteen or twenty minutes. But it works straight onto your brain. I love crack, but it's too expensive.'

Dadinha said cocaine and crack made her hyperactive and she needed a dose of heroin afterwards to bring her 'down'. This habit of mixing heroin and cocaine proved almost fatal when she started injecting herself with 'speedballs' – heroin mixed with cocaine. Addicts say it's the ultimate narcotic high and describe it as an erratic chemical voyage that see-saws between mania and tranquillity.

'I was confused. I took a gram of cocaine and two doses of heroin. I shot it up my arm. It was just poof! and I was gone. I woke up much later in hospital,' she said. Dadinha suffered permanent brain damage, which caused epilepsy and amnesia. She was never able to work again.

Dadinha suffered several more overdoses. 'I used ten grams of cocaine in three days and smoked rocks in between. I don't remember what happened. Carlos will remember.'

She also attempted suicide more than once. 'I took lots of drugs and was very depressed and couldn't sleep. So I took all my sleeping pills. But I didn't die. I woke up in hospital and was paralysed for a whole month. Carlos was next to my bed all the time.'

Carlos and Dadinha locked themselves in their bedroom for hours while spiking or smoking heroin and cocaine. They didn't cook or eat. They would promise their daughters weekends away or movies and ice cream, but instead would lie in a stupor in the bedroom. They forgot their children's birthdays. Katia and Yara walked in on one of their drug orgies and found needles dangling from their arms. They once forgot to fetch the children from a resort in southern Mozambique where they had been on holiday with friends.

Dadinha's former husband sued for custody of Debbie. The court declared Dadinha an unfit mother and placed the child in her father's care. Life had also become unbearable for Katia and Yara, and they went to live with their mother. Dadinha's foster mother told her not to visit the family again.

Tears welled up in Dadinha's eyes. 'The worst is the children,' she said. 'The family we lost.' She burst into tears and sobbed uncontrollably. Carlos put an arm around her. 'Dadi, Dadi.' He stroked her head. Sitting opposite them on the floor, I had a lump in my throat.

'How they had to suffer because of us,' she wept. 'And it is not that they did not have clothes or food. They had everything. But they never had us. They never had their parents.'

She scratched around in the basket again and passed me three small passport photographs. 'This one is Katia. She is twenty-three and at university. The second is Yara. She is also at university. And the last one is Debbie. She is still at school.'

'We didn't raise them and it hurts a lot,' said Carlos. 'They visit us now and then, but that is all.'

'Towards the end we were not looking after them any more, but they had to look after us. I am not their mother, they are my mother,' said Dadinha.

By 1998 they had run out of money and started selling furniture in order to maintain their habit. A year later, they sold their house and cars for $120 000. Carlos stopped working. 'Then we dived into cocaine. Within one year, we had used all that money. We smoked and smoked. And when that money was finished, we went to the bank to get more,' said Carlos.

By 2000, they were down and out. The children were gone, the family had rejected them, they had no house and no money, no friends and Dadinha had suffered brain damage.

'I went to my mother to borrow money. She said, I'm giving you this fucking money but I'm helping you to kill yourself! It's horrible. I just want to finish this as quickly as I can and tell them how guilty or sorry I feel for what I did to them,' Dadinha wailed.

For several years they were confined to their rundown and bare one-bedroom flat, and their existence centred on the dealers and drug houses of Little Colombia.

'It's not easy. I am unemployed and I don't have friends,' said Dadinha. 'The people there have no education and no culture. I cannot talk to them about politics or economics. I stay at home. I read and I write poetry.'

The junkies in Little Colombia called Dadinha auntie. 'They respect me too much because they know who I once was. They know I come from an important family and that we had a big house and that I worked for the United Nations.'

Dadinha said one of the dealers had tried to poison her the year before because they owed him money and couldn't pay. 'So he gave me a dose with very bad things inside. I injected, but after half an hour I was freezing and I had fever. I took another shot. It got worse. Carlos had to take me to hospital.'

'Yes, I saved her life. She was nearly dead. If you owe money to these people you must pay or you are going to die,' said Carlos.

They hardly ever saw their daughters. 'Sometimes, about once a month, we have lunch with them. Or they come here to feed us. But they are afraid to visit us. It is not a nice area and they don't know in what condition they are going to find us.'

Debbie had sent Dadinha a Christmas card the year before in which she wrote: 'Mom, you can be the happiest person in the world. Pray as much as you can. God exists.'

'She is a sick little girl. Very depressed,' Dadinha said. 'She needs me, but the father uses my sickness to keep her away from me. She's very religious and last year was her confirmation and she wanted us to be there. So we went. But when it was time for the party afterwards, the father said we are not welcome. Debbie cried and I said don't worry, take some pictures and show me later.'

The couple's situation had turned desperate. 'I have nothing else to sell,' said Dadinha.

'We have lots of debt and nobody will give us anything until we can pay,' Carlos added.

'The money that Carlos gets is not enough for drugs and food and the rent,' said Dadinha.

'We don't steal things. I have no money in the bank,' Carlos added.

'We will have to stop,' said Dadinha.

'Ja, we will stop. We will stop,' Carlos promised.

Two hours after we had started the interview, they were both exhausted; I was drained and Jan had cramps in his legs from the sitting-kneeling-crouching position in which he had filmed the two addicts.

'I have to call the daughters and tell them what has happened today,' said Dadinha. 'They will be happy. This was also a surprise for me and I think it was good for us.'

'We will do the best for all of them,' said Carlos. 'We will stop and get healthy again.'

Dadinha embraced me and kissed me on both cheeks as we left. 'So when are we seeing you again?' she asked.

'Soon,' I said. 'We'll be back soon.'

As we drove away and headed for the border post, I said to Jan: 'Do you know what?'

'What?'

'We're their last hope'.

CHAPTER 17

A junky journey through junkie life

This was to be my final hit. But let's be clear about this: there's final hits and final hits. What kind was this to be? Some final hits are actually terminal one way or another, while others are merely transit points as you travel from station to station on the junky journey through junkie life. — Renton in the movie *Trainspotting*

CARLOS FELNER'S TEN-YEAR LOVE AFFAIR WITH THE GRANDDADDY of all narcotics was about to be terminated. How long the abstention might last, nobody could tell. A day, a week, a month, who knew? Less than one in twenty heroin addicts stay clean after kicking the habit. But whatever the future held, Carlos was not about to go quietly into the next chapter of his junky life. For the camera's sake, he greedily tucked into his own version of a 'last supper'.

He sprinkled powdered heroin into a teaspoon and cooked it over an open flame with water and a drop of lemon juice. He filled a syringe with the brownish liquid and held it in the air in front of him. There was nothing unusual about this spectacle. Carlos had done it thousands of times before.

But this was supposed to be where his heroin journey ended. He was about to be bundled into a car and whisked off to the Ressano Garcia border post, clear customs and race to Johannesburg, where a team of drug counsellors awaited his arrival. The journey would take at least six hours and he had to reach rehab before his craving body began to react with uncontrollable convulsions.

Colleagues Anna-Maria Lombard and Dudley Saunders were witness to his farewell fix and had the unenviable task of driving him to Johannesburg. Dudley's camera hovered a few inches from Carlos's hands and perfectly captured a drop of ballooning liquid at the tip of the needle. The addict bound a piece of string around his upper arm and plunged the needle into his flesh, but pulled it out almost immediately. He couldn't find a vein. He tapped with his forefinger on another vessel and tried again … and again. He found his target, drew a few drops of blood into the syringe and shot the concoction into his body. As the analgesic opiate permeated his brain and catapulted him through heaven's gates, he closed his eyes and became relaxed, content and gratified.

Carlos held the empty syringe in the air and paused for a moment to let Dudley focus on his hands. Then he snapped it in two, dropped the pieces on the floor and said: 'I'm finished. This was the last one.' He made wild gestures with his hands and stuck his thumbs triumphantly in the air.

I later watched this footage with disdain. Carlos was clearly relishing the attention and playing to the camera. Dudley's lens had almost sensitised his macabre act and elevated him from the desperado he was to the status of a *célèbre fatal*. He had, after all, devoted the last decade of his life to heroin and, although it had shackled and subjugated his whole being, he saw himself as a survivor who had grappled and endured.

This is your story, I had told Anna-Maria when I walked into the office the morning after we had found the two addicts a few weeks earlier in Maputo. I showed her the footage of Carlos and Dadinha and said we had to find them rehabilitation in Johannesburg and make a deal to film them.

What Anna-Maria thought was going to be a relatively easy story turned into a nightmare the moment she set foot in Maputo. Drug addiction spawns bandits, beggars and bloodsuckers, and Carlos and Dadinha were no different. Anna-Maria was a pot of gold waltzing into their wretched lives.

It was strictly off-limits to buy the two any drugs and Anna-Maria told them so, but they demanded money for food, medicine, clothes and shoes. They told her there were unpaid medical bills and money owed to several drug dealers. Carlos pleaded and tears rolled down Dadinha's cheeks. You have to help us, otherwise they will kill us when we get back, the addicts wailed. When that didn't help, they threatened to cancel our agreement.

Before long, they openly demanded heroin. 'Anna-Maria, it's like medicine for us. If you have a headache, you take aspirin. If we don't take our dose, we suffer from withdrawal and cannot function. We cannot talk to you,' Carlos said.

Anna-Maria finally relented under emotional blackmail and gave them money to pay off some of their debt. The gesture propelled the two into a drug binge. They probably argued they were soon going into rehabilitation and might as well indulge in a last spike or two. It's highly unlikely that any of the money went towards settling unpaid scores.

Anna-Maria spent much longer in Maputo than we had anticipated. Carlos and Dadinha had long since sold their passports to drug dealers. In fact, every article worth a dime had been 'invested' in Little Colombia. Carlos had even exchanged the door handles from their apartment and the golden seal on his university graduation certificate for heroin. It could take months to replace a lost or stolen passport in Mozambique, and in the end Carlos and Dadinha had to bribe officials to get new ones.

Dudley shot endless rolls of film of Dadinha standing in front of the mirror with a needle in her neck and blood dripping from the wound. At times like that she would babble relentlessly. 'Hey man, I'm feeling relaxed now. Before this dose I couldn't speak much. But now the sweating has stopped. I feel normal.'

She wiped the blood from her neck. 'I have to use my neck because I have no more veins on my legs, my arms and even my feet.'

Carlos would come back from work for a midday spike. As he cleaned the syringe and rubbed his leg where he had just injected himself, he said: 'I was lazy and had pain in my back. Now the pain is gone and my body feels strong.'

Dadinha: 'We will need another dose for tonight.'

Carlos: 'But we don't know how we can get it.'

Dadinha: 'And there is nothing more to sell.'

Carlos: 'We don't steal things. But there's no money in the bank.'

Dadinha: 'We will have to beg the dealer for another dose.'

For almost two weeks, Anna-Maria had lived under a barrage of manipulation. She realised the rehabilitation mission might be futile and doomed. Dadinha seemed ready to kick the habit, but Carlos loved his heroin and was under the illusion that he was in complete control of himself. And for as long as he was hooked, he would always draw Dadinha back into the habit.

When I asked Anna-Maria how it was going, she said: 'Dadinha? Maybe. Carlos? No way in hell.'

Their family was equally sceptical about yet another attempt to get clean. Agonising memories had laid waste to any faith Yara and Katia had in their parents. 'When we caught them taking drugs, they lied and said it's a Chinese cigarette. At first we believed them, but then we found them passed out. We cried and didn't know what to do. The next day they were sorry and promised to stop. But they never did,' said Katia.

'We've lost trust in them because they lied so much. They always told us they'd stopped, but we found them on the bed with needles in their arms and blood on their fingers,' said Yara. 'My father's getting weaker and weaker. If this fails I don't think he will try and fight again. He might die.'

Anna-Maria had arranged for Dadinha to go into rehab first. The plan was to take her to Phoenix House in Johannesburg and return two weeks later to take Carlos to Mercy House on Johannesburg's East Rand. Both institutions warned from the beginning that it would be a miracle if they could rehabilitate just one of the two.

On an August morning in 2003, Dadinha stood in front of the bathroom mirror, jabbed a needle into her neck and shot the brown liquid into a vein. As she cleaned the syringe, she vowed it would be her last spike.

Minutes later, after embracing Carlos, who wiped a drop of blood from her neck, she was in the car with Dudley and Anna-Maria, speeding towards the border post.

I saw her a few days later. Although Dadinha was still on medication, she looked rested and relaxed. 'I slept like an angel. And I woke up smiling and happy. If I were in Maputo, I would already have had my first spike. But I don't miss it.'

Dadinha, adored by both patients and staff, soon struck a special affinity with her therapist, Ian Opperman. Apart from her addiction, there was a lifetime of calamity the two had to work through: an abusive father, a mother who had abandoned her, the adoption, the rape, her brother's suicide, the ambush, the drugs, bankruptcy, brain damage and failed motherhood.

Ian told her she would have to separate from Carlos. 'If she goes back to Carlos,' he said, 'there's a very good chance she will end up dead. If the one starts, it will get the other one back onto drugs. She's smaller and weaker than Carlos but takes equal amounts of drugs. He will wake up one morning and she'll be dead next to him.'

Carlos was setting himself up for failure. He said he couldn't afford to be away from work for more than six weeks. His therapist, Ruby Weber, said it was a drop in the ocean. 'It's not enough. There is no way you can be rehabilitated in only six weeks.'

Halfway through his programme, Carlos declared: 'I'm completely recovered. I feel very positive about our future. I'm not worried. I think I can now control my life.'

In the meanwhile, Dadinha had decided to continue with a secondary care programme after her initial rehabilitation at Phoenix House. She also decided to leave Carlos. 'He's my husband and my friend and my lover, but if I don't get away from him, we will kill one another.'

She broke the news to him in a letter. He was devastated. 'I can't think how my life will be without Dadi. I don't know how to live alone. I've never been alone.'

Soon afterwards they discussed the separation at a joint therapy session. 'For me, this is about life and death,' Dadinha said, 'and if we have to live apart to live healthy and clean lives, then we have to do it.'

'I want to have a new life with Dadi,' Carlos said. 'We need to work together and be together. We can give one another strength.'

'No, we have to save one another. Maybe we can be together again after a few months. It's not divorce, it's something like separate holidays,' Dadinha said.

'Then I will go back to Maputo alone. I will get us a new house and buy nice furniture so that when you come back, it will be ready for you.'

I saw Carlos only once during his rehabilitation and that was for a reconciliatory meeting when he threatened not to speak to us any longer. As he sobered up and got a new perspective on life, he obviously mulled over the idea of appearing in another television documentary. He believed we were cashing in on his predicament and that he was entitled to a share.

I had a screaming match with Carlos in Ruby Weber's office. We entered into a written agreement whereby he could see the documentary before broadcast and give his approval. It was a highly unsatisfactory arrangement, but we had no option. It was then that I decided Carlos was mean, manipulative and devious.

He walked out of rehab looking healthy and clean and with a new set of teeth. By then Katia and Yara had arrived in Johannesburg to marvel at Carlos and Dadinha's sobriety and to pose for good-news pictures. The family had lunch at a Johannesburg restaurant, where they chuckled and laughed and said all the right things. It was simply too good to be true.

As Dadinha went off to the Southern Cape for her secondary care programme, Carlos returned to Maputo. Ruby Weber was not convinced that he genuinely wanted to stop using drugs. During rehabilitation he had often expressed his fear of being alone. And yet, instead of going into secondary care, he chose to return to Maputo where he would be miserable without Dadinha and forced into an almost reclusive life. He had no friends and he would depend on two daughters whom he had deprived of a childhood and who had in the meantime gone on with their own lives.

In the end, his only cronies might be the drug dealers around the corner in Little Colombia. And wouldn't they love to make his acquaintance again!

Anna-Maria's documentary had caused a huge response, with hundreds, if not thousands, of messages of good luck and offers of money and further recovery programmes. Dadinha settled in Johannesburg after her secondary therapy and found herself a flat and a job as a receptionist. She was a model patient and seemed to be among the fortunate few addicts who would make a complete recovery.

In Maputo, Carlos had gone back to work and found a new flat – further away from Little Colombia. He was, however, unbearably lonely and frequently phoned Ruby Weber to lament his predicament. She urged him to return to Johannesburg, but he said he couldn't. Then both Felners dropped off our radar screen.

It was not until a year later, in November 2004, that I gave Carlos and Dadinha another thought. Alex and I were in Maputo trying to track down a wanted rapist. In between our (futile) stalking of the suspect, we had a day or two with nothing to do. As we languished on the veranda of the Café Costa do Sol gazing at the Indian Ocean and trying to escape Maputo's sticky heat, I said to him: 'Let's see how Carlos is.'

Alex found Carlos at his office and arranged that we would see him later at the Café Continental, a landmark eatery in downtown Maputo. 'He doesn't look good and I don't think he was happy to see me. He might be back on drugs,' Alex reported.

We waited for two hours at the café, but Carlos never pitched up. We went back to our hotel and were about to go out for a late-night dinner when the concierge called to say someone was waiting in the pool restaurant downstairs for me.

It was Carlos. Sitting next to him was Dadinha. She was obviously back in Maputo and back with Carlos. Her presence did not bode well. When I walked closer, Dadinha looked up and gave me a sullen stare. She cut a piteous figure and little remained of the buoyancy of a year ago.

Carlos appeared equally woeful. His hair was greasy and he was shabbily clothed. They're back on drugs, was my thought. Next to Carlos on the ground were a sling bag and two plastic bags.

Carlos greeted me, but Dadinha said nothing. 'How are you two?' I asked as I sat down. It was a silly question, but I didn't know what else to say.

'We are not well,' Carlos said. 'We have no money and I'm very sick.' His skin had a pasty colour and the only memento that remained of his Joburg junket was a row of false white teeth.

'What's wrong, Carlos?' I asked him.

'I've been in hospital for a long time and I have to go back again. I nearly died,' he said.

Dadinha mumbled something to him in Portuguese. Carlos called a man who was standing a few yards away from us. It turned out to be a taxi driver they had hired to drive them around Maputo to look for us. We were staying in a smallish suburban hotel and it seemed to have been just about the last place they had stopped to search for us. It was a huge bill.

'We waited for you at Continental. Where were you?' I asked Carlos as I counted out a wad of meticais for the taxi driver. I was pissed off and instantly regretted the impulse to look them up.

'We were busy,' he said.

Yes, I wanted to say to him, busy shooting shit into your miserable bodies.

Dadinha spoke for the first time. She had an icy tone in her voice. 'So, Jacques, what do you want from us? Why are you here?'

I told her we were on another assignment in Maputo and decided to see how Carlos was doing. *Special Assignment*'s viewers frequently enquired about his welfare.

'It's only when you need us that we see you. When we need you, you are nowhere,' she said.

'What do you mean?' I asked.

'We haven't heard from you for months. And now suddenly you're back. Why?'

'Because I was hoping to interview Carlos and do a short follow-up.'

'You have used and abused us. You don't really care,' she said.

I could see where the conversation was going and didn't have the strength to squabble with either of them. Dadinha wasn't letting go: 'When Carlos was sick I tried to phone Anna-Maria, but she didn't answer my calls.'

I said Anna-Maria had resigned and was meditating on a mountain somewhere in the Limpopo Province. I should have told her it was because of her persistent and insidious demands over a period of months that Anna-Maria had decided she was *gatvol* and needed a break from journalism.

'And where's the air ticket from Johannesburg to Maputo you promised me?'

'What are you talking to about? You decided to stay on in Johannesburg!'

'In your agreement with Carlos you promised to fly me back to Maputo. You didn't. When Carlos needed me, I had to take the bus and use my own money.'

I explained to her we had fulfilled every undertaking. More than that, we had found her secondary care in the Southern Cape, flown her there and helped her to settle in Johannesburg.

'If you want to interview Carlos and me,' she said, 'it will cost you R5 000.'

'Yes, R5 000,' Carlos confirmed. 'We need the money.'

I stared at them in disbelief. 'Go to hell,' tumbled over my lips, something I'd wanted to tell them a long time ago. I got up. 'I hope you're better soon, Carlos,' I said, and started to walk away.

'Would you mind if we order a meal?' he asked. 'We haven't eaten today.'

I pretended not to hear and went to my room. When we left for dinner a few minutes later, the two were still sitting at the same table. I told a waiter to get them food and put it on my bill.

My appetite had disappeared. 'I think they're on the streets,' I said to Alex. 'They've got nowhere to go.'

And what do you plan to do about it?' he asked me.

'Nothing,' I said.

I drank far more wine than I should have and we returned to the hotel after midnight. The place was almost dark and deserted except for a clerk at the front desk. He pointed towards the pool area as we walked in.

At the same table, as though they hadn't moved a muscle since we left two or three hours earlier, sat Carlos and Dadinha. I couldn't ignore them again. 'Why are you still here?' I asked them.

Carlos said they could sleep at a friend's house but that they didn't have taxi fare. I gave them money. 'Is there no other way you can help us?' Dadinha asked.

'I can't give you money. But come back tomorrow morning at nine and we can discuss it,' I said.

'You're a sucker!' Alex said as we walked to our rooms.

The next morning, the two arrived at the hotel promptly at nine, still clutching their plastic bags but far more amicable than the night before and prepared to accept whatever I could offer. I said I'd book them into a *pensão* for a few days and pay for their meals in exchange for an interview. They greedily accepted.

Shortly afterwards, they sat opposite me on a bed at the Pensão Central and chronicled yet another instalment in their lives for an insatiable *Special Assignment* audience that couldn't get enough of them.

On returning to Maputo, Carlos had spent hours and days crying in his one-bedroom apartment. He yearned for Dadinha, had no friends and his daughters were not taking care of him. When Katia celebrated her birthday, she invited Carlos to spend the day with her. He waited the whole day, but she forgot to pick him up. He then invited his daughters for lunch at his new apartment. He shopped and cooked, but again waited all day. They never came.

Carlos soon discovered he was powerless to deal with the incredulity that surrounded his restored status. People had seen it too many times before. He worked harder than ever, but returned every night to an empty and cold place.

As his therapist had predicted, Carlos was incapable of dealing with his solitude. He started drinking – a taboo for recovering drug addicts because it is often the first step towards drug relapse.

Three months after Carlos returned to Maputo, he stumbled across a busy intersection and was run down by a car. He was drunk. He landed in hospital with a smashed hip. Lying there in unfathomable pain, Carlos made a call. He phoned a drug dealer. Minutes later, the merchant walked into his hospital room with a syringe full of heroin and injected Carlos in his bed.

He then made another call – to Dadinha, who had made a new life for herself in Johannesburg. 'Life was enjoyable. I had everything I needed. I had a job and I had friends. Real friends. Something I haven't had for a very long time. It was a beautiful life.'

In an act of incredible selfishness, Carlos begged her to return to Maputo. I'm in hospital and will die if you don't come and take care of me. Get here as soon as possible.

A few days later, Dadinha was on the bus. 'I knew Carlos was back on drugs and that I was heading for my own relapse. It was out there waiting for me, but there was nothing I could do. I had to go back.'

Carlos had already been released from hospital and Dadinha found him at his flat. He was unkempt, skinny and scruffy. He greeted her with a dose of heroin. He injected and she smoked. 'I just did it. It wasn't good, and it wasn't bad. It was just the same thing. It was just like before.'

Her new life went up in smoke and she was once again hooked. 'I was thirty-seven years old and couldn't afford to be a junkie again. I didn't want to be back in Maputo and creep around Little Colombia in search of the next dose.'

Dadinha took an overdose of sleeping pills and was hospitalised. But much worse was still to come. Two or three weeks after her arrival, armed men entered their apartment while they were asleep. Carlos said it was robbers, but it might also have been drug dealers settling unpaid debt. Whatever the case, they took the couple's cellphones, money and clothes – and raped Dadinha.

She had barely come to terms with her first rape more than twenty years earlier on a deserted beach in Maputo. 'I am still working on that. My therapist in Johannesburg did a great job. And then it happened all over again. It was something I cannot describe.'

Now, sitting across from me on a wood-carved double bed, Carlos hunched forward and held his head in his hands. 'When I was in hospital there was only one person I could turn to and that was Dadinha. And when she was raped there was only one person that could help her and that was me. From now on we will be together. No more separation.'

They held hands. 'But there is another problem,' Carlos said, 'and a very serious one.' He kept quiet for a second or two. 'In July I got hepatitis. I started thinking that something else might be wrong.'

Carlos went for an AIDS test. He was HIV-positive. His immunity was severely depleted. His body had virtually lost its natural defences. The doctor told Carlos he had to start taking antiretrovirals, but this would be impossible as long as he was using drugs. The medicine would poison his body and hasten his end.

Two weeks later, he was admitted to hospital with dysentery and diarrhoea. 'Carlos was dying. It was then that I realised I really loved this man and I would be with him until the end.'

Dadinha set up camp in hospital to be with Carlos. The doctor advised her to take an AIDS test, and she, too, tested HIV-positive. 'When they told me, I said, okay, I'm done. I'm tired. So God is easing things for me. I am not willing to fight this disease.'

Carlos and Dadinha had both tested HIV-negative when they entered rehabilitation in Johannesburg. How did you get infected, I asked them. Dirty needles? Dadinha's rape? Maybe Carlos had had an HIV-positive girlfriend while Dadinha was in Johannesburg?

'We don't ask that question,' Dadinha said. 'It's not important. All that is important now is that Carlos must live.'

Carlos was in hospital for more than a month and at some point his doctor thought that he might die. He was on the verge of contracting full-blown AIDS. 'Life! The struggle for life!' said Carlos as he started crying. 'It is stronger than anything else. I've got lots of things I want to do in the next five years of my life. And if I use drugs, I will die. And I don't want to die. Oh please, I don't want to die!'

Tears rolled down his cheeks. 'I'm struggling. Everything has gone wrong. HIV, relapse, rape, accident, theft. I have been robbed three times. I've lost my cellphone three times. My glasses, my flat, our children, everything.'

Dadinha turned towards him and put her arm around him. 'I want him alive. I want this man alive.'

'But you need to be alive as well,' he said.

'We'll be together,' Dadinha said. And then, in an act of almost sardonic humour, she laughed and added: 'Maybe we'll have a funeral at the same time.'

'Yes,' said Carlos, as he wiped his tears, 'because if Dadinha dies, I will not live for more than two or three months. And If I die, she won't live for more than a month or two.'

'There is only the two of us,' Dadinha said. 'And we will either live or we will both die.'

Still holding hands and sitting close to each other, they fell silent. It was an awkward moment and I told the cameraman to wrap up. What on earth do you say to people like Carlos and Dadinha? Good luck? Hope to see you again soon?

As we drove away, they were in surprisingly high spirits and waved goodbye to us from the pavement. Carlos said he was going to hospital the following week, would stop using drugs and start taking his antiretrovirals.

'What now?' Alex asked.

'I'm not sure,' I said. 'I suppose we'll be back for his funeral. And we'll probably have to pay for it.' I was convinced I would never see him alive again and that she would die shortly afterwards.

Seven months later, Alex was back in Mozambique to look at a piece of coastal land north of the city that he wanted to buy. Diligent as always, he went looking for the couple – or whatever might have remained of them. He phoned me the next day.

'You won't believe what I found!' he said excitedly.

I thought he was talking about a stretch of white sand with waving palm trees that someone wanted to sell for a song.

'What?' I asked him.

'I found Carlos and Dadinha!'

'And?'

'Carlos is fat and healthy! And he's working again. They have a big flat and Dadinha is a housewife. It's going very well.'

'And drugs?'

'They say they're not touching it. And I think it's true. You can see they're clean.'

'For how long?'

'You should see them. I think this is for real.'

I was in Maputo within days. Alex and I picked Carlos up in front of the Ministry of Agriculture. He was going to show us land north of Maputo that was for sale. He looked remarkably fit and healthy as he directed us out of the city. He had gained fifteen kilograms and spoke non-stop as we negotiated our way around potholes and through pools of rainwater to the coast.

Carlos told us that two days after we had last seen them, he admitted himself to a Roman Catholic care centre on the outskirts of Maputo. His immunity was waning and he faced a long and agonising sickbed. Dadinha moved in with him.

He knew he was dying. Dadinha, watching him grow weaker, said they had one final chance. They had to stop using drugs and he had to start taking antiretrovirals. And if you stop, she promised him, I will also stop. I will suffer with you because we have to live.

'And I have a surprise for you,' she said. A few hours later, Yara walked into his room. 'Pappa,' she said, 'I'm pregnant. I'm going to be a mother and you are going to become a grandfather.'

A month later, Carlos walked out of hospital. He had gained weight and looked healthier. He was on antiretrovirals and, even more importantly, off drugs. It's highly unusual for heroin addicts to stop just like that. How did they manage to do it?

'I wasn't ready to die,' said Carlos. 'The will to live is stronger than anything else we know. And my grandchild. I wanted to see him before I die.'

He was holding down several jobs. He had just been appointed as a special advisor to the Minister of Agriculture and was still a director of his veterinary company. He had also started farming again south of Maputo and had been approached to run an AIDS campaign in the rural areas.

'When you saw me the last time I was in a bad state,' he said, and laughed.

'And then you stopped?' I asked him.

'Yes,' he said, 'we stopped. We just stopped. Now life is normal. It's beautiful.'

Gone was the conniving and disingenuous behaviour I had come to associate with Carlos. At a certain point of our journey, the 4×4 couldn't go any further and we had to climb a high sand dune to get to the beach. He got to the top long before Alex and me. When the vehicle slid off the muddy track and the wheels sank into a swamp, Carlos quickly assembled a team of locals and pushed as hard as any of them to get us out.

He directed us to a beachfront restaurant for lunch and ordered *frango zambezia* – barbecued chicken drenched in a rich coconut sauce – and devoured it with gusto. 'It brings back memories of my childhood,' he said. 'I grew up with this.'

I was invited the next day for tea and cake at their apartment. Waiting for me was a chubby Dadinha and a skinny girl with a ponytail and sparkling eyes. It was Debbie, Dadinha's daughter from her first marriage.

Debbie, who was in her final school year, still lived with her father but spent most of her weekends with Carlos and Dadinha. Mother and daughter were planning her eighteenth birthday celebration when we walked in. Dadinha seemed genuinely happy to see us.

'Welcome to our home,' she said, and took me through the apartment. It was modestly furnished, but friendly, comfortable and light. On a dressing table was a picture of a baby boy.

'That's my grandson,' said Carlos. 'He was born two weeks ago.'

'Carlos has never been one for babies,' said Dadinha, 'but when he saw the baby for the first time he touched him and said to me: "Oh Dadinha, isn't he beautiful?" That was when I knew this man is changing.'

'The question of drugs is not even in my mind. A week or ten days pass and I don't think about it,' said Carlos.

'It's different for me,' said Dadinha. 'I cannot forget that for fourteen years of my life I was on another planet. And we are both HIV and must live life carefully.'

Carlos had a new lease on life and seemed bent on making up for lost time. The morning after the tea party, Alex got a phone call from him. He said he was somewhere in a bar and we had to come immediately.

'What's it about?' I asked Alex as we sped off.

'I don't know, except he said he's in shit.'

The bar wasn't far from the couple's apartment. Carlos was sitting with a young, plump girl in a corner and gave an awkward grin when we walked in. His eyes were bloodshot and it looked as if he hadn't closed an eye all night. He got up, took Alex aside and spoke softly to him. He smelt of cheap booze.

The girl was his mistress and he had spent the night with her. He had told Dadinha that he couldn't sleep and was going for a late-night stroll. He met the girl in the bar, started drinking and went back to her place. He fell asleep in the early hours of the morning and woke up as the sun rose.

He begged us to concoct a story that he had been with us the night before. We had to tell Dadinha we had drunk too much and that he had fallen asleep in one of our rooms. His predicament seemed desperate and we agreed to help him.

'Is she your girlfriend?' Alex asked him on the way back to the apartment.

'Yes,' he said, 'she's in love with me. But for me it's nothing.'

Carlos was playing Russian roulette with his health and treating the woman who had stood by him through thick and thin with contempt and disdain. And I didn't even want to think about whether he was using condoms.

Needless to say, Dadinha was seething with rage and anxiety when Carlos swung the back door open. She had been up all night and was convinced Carlos had gone back to Little Colombia. She virtually attacked Alex when he told her Carlos had been with us. It took lots of bullshitting before she calmed down. We left shortly afterwards.

Can you imagine what would happen if Carlos left Dadinha, I asked Alex as we drove away. It would catapult her back into the darkest dungeons of Little Colombia. Or if he tried to reclaim those years he spent with a needle in his neck, ignored his HIV status and behaved like a thirtysomething stud? He would be on his deathbed in no time.

I never saw or heard from Carlos and Dadinha again. I don't know if they managed to maintain their abstinence or if common sense prevailed over his stupidity. But whether hooked or clean, alive or dead, nothing about Carlos and Dadinha would surprise me.

I had long observed their lives as roller-coaster rides of ascent and descent that could change direction at any moment and surge towards victory or derail and plunge into calamity.

As Renton would have said in *Trainspotting*, they had merely arrived at yet another station on their junky journey through junkie life.

CHAPTER 18

Marauding miscreants in blue

Avoid being seized by the police. The cops are not your friends. Don't tell them anything.   – Hunter S Thompson

A T THE END OF 2003, FOLLOWING OUR EXPOSURE OF THE HEROIN drug route from Afghanistan to East Africa, Alex had a yen to go back into law enforcement. When his contract with me expired, he wanted nothing less than to be a Scorpion – one of South Africa's so-called super cops!

The Scorpions were eager to bust drug syndicates and expand their investigations beyond South Africa's borders. Alex had names and numbers. I brokered a meeting between him and senior Scorpions officials, who agreed to employ him to find and bust a drug syndicate in Johannesburg. If successful, they said, they would offer him a longer contract.

I was sceptical from the outset. I'd never had a happy relationship with the police, but it transpired that they held Alex Stellianos in such low esteem that they would seemingly go to any lengths to discredit him.

Among the Scorpions in charge of Alex's trial operation were two of the agents who had blundered the arrest of Rwandan *génocidaire* Bishop Samuel Musabyimana. Alex's handler was a whisky-nosed buffoon whose office desk seemed to be in the bar at the Ellis Park Hotel. But Alex was beaming from ear to ear and immediately telephoned his closest relative and told her excitedly: 'Guess what? I'm going to be a Scorpion!'

Within days, he had infiltrated two Nigerian drug syndicates in Hillbrow. All his meetings were recorded on spy camera. One of the syndicates operated from a pawnshop and wanted Alex to fly to Brazil to pick up a consignment of cocaine. Before long the second syndicate also tried to recruit Alex as a drug courier. At the head of one of the syndicates were two Colombians who procured their cocaine directly from that country. Alex thought this terribly important, as it might indicate the influx of Colombian drug cartels to our shores.

The Scorpions thought differently. Despite two intelligence reports detailing his meetings with the syndicates, five spy camera tapes and names, and telephone and car registration numbers, his handlers said the information was useless and fired him without payment.

After just a month as a Scorpion, Alex was back at *Special Assignment*. I gave him a contract to continue infiltrating the drug rings. Then, in an act of in-credible deviousness and without telling Alex, the Scorpions raided one of the syndicates. Of course they didn't find drugs – but that didn't seem to be their main purpose. They wanted to set Alex up. They told the Nigerians they were actually looking for a middle-aged white man with grey hair who visited them every day. The description could only have fitted Alex.

When he walked into the shop later the same day, the Nigerians slammed the door behind him, surrounded him and accused him of being an informer. All the while the spy camera was rolling. The footage was a see-saw of black and white and voices hurling abuse at one another before the door opened and Alex stumbled back onto the pavement.

I phoned one of the Scorpions. 'You could have killed Alex!' I said. 'How could you?'

'We were merely verifying his information,' was the ludicrous response.

'How come you fired Alex for useless information when you hadn't yet verified any of it?'

He launched into a stream of abuse. 'We refuse to work with such a sleaze-ball! Do you know who this man is?'

'Who do you get to infiltrate drug syndicates?' I asked him. 'Sunday school teachers and nuns?'

Scorpions head Leonard McCarthy responded by saying: 'The turn of events has been unfortunate.' It turned even more bizarre when he advised Alex to hand himself over to the Booysens police, as there was an outstanding warrant for his arrest. 'I am further informed that the complainant in this matter is ready and willing to testify in court,' he said, and provided me with a case number.

Alex was perplexed – and so was a police sergeant at the Booysens police station. He said there had been a warrant for Alex's arrest several years ago, but the case had long since been withdrawn. There was no complainant willing to testify. What puzzled the sergeant, he said, was that two Scorpions – one of whom was Alex's ruddy-faced handler – had visited him and pleaded with him to reissue the warrant. He refused and told them he had no case.

Since then, Alex had worked for *Special Assignment* continuously and kept chipping away at corrupt policemen and Home Affairs officials, drug and gun dealers, and paedophiles. In the process the police withdrew virtually all coop-eration with me and my colleagues, saying that we only showed 'negative things'.

The perception that *Special Assignment* harboured a grudge against the police had started long before Alex's arrival, probably with the broadcast of the infamous 'police dog video'. In 2001, a Benoni traffic cop approached *Special Assignment* with an explosive homemade video showing members of the East Rand Dog Unit training their animals by letting them loose against three illegal

Mozambican immigrants. Six white members of the unit arrested the aliens and took them to a deserted gold mine. With the immigrants begging and pleading for mercy, the policemen ordered their dogs to attack. The cops shrieked in delight as their beasts mauled the hapless victims, inflicting serious wounds and bite marks. One of the policemen had a video camera and filmed the macabre spectacle.

The video became something of a party trick on the police braai circuit. As soon as the *polisiekoffie* had taken effect, the cops would screen it for their friends. The traffic cop watched it, stole the tape and put it up for sale for R100 000. After watching it, I bargained him down to R50 000. I persuaded my editor to put up the money, stuffed it in a bag, drove to Benoni and bought the video. After verifying its authenticity, we broadcast it a week or two later.

It made international headlines and was shown around the world. The policemen were arrested, dismissed from the force, charged, and eventually sentenced to between five and seven years' imprisonment. The video caused great embarrassment to the 'new' South African Police Service and its critics had a field day using it as evidence that racism was alive and well and living in blue uniforms.

I then did a documentary on a police unit in Durban that specialised in tracking down and arresting Nigerian drug dealers. The commander gave me unlimited access to his men and their operations as they raided seedy nightclubs and swooped on dealers standing on street corners. They broke and kicked down doors, pinned dealers to the ground and flung them into the back of vans.

Celebrating their success, the unit had a *potjiekos* (a traditional stew cooked in a cast-iron pot) evening where members washed down 9-mm bullets with a vile alcoholic concoction in full view of the camera. They congratulated one another on 'hunting down the Ni-gees'.

The commander bestowed honorary membership on cameraman Jan de Klerk, soundman Mandla Mlambo and me, but the unit's highest accolade came with a price – each of us had to wash down two bullets with the concoction! Jan gulped down a third. I had endless problems when I arrived home and tried to explain to my girlfriend Sam why I had willingly embarked on such an enterprise. It didn't help when I said it was all about maintaining a good relationship with the cops. 'I told you never to bring bullets into the house!' she said. I walked around with the lead in my stomach for a day or two until Sam shrieked one morning: 'Come and have a look!' At the bottom of the toilet lay the bullet. 'Get it out!' she ordered. 'I never want to see it again!'

I showed the cops swallowing the bullets in my documentary. This was too much for the Nigerian consul general. He launched an attack on the unit and accused them of xenophobia and victimising his countrymen. The police apologised, and not long afterwards the unit was disbanded. I was never again able to obtain police permission to spend time with any unit.

Relations with the cops deteriorated even more when Alex and accomplished *Special Assignment* journalist Jessica Pitchford exposed policemen in Johannesburg's northern suburbs who extorted money from prostitutes and their clients. The cops waited for a potential customer to pull up next to a woman and clinch a deal with her. The moment the prostitute got into the car, the policemen pounced and arrested both. The client was given a choice: either you pay a fine now or we take you to the station and formally charge you. Eager to shroud their seedy secrets, clients paid.

Alex and *Special Assignment*'s production secretary simply parked a car in Oxford Road, Rosebank, and waited for the cops to apprehend them. It didn't take long. They threw the secretary in the back of the van and asked Alex, sitting with the spy camera on his lap, if he was a married man.

'Why?' Alex asked.

'Because you have a choice. We can either solve the problem now, or we can take you to the police station and book you.'

'No, I would like to solve it now,' said Alex.

'Then it will cost you.'

'How much?'

'At least R800.'

The policeman marched Alex off to an electronic cash teller and greedily pocketed the money he withdrew. Alex repeated the exercise several times, and when the programme was broadcast, six policemen were arrested, suspended and charged. However, the police investigation fell apart when we refused to hand over our tapes. I wasn't going to let Alex appear in court, reveal details of our operation and be cross-examined. They had pictures and names and there were plenty of prostitutes who could testify to the corruption. The police did nothing further and accused us of sabotaging the investigation.

In the spring of 2005, I invited police commissioner Jackie Selebi to come to *Special Assignment* to watch evidence of more corruption in his force. He sent his Gauteng deputy Perumal Naidoo and a team of senior policemen to our offices instead. Commissioner Naidoo, not exactly known for his good relationship with the media, marched into the edit suite with a curt nod and sat down.

When he left an hour later, it was with a sullen and sour expression, largely thanks to a thickset policeman with a frog-like appearance and bulging eyes. Japie Mahidi, an old-timer who had been with the police since their main task was to enforce apartheid laws, was the head of a unit responsible for investigating, apprehending and processing illegal immigrants. Known as the

Raiding Squad, the unit was based at the Booysens police station south of Johannesburg.

When a slightly built Zimbabwean with a boyish face knocked on his office door at about nine o'clock one winter's night in 2005, Mahidi turned around, clearly irritated, and stared at the young man. Over his shoulder was a grey sling bag.

He greeted Mahidi in a subservient tone. '*Sawubona*.'

'*Sawubona* who?'

'*Sawubona*, sir.'

'Can't you see I'm busy?' snapped Mahidi.

'I can see, sir. But I've come to enquire about my brother over there wearing the blue sweater, sir.'

Sitting on the floor in front of Mahidi were some thirty immigrants who had been arrested earlier that afternoon on the streets of Johannesburg's southern suburbs. Mahidi swatted the Zimbabwean away as if he were a fly and continued writing their names in a book.

At first glance, Mahidi cut an intimidating and no-nonsense figure, the dedicated policeman doing his duty. But it was all a sham. Underneath the bluster was a marauding miscreant whose blue uniform was simply a passport to riches.

Another policeman walked into the room and told the Zimbabwean to follow him outside. He stopped in the dimly lit passage. 'How much do you have?' he asked the Zimbabwean. It was all prearranged and later the cops would share the loot.

'R250.'

'It's not enough,' said the policeman. 'The price is 300.'

'Okay, I've got 300.'

'Follow me,' he said, and turned around. The Zimbabwean followed him into a dimly lit toilet, counted out the money and pushed the notes into the policeman's hand. 'If this ever comes out, you're a dead man,' the policeman said, and went to fetch the immigrant the Zimbabwean had just bribed out of jail.

Business was brisk, and an hour or two later there were only five or six immigrants left. Despite being shown to a telephone from where they could call friends and family, they had failed to raise R300 to buy their freedom. The next morning, they were sent to the Lindela repatriation camp, where they would be detained until they could be sent back to where they came from.

Around midnight, Mahidi got into his brand new pickup and drove with bulging pockets to his walled residence in one of Johannesburg's middle-class suburbs. He and his Raiding Squad had been extorting money from illegal aliens for years. Before that, several people claimed, he had bullied financial rewards from his brothers trapped in apartheid's demonic race laws.

The story started with Alex and me venturing into Rosettenville to produce a documentary on the immeasurable changes that had taken place in the area over the previous ten years. Nestled between mine dumps, Rosettenville had once been home to large numbers of Johannesburg's middle-class Portuguese community. With democracy washing up on our shores, many feared another Mozambique or Angola and returned to the fatherland. Their homes were quickly occupied by the city's new black residents. Before long, drug dealers and pimps, smelling promise in the southern suburbs, swamped Rosettenville and the nearby suburbs of Turffontein and Booysens. Emaciated girls in tight jeans and high heels stood under lamp posts and crack and heroin houses sprouted up on street corners. Rosettenville became the crucible of lower-class 'old' South Africans clinging to bygone times, African immigrants, drug dealers, prostitutes, and decent and ordinary people trying to raise their families anywhere but in an informal settlement.

The story took on a new dimension when we spoke to immigrants. They told us of a white truck that roamed the suburbs and policemen who arrested them. Whether they were in the country legally or not, they all paid. Those with money settled their bribes upon arrest and were immediately released. The rest landed up in the truck and were taken to a room at the Booysens police station, where they were held until families or friends paid their way out. Those who remained were handed over to the Department of Home Affairs for deportation.

A few days later, Alex and I were hunkered down behind our cars at a scrap-metal dealership across the road from the police station, waiting for the truck to appear. It was a cold and typically bleak and chilly winter's night. If anybody ever had any notion that investigative journalism was glamorous, this was the story to shatter the illusion.

By then we had made contact with a Zimbabwean student who had been arrested several times by the Raiding Squad and knew the drill. He agreed to help us and carry the spy camera into the station.

As the white truck, loaded with immigrants, crawled into the station that night, the Zimbabwean threw the grey bag over his shoulder and strolled across the street. When he returned half an hour later, he was grinning widely. 'I think I got them,' he said. 'I paid the cop R300.'

'Very good,' I said to him after we'd watched the footage, 'but we'll have to go back again.'

He looked perplexed. 'Why?' he asked.

'You can't see the money changing hands. We have to show policemen taking money.'

Two weeks later, the Zimbabwean was back. Mahidi was eating *slaptjips* and was perched like a king on a throne behind his desk, looking down at the band of potential money-makers seated on his office floor. A Zambian immigrant didn't have enough money, but offered Japie his cellphone in exchange for the release of his Congolese friend. As boorish as ever, Japie dismissed him and chased him out of the office. The Zambian eventually borrowed more money and was instructed to leave it in the telephone booth. Minutes after he had done so, his friend was released.

Two policemen sitting in a van collected the Zimbabwean's money that night. They called him to the vehicle, opened the door and told him to throw the money on the floor.

'Not good enough?' asked our dejected collaborator as we watched the footage the next morning.

'It's very good. You can hear what they say, but we still need to see a policeman actually taking the cash from you. We'll try again.'

We had to wait almost a month before the Raiding Squad arrested someone that the Zimbabwean said he knew. 'Have you brought the things?' a policeman asked him as he walked into the station.

'Yes, sir, I have.'

'Hey, young man, have I not seen you here before?'

'You have, sir. I came to fetch my brother's friend.'

'And now?'

'I am here to fetch my sister Ellen. She's the one sitting in the corner over there.'

'Go and speak to the policeman outside,' he said, dismissing the Zimbabwean.

Perhaps the designated cop was careless or maybe overwhelmed by greed, but in full view of the spy camera and under the station's glaring spotlights he told our man to hand over the money. He slowly counted out the notes, one by one.

'Come, come!' the policeman said. 'Hurry up!'

He stuck the money in his pocket and walked away. We had the evidence we needed.

If I had to make a list of the most reprehensible scoundrels I've encountered in my life, Nigerian drug dealer Justin Okyeokwu would be close to the top. Suave and nonchalant, he was a clean-shaven character who could reminisce engagingly about his childhood in rural south-east Nigeria, the spicy goat stew he missed so much and his decision to come to South Africa to seek, as he called it, 'greener pastures'.

Those pastures were drug deals, and since his arrival in Rosettenville two years before, he had created an enclave of several heroin and crack houses, dealers and prostitutes. Everybody, it seemed – including the police – knew about the goings-on in and around his houses, but Justin and his accomplices went about their daily business without fear of the long arm of the law. Policemen frequently searched and ransacked his house and once found crack and heroin on him. He simply paid them and the docket disappeared. Whenever the Raiding Squad apprehended him or one of his friends, they merely paid their way back to their street corners.

Justin's girlfriend Megan was a down-and-out, woebegone heroin addict with septic pockmarks on her hands and face. He provided her with heroin, and in return she worked the streets and screwed as many men as she physically could. Years of hardened heroin abuse and cold nights in strange cars had turned the twentysomething into a wretched bag of bones. Looking at her, one had the sinking feeling she was slowly killing herself and wouldn't live long.

Justin pimped her on the street corner outside their house where customers pulled up and she got into their cars. If she complained she was tired or sick, Justin tied her up, lashed her with his belt and withheld heroin from her. She had scars on her back from all the beatings.

'Megan looks sick,' I said to Justin over a lunch of coconut chicken curry and *katembes* (Coke and red wine) at an old-style Portuguese restaurant in Rosettenville.

'She's not well,' he said. 'She takes too much heroin.'

'You must help her to stop,' Alex said.

'I can't,' he said. 'She's too far gone.'

'She's going to die, Justin,' Alex told him.

'I know she is. But what can I do?' he said, and sneered. 'She must bring in the rent.'

'Does she still get lots of clients?' Alex asked.

'Oh yes,' he said. 'When she stands under a street lamp at night you can't see her properly. She looks okay.'

One day Megan called Alex aside and told him that she was pregnant. 'It's twins,' she said, 'and Justin is over the moon with joy.'

In fact, Justin was fuming. He said she was building sandcastles, and even if she was pregnant, anybody could be the father. 'I don't know who fucks her with a condom and who not,' he said. He apparently told her this, and in an outburst of fury she tried to inject him with heroin. He beat her senseless.

A few days later, cameraman Jan, Alex and I were filming in Rosettenville. Alex wanted to know how Megan was and decided to stop at Justin's house. He was on the street corner but Megan was asleep in the house. He said he'd go and call her.

A few minutes later the mother-to-be pranced around the corner. It was a sight to behold. She was in pyjamas – a screaming pink outfit with Mickey Mouse motifs – and strawberry-coloured woolly slippers. She had just woken up and wore no make-up. She was a pink ghost.

We were too thunderstruck to say a word. She babbled away about her twins and took Alex's hand and put it on her tummy. She then leant through the window and greeted Jan. He hesitantly shook her hand.

Jan was at the doctor two days later, convinced he had contracted an infection from Megan. He had had a small cut in the palm of his hand when he'd exchanged greetings with Megan, and it became inflamed the very next day. 'It's that woman,' he growled. 'I should never have shaken her hand.'

Justin agreed to show us how easy it was to bribe one of his friends or co-dealers out of police custody. He said he would carry the spy camera into the Booysens police station and pay a cop. I'm still not sure why he agreed to do it, but by then he trusted Alex implicitly. He knew we were journalists, but probably never thought we would betray his trust or set him up.

How wrong he was. We were planning his exposure and downfall all along. He was a depraved creature and I had absolutely no qualms about plunging my journalistic knife into him as deeply as I could.

Admittedly, this is one of the murkier sides of journalism: winning someone's trust just to betray him in the end. In the process journalists usually lie, deceive and mislead. Journalistic values and ethics tend to fade into the distance when dealing with a hooligan like Justin.

Alex got a call from Justin. The Booysens Raiding Squad had picked up his friend. Alex met him in front of the police station, but when he passed the sling bag to Justin, the drug dealer got scared and bailed out. Alex phoned the Zimbabwean. Would he go with Justin and carry the camera? Our Zimbabwean associate agreed, and an hour later the two walked into the station.

Justin made a crucial mistake by allowing the Zimbabwean to accompany him, because his face was now on camera! Our footage showed him phoning Mahidi's second in command, Michael Majozi, who he said was his contact. We filmed Justin cosily chit-chatting with the policeman. Eventually Majozi ordered everyone but Justin out of the station. As the Zimbabwean walked out, the camera showed Majozi and Justin walking into a dark corner.

The Zimbabwean had to wait outside, but a few minutes later Majozi escorted Justin and his dealer friend out of the police station, offered to get them a taxi and wished them good luck.

It was damning evidence. Not only were both Justin and his friend illegally in the country, but we could show the police putting two known criminals back on the street. Even if the authorities couldn't nail them for drugs, they could at least deport them back to Nigeria.

Justin agreed to be interviewed. He had decided to leave Rosettenville, as there was infighting among dealers in the neighbourhood. According to him, there were brilliant new opportunities for him and Megan in Pretoria.

I rented a room in a decrepit hotel. We darkened the room with blankets and cameraman Dudley Saunders put one spotlight on Justin's face. The secret of interviewing someone like Justin was to keep him talking for as long as possible. He was eventually going to make a mistake and say something he shouldn't. This was no exception. His arrogance finally got the better of him. He told us how he had bribed Majozi and how corrupt the Raiding Squad was.

'He just took the money and then set my friend free,' he said.

'You're not afraid of being sent back to Nigeria. You just pay? Am I right?' I asked him.

'Yes, I pay,' he answered.

'So there's no chance of being sent back?'

'No. No possibility.'

I asked him if he sold drugs. At first he wouldn't answer and just laughed. Then he said he didn't. It was clear he was lying. So how then do you earn a living, I asked him.

'Stop the camera first,' Justin said. Dudley lifted his head and stood away from the camera. Justin presumed it had been switched off. It hadn't.

'I am a drug dealer. You know that,' he said. 'If I talk about prostitution and drugs – because that is what I do – they'll find a way to come to my house.'

'You're not going to use the stuff about the police or the drugs, are you?' he wanted to know when we packed up.

'Don't worry,' I assured him. 'You can trust us.'

The final nail in the coffin of Mahidi's Raiding Squad was a Congolese woman soaked in blood and with a hole in her head. Alex called me one Sunday around lunchtime.

'Come to Rosettenville immediately,' he said excitedly.

'Why?' I asked him.

'They've beaten up a woman. She's still covered in blood!'

'I'm coming,' I said. 'Tell her not to wash!'

Jolly Tambwe waited for us at her Rosettenville home with a crust of dried blood covering the side of her face. Her white jersey had turned maroon.

'I've been beaten by the Booysens cops,' she said, 'with a wheel spanner.'

Jolly and her Nigerian partner, Jerry Anyaechie, had been cooking in the kitchen when there was a loud knock on the door. It was Jerry's friends from downtown Johannesburg who were expected for lunch. They were in a state of panic.

Mahidi and his squad were coming down the street in their white truck when they spotted the two men and ordered them to stop. They were scared and ran into Jerry and Jolly's yard. The policemen followed, and seconds later started forcing the kitchen door open with a wheel spanner. Jerry unlocked the door and they burst into the house.

Where's the *makwere-kwere* (South African street slang for foreigners), the policemen barked, and demanded to see everyone's papers. Jolly, Jerry and their guests produced their refugee certificates. 'Fucking Nigerians. *Makwere-kwere*,' a policeman said, and threw the papers on the ground.

'Sir, why are you calling us that word, *makwere-kwere*?' Jolly asked him.

A cop holding the wheel spanner stepped forward and whacked her against the side of her head. She fell to the ground, bleeding. We later took her to hospital, where she needed ten stitches.

The cops then pointed a gun at Jerry's head and arrested him for interfering with a police investigation. It was nothing but an attempt to intimidate the couple, and charges were later dropped.

There had been countless allegations of assault and abuse against the Raiding Squad, but foreigners were too scared to press charges. This time, however, they had messed with the wrong people. Jerry and Jolly hired a lawyer and laid charges of assault with intent to do grievous bodily harm, illegal arrest, illegal pointing of a firearm, intimidation and malicious damage to property.

Following the broadcast of our documentary, Jerry, Jolly and the Zimbabwean went into witness protection and testified against the crooked policemen. I once again refused to hand over our spy camera tapes, but this time a proper investigation was done. Mahidi and virtually all the members of his unit were suspended, arrested and charged with crimes ranging from fraud and bribery to assault and malicious damage to property. At the time of writing, their case was still pending.

As for Justin and Megan, they relocated to Pretoria and set up business in a flat. Not long afterwards he was locked up for a few hours after once again beating Megan. She decided she'd had enough and called the police. The cops took Justin away but released him as soon as they got to the nearest police station. Megan lost no time phoning Alex, who whisked her off to a drug rehabilitation centre north of Pretoria. They examined her and said she was one of the worst cases of drug abuse they had ever come across – and she also had a brain tumour.

But a few days later, Megan escaped and went back to Justin. The last I heard, she was once again standing on a street corner, semi-comatose and spaced out and slipping into heroin's dark abyss.

Alex's information was almost always impeccable, except once in Maputo, when he was convinced he had traced one of South Africa's most notorious wanted rapists and murderers.

He rushed into my office frantically one day. A Mozambican friend had told him the whereabouts of one of the so-called Grasmere rapists and killers. In 2003 a family was abducted when they stopped at the Grasmere toll plaza on the national road south of Johannesburg. The three kidnappers took them to a piece of deserted veld, where they shot and killed the husband and raped the woman and her young daughter. The killers had been on the loose ever since and were among South Africa's most wanted criminals. The police identified one of the gang members as a Mozambican by the name of Dito.

Alex knew Dito's former girlfriend in Johannesburg, who said he was hiding in the Maputo suburb of Matola. I gave Alex the green light to launch an elaborate seek-and-film operation in the Mozambican capital. It wasn't long before he said he had traced the fugitive. Alex recruited a young woman and her boyfriend to befriend Dito and film him with the spy camera. With the overexposed footage back in South Africa, I met with the investigating officer to try to positively identify the man we had filmed in Maputo. The policeman had an old photograph of Dito. There were similarities but also discrepancies and we couldn't be sure.

The killers were wanted for a spate of car hijackings, rapes and robberies in South Africa. With the assistance of the police, we traced three victims. One identified the man on our footage positively; the second wasn't sure, but the third was convinced we had the wrong man. The raped woman and her daughter refused to look at the film.

The woman and her boyfriend tracking Dito reported that the man they had befriended and filmed spoke English, had lived in South Africa, and was selling stolen CD players, hi-fi sets and video recorders. Alex was convinced we had the right man, but I was still not sure.

We decided we had at least enough evidence to confront him. We devised an elaborate plot whereby the woman and her boyfriend would take him to a bar and buy him a drink. At some point they would leave, and that would be our signal to move in with the camera.

I was rather nervous and warned Alex that we had to be vigilant. Neither of us was a youngster and our quarry might be armed and dangerous. Just don't block the door, I told the cameraman. We didn't want the suspect to shoot his way out.

When the girl and her boyfriend left, the three of us marched into the bar, swooped down on our victim and pushed the camera into his face. He was stunned.

'Are you Dito?' I asked him.

'No,' he said a few seconds later in a tiny voice.

'Who are you then?'

'My name is Pappa Joe.'

'You're lying! You are Dito!'

'My name is Pappa Joe.'

'Have you ever been in South Africa?'

'Yes, I lived there.'

By now silence had descended on the bar and patrons were frozen with Laurentinas in their hands. I had expected our suspect to jump up and make for the door, but instead he sat looking bewildered and perplexed.

'I want to put it to you that you are wanted for rape and murder in South Africa.'

'For what?'

'Rape and murder.'

'No.'

'Yes, you are. What do you have to say to that?'

'It's not true.'

'Where did you live in South Africa?'

'Johannesburg.'

'And what were you doing there?'

'Business.'

By then it had dawned on me that the man in front of me bore no resemblance to the man in the police photograph. Pappa Joe was small-framed and skinny with two gold front teeth, gold chains and a mop of dreadlocks. None of Dito's victims had mentioned gold teeth. And as far as I could remember, the woman and her daughter had described their rapists as muscular and powerful. The man in front of me might have been a criminal of some kind, but he was not the Grasmere rapist.

Alex was also getting in on the interrogation. 'When did you put the gold teeth in?' he asked.

'Huh?'

'Where did you get those teeth?'

'I've had it for a long time.'

I pushed on for another minute or so, but Pappa Joe stuck to his story. The more I looked at him, the more I realised it was a matter of mistaken identity. By then I was the one looking for a way out! I gave up and told the cameraman to stop filming. I feebly shook Pappa Joe's hand, waved at the patrons and left the bar with my tail between my legs. It wasn't my finest moment in journalism.

'I'm sure he's changed his looks,' Alex said in the car. I said nothing, but when he approached me a few weeks later about another sighting of Dito in Maputo, I told him to find something else to do. He persisted and later produced a picture of the 'new' Dito. I didn't even look at the photograph and ordered him to drop the story.

The second time around, Alex was right. At the end of 2005, Dito died in a shoot-out with Mozambican police. He was also wanted for a host of crimes in Maputo. A while later, Alex produced a photograph of the dead man lying on a slab in a Maputo morgue.

'That's Dito,' he said.

CHAPTER 19

Manna from heaven

*With a white man, not just any white man, but one who can interpret
like you, ah, the movie is done!* — **Chinny Ahaneku**

S HE WAS A COY AND PIMPLY-FACED VILLAGE GIRL OF ABOUT
eighteen with a white and blue kikoi wrapped around her plump body. She
approached me in an almost subservient manner, her head bowed and her body
stooped slightly forward. In one hand she clutched a Kodak Instamatic. When she
looked up at me, her eyes shone with unadulterated adoration. 'Father? Would
you mind if we take a photograph together?'

Behind her stood a circle of more admirers, all staring at me. I felt agonisingly uncomfortable. The white robe spanned my midriff like a second skin. I
could hardly breathe, and the button at my belly had already popped off. I felt
like a tightly stuffed pork sausage sizzling in the tropical midday sun.

I stood up and sucked in my tummy to prevent white and flabby flesh protruding from the gap left by the missing button. 'Of course not,' I said, and smiled
politely. One of the villagers dashed forward and took the camera from the girl.
She said her name was Frances, and she manoeuvred herself closer to me. I put
my arm around her in a chivalrous manner and grinned for the camera.

'When I grow up, Father,' she said, as the photographer set the camera for
another picture, 'I want to be a good actor like you.'

'I'm sure you will be,' I answered, and smiled again.

'That's my big dream, Father. Even when I sleep, even when I eat, I just dream
about acting.'

'I'm sure you will be a good actress.'

'I can feel it in my bones, Father. I feel I'm going to be a great actress.'

'I have no doubt you will be.'

By then the photographer had taken four or five pictures. I felt exceedingly
sheepish, but behind Frances was a line of people awaiting an audience with
me. A villager with a Polaroid camera had in the meantime grasped a business
opportunity and was selling photographs of admirers posing with the 'priest'.

Next were two young boys in maroon school uniforms. With one perched
on each of my knees, they asked me to sign my name in an exercise book.
'Where do you come from, Father?'

'South Africa,' I said.

'Where's that, Father?' one asked.

'Where Nelson Mandela comes from.'

They smiled broadly, got up and ran off, probably to tell their folks they had seen a real movie set and shaken the hand of a celebrated white actor who came from Nelson Mandela–land.

Director/producer/scriptwriter/actress Chinny Ahaneku saved me. 'Come, come, come,' she called from a distance.

'What now?' I asked as I got up and waved goodbye to the disappointed admirers still queuing up to have their pictures taken with me.

'It's time for the next scene. The one where the evil king wants to chop your head off,' she said as we strode towards a hut where a make-up artist was ready to slap powder on my sweaty face.

'I'm not really a powder-and-lipstick person,' Jude said, sweeping his brush over my cheeks and forehead. 'I like more challenging things.' Earlier, he had poured red liquid over a cow's skull in front of the royal hut where I was about to face the wrath of the murderous monarch.

My robe was made of thick nylon, enveloping me in what felt like a scorching oven. Drops of sweat spouted on my forehead and poured down my cheeks in tiny streams, washing Jude's powder off and staining my white ecclesiastical collar a rusty brown.

The make-up artist gave up on me and turned his attention to a hulking man sitting opposite. Colourful cotton sarongs were draped over his broad shoulders. Jude applied red and yellow warpaint to his face. He was the evil king, a man notorious for sacrificing twins and despising white missionaries.

'Do you know your words?' Chinny asked me.

'Sort of,' I said. The script didn't always make sense and I was making up my own lines as we went along.

'Remember to look scared,' she ordered.

'I'll do my best.'

'And don't forget your Bible. Hold it in your right hand.'

'Action, action!' shouted the director of photography – addressed as DOP by the crew – outside the royal hut, his aged video camera set up for scene number twenty-seven of *Deceit of the Gods*.

The evil king, surrounded by a council of half-naked elders, took his seat on a throne. It was covered with buckskin and decorated with grisly-looking masks. Behind the king stood two muscled warriors armed with spears.

'You stand here,' ordered Chinny, marking a spot in the dust with her foot. 'And you stand here,' she ordered a tiny man dressed in khaki shorts and shirt. He played the role of my interpreter. I was sure the two of us looked like colonial relics from a Tintin cartoon.

'And action!' screamed DOP.

'Action!' followed Chinny, crouched behind a monitor.

A young man clad only in a loincloth scurried into the hut, fell down on skins in front of the throne and cried out: 'Your majesty, that white man has come!'

'Send him in,' ordered the monarch.

Guards waved the interpreter and the priest into the royal hut. Before the priest could present the king with gifts or tell him of the wondrous message of God Almighty, the king shut him up and said: 'If ever I see you again, white man, I will cut your head off.'

As the interpreter grabbed my hand, pulled me out of the hut and hurried me through the village, from the corner of my eye I could see Jan de Klerk folded almost double with laughter. He had been pissing himself the whole day. And I couldn't blame him.

If Sudan was my worst journey, Rwanda my most harrowing and the Congo my most precarious, Nollywood was without a doubt the most bizarre. This could only have happened in Nigeria, where nothing should come as a surprise. The country and its people are big, eccentric and flamboyant, and they live life with an equal share of excess and outlandishness.

I'd always been fascinated by Nigeria, usually branded as grim, hideous, overcrowded, hot as hell and religiously zealous, its citizens swollen-headed, brazen, chaotic, coup-crazed, conniving and lawless. But with a population of 130 million, one out of every six Africans is Nigerian. It is the world's sixth largest producer of oil and ranks fifth in natural gas reserves. If Africa is to succeed, two countries will have to lead the way: South Africa and Nigeria.

Nigerians possess two special traits: they're survivors and entrepreneurs. No surprise, then, that the West African country's movie industry, aptly named Nollywood, has grown to be the third biggest in the world behind those of Bollywood (India) and Hollywood. In just thirteen years it has gone from nothing to more than 1000 titles a year and an annual turnover of about $200 million. And this in a country where there are virtually no cinemas. Most were turned into churches during the political instability and economic depression of the 1980s. Nollywood productions are aimed at the home video market – seventy million VHS and CD players in 2005 – and sold across the continent and to the African diaspora via markets in the West.

Lurid, sensational, trashy and cheap are words most often used to describe Nollywood movies. But they aren't all that different from the heart-rending slush churned out by Bollywood or, for that matter, the illusory Hollywood spectaculars. Nollywood plots might be paper-thin and the sound quality appalling, but what can people expect from movies shot on shoestring budgets and often in a matter of days? When actress Charlize Theron told reporters that her Oscar-winning performance in *Monster* took just twenty-eight days to film, it became a talking point in Hollywood. In contrast, very few – if any – Nollywood movies take that long to shoot. Production usually wraps within five to ten days. The themes are basically the same: good versus bad and the triumph of good over evil. There are no pretensions of high art. Like the rest of Nigeria, Nollywood is about making money.

It was just too captivating to ignore. It took weeks to convince the embassy to grant me a visa. I'd done far too many stories on Nigerian drug dealers seeking a foothold in South Africa for their liking. Now suddenly I was interested in something as bubblegum as Nollywood. At first the embassy didn't buy it. Later, they hesitantly pasted a visa into my passport.

Nothing comes to fruition in Nigeria without intervention from a higher power or influential hand. In our case it was movie producer Ralph Nwadike, a Nollywood legend with more than forty titles under his belt. He had agreed – obviously for a substantial fee – to open doors for us. A genial man with a wide smile, he also met us at the airport and whisked us through immigration and customs.

I'd been to Lagos several times and the sheer volume of cars slithering along the city's highways and byways never ceased to amaze me. It took us almost three hours to cross the lagoon – a rotten stew of garbage, industrial waste and raw sewage – to our hotel in the upmarket suburb of Victoria Island.

Ralph spoke non-stop: 'Did you watch the Oscars this morning?'

'No,' I said, 'I didn't.'

'I woke up at six and watched,' he said. 'And I thought that if I had their budgets, believe me, next Oscars and Ralph Nwadike will be there!'

'Oh, really?'

'Oh, yes. Like everyone else,' he said, 'I dream to be in Hollywood. But for now, I'm in Nollywood. Here I consider myself among the best, if not the very best.'

Ralph had fallen on hard times. Weeks earlier he had finished a Nollywood blockbuster called *Armageddon King* that took an almost unprecedented three weeks to shoot. The movie was a vampire thriller, a Nollywood version of *Dracula* with a gory dash of *The Texas Chainsaw Massacre* and *Nightmare on Elm Street* thrown in.

An army of black vampires invades a Nigerian city and terrorises residents. Camouflaged as prostitutes, priests and policemen, the vampires spare no one and turn the city into an orgy of bloodsucking. By the end of part one, blood is literally dripping from their teeth. And whenever one of the beasts is trapped, it dissipates with a 'swoosh' into the humid air and changes into a crow.

To create his masterpiece, Ralph had commissioned a dentist to craft sets of vampire teeth, had costumes designed and employed graphic artists to create special effects. He forked out $50 000 for the production and, in an attempt to recoup his money, decided to market and distribute the film himself. He released it under the title *Survival*.

Ralph's solo enterprise resulted in him locking horns with Nollywood's distributors – described as a mafia that wielded the real power in the industry. Not only did they obstruct his release and prevent outlets from selling *Survival*, they threatened to kill him and his family.

'They said I'm trying to run them out of business,' Ralph lamented. 'It's a dog-eat-dog business.' Fearing for his life and facing financial ruin, Ralph withdrew his movie, repackaged it as *Armageddon King* and surrendered it to a mainstream distributor.

At the heart of Nollywood lies Surelere, once a drab neighbourhood with sewage-lined streets, single or two-storey grey buildings and a Western Union on virtually every street corner where Nigerians collect dollars from family members who have cracked it in America, Europe or South Africa. Pulp movies have transformed Surelere into a crucible of dreams and desires. The streets are adorned with gigantic movie posters and lined with production houses and video stores. A steady stream of aspiring actors and actresses mill in front of notice boards displaying ads for auditions, roles and 'extras'. The heartbeat of Surelere is the legendary Winis, a rundown hotel and haunt for directors, producers and actors making deals over Gulder beer, pepper soup and goat stew. This is also where ordinary Nigerians went to do star spotting.

Ralph ran his studio with two generators. Just before our arrival, one had belched black smoke and ground to a halt. He pointed at the machine and said: 'This is why I will not pay a dime of tax, and I'm ready to go to court or jail for it. Virtually nothing works. Why should I pay for anything in this country? The roads are bad. My two cars are almost off the road. The electricity doesn't function. Water supply is epileptic. Sometimes I'm ashamed to be Nigerian. My country has disappointed me.'

Movie producers were up against tremendous odds. Not only did they have to cope with a crumbling infrastructure and rampant corruption, they were also forced to fund a censorship board that hacked their movies to smithereens in the capital of Abuja. In a country where religious tension between Muslims and Christians often exploded in bloodshed, issues of faith were all but taboo. French kissing was deemed obscene, and in scenes of passion actors merely rubbed their lips together.

'As though Nigerians don't fuck!' laughed Ralph as we drove in his battered Merc to a movie set in one of the suburbs. Minutes later, as we came to a standstill in a go-slow (that's what traffic jams in Lagos are called), Ralph said: 'Now you try and make a movie with traffic like this!' Actors were often hours late for shoots and directors were forced to book crews into nearby hotels to ensure they were on set on time.

Ralph roared with laughter when I suggested he should make a movie about the traffic. 'That will be an epic of unprecedented sadness and horror,' he said.

The traffic spared no one. The man who gave his name to the city's international airport, former head of state Murtala Mohammed, was assassinated in a go-slow. The former wife of Nigerian president Olusegun Obasanjo was shot dead in traffic in downtown Lagos when gunmen tried to hijack her car (his last wife died while undergoing cosmetic surgery in Spain).

Even if the traffic was merciful and the DOP could get to a generator to charge his batteries overnight, neighbourhood gangs – known as area-boys – were sure to spoil the action unless they were paid handsomely. These juvenile thugs ran amok on the streets of the city and were in cahoots with the police.

They were spoiling our shoot as well. When we took a Nigerian actress to a public beach one Sunday morning, we ran into a makeshift roadblock of branches erected by area-boys who demanded money before allowing motorists to pass. When they saw white faces, the price rose. When they saw the camera, the price skyrocketed. We could do nothing but pay. Just a little further down the road was a police station.

When we got to the beach, more area-boys descended on us and demanded entrance and shooting fees. By then Jan had lost patience with the riff-raff and threatened to smash their heads to a pulp with his camera. They gave him one glance and retreated.

It didn't take long to grasp the ingenuity and uniqueness of Nollywood, its stories and its people. A week or two after shooting ended, the movies flooded the markets, where they were sold for about three dollars. Restaurants, taverns, video centres or even private homes operating as movie outlets showed them to the public for a few cents. An average movie sold about 50 000 copies, a block-buster or epic six times as many.

As we threw pints of Gulder down our throats and nibbled on a whole fish marinated in a fiery chilli sauce and barbecued in front of us on the beach, a vendor with a basket filled with Nollywood movies approached our table. Ralph pulled out *Armageddon King* and held it triumphantly in the air.

'Nigerians are known to be warriors,' he said. 'We fight and fight until we fall down or get what we want. That's why Nigeria is on my lips and I defend it wherever I go. Where else in the world can you sit on the beach and buy your own movie?'

While Ralph Nwadike's star was fading on Nollywood's western horizon, that of Emmanuel Ugo was hurtling like a meteor through the Milky Way. A producer of fifty movies, his latest release, *King of the Jungle*, had captured the imagination of millions of Nigerians and was selling like hot cakes. Even though the movie cost $140 000 to produce, Emmanuel was smiling all the way to the bank.

'The interpretation of the story by the different characters is so superb,' he blustered in typical Nigerian fashion, 'and the technical input is wonderful. Every part of the film was executed with so much detail and everything was done painstakingly. It would keep you engrossed for a long, long time.'

King of the Jungle told the story of a gangster who sowed death, mayhem and destruction throughout the land to the point where he dethroned the monarch and declared himself king.

One of Nollywood's biggest heartthrobs played the role of the treacherous rebel king. He was Hank Anuku, the fortyish star of many blockbusters and one of the highest paid actors in Nigeria. Ralph described him as a home-grown Jean-Claude van Damme or Chuck Norris.

Hank was known more for swinging his fists and shooting his enemies full of holes than engaging in meaningful dialogue. When he finally spoke on screen, his few lines were richly spiced with a heavy American accent. In *King of the Jungle* his killing spree ended with his capture and summary execution by firing squad. As the soldiers cocked their rifles, he looked into the camera and muttered: 'If God doesn't destroy this town with fire and brimstone, then God made a mistake by destroying Sodom and Gomorrah.'

As the bullets tore into his body and splattered his face and sunglasses with blood – he took a very long time to die – a Bible verse appeared on the screen: Genesis 9:6: *Whosoever sheds Man's blood, By Man his blood shall be shed.*

We met Hank at the offices of the Actor's Guild of Nigeria, where he was negotiating a new movie deal. Tall and lanky with a thin moustache, and adorned with gold bracelets, chains and a silver dragon around his neck, Hank resembled a freak show on legs. With a Stars-and-Stripes bandanna wrapped around his head, he was as Yankee as Starbucks or George Bush. He drove us in his Oldsmobile to his house in Surelere. As the V8 roared through the traffic with American rap blasting from the loudspeakers, onlookers and passers-by came to a standstill, gaping in wonderment at the Nollywood beau blowing kisses at them from his coupé.

The street in front of his house resembled a designer scrapyard with several luxury automobiles standing on blocks. 'This is a BMW 730. It's German,' he bawled in a Southern twang. 'That one is a 24-valve. Mean machine. Also German. They'll soon be on the road again. The next thing I'm getting is a boat. It's gonna to be a love boat and I'm taking everybody onto the other side. You know how it is, hey?'

A son of a tribal chief and former cabinet minister, Hank had lived in the United States, England and Italy before somebody suggested he audition for a role and become an actor.

'Why?' he wanted to know.

'Because you walk the walk,' said the friend, and before long a Nollywood star was born.

It was almost impossible to interview Hank, as his cellphone rang non-stop. 'Can't switch it off,' he said, "cause it might be God Almighty or the angel of mercy calling from heaven to come and save every one of us here in Nigeria.'

One of Hank's all-time favourite movies, which was a smash hit, was *Blood Diamonds*, shot in Sierra Leone and with real-life drama as its theme. According to the plot, rebel leader Foday Sankoh had hidden a stash of diamonds worth three billion dollars before his arrest and subsequent death.

'Jesus God,' exclaimed the Sierra Leonean security chief when he heard the news. 'That's enough to turn around the whole economy of this country.'

Former Liberian president Charles Taylor, in exile in Nigeria, was trying to lay his hands on the bounty. He sent a team of mercenaries into Sierra Leone to find the diamonds. Hank Anuku played one of the soldiers of fortune.

The movie contained spicy love scenes. In one, the villain and guardian of the diamonds was sitting in a dimly lit lounge with his fiancée, a buxom vamp in a skimpy miniskirt. She ran her hand over his leg.

'Make love to me. Please!' she begged.

'Will you shut up, please? I've got better things to think about than a sex maniac fiancée who thinks of sex all the time.'

'You are starving me,' she said, as her hand crept towards his crotch. He slapped her and she fell down on the floor. The fiancée jumped up, put pink shoes on and waddled off in disgust.

The scene cut to her standing on a beach with tears in her eyes. Who should walk past and see her in distress? None other than our hero. He stopped, looked at her and said: 'You are the most delectable damsel I have seen in a long time.'

'I haven't heard that for a long time,' she said with pouting red lips.

'You're kidding! If you give me a chance in your life, I will make you realise the potential to be the queen of the world.'

He took her hand and kissed it. The lovebirds strolled off into the sunset, stopped, and with the shallow waves washing up against their ankles, hungrily rubbed their mouths together. She murmured: 'Loverboy, you're the greatest man I've ever known in my whole life.'

After roaming Lagos for several days trying without success to get onto a movie set – directors were afraid we were spying or might steal their ideas – Ralph arrived at the hotel with a broad smile. 'Pack your bags, boys,' he said as he got out of the car. 'We're going to Enugu.'

'Why Enugu?' I asked him.

'A good friend of mine is shooting a big movie near Enugu and she says we can film everything we need and speak to whomever we want,' he said. 'We must fly this afternoon.'

Flying in Nigeria is a terrifying prospect. The national airline had gone bust (imagine a nation of 130 million without a national airline!) and its void was filled by a host of domestic airlines operating time-worn 727s and 737s that more reputable airlines would have grounded a long time ago. In 2005, two aircraft crashed in Nigeria, killing hundreds.

While the horridness of Lagos is impossible to exaggerate, Enugu, by contrast, was airy, spacious and hospitable. And movie director Chinny Ahaneku was sweet, smart and seductive. She greeted us like long-lost friends and said: 'Whatever you need, just ask. I'm at your service.'

Chinny was a twenty-five-year-old rather vivacious actress who was directing her second movie with money she had borrowed from her husband, an engineer on the oil rigs. She had a rasping and scratchy voice and as an actress could never land major roles. 'No matter how good I was at audition,' she said. 'I was always told that I'm playing the secretary. Sometimes I was the nurse.' She decided to try her hand at directing.

Her first movie was *Castaway*, a story of parents adopting children and their struggle to provide them with a better life. The movie led to Chinny's financial ruin when her co-financier turned on her and claimed she had misled him and forged documents to secure loans. She was locked up for a week and was still involved in a civil court battle.

Unperturbed by the initial setback, Chinny embarked on a quest to produce a movie about an evil forest near her home village in Enugu state, where she grew up. According to a seventeenth-century Ibo legend, an evil king and a wicked sorcerer had cast a spell on the forest and sacrificed twins in the woods. 'I knew it wasn't evil,' said Chinny, 'because as a child I played in the forest and nothing happened to me. It had to be a deceit from the gods.'

And so was born *Deceit of the Gods*. Chinny managed to scrape together $20 000, assembled a cast and crew of 120, and rented a kraal in an Ibo village set under waving palm trees and next to a silver stream. She managed to secure some of Nigeria's foremost actors and actresses for her movie.

Larry Morgan Briggs, a grey-bearded veteran of thirty films, played the role of King Izigbo, the good monarch who sees the wickedness in the tradition of sending twin children into the evil forest to be sacrificed to the gods. The script described him as a twentieth-century king living in the seventeenth century.

Chudi Kashimawu, a thickset, dark-skinned actor with a mop of unruly hair, played the evil priest. He'd become known in Nigeria for villainous roles. 'When I walk on the streets, people go away because they fear my spiritual powers. On aeroplanes I'm always assured of having the seat next to me open,' he said.

His baleful spell on the peasants is finally broken through the forceful intervention of King Izigbo and a young British missionary who travels to the Dark Continent, sees the sacrifice of the twins and sets out to abolish the practice. The whole cast was as black as the Enugu night, but it never occurred to me to ask where the white missionary was. Under a tree, alongside rows of costumes, hung a priest's robe.

'Action!' Chinny yelled as scene one got under way. In front of a hut sat a wailing mother with her dead child on her lap. The boy had died after a deadly curse from the gods. Minutes earlier, Chinny had picked a little boy from the crowd of bystanders, dressed him in a traditional loincloth and ordered him to lie down and close his eyes.

'Play dead,' she told the boy, who shut his eyes tightly. Chinny pointed at the mother and said: 'You, cry!' She walked back to the monitor, crouched behind it and yelled: 'Action!'

As easily as switching on a radio, the woman threw her arms in the air, burst into woebegone grief and wept: 'Oh God, what have I done? What have I done to deserve this?' According to the script, her husband, a spear and dead chicken in his hand, would stroll into the village and see the dead boy sprawled on his wife's lap. He would then throw down his spear and the chicken, kneel next to the boy's body and lament the passing of his first-born.

As Chinny waved him into shot, he said: 'Where's my chicken? I don't have the chicken!'

Chinny threw her arms up in frustration. 'Stop! Where's the dead fowl?'

'It's not dead. It's alive now,' said the DOP. Next to him stood a man wringing the chicken's neck. He wrung and wrung and wrung, but the bird refused to die. When it finally stopped kicking, Chinny again screamed: 'Action!' As the woman's wails echoed through the village and her husband flung his spear and the chicken in the dust, Chinny jumped up and screamed: 'Stop! Stop! Stop!'

She angrily pointed at the throng of curious onlookers pushing and shoving ever closer to the set. 'Why are you spoiling everything? Why are you so loud?'

Cast members armed with bamboo canes drove the crowd about twenty metres back from where they gaped wide-eyed as scene one was acted out to Chinny's complete satisfaction. The mother's grief and the father's torment would be, in Chinny's words, 'too much for anyone to bear'.

'And the little boy was just a magician,' she said. 'He was so real. He never opened his eyes once.'

At the end of day two of our stay in Enugu, Chinny had completed only the first three scenes and was already behind schedule. First the bus with the crew broke down on the road from Enugu to the village. Then a set of baby twins needed for the scene showing a human sacrifice fell ill and replacements had to be sought in neighbouring villages. On top of that the local chief brought shooting to a standstill when he chased the crew out of his village and demanded more money for using the location. Chinny succumbed.

'Scene 26,' announced Chinny on the morning of day three. Ralph, Jan and I were booked back from Enugu to Lagos later that afternoon.

'What's scene 26?' I asked one of the actors as make-up artist Jude decorated the royal hut with animal skins, masks and skulls. King Izigbo was already draped in flowing white and red robes and wore a crown of buckskin decorated with shells.

'The good king and the priest,' he said.

'Where's the priest?' I wanted to know.

'Dunno,' said the actor.

Ralph called me. 'Chinny wants to have a word with you,' he said. As we walked towards the royal hut, it had still not dawned on me that there was nobody to play the white priest and that I was earmarked for greater things.

'I have a problem,' said Chinny. She was addressing Ralph and didn't look at me.

'What's that?' he asked.

'You know it's now time for the white priest?'

'Yes?'

'Well, I don't have a white priest.'

'So what are you going to do? Fetch one in Enugu?'

'There's no time. And I don't know anybody who can do it.'

The full impact of this conversation suddenly hit me. Ralph asked: 'So what are you going to do? Paint a black man white?'

Chinny laughed and glanced at me. 'I want to plead with you to help me. Without a white priest, my movie will be a failure.'

By now Jude was standing next to me, holding the white robe in the air. 'It's really not something very big,' she said. 'Just put that on and say a few lines. Please, I beg you.'

I had never acted before and had no desire to star in a Nollywood movie. And the last role I would ever have wanted to play was that of a Bible-toting fanatic bringing his message of light and salvation to the peasants.

I sought an escape. 'I don't know how to act,' I told her.

'Acting starts in a day,' she said. 'Everything starts in a day.'

'I'll never fit into that,' I said, and pointed at the robe.

'You will,' said Chinny. 'We'll press you into it.'

A few minutes later I wriggled myself into the robe, which was probably two sizes too small. One of the buttons snapped off immediately. I exchanged my sneakers for Nigerian sandals, a plastic white cross was draped around my neck and a Bible pushed into my hand.

'What do I have to do?' I asked Chinny.

'Give the king some gifts and bring Christianity to this kingdom.'

She gave me the script to read. 'Chinny,' I said, 'this is not just a few words. This is a whole dialogue!'

'A few lines plus a little bit more,' she said, and laughed.

'Idol worship and human sacrifice are from the devil! But if you accept God Almighty, He will save you from all evil!'

I had never thought these words would roll off my lips, but for several minutes, with one hand in the air and a Bible clutched in the other, I chastised King Izigbo about the ungodly and barbaric conduct of his people. By the end of my raving and ranting, he was a changed man. He shook his head and agreed to spread God's word among his subjects and abolish the sacrifice of twins.

As Chinny called out 'Cut!', the crew applauded. 'It was fantastic,' she exclaimed. 'You didn't tell us you're an actor. You didn't even miss a line.'

'Can I go now?' I asked her, frantic to get out of the robe. We had probably already missed our flight back to Lagos.

'No, please,' she said. 'It's not over yet.'

The priest played a major role in the story and appeared in several more scenes, including one where the bad king threatened to chop off his head, one where he rescued twins from being sacrificed, another where he confronted the evil priest, and the final, joyous spectacle where the tribe celebrated the triumph of good over evil. King Izigbo marries the princess and the priest blesses the village and assures his new flock that with Christ as their saviour, a future of prosperity and fertility awaits.

'What do we do?' I asked Jan.

'You can't let them down,' he said, 'and we'll make it part of the documentary. It shows the bizarreness of Nollywood.'

When we arrived on set the next morning, a journalist from a local newspaper was waiting for me. 'How long have you been acting?' he asked.

'One day,' I told him. He had a perplexed expression on his face.

'How then do you manage to deliver such a solid performance?'

I told him that my great-grandfather had been an eminent missionary (it's true, he was a founder of the NG Sendingkerk, the Dutch Reformed Church for so-called coloured people), and said in pompous Nigerian fashion: 'I suppose playing the role of a missionary comes naturally.'

More than 100 actors and extras, dressed in colourful sarongs and loincloths and adorned with body paint, beads and bracelets, partook in the final wedding scene. The bad king had been driven into a far-off forest and the evil priest killed. As King Izigbo took his seat on his throne, drummers and dancers introduced the festivities.

'Today is the beginning of a new dawn for our people,' said King Izigbo as his subjects presented him with gifts of fruit, vegetables and calabashes of beer. 'Let the music play, for this is a day of celebration, of progress and prosperity.'

One of the calabashes found its way to a puny little man sitting next to me. For two days he'd been trying to get close to the priest and now had finally wiggled his way into the seat next to mine. He proudly presented me with the calabash and watched expectantly as I took a mouthful. The concoction tasted sour, but it was refreshing and kicked like hell. We swigged away at it while Chinny, playing the radiant bride, was presented to her charming prince, his muscles glistening in the late afternoon sun. Every time the DOP aimed his camera in my direction, I endeavoured to present a stern and unrelenting visage of piety and godliness.

It was time for my sermon. I stumbled to my feet, forgot my lines, but rambled on in a raucous voice about the greatness of God and how Her Majesty the Queen (never mind my Afrikaans accent) was going to bring civilisation to this dark corner of the world by building clinics and schools. 'These gods, these other gods, have no right to take people away. But God Almighty, he loves you and can save you and take you to heaven.'

By the time the ceremony ended, King Izigbo – who had also taken a few generous swallows from the calabash – was on his feet, dancing with the rapturous maidens and waving his buckskin crown in the air above his head. By then the sun was plunging into the forest and it was time to bid the cast farewell and return to Enugu. We were scheduled to fly back to Lagos early the next morning. Chinny pushed a brown envelope stacked with Nigerian naira notes into my hand: 'This is for you. Payment for the priest. You deserve it.' I gave it back to her and told her to buy crates of beer and food for the crew.

'I will drink on the priest,' she said. Then she put her arms around me, planted a kiss on my mouth, and said: 'When I saw you, I knew you were like manna from heaven.'

CHAPTER 20

In the heart of Conrad's darkness

The offing was barred by a black bank of clouds, and the tranquil waterway leading to the uttermost ends of the earth flowed sombre under an overcast sky – it seemed to lead into the heart of an immense darkness. – Joseph Conrad, *Heart of Darkness*

'WHY ON EARTH ARE WE FLYING HEWA BORA?' JAN ASKED. HE had the aisle seat in the aged Boeing 727. I was sitting at the window. Squashed between us was our Congolese colleague, Michael Mutombo.

'Because it's cheap. Half of what SAA costs,' I told him.

'I can see that,' he mumbled grumpily.

Pandemonium had broken out on our flight from Johannesburg to Kinshasa, courtesy of Hewa Bora, the rejuvenated Congo Airlines. It was overbooked and four people had to get off the aircraft before it departed. With a few other exceptions, Jan and I were the only white passengers and I was confident that our pale faces would save us from ejection. Michael crouched down in his seat and tried not to make eye contact with the captain, who had emerged from the cockpit and was personally taking charge of the fracas on his craft.

The captain was short and pot-bellied with a dark red, blotchy nose that blurted out his drinking habits. He barked commands in French to a few hapless passengers who had to collect their belongings and disembark. One, who objected fiercely, was told he would get a free night at the Holiday Inn and could board the next Hewa Bora flight to Kinshasa. He seemed more than happy and, cradling a cardboard box containing a television set or a hi-fi, scrambled down the steps to the runway.

Three hours after the scheduled departure, the aircraft creaked and hissed into the air and headed north for the Democratic Republic of Congo (DRC). Always petrified of flying, my thoughts were fixed on the French pilot in whose doddering hands my life now rested. He had probably worn the livery of Air France until he was sacked for boozing on duty. Idle and unemployable in Europe, he might then have landed a job with Hewa Bora, but in all likelihood despised his feeble aircraft, rowdy passengers and flying out of a pit like Kinshasa.

As we nose-dived towards the DRC capital four hours later, I looked out of the window. Far below was the Congo River, wide and thick and glimmering in the late afternoon light like a solid stream of black ink.

Jan was reading *Heart of Darkness*, in which Joseph Conrad portrayed the river as a symbolic highway to the outer reaches of the human soul. 'Going up that river was like travelling back to the earliest beginnings of the world, when vegetation rioted on the earth and the big trees were kings. An empty stream, a great silence, an impenetrable forest. The air is hot, humid, heavy, languid,' Conrad had written more than a century before.

I had a more recent chronicle of a Congo River journey on my lap. *Facing the Congo* told how American-born journalist Jeffrey Tayler had left a comfortable existence in Moscow for a taste of adventure on the African equator. His goal was to navigate the river in a hand-carved pirogue and with a single guide for more than 1700 kilometres from the jungle city of Kisangani to Kinshasa. Four weeks after setting out on his all but impossible mission, he had to abandon the journey, depleted, exhausted and hunted by hostile tribes.

A small library could be filled with books about this great river of the world. Many had wanted to travel the mighty waterway. Some, like Tayler, hoped to dispel their boredom through suffering and achievement and the conquest of fear. Others were inspired by the myths and legends of darkest Africa where, in pristine jungles and on the banks of rivers alive with crocodiles, were to be found cannibals, pygmies, great apes, predators, parrots and pythons as thick as a man's thigh. A few were doubtless undaunted by the Hollywood stereotype of cannibals boiling a mercenary in a pot and serving him for dinner.

Washington Post journalist Blaine Harden used a river journey in *Africa: Dispatches from a Fragile Continent* as a narrow but revealing window on so-called Mobutuism – a system created by the post-colonial dictator who reinvented the Congo and made up the vulturine rules by which it continued to be run after his demise. Mobuto Sese Seko first renamed himself. Then he renamed the country and the river, initiating an era of corruption and plunder unrivalled on the African continent.

I also wanted to travel on the Congo River. The more I was told that it was a hazardous, perilous, steamy, sticky, dirty and potentially deadly journey, the more I wanted to board a barge and sail across the equator, be encircled by rainforest so dense that it lacked any colour. I envisaged Africa as it once was: a land ruled by the jungle and where men spoke to one another through the beat of a drum. Of course, mine was an incredibly naive notion of life in the Congo.

'Where are you going to sleep?' people asked me.

'I don't care,' I would reply. 'On the boat somewhere. I'm sure there are cabins.'

'And what are you going to eat?'

'I don't know. There must be food on the boat. Or I'll take my own.'

'And where are you going to shit?'

That was the only predicament I foresaw. 'I'll find a place. There must be toilets. I'll make a plan.'

In the autumn of 1995, cameraman Jan de Klerk and I had undertaken a two-month overland journey from Johannesburg to Uganda, during which we made three television documentaries. We travelled through Botswana, Zambia, Tanzania, Burundi and Rwanda. For 600 kilometres, we traversed Lake Tanganyika, the longest and second deepest freshwater body in the world, on the Tanzanian boat the MV *Liemba*. We boarded the motorised vehicle at the Zambian port of Mpulungu, loaded our 4×4 and fared northwards on the emerald waters for a week before reaching the Burundian capital of Bujumbura.

The *Liemba* was no ordinary boat. Reputed to be the oldest cargo-carrier afloat, it had been built during the First World War by German colonialists and christened the *Graf van Goetzen*. Even before embarking on its maiden voyage in what was then known as German East Africa, the boat was scuttled by the authorities to prevent it falling into enemy hands. In 1924 it was salvaged, restored and renamed, and had steamed up and down the lake ever since.

It was an enthralling voyage that cut through the heart of Africa, with Zaire (as the DRC was then called) on the one side and Tanzania on the other. There were hundreds of traders on board taking bags of rice and kapenta (small dried fish) to markets along the shore.

The boat had recently been refurbished by a Danish aid agency and Jan and I travelled first class. We had a perfectly comfortable cabin, there was a well-stocked bar and the food was edible. It was on that trip that we decided we were going to travel on what local inhabitants call Nzere (the river that swallows all rivers) in the near future.

In a country where corruption had seen jungle reclaim what used to be the road network, the river was the only east–west thoroughfare. A quarter of a million passengers and a million tons of freight moved each year on the 15 000 kilometres of navigable water offered by the Congo and its tributaries.

The further downstream one sails, the wider the Congo becomes as it absorbs other rivers. Nzere drains the Congo basin, the second largest rainforest in the world, and is second only to the Amazon in the amount of water it deposits into the ocean.

Harden described the Congo River fleet as a stinking, noisy, overheated, over-crowded African market that is part supermarket, part disco, part abattoir and part brothel, open twenty-four hours a day for business. The boats that plied the river had a notorious reputation, but nothing could dissuade us, and towards the middle of 1996 I was ready to embark on my Zaire River adventure. I had a guide in Kinshasa looking for a suitable boat, and he told me it would be easier to make the journey from Kisangani to Kinshasa, as it was downstream and faster.

'How long?' I asked.

'Ten days. Two weeks. But maybe three. It's difficult to tell,' he croaked over the bad telephone line.

'And where are we going to sleep?'

'Ah, that's no problem.'

'What do you mean?'

'We'll get you a cabin.'

'Really?'

'Oh yes,' he said. 'With air conditioning and everything.'

But before we could board an aircraft, four rebel groups in eastern Zaire had formed a coalition and, with the support of neighbouring Uganda and Rwanda, mounted a military campaign aimed at overthrowing dictator Mobutu Sese Seko. Laurent Kabila, a little-known communist with a portly physique and a head resembling a soccer ball, emerged as the rebel leader.

With his forces moving towards the interior, we had to abandon our plans. In May 1997, after a lightning military campaign, the rebels reached Kinshasa. By then, Mobutu was battling cancer and living on his heavily protected yacht – complete with on-board helipad – in the middle of the river. But Kabila got him before the tumour did. Mobutu fled to Morocco, where he died shortly afterwards, and Kabila declared himself president. He renamed the country and almost immediately cracked down on the opposition, banning all political parties but his own. Despite his promise of bringing peace and stability to the country, the DRC slid back into anarchy as Rwanda and Uganda turned on Kabila and invaded from the east. One massacre followed another.

Our plan to sail the Congo seemed permanently shelved when Kabila closed the river to all traffic. Boats could no longer go upstream to Kisangani and were forced to stop at the town of Mbandaka. The DRC's interior became a land of forgotten and isolated outposts.

Ten days after one of his bodyguards assassinated Kabila in January 2001, his son Joseph was sworn in as president of the DRC. All that the world knew of him was that he had been the head of the Congolese army and, at the age of twenty-nine, was the world's youngest head of state.

By then, the war had killed an estimated three million people, mostly through disease and starvation, while another 2.5 million had been driven from their homes. The country had been sliced into several pieces and was ruled by an array of militias and foreign powers scrambling for its natural riches.

The elusive Joseph turned out to be much more of a pragmatist than his father and entered into agreements with Rwanda and Uganda for their withdrawal from the eastern reaches of the DRC. He also allowed United Nations peacekeepers into the country. The river was reopened in July 2003, and soon afterwards the first commercial barge, loaded with cement and fuel, crawled upstream towards Kisangani.

Although the river was officially open again, I couldn't find any information about the frequency of boat travel or the security situation, except that the area around Kisangani was highly volatile and that armed soldiers with hungry stomachs prowled the environs. The Congolese ambassador to South Africa, a tall and elegant man in flowing robes who spoke perfect English, told me that river traffic was almost back to normal. Ambassador Bene Mpoko gave us visas, the name and number of a boat owner in Kinshasa, and an official letter stating that the Office of the President had approved our mission and that we should be assisted and supported wherever we went.

Jan, Michael and I boarded the Hewa Bora flight for Kinshasa in May 2004. Michael was born in the Congo, but had refugee status in South Africa and worked as a cameraman in the SABC's news department. He would act as our interpreter, guide and second cameraman. As our pilot landed the 727 with a thump and brought the aircraft to a stop in front of the terminal at Kinshasa airport, I joined in the applause that customarily acknowledges a safe landing in Africa.

I had always resisted paying bribes, no matter where my continental travels took me, and found the tales of fellow travellers and journalists about obligatory payola and extortion highly exaggerated. The exception was the Congo, where corruption went all the way to the top and then down the ladder again.

Trapped at the bottom were the peasants – the passengers on the boats, the farmers in the fields, the hunters in the forests, and the traders on street corners and in markets trying to sell plastic sandals, cigarettes, tomatoes and bananas. For their right to get assistance from a public servant, have their children enrolled in school, obtain medical care or get someone to investigate a crime, they had to pay *matabiches*, bribes usually extorted by government officials, policemen, soldiers, teachers, magistrates, customs officers and health workers, who seemed to be interminably waiting for their salaries to be paid. In order to maintain some semblance of their former bourgeois lifestyle, they were forced to recoup lost earnings from peasants and foreigners.

Most of the elite not only remunerated themselves generously, but were entitled to 'commissions' from government contracts and demanded gifts from investors. They lived in compounds on the river behind high walls in order to keep the proletariat shantytowns out of sight. Once embedded at the top of the ladder, the ranks of the elite ballooned as quickly as ticks feasting on the blood of pedigreed dogs. Their roly-poly physiques filled the business and first-class seats on the Air France flights to Paris. Once in the French capital, they gorged themselves on *pâté de foie gras* and *confit de canard* while madame binge-shopped at the haute couture salons on Avenue Montaigne in the eighth arrondissement.

The leeches started sucking at us the moment we got off the aircraft. The health official who checked my yellow fever vaccination certificate huffed and puffed that it was valid for only another six months and that I could thus not enter the country.

'*Guest la Presidenté,*' I mumbled in broken French as I shoved Ambassador Mpoko's letter in his glutton face and walked on. It worked. The letter also got us past the customs officer who demanded *cold drink*, one of the accepted terms for a bribe.

But that was just about the last time the diplomat's *lettre de recommendation* made an impact on anyone in the DRC. Soldiers manning a roadblock on our way to the hotel refused to even look at it.

'*Stop! Tes papiers. Tes papiers tout de suite!*' Although our papers were absolutely in order, the soldiers soon had their 'cold drink'.

Kinshasa was an angry city. Just before our arrival, rebels had rowed across the river from Congo-Brazzaville and attacked the army barracks and television station in the capital. The invasion was repelled, but fear and apprehension lay like a blanket of smog over the city.

A precarious peace agreement had seen Joseph Kabila's two main rivals return to Kinshasa as members of a power-sharing government. Both rebel leaders brought hordes of their own soldiers to protect them. They set up their headquarters along the river – the city's prime real estate and the best escape route should the agreement disintegrate. One kept his white helicopter parked in his back garden.

Kinshasa's airport and the walls of government buildings were adorned with posters of the new cabinet of national unity, comprising a staggering three vice-presidents and seventy ministers and deputies. Suddenly the Congo had ministers of tourism and scientific development! The new elite were cruising the capital in shiny black limousines with wailing sirens and gun-toting escorts.

It took us two days – and a $150-dollar 'shooting permit', for which we got a receipt with a stamp – to obtain accreditation to film on and around the river. Then we set off to meet Dieudonné Bongumba, the boat owner whom the ambassador had suggested we contact. A tall, elegant man with a strong face and a broad smile, his news was bad. There were no boats in the harbour and only a handful of craft had made the journey all the way to Kisangani. His own boats went only as far as Mbandaka, about halfway up the river.

Dieudonné in turn introduced us to Jean Kasango, the director of Onatra, the Congolese shipping company that had gone bankrupt but was in the process of being resuscitated. He was the exemplary public servant, dressed in a black suit and starched white shirt behind a desk stacked with moth-eaten files.

'Ah, my friends,' he said, 'you're too late or maybe too early! Depends on how you see it. You should have been here six years ago and you would have been on a boat already. Or maybe you must come back in a year's time and we might have fixed a boat or two. But for now, we have nothing.'

Accompanied by the two men, we headed for The Beach, a series of docks lining the Kinshasa waterfront. One side of the harbour belonged to Onatra, the other was for private vessels bearing cargo from further upstream or from Brazzaville, on the opposite bank of the river. The dockland was choked with shoving, competing and jostling human flesh. Shirtless boys in ragged shorts balanced sacks of rice and corn on their backs as traders, mostly women, kicked and pushed against the fence while shouting bids in the local language of Lingala. There were as many wailing beggars as AK-wielding soldiers. The harbour was a security area and armed men immediately stopped us. '*Vos papiers!*'

Jean Kasango might not have had a viable job since the closure of the river, but his identity card gave him unlimited access to all parts of the harbour and his official position still carried weight. The soldiers waved us through.

The shallow waters of the harbour had become a graveyard for rusting and derelict heaps of warped steel. What had once been barges that routinely pushed upriver to Kisangani were now hideouts for squatters. A hundred or so metres away, four three-storey tugs were docked in a row.

'The last time their engines fired was six years ago,' Jean said. 'Some have been emptied out. I don't know if they can still start. We want to overhaul them, but it will take a long time.'

It was a depressing afternoon. Almost none of the old river boats were back on the water. The civil war had sent them to a demeaning end on Kinshasa's Beach, where they were looted and became shelters for the homeless. Eyes squinted at us from glassless portholes and the orange flicker of cooking fires emerged from the hulls.

Jean said only two privately owned boats had left Kinshasa for Kisangani in the previous couple of months. One was chartered by the UN to transport food to the interior and carried no passengers. The other was a smaller craft called the *Tshopo*, but it was old and slow and had taken six weeks to reach Kisangani. He had been told that it was docked there, but would soon depart for the down-river journey to Kinshasa.

'Should we try and get onto it?' I wanted to know.

'Beware of getting onto just any boat,' he warned. 'There are many un-scrupulous owners who are trying to make a quick buck. Many of the boats are unsafe.'

The next morning, we were on a flight to Kisangani to look for the *Tshopo*, named after one of the Congo's tributaries. A glistening shimmer of water danced off the black tarmac when we landed around midday at Kisangani's international airport (or what remained of it). As we walked into the airport building, a policeman gave our camera equipment one look and ordered us to follow him into a squalid office with dirty walls and piles of yellowed immigration papers.

'*Passeport et vos papiers!*' bawled the famished leech.

Just fifty kilometres north of the equator, Kisangani was an isolated, choking and steamy urban sprawl, encircled and strangled by an impregnable forest. It was chiselled out of the forest at the end of a series of smaller river harbours and situated at the point beyond which no boat could sail.

Long a hub of the diamond, gold and ivory trade, for most of its existence Kisangani had teetered between periods of tropical languor and fervid violence. It was a slave depot for Arabs from Zanzibar before Belgian racketeers drove them out. The city was bloodied by rebellions at independence and pillaged during a series of uprisings in the early 1990s. During a six-day battle in June 2000, more than 1200 civilians were killed and many thousands wounded as Rwandan and Ugandan forces battled for control of Kisangani. Scores of civilians also died during clashes in August 1999 and May 2000.

Decades of fighting and corruption had reduced Kisangani to a ramshackle city, with buildings pockmarked by bullets and torn apart by bombs, and roads that were nothing but clusters of broken asphalt. We headed for the harbour, which had a decrepit and desolate appearance, the water studded with disused barges and rusting cranes.

'Where's the *Tshopo*?' Michael asked an official.

'It's moored downstream outside the harbour,' he said. 'The captain is trying to avoid paying harbour tax.'

The *Tshopo*, tied up at a fishing dock, consisted of a small, squat tug and two barges. It was a frightful vision, best likened to one of Jean Kasango's ramshackle boats that had been pulled off the scrap heap and put to task. It was rusty and crumbling. The hull of the bigger barge, about twenty metres long, resembled a moonscape and was covered in dents and bulges that looked like cancerous growths, ready to explode or burst open at any moment. About a hundred passengers were squatting under woven mats or plastic sheeting on the deck.

I should have turned around and walked away after my first look at the *Tshopo*. The boat was obviously a disaster waiting to happen, but I had become obsessed by the desire to board a boat – any boat, even the *Tshopo*.

We ventured up the walkway and asked to speak to the captain. A stocky fellow emerged from the boat's depths and introduced himself as Freddy

Kibombo, the manager. (He lied. He turned out to be only the loading master.) We told him we were looking for a boat to take us downriver.

'Welcome to the *Tshopo*,' he said.

'We want to travel to Kinshasa,' I told him.

'You are at the right place,' he said. 'You will have a most pleasant journey.'

'And where will we stay?' I asked. 'Are there cabins?'

He laughed and said: 'Only one cabin. And that's for the captain. It's for him and his wife and three children.'

'Where then?' I asked.

He took us to the bow of the smaller barge and lifted a trapdoor. I stuck my head into the hole. It was a windowless chamber, designed for carrying freight. It was pitch-black, damp and had the temperature of a hothouse, as well as a musty smell. It was empty, but at the bottom I glimpsed a layer of water.

'Is this it?' I asked Freddy.

'*Cabine de luxe*,' he said, and laughed. By then we were surrounded by an animated crowd engaged in a lively discussion. They were clearly deliberating what the hell the two *mondeles* (whites) were up to.

Faced with the black hole, Jan was as eminently practical as ever. 'This is not bad,' he said. 'We can store the equipment in the hole and sleep on the deck. We'll buy plastic sheeting and make a canopy.'

I had already noted – or rather, nosed – the toilet situation on board. There was one *pissoir* in the stern and another at the front end of the barge. As I mused over my options, the door of one privy swung open. It was grimy and as small as a telephone booth, and although we were a good fifteen metres away, the rancid whiff engulfed us. It was at that moment that I promised myself, no matter how urgently nature called, I would venture nowhere near the *Tshopo*'s toxic toilets.

'So, do you take it?' Freddy wanted to know.

'Yes, but how much?'

'You'll have to speak to the captain,' he said.

'We'll come back later,' I replied.

'But there's one small problem,' he added. 'We're leaving at five this afternoon.'

It was impossible for us to sail two hours later. We had to get supplies, such as food and water, register with customs and immigration (we were told in Kinshasa that this was a prerequisite for travelling on a river boat), and get our equipment ready.

Freddy sensed our desperation. 'If we don't leave at five, we will take a big loss.'

'Can't you postpone for a day or two?'

'Only if you cover that loss.'

'How much?'

'Five hundred dollars.'

Michael quickly beat Freddy down to $50. He smiled as he pocketed the note and said: 'The boat will not leave today.'

We were conned. The boat didn't leave for the next six days.

Oggi Saidi found us at the Wagenia cataracts, a series of rapids a kilometre upstream from Kisangani that prevents the river boats from sailing further east. We wanted to get a few shots of the city and the area before boarding the boat. The previous afternoon we had shopped for foam mattresses, tinned food, water, fuel for the generator that we had carried all the way from Johannesburg, plastic sheeting, mosquito repellent and, Jan insisted, a fan. He said we had to keep the equipment cool. We then registered at immigration, where we had to pay another $50 as a 'shooting fee'.

Earlier that morning we had gone back to the boat and Freddy had assured us that we would leave by five. 'The captain is finalising the papers. Be ready to leave.'

At the cataracts, while filming fishermen perched on bamboo poles in the middle of the roaring waters as they lowered conical raffia baskets into the rapids, a slight, sinewy man standing next to me said: 'I'm sorry, but you cannot do this. It is not allowed.'

Speaking in English, he continued: 'This place is under the control of our chief. You cannot just bring your camera here. You have to get permission first.'

'And who are you?' I asked him.

'My name is Oggi and I belong to the same village. I am speaking on behalf of the chief.'

'And what do we have to do to get permission?' I wanted to know.

Irritatingly, Jan moved away from his camera. We had been in the Congo for almost a week and this was the first time we had managed to film anything.

'You have to pay a fee,' said Oggi.

'How much?'

'Hundred dollars.'

I told Jan to pack his equipment. We would probably not need the cataract shots in any case. I turned and started walking back to the taxi. Oggi ran after me. 'Please, don't go. This can all be negotiated.'

'I am sick and tired of negotiating,' I said. 'I'm not interested in your pictures.'

'Twenty dollars,' he said, 'and then I'll get a boat and take you to our island and show you my village. Then you can take pictures of everything you want. There's a good view of Kisangani.'

A few minutes later, we clambered into a pirogue just below the cataract. Two half-naked young men with glistening muscles dug their paddles deep into the water as they pushed us over a stretch of river to an island in the middle of the Congo.

'How come your English is so good?' I asked Oggi.

'I have been a tourist guide for a long time,' he said, 'but we haven't had any visitors for many years. You are the first.'

I told him we were journalists rather than tourists, and intended travelling downriver to Kinshasa on the *Tshopo*. He burst out laughing and nearly capsized the boat. 'You can't be serious!' he shrieked.

'Yes, we are,' I said, slightly taken aback. 'Why are you laughing?'

'There are many stories about that boat,' he said. 'Many, many stories.'

'Like what?'

'That some barges sank in the river on the way up from Kinshasa. That's why it took the *Tshopo* so long to get here. Now the captain can't pay for the lost freight and they won't allow him to leave. They say he's a crook.'

Jan, Michael and I glanced at one another. 'The boat manager said we're leaving at five this afternoon,' I said.

Oggi chuckled again. 'The boat will not leave this afternoon or tomorrow or the day after that.'

'How do you know?'

'I grew up in Kisangani. I've travelled on hundreds of boats. Believe me, I know how it works. Maybe five days from today. But not today or tomorrow.'

Oggi Saidi, thirty-two years old and married with several children, lived on an idyllic hilly outcrop on the island. Behind his home were the rumbling cataracts and in front stretched the gleaming waters of the Congo River, more than a kilometre wide with a curtain of forest on one side and Kisangani on the other.

Oggi had studied African culture and English at the local university, and became a guide for adventurous tourists, aid workers, diamond dealers and foreign traders. He remembered a time when he would take visitors daily to see the fishermen at the cataracts, make a cultural tour of his village, where they were greeted by the chief to the beat of a drum, and paddle them for a kilometre or two down the river. He sometimes accompanied tourists on a river boat from Kisangani to Kinshasa.

That, he said, was all in the 'good old days' of Mobutu Sese Seko. 'When he was president, we had peace. There was no war. Boats were many, food was plenty and everybody had a job.'

One of the highlights of Oggi's life was when Mobutu visited not just Kisangani, but his village. He arrived in a helicopter while the villagers sang: '*The Father has come. Bless him because we are not going to be hungry.*'

'He brought many presents,' said Oggi. 'He gave each of us lots of money. He did a lot for the Congo. He built a big football stadium in Kinshasa and very high buildings. He was our father.'

'But he stole most of the money,' I said. 'He was a thief.'

'In Congo, everybody steals,' said Oggi. 'Mobutu is dead, but people still steal. When Mobutu was here, there was no war. When he left, soldiers came and killed our children.'

It was difficult to argue with Oggi. He told me about the six-day war when bombs had rained on the city and all sides had poured indiscriminate firepower into houses, schools, churches and workplaces. His brother was killed by a bomb and Oggi was wounded when he tried to go to Kisangani to get food and salt for the village. His mother, a trader, was in Kinshasa when the fighting broke out and had still not been able to return to Kisangani.

He offered to show us Mobutu's former palace, a riverfront estate on the city's outskirts, one of eleven mansions the dictator had built throughout the country. It had been destroyed and looted during the war and only a shell remained of what was a monument to the greed and megalomania that epitomised Mobutu's reign.

His ghost still loomed large and real over the Congo. His name crept into every conversation and life was still played according to his rules. It would be impossible to grasp the woes of the Congo without appreciating what Mobutuism was all about.

Mobutu was born a peasant, the son of a cook and a maid. After attending mission school, he joined the colonial Force Publique and rose to the rank of sergeant major, the highest military position then open to Congolese. He left the army to become a journalist, and on a trip to Belgium in 1959, made contact with America's Central Intelligence Agency and was soon on their payroll. The Cold War was at its zenith and Washington was terrified that the Congo's untapped wealth might fall into communist hands. Mobutu soon became the CIA's main man in Kinshasa.

When Congo became independent in 1960, a fiery and outspoken critic of the West by the name of Patrice Lumumba became its first prime minister. He set off alarm bells in Western capitals when he said the continent had to cease being an economic colony of Europe. Not only couldn't Lumumba be bought, but he signed his own death warrant when he turned to the Soviet Union for aid. A US National Security Council subcommittee on covert operations authorised his assassination.

It proved impossible to get close enough to Lumumba to shoot him. The CIA plotted his downfall by supporting anti-Lumumba factions in the Congolese government. Washington's choice to unseat the prime minister was Mobutu, then army chief of staff. The CIA conspired with Mobutu to have Lumumba murdered and then approvingly watched as he became ruler for life of Africa's second largest country.

The West richly rewarded their favourite dictator for getting rid of that nasty communist, Lumumba. The US gave him more than a billion dollars in civilian and military aid. European powers gave even more. Ronald Reagan received him at the White House several times and praised him as 'a voice of good sense and good will'. George Bush senior called him a 'valued friend'.

The man who had been christened Joseph Desiré Mobutu transmuted himself into Mobutu Sese Seko Koko wa za Banga. According to an official government translation, the name meant 'The All-Conquering Warrior Who, Because Of His Endurance And Inflexible Will To Win, Will Go From Conquest To Conquest Leaving Fire In His Wake'. He cut a flamboyant image with a leopard-skin cap perched at an angle on his head, and wasted little time immortalising himself. He labelled himself *The Messiah, The Sun President, The Guide.*

'What did you call Mobutu?' I asked Oggi.

'Father. For us, he was father.'

'And is it true,' I wanted to know, 'that bullets couldn't harm him?'

'Oh yes! Bullets just bounced off his body. You couldn't do anything to Mobutu. He had many enemies, but nobody could kill him.'

Oggi said that God's name had been replaced by that of Mobutu in some of the hymns the Congolese sang at church. 'The priests didn't like it, but there was nothing they could do. That is how powerful Mobutu was.'

In 1970, Mobutu engineered his *authenticité* programme in order to rid his country of the blemishes of colonialism. He dumped the name of Congo in favour of Zaire for both the country and the river. He named the country's biggest lake after himself. Stanleyville became Kisangani. He banned Christmas and neckties because they were 'un-African'.

Mobutu amassed his wealth according to what became the blueprint for African dictators – he snitched it and stashed it in offshore bank accounts and real estate. He plundered his country to such an extent that he spawned a new term in political philosophy: kleptocracy. From the moment he became president for life, he diverted revenues from copper, cobalt, diamonds, tin and zinc mines into his private Swiss and French bank accounts.

He pillaged the national coffers to the extent that the state virtually ceased to exist. Mobutu legitimised corruption and it became endemic in every sphere of life and at all levels of society. It was the only means by which those at the bottom of the ladder could survive and enabled those climbing to the top to grow rich along the way.

Mobutu's private fortune was estimated at $4 billion. Besides his eleven palaces in Zaire, he owned estates and villas all over Europe. He once despatched a government-owned jet more than thirty times to Venezuela to collect 5000 longhaired sheep for his ranch at his ancestral village of Gbadolite. It became known as the 'Versailles of Africa'. He regularly flew to Europe and America in a chartered French Concorde.

'If you want to steal, show a minimum of intelligence,' he told public servants at Kinshasa's sport stadium in the 1970s. 'If you steal too much [in order] to become rich overnight, you'll be caught.'

Unfortunately for Mobutu, his speech was broadcast on television and radio. Following an outcry, his aides said it had been misinterpreted and it was removed from later broadcasts. But it had been said.

By four o'clock on the afternoon that we met Oggi, we were at the boat with two taxicabs, loaded with our equipment and provisions. Freddy looked despondent. 'I have bad news, guys,' he said. 'Our papers have not been cleared yet. We will not leave today. But I'm sure we will go tomorrow.'

'What about the fifty dollars we paid you, Freddy?' I asked.

'Sorry guys, but it's already been paid to other people. There's nothing I can do.'

Of course he was lying, but for the moment there was nothing we could do. 'I want to speak to the captain,' I told him.

'He's with the customs people trying to clear the papers,' said Freddy.

'But he's been with the customs people for two days!'

'That's how it is,' Freddy said. 'There are lots of people we have to keep happy.'

Meanwhile, more leeches homed in on us. Several soldiers and customs officials were hanging around the boat waiting for the right moment to strike. We decided to 'commission' one or two soldiers at a generous fee to keep the others at bay.

The soldiers had not been paid for five months (their last salary had been $12) and the customs officials had been waiting eight months for their money. A young soldier who begged us for a piece of bread had lost the use of an arm to a piece of shrapnel. The limb was completely feeble and he couldn't carry the gun that would have empowered him to bully food from peasants. He had become a low-level scrounger. The hospital had run out of even the most basic painkillers and told him to travel to Kinshasa for an operation. He had no money to make the trip.

We returned to the Palm Beach Hotel. The clerk at reception had our rooms ready and laughed when he saw us. He obviously also knew that the boat would not leave as promised.

'Do you realise that we might never get onto a boat?' I asked Michael and

Jan over dinner that night. The Congo was an expensive place and every day in Kisangani increased our chances of going home empty-handed. We simply had to wait and hope the situation would soon improve.

It was frightening to imagine life in our steel capsule aboard an over-loaded, decrepit and smelly river boat. It had taken the *Tshopo* six weeks to reach Kisangani. It might well take just as long to get back to Kinshasa. When other journalists and adventurers travelled the river it was on faster, more reliable and relatively comfortable boats. The *Tshopo* was a hellhole.

There were only three ports along the way where we could leave the boat and fly back to Kinshasa: Bumba, Lisala and Mbandaka. Between them was nothing but jungle. Mbandaka was a sizeable town, but Lisala and Bumba were isolated and lawless outposts.

'What about the toilet?' I asked my colleagues.

'I had a look at it today,' Jan said.

'And?'

'How the fuck do you manage to get shit on the ceiling?' he growled. Jan and Michael were adamant they wouldn't go near the latrines. The boat docked from time to time at small villages and Jan said he'd wait for opportunities like that to seek relief in the bush. The dilemma was that a white man in rural Africa was something of a curiosity and was always followed by a host of onlookers.

I had another solution: a hunger strike. I told them I would eat a banana and a slice of pineapple every day and supplement my meagre diet with vitamin tablets I had brought along. That should keep nature under control.

After dinner there was a knock on the door. It was Oggi, who had rowed all the way from his village to Kisangani to come and see us. 'I am going with,' he announced. 'I'm not going to let you get onto that boat without me. I know these boats and I want to go to Kinshasa to fetch my mother.'

I had thought about hiring Oggi as a guide but was concerned about spending too much money. Useful as he was, Michael knew nothing about boats or the river. Oggi could be invaluable, and both Jan and Michael agreed that we should sign him on as the fourth member of our team. He there and then agreed to go and sleep on the boat to find out what was going on.

When we arrived at the fishing port the next morning, the *Tshopo* – and Oggi with it – was gone! It turned out the captain had moved the boat further downstream in the dark of night to avoid customs officials who were pressing him for port tax.

'Bad news,' Oggi said when we found him. 'We won't move today. And I don't think tomorrow either. The captain is trying to find money for the goods they lost when the one barge sank.'

Oggi had heard that there had been two accidents on the way up. 'They first hit a sandbank and then a rock. I don't think anybody died. I heard the captain is also looking for a new steersman to replace the one that crashed the boat.'

The boat was anchored in the shadow of a Roman Catholic mission – made famous by a visit from Pope John Paul II in the 1980s. We relocated from the Palm Beach Hotel to the church hostel in order to be near the boat. Oggi was sure the captain would leave virtually unannounced in order to elude the hungry customs officials.

The number of passengers on board had grown from 100 three days earlier to more than 300. People, luggage, baskets of dried fish, smoked monkey and goats took up virtually every inch of the deck. Oggi was bravely holding onto our black hole and had cordoned off an area of about four square metres with a rope.

The early morning sun was scorching down on the steel structure when we were called to meet the captain. To my surprise, Laurent Esperant could speak English. As a young man he had worked on a South African mine. He then studied medicine for several years, but had to abandon university when he ran out of money. He wasn't a professional skipper but had hired the tug and two barges in an attempt to get a transport business off the ground, sailing between Kinshasa and Kisangani. But he faced financial ruin after the barge ran aground on the voyage upstream to Kisangani. The hull was ripped open by a rock and much of the cargo of sugar got wet. Several people fell in the river, but all were rescued.

Laurent was trying to recoup his losses from us. 'Thousand dollars,' he demanded, 'and that includes the whole journey, the deck space and the cabin.'

'Oh come on, what cabin? This is not the *Queen Elizabeth*,' I told him. A few minutes later we settled on $250.

Oggi had by then made a frightening discovery. Our *cabine de luxe* was leaking water! The decaying hull was full of little holes plugged with wooden pegs. I should have had a closer look when I saw the water at the bottom when Freddy showed us the space a few days earlier.

'This boat is very dangerous,' Oggi said. 'Maybe it will not make Kinshasa.'

'Don't worry,' Laurent laughed. 'We have a big pump and I don't think too much water will get into the boat.'

Besides guarding our equipment, Oggi was given a new task: to scoop water from our hole and keep everything dry.

By the next morning the passengers were up in arms. The boat was moored near an army camp and during the night soldiers had sneaked on board and raided the passengers. The longer the boat lingered in Kisangani, the more leeches it attracted. The problem was that they were targeting us as well.

Our white skins protected Jan and me to some extent, but when Michael wandered off to take pictures of the harbour, he was duly arrested. We had to pay a spot fine of $30. Three men in civilian clothes then arrived in a car and identified themselves as secret police officers. They showed us a warrant – with an array of stamps – for Oggi's arrest for not having informed them that he was working for foreigners.

'And what law is that?' I asked them.

They shoved the warrant under my nose and threatened to take Oggi into custody. I had no doubt they had the authority to take him away and, if they so desired, make him disappear. Law and order in Kisangani was meted out over the barrel of a gun.

'What's the fine?' I asked them.

'Hundred dollars.'

'It's too much.'

We haggled them down to $30. They were cocky enough to allow us to film the whole exchange. In their eyes they had done absolutely nothing wrong and had merely supplemented their meagre income. Oggi stood a few metres away with tears in his eyes, and after they had left, said: 'Now you know how fucked up this country is! We have to live with this every day. Now you know what the Congo has become.'

After he had regained his composure, he said to me: 'Do you know where those people studied?

'No, where?'

'The Kisangani University of Corruption!'

At five the next afternoon, the *Tshopo*'s diesels rumbled to life. As we boarded the boat with our equipment, the passengers cheered. They knew with *mondeles* on board, the boat was sure to leave. The deck was by then already jammed with passengers, their children, their animals, their goods and their livestock.

Looking back at our decision to fare on the *Tshopo*, we must have been mad to get on board, but by then we felt we had no choice. Joseph Conrad wrote: 'I went a little farther, then still a little farther till I had gone so far that I don't know how I'll ever get back.'

As we edged away from the quay, people cheered from the shore, tinny Zairean reggae music blared from somewhere among the passengers and two young men gyrated to the rhythm on the roof of the tug. The atmosphere was festive, to be sure.

As the sun cast a saffron lick across the kilometre-wide river and Kisangani slipped out of sight, the forest enveloped us. Solid barriers of vegetation sprang up on both banks. Many of the big trees that Conrad wrote about were still kings, brooding noblemen on the shore, their sinewy and knobbly limbs slumped in the water.

And then, as the tangerine ball plunged below the horizon and night folded around us like black satin, the arrow-like profiles of pirogues loomed out of nowhere. From each village the *Tshopo* passed, pirogues carrying a couple of bare-chested young men and a woman or two between them would frantically paddle towards the boat. When they came alongside, one of them would throw down the paddle, jump onto the river boat and secure the pirogue. The women had crates of dried catfish, smoked monkey, maggots, bananas and an assortment of small, live animals that they traded for clothes, shoes, sugar and oil. This happened day and night.

The first few hours on the *Tshopo* were magical, exactly as I had imagined a voyage on the Congo. Travelling on or near the equator is a peculiar experience. Days are sliced almost perfectly in half: twelve hours of sunlight and twelve hours of darkness. Dawn and dusk are brief and intense and the sun rises and sets in colourful bursts.

We must have presented an outlandish sight to our Congolese travelling companions as we sipped from a bottle of French cognac that we'd procured from a Lebanese trader in Kisangani, with Jan's fan, connected to our murmuring portable generator, blowing cool air over us.

As the boat growled downriver through a black rainforest, two giant searchlights on the *Tshopo*'s roof came to life. These were the captain's night eyes, gleaming back and forth across the water in search of channel buoys that would guide him to deep, safe waters.

I had taken a sleeping pill and was nestled snugly between Jan and Michael on the deck when the boat suddenly jerked to a halt. The plastic sheeting we had rigged overhead for shelter was ripped loose and Michael was nearly cast overboard. Women screamed, babies cried and men cursed. The *Tshopo* had hit a sandbank.

Oggi scrambled from the cargo hold below the deck where he had been sleeping and asked anxiously: 'Are you okay?' We were in the middle of nowhere. A half-moon cast a flicker of light across the river. 'The new steersman obviously doesn't know what he's doing,' said Oggi. 'I don't think he's ever been on the river!' If the boat had run aground during the day, he said, scores of people would have been thrown off balance and might have broken arms or legs.

It took more than an hour to manoeuvre the boat off the sandbank and back on course. Jan, Michael and I stayed awake for the rest of the night. Hours later, I watched the sun raise its crown over the mist-covered river. The boat slowly came to life. A cacophony of radios blared, a goat bleated above the good-natured yelling of people and in the group next to us, a man triumphantly held aloft a monkey with a white tuft of hair and a red beard. It had been delivered by pirogue earlier that morning and was due to be butchered later in the day.

Monkey seemed to be the preferred dish and came both smoked and fresh. The animals were carried on board in bunches with their tails curled around their necks. I tried to ignore the doomed animals gasping for air and water while lying bound together on the blazing hot steel deck, awaiting their fate. Most landed up roasted or smoked. Their mouths and eyes were wide open and I couldn't help but think they had met their ends in sheer terror.

Oggi declined our offer of tinned meat and fish, opting instead to patronise the little food kiosks along the deck, where he ate monkey and thumb-sized white maggots that had been sautéed with onions. All over the boat, women in rainbow robes were frying little dough balls and pounding white roots into mash. People were washing themselves with water scooped from the river in plastic buckets. A few feet away our neighbour soaped his young son from head to toe, the child standing perfectly still in the hot and humid air.

Throughout the day, impromptu bars sprang up, serving palm wine and hot Primus beer. A hair salon opened for business near the stern, and somewhere even further to the rear, a makeshift slaughterhouse swung into operation. That was where our neighbour's monkey met its end. He returned with the carcass and spread it out over a fire to burn off the hair. It looked like a toddler on the grill. An hour or so later, our fellow traveller kindly offered to share his meal with us. Michael, Jan and I politely declined, but Oggi greedily gobbled down a chunk of meat.

Oggi told me he had once been on a boat where scores of passengers died of food poisoning after the kitchen on the barge had served up a rancid rice and monkey stew.

As our journey continued, I mused on the astonishing fact that all the waters of the Congo River and its tributaries, all the rainforest in its basin and all the people that subsisted on its shores had once belonged to a single man: a big-nosed and maniacal monarch by the name of King Leopold II of Belgium. He didn't just rule the Congo, he owned it!

The colonial history of Congo is the most grotesque in the scramble for Africa. The British explorer Henry Morton Stanley opened up the Congo in the 1870s by navigating its rivers. His expeditions set up Central Africa for European profiteering. The British regarded the area as of no value, and in 1885, King Leopold took over the territory through which Stanley had travelled, named it the Congo Free State and ran it as his private estate.

The invention of the motor car had led to an unquenchable demand for rubber. Leopold set up a series of river stations and rubber plantations along the Congo River. It was a brutal operation, and historians estimate that up to eight million people died in what became known as the 'rubber terror'. Every village had to provide four labourers a year to work for the Free State as full-time slaves. Villagers who defaulted on their quotas were lashed, raped or had their hands and penises cut off.

Joseph Conrad branded it the 'vilest scramble for loot that ever disfigured the history of human conscience'. Evidence of Leopold's operations eventually reached the power echelons of Europe, and in 1908 the king was forced to hand over the Congo to the Belgian government. It became a colony until, along with the rest of Africa, the Congolese people demanded independence. It came in 1960 as an ungovernable brew of 200 tribes.

'Those who are conquered, always want to imitate the conqueror in his main characteristics,' wrote Adam Hochschild in *King Leopold's Ghost*. 'Consider Mobutu again. Aside from the colour of his skin, there were very few ways in which he did not resemble the monarch who governed the same territory a hundred years earlier. His one-man rule. His great wealth taken from the land. His appropriation of state possessions as his own.'

Mobutu acquired one of the finest chateaux in France, the pink-and-white-marble-colonnaded Villa del Mare at Roquebrune-Cap-Martin on the Riviera. Complete with indoor and outdoor swimming pools, gold-fitted bathrooms and decorated with Louis XV furnishings, Hochschild pointed out that it was only a stone's throw from the equally ostentatious estates Leopold had once owned at Cap Ferrat. One cape can be seen from the other.

By the end of the second day, our initial enchantment with our Congo River boat journey had dissipated. Blaine Harden spoke in his book about boats that approached 'human-barnyard gridlock' and one that became 'a garrulous whore in a gloomy church'. So did ours. People and livestock – alive and dead, smoked and dried, fresh and rotting – were everywhere. The smell of the boat was unforgettable. It was a mix of smoked fish, roast monkey, half-rotten meat, diesel fumes, urine, unwashed bodies, and animal and human excrement.

On a professional level, Jan and Michael were fantastic. They were up and down the boat, fighting their way with the camera and the tripod through the walls of bodies and goods. Every time a pirogue secured itself to the *Tshopo* and yet another strange forest animal was thrown on board for lunch or dinner, I would call to Jan: 'Did you see that? Did you get it?'

'How many more fucking monkeys do you want me to film?' he snapped back, sweat rolling off him. 'We've got hours of it.'

It was Jan who first noticed that our barge was drifting unevenly in the water. 'Something is wrong,' he said. 'It's taking water,' said Oggi. Minutes later, pandemonium broke out as crew members scrambled onto our barge with a generator and a pump. Our neighbours had to evacuate their section of the barge. It had five compartments – including ours, where the holes were sealed with wooden pegs – of which two were completely flooded.

'If another compartment gets flooded, we'll sink. Look how low in the water we are,' Jan said as a thick stream of water spewed out of the pump. He was probably right. The crew continued to pump water out of the barge throughout the night and the next morning.

Laurent was suddenly not as buoyant as before. 'The boat is not so safe,' he admitted. 'But I think we'll reach Bumba tomorrow morning. We have to trust in God. Don't worry, I think we'll make it.'

Oggi was not as optimistic. 'We might die on the river. I might not see my children again,' he said. 'There's a dangerous stretch with lots of islands. If we hit a sandbank again, we'll go down.'

None of us – or any of the passengers – thought about sleep as we entered our third night on the river. Though Laurent knew the *Tshopo* was in a perilous state, he had taken on more and more passengers during the day and every square inch of deck was crammed with people, animals and goods. It was an indictment of how poor people are forced to travel in one of the world's least developed yet potentially richest countries. The known and untapped natural resources of the Congo are worth a king's ransom, but the vast majority of its inhabitants subsist in dire poverty.

As the half-moon rose above the forest, the *Tshopo* sailed forth into the night. 'This is a big mistake,' Oggi said. 'There's islands, and the steersman doesn't know the river. If we sink tonight, the crocodiles will eat all of us.'

After an hour or so we saw the outline of land and bush in the moonlight. The searchlights were scanning the shores for the markers while one of the crew members stood on the front toilet's roof with a torch, giving directions to the steersman.

I rushed to the tug to speak to Laurent. He was drinking beer with Freddy in his crummy cabin and reeked like a canteen. His eyes had the colour of blood oranges in the dim light. 'You have to stop the boat!' I pleaded with him. 'We're in danger!'

He laughed. 'Don't worry! Everything is fine. There's no problem! Enjoy the ride.'

I was getting nowhere with him and went back to our space on the deck. The passengers were petrified. Nobody was cooking, playing music or drinking. The only sound was the diesels pushing the boat towards the islands.

'Crocodiles!' Jan said at one point. I refused to look, although it was common knowledge that the river was infested with the beasts. Jan swore he saw their eyes blink in the water and that they were colossal.

The four of us peered into the night when Oggi pointed ahead of him. In the faint moonlight we made out the silhouette of two small islands. Between them was a narrow gap. It looked hardly big enough for the boat to get through, but the *Tshopo* was steering straight towards the channel.

'The man is mad,' Oggi said. 'Here comes a big problem.'

I had never been scared in my life. Not in Rwanda, Sudan, Ethiopia, Eritrea, Algeria, Sierra Leone, Burundi or anywhere else. But that night on the *Tshopo*, I thought I might die. There was a real chance that we would hit an island or a sandbank and be dropped into the hungry jaws of crocodiles.

We headed at full speed (about fifteen kilometres per hour) for the islands. Several people started screaming, and the watchman with the torch frantically waved his left arm up and down. At the very last moment the steersman veered to the left in an attempt to miss the island. It was too late. I was sure we were going to crash into it. I instinctively got up and braced myself for the impact.

We ploughed through a huge clump of floating water hyacinths attached to the island. The boat creaked and moaned as its bottom scraped the surface. Then we burst into the plant undergrowth that hung over the river. Leaves brushed our faces. A branch ripped off plastic sheeting at the back of the boat. For a moment it felt as if the *Tshopo* was stuck in the shallow waters and entangled in the overgrowth. Then the diesels propelled the boat through the shrubbery, and with the barges creaking and croaking, we burst into open water.

There was a commotion on board. Passengers were on their feet and bawling abuse at the captain and the crew. 'The boat has to stop! We can't carry on!' Oggi said feverishly. 'Do something, please! There's more islands!'

I told Jan to come with me. We were ready to lead a mutiny. Laurent stood outside his cabin, wobbly on his feet. 'Stop this fucking boat!' I screamed at him. He heaved himself out of his drunken stupor and stared at us. 'We are going to sink!' I told him. Jan stepped forward and ominously towered over him.

I took out Ambassador Mpoko's *lettre de recommendation* and shoved it in his face. 'Have you seen this letter yet?'

He shook his head. I raved on: 'This is a letter from your ambassador in my country. It says that your President Kabila has invited us to come to your country to film the river.' I pushed my finger against his chest. 'Do you know what will happen to you if this boat sinks tonight?'

He shook his head as I continued: 'You will sit for the rest of your miserable fucking life in prison!'

'You will stop the boat now!' Jan barked. 'Now!'

Esperant kept silent for a moment or two. 'Okay, okay,' he slurred, 'I'll stop the boat. We will stop for the night.'

A short while later we dropped anchor next to one of the islands. Within seconds, swarms of mosquitoes descended on the boat. We doused ourselves in repellent and spread our mattresses on the deck. I didn't close an eye. It was my third night without sleep.

When we discussed the incident the next morning, we discovered that Jan and I had plotted exactly the same escape in the event of a crash. I reckoned that should the boat hit land, I would throw myself off the deck and scramble up the riverbank in order to avoid the crocodiles. But should we sink and be dumped in the water, I thought it imperative to get away from the sinking craft and its squirming and horror-struck human load as quickly as possible That was obviously where the crocodiles would head. I reckoned the secret of survival was to keep myself afloat and quietly drift downstream away from the calamity, until I could paddle to shore. Jan had had exactly the same plan!

A joyous ovation erupted on board the *Tshopo* as Bumba came into view. Reggae blared, youngsters danced and everybody smiled. Oggi beamed from ear to ear. 'We've made it,' he said.

'Yes, we have,' I answered him. 'Is there a hotel in Bumba?'

'Oh yes, a very good one. I stayed there with tourists. Lots of cold beer.'

'Let's hope it still exists,' I said.

Jan and Michael filmed our docking. As we gathered our equipment, armed soldiers boarded the *Tshopo* and headed straight for us. A sinewy, narrow-eyed man with a fiendish face accompanied them. He spelt trouble. He spoke to Michael as the soldiers formed a circle around us.

'Bad news, guys,' Michael said. 'We've been arrested.'

'What for?' I asked the sinewy man.

'There is a serious problem,' he said with a twisted little smile. '*Un grand probléme. Trés, trés sérieux!*'

We followed him to a dingy office at the back of the harbour. He slumped into his chair and looked at us with a perverse sneer on his face. He was a repugnant character, and I could imagine him torturing, raping and killing with grotesque abandon.

He spoke and Michael translated. 'You have committed a very serious crime. *Trés, trés sérieux!* You have filmed the harbour and that is not allowed.'

I showed him the ambassador's letter. He threw it back at me. 'Here in Bumba,' he snarled, 'I'm the chief of security. I'm the FBI of Bumba! Here we work like the FBI.'

'If we have broken the law,' I said courteously, 'is there a fine we can pay?'

'I am afraid not,' he said. 'You have committed a serious offence. *Trés, trés sérieux!*'

I had no fear of being locked up. I'd been to the Congo enough times to know that *Monsieur FBI* was merely setting us up and stringing us along for a bigger bribe. In the meantime his friend, who introduced himself as the head of customs, also arrived and was inspecting our equipment. He demanded our customs papers and started checking the serial numbers of every piece of equipment against our declared list. He shrieked in delight when he found a mistake. The secretary who had typed the list had swapped around two numbers. They now had us on two offences.

'*Trés, trés sérieux!*' said the customs man. This leech was now also eligible for a healthy gulp of blood.

The FBI man could see we were fatigued, unwashed and hungry, but launched into a lengthy lecture about security in the Congo and the perils of travelling around without the proper documentation. At five o'clock, he said: 'I'll allow you to go to the hotel now, but you must report to me at nine tomorrow morning so that we can determine what to do with you.'

'Thank you very much, sir,' I said.

'Would you in the meantime be so kind as to buy us a cold drink?' he asked. I gave him $10.

'And I have to phone Kinshasa to report to my superiors,' he said. I gave him another $10.

Bumba was nothing more than a riverside post set at the edge of the jungle – and the world, it seemed. It was sort of an equatorial Pofadder or Putsonder-water. It had taken a terrible beating during the war and there was no water or electricity. A report from Amnesty International mentioned that thousands of civilians wounded and traumatised during the war remained without adequate medical care. Some still had not had shrapnel removed from their bodies. The banks had been looted and businesses cleaned out.

Little had remained of Oggi's tourist hotel. It was dirty and dilapidated. The windows were covered in only gauze and the doors didn't lock. The next aeroplane to Kinshasa was not due for four days. Until then we were at the mercy of Bumba's FBI.

We reported at nine the next morning. 'The crime you committed is serious. *Trés, trés sérieux!*' the FBI man ranted again. 'But because you are foreigners, we are not going to charge you. We will allow you to pay a fine.'

'Thank you, sir,' I said.

'*Que c'est sérieux!*' said the customs official. 'You broke the law by making a false declaration and you will have to pay a fine.'

We paid each of them $50. Later that morning we were invited for tea with the governor of the area. He lived in a ruined colonial villa on the edge of the water. I was scared another bribe was looming, but was pleasantly surprised by a grey-haired and polite gentleman dressed in a threadbare and shiny black suit with a broad, multicoloured tie. He offered us tea, welcomed us to his town and apologised for the behaviour of his officials. If we had any further problems, he said, we should let him know.

The rest of our stay in Bumba was rather uneventful, except for withered-looking soldiers looking at us with famished eyes. When a gun-toting boy attempted to arrest us at the market for filming catfish as big as grown men, monkeys tied to poles, dehydrated crocodiles with bound jaws, and rotting buck and buffalo meat, we literally told him to fuck off and go speak to the governor.

We found a woman running a makeshift restaurant from her house and she barbecued us chicken. A scruffy and suspicious-looking Lebanese trader had bottles of lukewarm Spanish wine and chocolate cookies on his shelves. By late afternoon, purple-bellied clouds rolled in over the forest and at night I lay awake in my bed listening to the sound of thunder and equatorial storms pounding the river.

Laurent Esperant sought our company at every possible opportunity to scrounge beer and lament his financial predicament. He didn't have insurance and was ruined, he said. The leaking barge on which we had travelled would have to be left behind in Bumba. Since he had delivered us safely, he pleaded, was there any possibility of supplementing the meagre fare he had charged us for a cabin and passage on his boat? I took a swig of ice-cold beer and ignored his pleas.

The passengers on the *Tshopo* were once again stranded. The boat was going to be docked in Bumba for God knows how long. For passengers it was next to impossible to find out what was going on or why.

Oggi had lost his enthusiasm for the journey. A bigger barge had in the meantime arrived from Kinshasa and was docked in Bumba for a day or two. Oggi wanted to take it back to Kisangani.

As we waited a few days later for the Canadian Buffalo cargo plane to land on the gravel strip to ferry us back to the luxury of Kinshasa, the FBI man and his customs friend showed up at the airport. As they were about to pounce on us for a last-minute fine, the governor arrived to bid us farewell. They retreated to a corner and stared at us with hungry eyes and hangdog faces.

'Oggi's going to have problems,' Jan said.

'Why?'

'Because they know he's staying behind and that we must have paid him.'

'Are you going to be okay?' I asked Oggi. That morning I had given him our agreed fee plus a handsome bonus, our mattresses, mosquito nets, the fan and food.

He had already booked a berth on the new boat and found a place on the deck to sleep. He said the boat was clean, organised and the captain was competent.

'I'll be fine. Don't worry.'

An hour or so later, the aircraft landed in a cloud of red dust. I gave Oggi a hug and we were off.

We spent another week in Kinshasa before flying back to Johannesburg courtesy of Hewa Bora. In contrast to our journey to the Congo, the aeroplane was empty. We had bought a bottle of cognac at the airport and were in buoyant mood.

Some time after our documentary was broadcast, I received a phone call from a British journalist who was on his way to the Congo to commemorate the centennial of Henry Stanley's death by attempting to travel in his footsteps. He had seen our piece on the Congo and wanted to get hold of Oggi to use him as a guide. I told him where Oggi could be found.

Weeks later, I received an envelope that had been posted in London. It was a one-page letter that Oggi had written in Kisangani and asked the British journalist to post.

> Dear Mr Jacques
> I am indebted to you for providing my name for further employment. It was a great success and I thank you and God so that I can send my children back to school.
>
> Everything is fine and we have enough to eat. There is also peace for now in Kisangani.
>
> I however regret to inform you of a great tragedy that struck me when you left Bumba. It was a great loss that pained me for a long time and I know that you will share it with me.
>
> It happened on that day that you and Mister Jan and Mister Michael left. That man from the military and his friend and two soldiers came on the boat during the night. They arrested me and they took me off the boat to that office where I was with you and Mister Jan and Mister Michael.
>
> They said I stole all the stuff you gave me. I said no, you gave to me as a present but they didn't believe. They found the 450 dollars you paid me and said it was also stolen. I said no it was money I worked for. They said it was a lie and they will keep it. I fought hard but they were too many and the one soldier hit me with his rifle.
>
> They let me go but I left Bumba with nothing. They said if I tell anyone they will kill me. I had no more food, no water, no blanket. I was scared of them.
>
> The boat left in the afternoon. For four days I had nothing to eat and slept badly at night. I found here and there something to eat but it was not enough.

I came home with nothing. The children cried because I promised them things that I could not buy.

But then God blessed me and I found this new employment. Thank you for that. Everybody is happy now and life is fine.

Will you please, Mister Jacques, every time you hear of someone coming to Kisangani give them my name and tell them that I am a knowledgeable and good guide?

You will like to know that the *Tshopo* was still in Bumba when I left. When I got to Kisangani it was still there. I don't think it will leave.

Greetings to Mister Jan and Mister Michael. It was an honour to be your guide and I hope you agree to use me again in future.

Your good guide and friend,

Oggi Saidi.

Epilogue

I have spent half my life trying to get away from journalism, but I'm still mired in it – a low trade and a habit worse than heroin, a strange, seedy world full of misfits and drunkards and failures.

– Hunter S Thompson

O N A SATURDAY NIGHT IN OCTOBER 2004, I STAGGERED TO MY feet and stumbled ten or twenty metres towards a stage. My name had just been announced as South Africa's Journalist of the Year and I had to collect a framed certificate and a prodigious amount of money. I did well to even reach the stage, shook several hands, and firmly clutched the certificate and the cheque.

Over a period of about fifteen years, I've won a host of local and international awards. Some colleagues and critics have accused me of making a business out of nabbing journalism's gold. True or not, some awards – especially those bestowed on me by my peers – have been sincerely cherished, and in the process I've pocketed a small fortune. The monetary rewards have enabled me to travel far and wide and parts of this book were written in places such as Vietnam, Cambodia and Madagascar.

But, it also has to be said, along the way I acquired a rather notorious reputation for my behaviour at award functions. At the October 2004 shindig, the chairman of the judging panel asked me to say a few words. It was a fatal mistake that he and an audience of eminent media personalities would deeply regret. I was sloshed out of my skull and let rip with a spate of execrable dribble. The standard was set for what became a custom whenever I was called to a platform to collect booty.

Long before the announcement crowning our three-month investigation into heroin smuggling through east and southern Africa – deemed by the judges to represent a new benchmark for current affairs television in South Africa – I had been overcome by trepidation and anxiety and had taken refuge in the bottles of wine on the table. I have no fear of speaking at a conference or lecturing students, but as soon as I have to get onto a stage, my mental constitution revolts against the attention and praise. Out jumps a ghoul who gobbles down anything alcoholic in sight.

Once I was up there and standing in front of the microphone – goggle-eyed and soused – I couldn't stop talking. I rambled on about Jan's artistry, my researcher's bravery and the nasty scourge of drugs. The chief judge of the awards, Phil Molefe – a former colleague and a dear friend – stood behind me. At some point, he whispered: 'Jacques, that's enough! Stop now!' I ignored him, continued to the point of exhaustion and only then relinquished my position on centre stage.

A few days later I received an e-mail. It said: 'You don't know who I am but I was at the awards on Saturday night. I don't know what you discovered in Mozambique or Tanzania, but some of it obviously found its way into your lungs or veins. That's the only way to explain the nonsense you spoke.'

My worst embarrassment had occurred a few years earlier when I travelled to the Italian resort town of Riccione to receive a major television documentary award. Somebody phoned me to say I had won an *Ilaria Alpi* for a documentary about the head of apartheid's chemical and biological warfare programme, Dr Wouter Basson. I needed little persuasion to travel to Italy and was on an aircraft a few days later.

The ceremony in the town hall was a rather jolly affair with a rowdy audience, flowing wine and plates of scrumptious antipasti. I'm still not sure why I won an award introduced to honour an Italian journalist who had died in Somalia, as the entire ceremony was – obviously – in Italian. My translator for the evening was the mayor's luscious daughter, a university student majoring in English. And although I didn't mind her whispering her sweet breath into my ear, her mastery of the language was not her best attribute. I couldn't make out what she was saying.

As the evening wore on – and it went on forever – I grew more and more anxious and threw back glass after glass of frascati. I could feel myself slipping away. I eventually wobbled onto the stage – translator in tow – way after midnight. I think everybody was plastered and rather rowdy by then. I accepted my award, received a standing ovation and was asked to speak. Instead of uttering a few words of gratitude and getting off the stage as quickly as possible, I rambled – and rambled. The mayor's daughter was desperately trying to keep up, but I didn't really give her an opportunity to tell the audience what I was saying. Halfway through my diatribe I could see some people leaving the hall. Then they started talking. And finally, someone clapped. When at last I stepped down, I threw back another frascati, went back to my hotel and left Riccione very early the next morning.

The same thing happened at every other award ceremony where my work was recognised. When I was named for the second year running as Africa's Journalist of the Year, I stumbled on to the stage without having prepared or thought about anything to say. I never expected a white man entering middle age to win again, so I stood dumbfounded behind the microphone for a second or two and then ripped loose: 'Winning again is like sex: it's always better the second time around!' Even in my intoxicated state I could feel the audience cringing.

A row of my awards is showcased at *Special Assignment*'s office; others are kept at my mother's house, while a few are gathering dust in plastic bags and boxes in my garage. Some date back more than ten years, and one of the reasons for this significant collection of accolades is that I've been a journalist for more than two decades.

In December 2004, I was in the exquisite city of Porto in northern Portugal to do a month-long language course. I had won an award that offered me a scholarship to study whatever I desired. I flunked out after only one or two lessons and instead embarked on a glorious voyage around the Iberian peninsula. Feeling guilty about wasting Dutch taxpayers' money (they sponsored my study trip), I started scribbling notes about the Congo river boat journey.

Almost two years later, as I was finishing this book, I was sitting with Max du Preez at the glorious Polana Hotel in Maputo when he turned to me and said: 'Do you realise you're one of the oldest working journalists in South Africa?'

We were in the Mozambican capital for the annual CNN African Journalist of the Year awards, sipping on *caparinhas* and nibbling on prawn cocktails when he added: 'If not *the* oldest!'

I momentarily froze, took a long gulp of my icy rum-and-lime cocktail and thought: 'That's fantastic! I'm proud of myself!'

I am at an age where most of my peers have long been promoted to editors or left the profession altogether to pursue more lucrative careers. Some have become businessmen, others Scorpion law enforcers and some lawyers. Max was much younger than me when he started his own newspaper. Anton Harber, also relishing the CNN freebie with Max and me in Maputo, had edited the *Weekly Mail* for a decade and a half and was my age when he was appointed a journalism professor at Wits.

I've never had any ambition to be an editor or to sit behind a desk making decisions. If I am to remain a journalist, it has to be in the field. I often feel I'm tired of journalism and wouldn't mind opening a beach bar or a restaurant, or, like Max, retiring to a quaint southern Cape village to write books.

Every time I feel – as Renton would have said in *Trainspotting* – that I've arrived at the final stop of my journalistic junket, a new idea pops up that propels me to the next station on my hack's journey.

As I write, Jan de Klerk and I are planning to venture into Liberia, Africa's oldest republic but better known for its long-running, ruinous civil war in the nineties and early 2000s that reduced the country to an economic disaster, overrun with weapons. Corruption is rife and unemployment and illiteracy are endemic. In a country with a population of fewer than four million, around 250 000 people were killed in the war and many thousands more fled the fighting.

It's one of those bloodstained spots on the African map that my mother would have difficulty locating. I can already hear her asking: 'Why on earth do you want to go there?'

Despite its turbulent history and battered people, Liberia holds a promise. In October 2005, Liberians flocked to the polls and voted into power an erudite politician who adopted the popular moniker 'The Iron Lady'.

I became intrigued and to a certain sense captivated by the resilience and charisma of Liberian president Ellen Johnson Sirleaf, who drew much of her support from women voters and from Liberia's small but educated elite. If there is one person who can restore peace and dignity to Liberia, it might be this Harvard-educated widow and mother of four.

Once jailed by tyrant Charles Taylor and almost executed, she tackled her country's legacy head-on and established a truth and reconciliation commission modelled on South Africa's. Whether Johnson will succeed in forcing cannibals, warlords and blood-diamond merchants to the confessional, only time will tell.

I had negotiated with one of Johnson's advisors to spend several days with Her Excellency in the hope of getting a close and intimate look at Africa's first elected female president. The question I would most like to ask her is: How do you plan to turn this mess around?

But I would also want to get under the skins of those who reduced the nation to rubble and plundered its wealth and hacked their countrymen to pieces and literally ate their flesh.

Jan has been murmuring for months about the softer and subtler lighting he wants to direct on the president and how he would juxtapose it with a harsher light on the perpetrators.

It's difficult to get to Liberia, as virtually no international airlines fly into the capital of Monrovia. I worked out a route that would take us via the Senegalese capital of Dakar, where we would board an aircraft operated by Slok Air of Gambia and make several stops en route before landing at Roberts International Airport, situated about forty kilometres outside Monrovia.

It would suit us just fine to fly via Dakar. The city is host to an offshore island called Gorée, once a major slave-trading centre through which millions of Africans passed on their forced journey to the New World. The *Maison des Esclaves* (House of Slaves) on the island has become a place of pilgrimage for everyone to reflect upon the horrors of the trade and the millions of souls who died because of it. Slok is erratic, and no doubt we would have to spend a few days in Dakar, giving us time to explore this World Heritage Site.

Monrovia remains without electricity and running water and still reeks of the mess that Charles Taylor left behind when he fled to Nigeria. Officials are underpaid and impoverished and no doubt they would smack their lips at the sight of two waxen-faced hacks in their benighted country. Liberia is littered with the brutal legacy of Taylor's storm troopers, traumatised and desperate boy-soldiers and their mutilated victims.

I've been told it's the kind of place you want to run away from.

It holds the promise of a great adventure, a captivating story and an invaluable learning experience. It's precisely where I want to go.

The Norwegian philosopher Søren Kierkegaard once said that journalists are the sewage disposals of society. If that's true, my hands are probably dirtier than most. A colleague recently wrote of me that I don't just collect the toilet buckets, but that I scratch around in the contents, turn them over and illuminate the excrement with my camera lights.

Few South Africans have done more investigative journalism. Fewer still have seen what I have seen and been where I have been in Africa. I'm way past forty and still scratching around in toilet buckets. And you know what? For as long as there are devils left to dance with, I wouldn't have it any other way.

References

CHAPTER 5

p. 67   Nyarubuye haunted everyone who went there ...: BBC, 7 June 2001.

p. 67   There was certainly no shortage of bloodletting ...: Human Rights
         Watch, 1999.

p. 68   On the hills of Biserero in western Rwanda, 50 000 Tutsi ...: Human
         Rights Watch, 1999.

p. 68   As the western resort town of Gisenyi was cleared of Tutsis ...: *Guardian*,
         2 December 1999.

p. 69   Most African countries are multi-tribal ...: Ryszard Kapuściński,
         The Shadow of the Sun.

p. 69   Juvénal Habyarimana, a Hutu, staged a coup d'état in 1973 ...: Human
         Rights Watch, 1999; Ryszard Kapuściński, *The Shadow of the Sun*.

p. 72   It is important to understand who the killers were ...: *Sunday Independent*,
         22 April 2001; Philip Gourevitch, *We Wish to Inform You that Tomorrow
         We Will Be Killed with Our Families: Stories from Rwanda*.

p. 72   Preparations for the 'cleansing' of Rwanda began ...: Ryszard Kapuściński,
         The Shadow of the Sun.

p. 72   The genocide was a true team effort, and as such ...: *Sunday Independent*,
         22 April 2001.

p. 73   Never was it truer that evil triumphed ...: Philip Gourevitch, *We Wish to
         Inform You that Tomorrow We Will Be Killed with Our Families*; Roméo
         Dallaire, *Shake Hands with the Devil: The Failure of Humanity in Rwanda*.

p. 73   Top of their list was Prime Minister ...: Human Rights Watch, 1999.

p. 74   Two days into the genocide ...: Roméo Dallaire, *Shake Hands with the Devil*.

p. 74   Some 500 Tsutsis had sought refuge ...: Linda Melvern, *A People Betrayed:
         The Role of the West in Rwanda's Genocide*.

p. 75   An African himself, he reckoned ...: Linda Melvern, *A People Betrayed*.

p. 75   With foreign embassies closed ...: Human Rights Watch, 1999.

p. 75   The genocide was preceded by a stockpiling ...: Philip Gourevitch, *We
         Wish to Inform You that Tomorrow We Will Be Killed with Our Families*.

p. 79   General Dallaire needed 100 armoured personnel carriers to be ...:
         Roméo Dallaire, *Shake Hands with the Devil*.

p. 79   The Ecole Technique Officielle (ETO) was a ...: African Rights, April 2001.

p. 80   The refugees settled on lava rock that stretched ...: Philip Gourevitch, *We
         Wish to Inform You that Tomorrow We Will Be Killed with our Families*.

p. 82   **Although the UNHCR administered the camps ...**: Philip Gourevitch, *We Wish to Inform You that Tomorrow We Will Be Killed with Our Families.*

p. 83   **General Dallaire realised the camps had become ...**: Roméo Dallaire, *Shake Hands with the Devil.*

p. 86   **In March 1998, American president Bill Clinton ...**: Philip Gourevitch, *We Wish to Inform You that Tomorrow We Will Be Killed with Our Families.*

CHAPTER 6

p. 87   **He was editor of the newspaper *Kangura* ...**: Philip Gourevitch, *We Wish to Inform You that Tomorrow We Will Be Killed with Our Families.*

p. 88   **In 1990, the Tutsi-dominated RPF invaded the country ...**: Philip Gourevitch, *We Wish to Inform You that Tomorrow We Will Be Killed with Our Families.*

p. 90   **They almost succeeded, and in the space of a hundred days ...**: Philip Gourevitch, *We Wish to Inform You that Tomorrow We Will Be Killed with Our Families*; *Sunday Independent*, 22 April 2001.

p. 91   **Tutsis were killed simply because they were born Tutsi ...**: Philip Gourevitch, *We Wish to Inform You that Tomorrow We Will Be Killed with Our Families*; Human Rights Watch 1999; Linda Melvern, *A People Betrayed.*

p. 94   **Radio des Milles Collines directed the killings ...**: Philip Gourevitch, *We Wish to Inform You that Tomorrow We Will Be Killed with Our Families*; Human Rights Watch, 1999.

p. 94   **As bodies accumulated next to the roads ...**: Human Rights Watch, 1999.

p. 95   **The world preferred to ignore compelling evidence ...**: Human Rights Watch, 1999.

p. 95   **The killings were more intense and effective ...**: Philip Gourevitch, *We Wish to Inform You that Tomorrow We Will Be Killed with Our Families*; Human Rights Watch, 1999.

p. 96   **Years later, then UN Secretary General Boutros Boutros-Ghali ...**: Linda Melvern, *A People Betrayed.*

p. 97   **According to Valentina, Gacumbitsi said ...**: Testimony of Valentina Izibagiza, Survivors Fund, 2000.

p. 97   **As night fell, only a few hundred had been killed ...**: Philip Gourevitch, *We Wish to Inform You that Tomorrow We Will Be Killed with Our Families*; Human Rights Watch, 1999.

p. 99   **With all the Tutsis gone, talk in the village was ...**: Human Rights Watch 1999.

p. 100   **As the RPG reached Kibungo, a quarter of a million ...**: Philip Gourevitch, *We Wish to Inform You that Tomorrow We Will Be Killed with Our Families.*

p. 102   **Sheer numbers overwhelmed the country's legal system ...**: Internews Rwanda, 6 November 2004.

p. 102 One of the first witnesses against Gacumbitsi …: Internews Rwanda, 6 November 2004.

p. 103 BBC journalist Fergal Keane was one of the first to show …: PBS Frontline, 1997.

CHAPTER 7

p. 106 The complicity of men and women of the cloth …: African Rights, 2 December 1998.

p. 107 He made no secret of his aversion to Tutsis …: African Rights, 6 April 1999.

p. 107 A mother superior and a nun at a convent in Sovu …: *The Cross and the Genocide*, Afrol News, November 2001.

p. 107 The two nuns were eventually arrested under new law …: *The Economist*, 16 June 2001.

p. 108 No less compromised was the Anglican archbishop …: Human Rights Watch, 1999; *Guardian*, 3 April 2004.

p. 108 At the height of the slaughter, Nsengiyumva …: *Guardian*, 3 April 2004.

p. 108 Seromba walked away from the bloodstained earth …: *New York Times*, 12 May 2002; African Rights, 2 November 1999.

p. 109 Fulgence and Lingo stayed in the forest for a week …: Internews Rwanda, 6 November 2004.

p. 110 It wasn't long before the human rights organisation …: African Rights, 2 December 1998.

p. 110 In June 1999, a Rwandan military tribunal convicted …: US Department of State, 23 February 2000.

p. 111 Professor Mugabo was a physician at the University …: *Rwanda – Not so Innocent*, African Rights, August 1995.

p. 111 In 1998, Rwanda was internationally castigated …: BBC, 22 April 1998; Amnesty International, 1998.

p. 112 Mugabo was fingered by survivors …: *Mail & Guardian*, 23 April 1999.

p. 123 On a Thursday in April 2001, more than eight months …: Episcopal News Service, 7 May 2001.

p. 124 Wearing episcopal robes at his first court appearance …: ICTR press release, 27 April 2001.

CHAPTER 10

p. 181 The book also said that down below lived herdsman …: Blaine Harden, *Africa: Dispatches from a Fragile Continent.*

p. 183 During the colonial era, Britain ruled Sudan …: Ryszard Kapuściński, *The Shadow of the Sun.*

p. 183 In 1983, a career colonel, John Garang, organised the Sudan People's Liberation Army …: Blaine Harden, *Africa: Dispatches from a Fragile Continent*; Ryszard Kapuściński, *The Shadow of the Sun.*

p. 184   Since the outbreak of civil war, government had barely existed ...:
Ryszard Kapuściński, *The Shadow of the Sun*; Blaine Harden, *Africa:
Dispatches from a Fragile Continent.*

p. 184   The number of victims in the Sudanese calamity ...: *Washington Post,*
6 July, 2002; *Guardian,* 4 May 1998; Inter-Church Coalition on Africa,
March 2000; *Crimes of War,* April 2002.

p. 186   Bol was a former army colonel who in 1983 led the mutiny ...:
Human Rights Watch, 23 July 1998.

p. 187   Aid agencies agreed that Bol's prints ...: Amnesty International, 1998;
Human Rights Watch, May 1998.

p. 189   The Dinka, sinewy, tall and dark-skinned, were once ...: Blaine Harden,
Africa: Dispatches from a Fragile Continent; *Courier-Journal,*
14 November 2005.

p. 190   As night fell, a bull's horn and the thump ...: *Washington Post,*
24 August 1997.

p. 194   Said French writer Antoine de Saint-Exupéry ...: Aidan Hartley,
The Zanzibar Chest: A Memoir of Love and War.

p. 195   Khartoum was a typical Arab city: noisy, dusty ...: Blaine Harden,
Africa: Dispatches from a Fragile Continent.

p. 196   Sudan implemented Sharia law in its purest form ...: *The Scotsman,*
18 January 2004.

p. 197   Not long after our return from Sudan ...: *East African,* 22 September 1999.

p. 197   In the meantime, however, a vast tract of land in the west ...: BBC News,
10 April 2004; *Guardian,* 30 March 2005, 3 June 2005; *The Economist,*
12 April 2001.

p. 198   In 1999, when NATO went to war against Slobodan ...: *Guardian,*
30 March 2005.

p. 198   Evidence of cruelty in Darfur piled up in report ...: *The Economist,*
13 May 2004.

CHAPTER 11

p. 199   The erstwhile photographer and lowly army corporal ...: *Cornerstone*
magazine, Vol. 29, Issue 119, 2000.

p. 200   Profiling Sankoh and Bockarie, the *Washington Post* said ...: *Washington
Post* magazine, 9 January 2000.

p. 201   The broker of the Lomé Peace Accord ...: *Insight* magazine, 25 July 2003.

p. 201   The cherry on Jesse's rotten fruitcake was the appointment ...: *Insight*
magazine, 25 July 2003.

p. 201   Suddenly a war criminal rubbed shoulders with world ...: CNN,
12 May 2000.

p. 203   The son of a peasant farmer, Foday Sankoh had received ...: BBC News,
12 May 2000; *Washington Post* magazine, 9 January 2000.

p. 203 Sankoh and the RUF, sponsored by Taylor, launched …: Ian Stewart, *Freetown Ambush: A War Reporter's Life on the Line.*

p. 204 When a former United Nations diplomat by the name …: *Washington Post* magazine, 9 January 2000; Ian Stewart, *Freetown Ambush.*

p. 204 Kabbah was overthrown in a military coup …: *Expotimes,* 15 August 2003.

p. 204 As they captured large parts of the capital, rebels went …: *Cornerstone* magazine, Vol. 29, Issue 119, 2000.

p. 204 By then Jesse Jackson was intent on reinventing …: *Insight* magazine, 25 July 2003.

p. 204 Jackson's timing was perfect. There was a crisis …: *Insight* magazine, 25 July 2003.

p. 204 According to a United Nations report at the time …: Report of the Panel to the United Nations on Sierra Leone, 2000.

p. 205 Freetown, nestled between green hills and the white …: Ian Stewart, *Freetown Ambush.*

p. 205 Human rights organisations documented an orgy of sexual abuse …: Making the Invisible War Crime Visible, *Harvard Human Rights Journal,* 2005; No Peace without Justice, 23 January 2002; Human Rights Watch, August 2004.

p. 214 Not long after our return to Johannesburg, the first cracks …: CNN, 12 May 2000.

p. 215 Nine months after it was signed, the Lomé …: *Insight* magazine, 25 July 2003

p. 215 A month after the capture of the UN soldiers, thousands …: *Expotimes,* 15 August 2003.

p. 215 Ten days later, a thirty-six-year-old stonecutter …: Voice of America, 15 May 2000.

p. 215 The soldier got together five friends and returned …: BBC, 15 August 2003.

p. 216 With Pappy in custody, the UN announced the formation …: *Observer,* 20 October 2002; International Center for Transitional Justice, March 2004; Special Court for Sierra Leone, 5 July 2004.

p. 216 The accused, said chief prosecutor David Crane …: Special Court for Sierra Leone, 5 July 2004.

p. 216 Tejan Kabbah won by a landslide, taking 70 per cent …: BBC, 30 July 2003; Associated Press, 30 July 2003.

p. 216 When Foday Sankoh finally emerged after …: International Center for Transitional Justice, March 2004.

p. 216 His comments were rambling. 'I'm a god …: BBC, 16 March 2003.

p. 216 As Sankoh's sanity continued to wither away …: BBC, 30 July 2003.

p. 216 Sam 'Mosquito' Bockarie never got to court …: International Center for Transitional Justice, March 2004.

p. 217   At 22h40 on Tuesday 30 July 2003, Foday ...: Associated Press, 30 July 2003.

p. 217   The first witness was a man from the north-eastern town ...: Special Court for Sierra Leone, 5 July 2004.

CHAPTER 16

p. 298   The turning point in Mozambique's struggle for independence ...: Paul Fauvet and Marcelo Mosse, *Carlos Cardoza: Telling the Truth in Mozambique.*

p. 299   By 1977, Mozambican independence and stability ...: Paul Fauvet and Marcelo Mosse, *Carlos Cardoza.*

p. 301   President Joaquim Chissano and RENAMO's Afonso Dhlakama ...: Paul Fauvet and Marcelo Mosse, *Carlos Cardoza.*

CHAPTER 19

p. 334   I'd always been fascinated by Nigeria, usually branded as grim ...: Blaine Harden, *Africa: Dispatches from a Fragile Continent.*

p. 334   No surprise, then, that its indigenous movie industry ...: *New York Times,* 16 September 2002; *Nigerian Village Square,* 2 August 2004.

p. 337   The man who gave his name to the city's international ...: Blaine Harden, *Africa: Dispatches from a Fragile Continent.*

CHAPTER 20

p. 346   Others were inspired by the myths and legends ...: Blaine Harden, *Africa: Dispatches from a Fragile Continent; Washington Post,* 28 November 2001.

p. 347   The *Liemba* was no ordinary boat ...: *Lonely Planet: East Africa,* 1994

p. 348   With his forces moving towards the interior, we had to abandon ...: Jeffrey Tayler, *Facing the Congo.*

p. 348   Ten days after one of his bodyguards assassinated ...: *Washington Post,* 28 November 2001.

p. 348   By then, the war had killed an estimated three million ...: Amnesty International, 1 April 2003; CBC News, 17 July 2003.

p. 349   Trapped at the bottom were the peasants ...: Blaine Harden, *Africa: Dispatches from a Fragile Continent;* Jeffrey Tayler, *Facing the Congo.*

p. 351   Accompanied by the two men, we headed for The Beach ...: Jeffrey Tayler, *Facing the Congo.*

p. 352   Just fifty kilometres north of the equator ...: Blaine Harden, *Africa: Dispatches from a Fragile Continent.*

p. 352   Long a hub of the diamond, gold and ivory trade ...: Jeffrey Tayler, *Facing the Congo;* Amnesty International, 1 April 2003; *New York Times,* 21 April 2004.

p. 356   Mobutu was born a peasant, the son of a cook ...: Blaine Harden, *Africa: Dispatches from a Fragile Continent.*

p. 356   **It proved impossible to get close enough ...**: Blaine Harden,
Africa: Dispatches from a Fragile Continent; Adam Hochschild,
King Leopold's Ghost.

p. 357   **The man who had been christened Joseph Desiré Mobutu ...**:
Jeffrey Tayler, *Facing the Congo*; Blaine Harden, *Africa: Dispatches from
a Fragile Continent.*

p. 357   **In 1970, Mobutu engineered his authenticité programme ...**:
Blaine Harden, *Africa: Dispatches from a Fragile Continent.*

p. 357   **Mobutu amassed his wealth according to ...**: Blaine Harden, *Africa:
Dispatches from a Fragile Continent.*

p. 357   **Mobutu's private fortune was estimated ...**: Blaine Harden, *Africa:
Dispatches from a Fragile Continent.*

p. 358   **If you want to steal, show a minimum of intelligence ...**: *Washington Post*,
28 November 2001.

p. 361   **As the sun cast a saffron lick across ...**: Blaine Harden, *Africa: Dispatches
from a Fragile Continent.*

p. 362   **And then, as the tangerine ball plunged below the horizon ...**: Blaine
Harden, *Africa: Dispatches from a Fragile Continent.*

p. 362   **Travelling on or near the equator is a peculiar experience ...**: Jeffrey
Tayler, *Facing the Congo.*

p. 363   **As our journey continued, I mused on the astonishing fact ...**: Blaine
Harden, *Africa: Dispatches from a Fragile Continent*; Adam Hochschild,
King Leopold's Ghost.

p. 363   **The colonial history of Congo is the most grotesque ...**: Jeffrey Tayler,
Facing the Congo.

p. 363   **The invention of the motor car had led to an unquenchable ...**: Jeffrey
Tayler, *Facing the Congo*; Adam Hochschild, *King Leopold's Ghost.*

Bibliography

Alagiah, George. *A Passage to Africa.* London: Little, Brown and Co, 2001

Arendt, Hannah. *Eichmann in Jerusalem: A Study in the Banality of Evil.* New York: Penguin, 1994

Conrad, Joseph. *Heart of Darkness.* New York: Penguin, 1983

Dallaire, Roméo. *Shake Hands with the Devil: The Failure of Humanity in Rwanda.* London: Arrow, 2003

De Kock, Eugene. *A Long Night's Damage: Working for the Apartheid State* (as told to Jeremy Gordin). Johannesburg: Contra Press, 1998

Des Forges, Alison. *Leave None to Tell the Story: Genocide in Rwanda.* New York: Human Rights Watch, 1999

De Villiers, Marq, and Sheila Hirtle. *Into Africa: A Journey through the Ancient Empires.* London: Phoenix Giant, 1997

Du Preez, Max. *Pale Native: Memories of a Renegade Reporter.* Cape Town: Zebra Press, 2003

———. *Oranje Blanje Blues: 'n nostalgiese trip.* Cape Town: Zebra Press, 2005

Fauvet, Paul, and Mosse Marcelo. *Carlos Cardoza: Telling the Truth in Mozambique.* Cape Town: Double Storey, 2003

Frankl, Viktor E. *Man's Search for Meaning.* Washington: Washington Square Press, 1984

Gobodo-Madikizela, Pumla. *A Human Being Died That Night: A Story of Forgiveness.* Cape Town: David Philip, 2003

Gourevitch, Philip. *We Wish to Inform You that Tomorrow We Will Be Killed with Our Families: Stories from Rwanda.* London: Picador, 1998

Harden, Blaine. *Africa: Dispatches from a Fragile Continent.* London: HarperCollins, 1993

Hartley, Aidan. *The Zanzibar Chest: A Memoir of Love and War.* Johannesburg: Jonathan Ball, 2003

Hochschild, Adam. *King Leopold's Ghost: A Story of Greed, Terror and Heroism in Colonial Africa.* New York: Mariner Books, 1998

Kapuściński, Ryszard. *The Shadow of the Sun: My African Life.* London: Penguin, 1998

Khan, Shaharyar. *The Shallow Graves of Rwanda.* London: IB Tauris, 2000

Kyemba, Henry. *A State of Blood.* Kampala: Fountain Publishers, 1997

Melvern, Linda. *A People Betrayed: The Role of the West in Rwanda's Genocide.* London: Zed Books, 2000

Naipaul, VS. *A Bend in the River*. London: Penguin, 1980

Omaar, Rakiya. *Rwanda: Death, Despair and Defiance*. London: African Rights, 1995

Pauw, Jacques. *Into the Heart of Darkness: Confessions of Apartheid's Assassins*. Johannesburg: Jonathan Ball, 1997

Peterson, Scott. *Me Against My Brother: At War in Somalia, Sudan and Rwanda*. New York: Routledge, 2000

Pilger, John. *Tell Me No Lies: Investigative Journalism and its Triumphs*. London: Vintage, 2004

Reader, John. *Africa: A Biography of a Continent*. New York: Alfred A Knopf, 1999

Rhodes, Richard. *Why They Kill: The Discoveries of a Maverick Criminologist*. New York: Vintage, 1999

Rosenberg, Tina. *The Haunted Land: Facing Europe's Ghosts after Communism*. New York: Random House, 1995

Sachs, Albie. *The Soft Vengeance of a Freedom Fighter*. Cape Town: David Philip, 1990

Sparks, Allister. *Beyond the Miracle: Inside the New South Africa*. Johannesburg: Jonathan Ball, 2003

Stewart, Ian. *Freetown Ambush: A War Reporter's Life on the Line*. London: Vision Paperbacks, 2002

Tayler, Jeffrey. *Facing the Congo*. London: Abacus, 2000

Index